Remote Freedoms

Politics, Personhood and Human Rights
in Aboriginal Central Australia

Sarah E. Holcombe

Stanford University Press
Stanford, California

Stanford University Press
Stanford, California

Printed in the United States of America on acid-free, archival-quality paper

Library of Congress Cataloging-in-Publication Data

Names: Holcombe, Sarah E. (Sarah Elizabeth), 1967- author.
Title: Remote freedoms : politics, personhood and human rights in Aboriginal central
    Australia / Sarah E. Holcombe.
Other titles: Stanford studies in human rights.
Description: Stanford, California : Stanford University Press, 2018.
Series: Stanford studies in human rights | Includes bibliographical references and
    index.
Identifiers: LCCN 2017045771 | ISBN 9781503605107 (cloth : alk. paper) |
    ISBN 9781503606470 (pbk. : alk. paper) | ISBN 9781503606487 (epub)
Subjects: LCSH: Aboriginal Australians—Civil rights. | Aboriginal Australians—
    Politics and government. | Indigenous peoples—Civil rights—Australia. |
    Human rights—Australia.
Classification: LCC DU124.C48 H65 2018 | DDC 323.1199/150942—dc23
    LC record available at https://lccn.loc.gov/2017045771

Typeset by Thompson Type in 10/14 Minion

For Elsey and Pira

Contents

Foreword

IN JUNE 1947, A. P. Elkin, professor of anthropology at the University of Sydney and a towering and controversial figure who oversaw the development of the discipline in Australia for decades, wrote an essay entitled "The Rights of Primitive Peoples." This essay was written at the request of UNESCO for a survey it was conducting on human rights, the results of which were intended to form the basis for the new declaration on human rights being drafted by the UN Commission on Human Rights, chaired by Eleanor Roosevelt. Elkin was one of only two anthropologists to participate in the UNESCO human rights survey; the other was the American scholar Melville Herskovits, a Boasian and vigorous proponent of cultural relativism whose "Statement on Human Rights" went on to achieve a certain notoriety decades later as the end of the Cold War unleashed what UN Secretary-General Kofi Annan described as the "age of human rights."

Part of what made Elkin so controversial was that he was among the most influential nonnative advocates for Australian Aborigines. He served for almost thirty years as the president of the Association for the Protection of Native Races (APNR) and vice president of the Aborigines Welfare Board. During the 1930s, Elkin and the APNR intervened during a highly charged criminal case brought against an Aboriginal man in the Northern Territories for the killing of a nonnative (described as a "white") man, for which the Aboriginal man had received a death sentence. Based on charges of racial bias and lack of due process, Elkin's public advocacy played a role in securing an appeal for the Aboriginal defendant through which he was eventually released. Yet Elkin's support for justice for Australia's Aboriginal people was grounded in the belief that their rights would best be served by being fully assimilated into majority Australian society, a position consistent with the then prevailing international legal doctrine regarding "indigenous and other tribal and semi-tribal populations" expressed in the 1957 International Labor Organization Convention 107.

But in developing a theory of human rights that could apply to Australia's Indigenous peoples in what would become the 1948 Universal Declaration of Human Rights, Elkin articulated a surprisingly nuanced and even radical position, one fully at odds with the dominant liberal conception of rights that centered on the abstract and idealized individual. As Elkin put it, in his UNESCO essay, "the question of Human Rights is one of the relationship of the individual to his fellows within a community, and of community to community. Fundamentally, the individual is a social personality, and his rights are an integral part of his place and role in his society and in its external relationships. Apart from the society he would have no rights."

As Sarah Holcombe's pioneering *Remote Freedoms* demonstrates, questions of vernacularization of human rights are not only, or even most importantly, about translation—the rendering of concepts in a way that preserves a core of meaning despite changes in phrasing, the use of different words, and a lack of equivalence. Rather, just as Elkin's UNESCO's essay appears to recognize, *particular* conceptions of human rights embody *particular* worldviews, particular ways of conceptually organizing the worlds of the material and immaterial, of parsing their constituent categories, of classifying their chains of being (and not-being), and of laying down the moral ground rules through which humans can and should navigate within and in relation to these worlds. Thus, as *Remote Freedoms* reveals in unparalleled clarity, the outer limits of human rights activism are not defined by language or culture or political cynicism; they are defined by a thick, living pluralism that resists the gentle pull of even the most benevolent normative imperialism.

Ultimately, the struggle to promote human rights in a world of salutary diversity will not depend on what happens in the Human Rights Council in Geneva, or within the many international treaty monitoring bodies, or in politicized and historically fraught national debates in places like Canberra (coincidently, I write these words on January 26—known in Australia as either "Australia Day" or "Invasion Day"). Instead, the future of human rights will depend on what emerges from quiet, attentive, respectful dialogues in places like the Western Desert Lands of the Pintupi-Luritja people, in which human rights norms are fashioned into social artifacts around the fire and then, eventually, ideally, back-translated into circuits of transnational practice. For this to happen, it will be necessary to develop what Holcombe describes as the "ethno-epistemological" capacity to hear other ways of being in the world, other ways of conceiving of sociality, and to reflect critically on how "human rights"—open, contingent, normatively polyvalent—might fit into these epistemological and moral pluriverses. As the Luritja phrase for "conscience" has it, we must understand the meaning of human rights by *kulirra tjungungku wangkanyi* ("listening and talking together"). Holcombe's magnificent study is a window into how this alternative social life of rights might flourish.

Mark Goodale
Series Editor
Stanford Studies in Human Rights

Acknowledgments

AS ONE WOULD ANTICIPATE in a book that draws both from the immediate experiences of people and from my twenty years plus of experience, there are many people to thank. The first of these are the Anangu with whom I worked because, without their interest, support, and collaboration, there would be no book. These include Elsey Gorey (who died on September 15, 2014), Punata Stockman, Fabrianne, Tjunkata Allen, Jeanella, Sylvana, Sammy Butcher, Sid Anderson, Audrey, Jeanetta, Coral, Kumantjayi Nangala, Lance Macdonald, Amos Anderson, Norissa, Topsy, Shelia Joyce Dixon, Linda Leichleitner, and Isobel. And I also thank the *urlkumanu* (elderly women), especially Tilau Nangala, Mavis Nampitjinpa, Wintjia Napaltjarri, and Marilyn Nangala; too many have passed away in the last ten years.

I have also benefited from discussions over the years with Jeff Hulcombe, mainly in Papunya. Both of us understand the value of the long-term attachments developed with both people (*Anangu*) and place. Whereas he has worked in the region for many years in various roles, I joked that I had to find—dream up—other projects to be able to continue visiting. This book is, effectively, the result of one of those projects. A special thank you, also, goes to Alison Anderson, who has lived and worked across most of the intercultural spaces and places discussed in this book. I have sent drafts of various chapters and sections to her over the years, and she has been generous in her support, although I know that she has little time for anthropologists and "experts." Her enigmatic approach to the contents will, I respectfully anticipate, yield an ongoing debate.

I have also had many discussions with staff of the Regional Council, and I'd especially like to thank Ronnie and, in the health clinic, Danny. The police who were based in Papunya for three of the four years of this project, Richard and Susan, were such openhearted and good people, an example of police who want to be there to make a difference. Also a special thanks goes to Helen Puckey, manager at Papunya Tjupi Arts, for often providing the fabulous studio with the gorgeous view over the Ulamparu Ranges and for our walks. I also held many conversations with the store manager, Bruce, and others including Bec, who for a time shared her energy and compassion working with Anangu youth. I'd also like to acknowledge Jeanette Pastor and Jamie Millier, for our frank conversations, as they were based in Papunya during most of the book's field research. Over the years, I have also had many conversations with Glyness Wilkins (variously store manager, aged care manager in Haasts Bluff and Mount Liebig) and also Faye Cameron (nanny and aged care manager in Mount Liebig).

Waltja staff have been supportive and engaged by the project; special thanks to Kate Lawrence, Linda Brooks, and Sharynne King. Thanks are also due to the CLC staff over the years whom I have both interviewed and/or been colleagues with, especially David Ross, a leader worthy of respect, Steve Hodder-Watts, Elkie Wiseman, Alyson Wright, Frances Claffey, Brian Connolly, and Pete Donohue. Also, a special thank you to Graeme Pearce for his energy, openness, and enthusiasm to "make a difference." Without him there would not be a Cross Borders Indigenous Family Violence Program. And a special thanks goes to Ruth Morley for her pragmatic legal insights. Thanks also to Matthew Heffernan and Lizzie Ellis. I can't name most of the public servants spoken with here, and I hope the book does justice to the conversations held, notably with staff from the Alice Springs Women's Shelter Outreach Service, Relationships Australia, facilitators from the Cross Borders Indigenous Family Violence Program, staff from the NPY Women's Council, and the several locally based staff from the Indigenous Affairs Group (prime minister and cabinet) in Alice Springs. Of course, if there are omissions or misinterpretations from these discussions, then I am to blame.

Several chapters, or sections thereof, in this book have also benefited from being presented in various forms as seminars and lectures in the ANU Anthropology seminar series, the CAEPR seminar series, the CAEPR Indigenous Rights and Recognition Symposium, cross-campus guest lectures, at the CLC in Alice Springs, and at AAS and AAA conferences over several years. Thanks go to Alan Rumsey, Francesca Merlan, Julie Finlayson, and notably dear friend and colleague Melinda Hinkson, for their scholarly interest and input. I also benefited from attending several of Sally Merry's workshops in her visits to ANU and several meetings with her. In 2013, as the critical framework for the book was unfolding, I convened a course on Indigenous Human Rights in the ANU School of Archaeology and Anthropology, as research-led teaching, and I benefited from the engaged feedback of the students. Thanks also are due to Jane Simpson and David Nash for their interest in the interpretation and translation work. Indeed, I have David to thank for encouraging me to work with Ken Hansen, whom I learned so much from as we worked side-by-side during the final interpretations work. Thanks, also, of course go to Ken.

My dear friends and colleagues Inge Kral and Sean Kerins have provided unstinting support, humor, and discussions over sections of the text. I thank CAEPR for supplying an office space for the final write-up; Tracy Deasy, Jerry Schwab, Janet Hunt, Will Sanders, and especially to Denise Steele, a wonder of a center manager.

My friends in Alice Springs, Adelaide Church—thanks, Addy, for your hospitality and fabulous friendship over the years and for letting me store so much camping gear in your shed, and also to Megan Halliday, dear friend and sage counsel. Also thanks to my parents, Sandra and Bob, for their eternal support and to Steve who was always a willing and patient ear, especially through the difficult economic precariat period of the final write-up.

I also benefited from the close and thorough reading from the three Stanford University Press anonymous reviewers. I was also fortunate to have the expert guidance of Michelle Lipinski as the senior editor who assisted in shepherding this book through to completion.

Funding for this research was provided by the Australian Research Council who funded the four-year program of research from which this book is the major outcome: ARC Future Fellowship (FT 110100805). Finally, I'd like to acknowledge Amnesty International Australia for a small grant from their Human Rights Innovation Fund, which was essential to complete the interpretation and translation work on the UN Declaration of Human Rights into Pintupi-Luritja.

Indigenous Rights as Human Rights in Central Australia

Contemplating human rights in the abstract is a luxury that only the most isolated occupants of the ivory tower can afford . . . moral or cultural relativism does not need to underlie the view that that the understandings of human rights are particular.

Englund 2006: 47

THIS BOOK IS AN EXPLORATION OF THE DIVERSE WORK of human rights in several remote Aboriginal communities in central Australia. It attempts to make visible the implicit and the tacit and to start a conversation about the possibilities and the limitations of human rights to address the multiple and intersecting forms of social vulnerability that many Aboriginal people in remote central Australia experience. To do this I have worked with Anangu (as Pintupi-Luritja speakers refer to themselves) in the communities of Papunya and Mount Liebig and some members of the diaspora from these places in Alice Springs. Although this book is at once particular to central Australia and to these remote communities, it is a narrative with global reach. Human rights language, discourse, and institutions have become fundamental to the work of states and state sovereignty, most notably through the United Nations. Human rights underpin the tacit contract of modern citizenship in democratic liberal states, and they are the benchmark, though arguably largely symbolic, by which states are measured as "global citizens."

For Anangu this tacit contract of citizenship is increasingly being made explicit through the regulatory dimensions of rights and the acknowledged public goods of representation, accountability, and transparency. These liberal practices are framed through the responsibilization discourse, the work of which can increasingly be found through an extensive raft of Indigenous affairs policies and, likewise, increasingly through Indigenous nongovernmental organizations (NGOs). This regulatory dimension of human rights is now the dominant discourse in the channeling of neoliberal forms of citizenship. The growing body of critical scholarship on the entailments of human rights, as that "which we cannot not want" (Spivak, cited in Brown 2000: 230) and as the ideological gloss for an emerging empire through the concealment of powerful interests (Douzinas 2007; Englund 2006), is a recognition of how encompassing the discourse has become.

On the other hand, for marginal and subordinated groups globally, the language of human rights is the language of progressive politics and social justice, largely replacing the earlier discourses of revolution and socialism. As Hodgson explains:

> Despite the existence of alternative modes of understanding, defining, and promoting justice, "human rights" have become the dominant model for making positive (*for* free speech for example) and negative (such as *against* bodily violence) claims against individuals and collectivities (primarily states) in the contemporary world. (2011: 4)

One only has to watch a film such as *12 Years a Slave*[1] or to recall the horrors of the Holocaust from the Second World War to be reminded why we require universal standards of equality and human dignity and why the United Nations system of human rights has been one of the great moral achievements of the twentieth century (Kymlicka 2007). It is the hope inspired by this emancipatory discourse deployed to fight oppression and to act as morally generative that invigorates movements for social justice (Speed 2006). The tensions between the bounded and domesticating form of human rights, and its enfranchising and emancipatory possibilities, are ever present within this book.

This book is energized by Goodale's statement that "ethnography of human rights practices [are a] fertile source of new ideas about the complex relationships between normativity, agency, and social and political intentionality" (2012: 468). It seems to me that new ideas are needed to reconsider the conundrum of structural and intersectional "disadvantage" (to borrow a policy term) that has come to characterize the Anangu world. Arendt's now iconic phrase, "the right to have rights" or the right to belong to a sociopolitical community that can guarantee these rights, unfolds in central Australia within the nexus of the state and the local Aboriginal community and family.

In this context, it is telling to recast the issue in terms of "why Anangu don't seem to 'claim' their rights."

Thus, this book explores the tensions and contradictions between the possibilities that human rights offers within its parameters and limitations as it identifies intersections and ruptures from the norm. As Santos has said: "The other possible world may be many things, but never a world with no alternatives" (Santos 2006: 12).

So What Exactly Are Human Rights?

A number of the core human rights principles can be traced back to the Magna Carta, which established some fundamental principles, including the distinction between church and state, the rights of all free citizens to own and inherit property, the principles of due process and equality before the law, and so on. This charter was a turning point in the historical development of modern democracy and the freedoms of individuals. In 2015, an exhibition commemorating the 800th anniversary of the Magna Carta was held at the Old Parliament House in Canberra. The principles embodied in this charter developed in a concerted way during the Enlightenment of eighteenth-century Europe and coalesced in the French Declaration of the Rights of Man and Citizen of 1789 (see Hunt 2007). The philosopher John Locke is widely considered as one of the founders of contemporary rights discourse. Locke's doctrine of natural rights that are essentially rights to liberty is regarded as the first firm statement of the ideas of Western liberalism and a symptom of the growing individualism of Anglo culture (Raphael 1965). Locke's three principle "natural rights" are the rights to life, liberty, and property. Such rights are today associated with civil and political rights, or "first-generation rights."

The French Declaration incarnated the promise of universal human rights (per Hunt 2007: 17), which then consolidated with the emergence of the United Nations (UN) after the Second World War. After the horror of Nazi Germany's extermination of millions of Jews, Sinti and Romani (gypsies), homosexuals, and persons with disabilities, governments committed themselves to establishing the United Nations with the primary goal of bolstering international peace and preventing conflict. Eleanor Roosevelt, the widow of US President Franklin D. Roosevelt, led the development of the Universal Declaration of Human Rights (UDHR), which was adopted by the then fifty-six members of the United Nations in 1948. So-called second-generation rights—economic, social, and cultural rights—were articulated during the development of the

UDHR and so are more recent than civil and political rights. Both sets of rights have their own conventions and, at the time the Universal Declaration of Human Rights was developed, these two tiers of rights were reflective of Cold War politics. In 1993, at the end of the Cold War, there was an attempt to reconcile these two opposing ideologies and the qualitative division between these two conventions with the Vienna Declaration: "All human rights are universal, indivisible and interdependent and interrelated."

The Australian government is a party to the International Bill of Rights (which includes the Convention on Civil and Political Rights and the Convention on Economic, Social and Cultural Rights). Yet, there is little systematic relationship between the rights articulated within the International Bill of Rights and law in Australia (see also Byrnes, Charlesworth, and McKinnon 2009). Nonetheless, these normative concepts do work on a range of levels: as discursive political tools, as tacit elements of contemporary mainstream "culture," as a set of principles to which various governing bodies abide, as mere rhetoric, and as a moniker for modernity and globalization. Part of the reason this discourse is tacit, and in certain contexts not legitimate, is that Australia is without a national bill or charter of rights. Yet, the discursive effects of human rights are real as they structure the relations of power between Aboriginal people and the state, as revealed through interventionist socio-legal policies.

Many of the core principles of human rights are intrinsically permissive as they alternately speak to what it means to be human—consciousness, mortality, and family—*and* what it means to be a modern political person. The discourse of rights, as ideology and as politics, permeates all aspects of modern life so that they are almost common sense. In the modern nation state the concepts of rights are part and parcel of everyday speech and everyday institutions. Because we invoke these concepts frequently, we rarely think about their meaning.

It is this commonsense element that scholars such as Arendt (2003) and, more recently, Gundogdu (2012) have termed the *aporias of rights*. This Socratic mode of thinking starts with ordinary concepts of political life, in this case human rights, and calls into question their conventional understandings, opening up possibilities of thinking them anew (Gundogdu 2012: 5). Notwithstanding the aspirational intent of the Universal Declaration of Human Rights as it espouses the "inherent dignity, the equal and inalienable rights of all members of the human family," there is, however, nothing intrinsic, natural, or inherent in humans that leads to a conference of "rights." They are fundamentally sociopolitical constructs.

Limits on Legitimacy: The Rights Discourse in Australia (and Australianist Anthropology)

The suspicion is that there is something a little simple-minded about the entire conceptual structure that underlies the oratory on human rights.

Sen 1999: 227

As the only Western liberal democratic country without a national bill of rights[2] and where basic human rights (such as the right to life) are not enshrined in the constitution, Australia has a deeply ambivalent relationship with human rights.[3] Although various rights principles appear in some laws, such as the Racial Discrimination Act 1975 (Cwlth) and the Disability Discrimination Act 1992 (Cwlth), "existing [human rights] protections are piecemeal" (Brynes, Charlesworth, and McKinnon 2009: 21). This is particularly so in relation to the rights of minority groups, including Indigenous Australians. Indeed, although the concept of "rights," ubiquitously referred to by the unique Anglo-Australian concept of the "fair go," permeates Australian public discourse, it tends to be the comfortable carriage of the mainstream who can afford to take human rights for granted.

According to the constitutional legal scholar George Williams: "Every Australian federal Labor government since the 2nd World War had sought to bring about major change to national protection for human rights" (2010). The Rudd Labor government, the fourth to go down this track, established the National Human Rights Consultation Committee. After an exhaustive process of research and public forums, the Brennan Committee reported in late 2009 that of the over 35,000 submissions, 87 percent were in support of a human rights act, although many wanted more, in the form of a constitutional bill of rights (Commonwealth of Australia 2009). In 2010 the government announced that it would not act on the recommendations of its own Human Rights Committee inquiry and that it would adopt only a small number of its findings. Instead of a National Human Rights Act, in 2011 we got a Human Rights Framework and a Human Rights Action Plan. However, because this was effectively only policy, major elements of both the Framework and the Plan were disregarded by the incoming conservative Abbott coalition government in 2013. Nevertheless, importantly, the Labor party did pursue one of the Brennan Committee recommendations and legislated to establish a

Parliamentary Joint Committee on Human Rights. The main function of this committee is to examine all bills and legislative instruments for compatibility with human rights and to report to both Houses of Parliament on its findings.[4] This committee has been described as the "big ticket item" (personal communication with Sarah Joseph, March 12, 2015) as it examines all commonwealth legislation for compatibility with human rights standards (Commonwealth of Australia 2015).

Although such parliamentary scrutiny on human rights standards is an essential, and overdue, element in democratic process, it is not a mechanism that is specifically enabling or inciting of broader public discourse. As stated by a senior public servant who leads the international reporting for several of the rights instruments that Australia is a party to:

> We don't have a rights discourse in Australia at all. Unlike the US and the UK we don't have anything to pin it onto. The constitution doesn't help—there are very few rights in that. So Australia has never had that basis for conversation . . . there is no ready narrative. (personal communication, February 2016)

In the Indigenous rights context, this lack of "ready narrative" is also fueled by the fact that Australia never made a treaty with the Indigenous inhabitants, unlike other settler states such as Canada, the United States, and New Zealand. Brennan and his coauthors note that historically it is unclear why the British took control of Australia without consent or a treaty, as it had been common practice in their role as colonizers elsewhere from the 1600s (Brennan et al. 2005: 4; see also Reynolds 1996). Australia is also a colonial anomaly. There is, however, a growing bipartisan political movement toward Indigenous recognition within the Constitution and, at least in some states such as South Australia and Victoria, the beginnings of treaty discussions.[5] Whether Indigenous Australians seek to be recognized within the Constitution or instead seek a treaty or treaties with the Commonwealth or other forms of political power is still unfolding.

Against this backdrop of historical political indifference to the language of rights, whether couched in the distinct human rights language of a "national bill of rights" or in terms of Indigenous treaties and sovereignty, it is perhaps no surprise that engagement with the concepts and practices of "rights" has not become an established field of research in Australianist anthropology. There are rights area specializations, such as Jon Altman's focus on customary economic rights leveraging off Indigenous property rights and the welfare economy, which he has conceptualized as a "hybrid economy" (Altman 1987; Altman and Kerins 2012). Elizabeth Povinelli has also critically engaged with the moral and ideological politics of recognition within liberal multiculturalism, under different forms of land rights legislation and judicial-legal categories that, to oversimplify, she maintains are essentially assimilatory and deeply patriarchal (2002). However, where she does move beyond a critique of property rights into civil rights and gender violence (in the chapter on "Sex Rites, Civil Rights" 2002: 111–152), rather than a contemporary ethnography, she limits herself to a textual account, drawing only on archival materials from the middle of the last century. As will be discussed in Chapter 2, Dianne Bell's work on gender violence, coauthored with Aboriginal woman Topsy Napurrula, has to date been the most explicit to engage with human rights principles, though at the time this approach was very contentious (Bell and Nelson 1989; Huggins et al. 1991)

Although there are exceptions, and I also include here the early work of Olive Pink on the central Australian colonial frontier of the 1930s–1940s, which speaks to an activist form of rights-based anthropology (Marcus 1993: 111–135), there has been a conspicuous silence around the ethnographic treatment of human rights in Australia.[6] Yet, the same can't be said for the disciplines of history and law—scholars of which have developed concerted fields of analysis in this area. In the discipline of history, Bain Attwood's *Rights for Aborigines* (2003) is one example, whereas in law there is an extensive body of research, much by Indigenous academics, such as Megan Davis (2007, 2008) and Larissa Behrendt (2005, 2011). Yet, perhaps Australianist anthropologists are simply reflecting the wider societal norm that, to quote Williams, "in the absence of a charter of rights, human rights ideas can lack legitimacy in the parliament and in the community" (2010).

Since the early 1970s the abiding preoccupation of Australianist anthropology has historically been on rights to land, beginning with the 1971 Justice Blackburn decision that culminated in the Aboriginal Land Rights (Northern Territory) Act of 1976. Anthropologists were strong advocates for the recognition of Indigenous property rights and were instrumental in developing the categories at law that now define Indigenous Australian land tenure in these legally discursive contexts. Since 1992, with the recognition of native title following the Mabo decision, even more anthropologists are involved in writing claims for recognition of native title or assisting with heritage clearances to facilitate land use agreements. And although the comfort of this historical fit has since been called into question, principally from within the discipline (see especially Sutton 2009), an outcome of this abiding disciplinary focus on land rights has been to the neglect of other aspects of Indigenous human rights.[7]

Although land rights have encompassed "regaining some fraction of the personal and group autonomy which existed prior to colonisation" (Peterson and Langton 1983: 3), the "performance of cultural continuity" (Povinelli 2002) required for the recognition of rights to land rarely transferred itself to other domains of Indigenous human rights. This tendency to focus on such a narrow form of cultural rights—expressed as land rights—has decoupled the anthropological project from the broader set of human rights concerns, such as substantive civil and political rights. This has created a legacy that is difficult to shift. However, we now know, for instance, that "land rights" is not enough on its own and has not been the answer to shifting Aboriginal "disadvantage" in the Northern Territory (Chesters 2009; Commonwealth of Australia 2009).

Why Human Rights and Not Indigenous Rights?

I did not begin this research with a specific focus on human rights. The impetus behind the research that led to this book was the Australian government's endorsement of the UN Declaration on the Rights of Indigenous Peoples (UN DRIP) in 2009, two years after it was adopted by the UN General Assembly. My initial focus was Indigenous rights, as I was struck by the disjuncture between this declaration of rights and social fact in the region where I have worked over many years. It is far from self-evident that the UN DRIP as a global instrument, in its potential as both resource and discourse, can effect change in a place like central Australia, where it is most required. What was the value of this instrument, which was twenty years in development, and was it making its way to central Australia? What significance do Aboriginal people in remote central Australia attach to this global rights instrument, as supposed beneficiaries? How do they come to see themselves in terms of Indigenous rights? It was with these questions at the fore that I began the research. Nevertheless, I had previously been engaged by the possibilities of this rights instrument, as I wrote for a seminar in 2009:

> The Declaration on the Rights of Indigenous Peoples is potentially a powerful instrument for Indigenous peoples. However, there is no point having rights unless they can be exercised and likewise, unless those who need to have them recognised and activated are aware that such rights exist.

As I more recently reread this statement it was initially with some horror: how could I be so naïve as to think that the "exercise" of rights was simply a matter of being aware of them? I have since grown to realize that although this is not the whole of the picture, it is indeed an important element of it. I was not far into the research when I had to take a step back. Very few Anangu, including community leaders in the communities where I was working, had heard the words "universal human rights." The concept of "Indigenous rights" was associated solely with Aboriginal land rights. So it seemed to me preemptive, like a false promise, to focus on Indigenous rights, when the Aboriginal people whom I knew had little access to the principles of human rights.

Although this lack of awareness of the words and meaning of "universal human rights" may be at the extreme end of the spectrum, it is by no means unusual. The 2009 National Human Rights Consultation also stated: "The Clearest finding from our work is that Australians know little about their human rights—what they are, where they come from and how they are protected" (National Human Rights Consultation Report 2009: Foreword).

Indigenous Human Rights: Parameters for Recognition

And thus, returning to this rights foundation was essential. Indigenous rights have emerged from the same normative stable as human rights. This has major implications for Indigenous peoples in a colonial democratic liberal state such as Australia. The United Nations is, as one might expect, deeply implicated in the development of the construct "Indigenous" and the associated international rights categories.[8] This new Indigenous rights instrument is firmly embedded within the UN human rights system, a system that is profoundly secular and antirelativist. As Kymlicka has pointed out: "Every international declaration and convention on these issues makes the same point—the rights of minorities and Indigenous peoples are an inseparable part of a larger human rights framework and operate within its limits" (2007: 7). These limits are prescribed by a liberal paradigm of democratic tolerance that underpins the Western political concept of multiculturalism. As Merry observed, there is a critical need for conceptual clarification of "culture" in human rights practice, as the word tends to be used to describe the developing world rather than the developed world and often has the legacy of premodern, as in preuniversal, human rights (2006a). Rajagopal described this conundrum in this way: "Human rights is to modernity what culture is to tradition" (2007: 274).

Although there has been a range of critiques about the ways in which the concept of "culture" has been essentialized within the liberal democratic discourse of multiculturalism (see especially Turner 1993 and Benhabib 2002), the polemic title of Phillips's book *Multiculturalism* without *Culture* pithily exposes the irony of pluralist constraint the discourse harbors (Phillips 2007; author's emphasis).[9] The concept of multiculturalism is both guided and constrained by a foundational commitment to principles of individual freedom and equality. Cultural practices that diverge from these principles butt up against the governmentality of tolerance (Brown 2006; see also Povinelli 2002). These limits are articulated within the UN Declaration on the Rights of Indigenous Peoples (UN DRIP) as follows (United Nations 2007; my emphasis):

> Article 1: Indigenous peoples have the right to the full enjoyment, as a collective or as individuals, of *all human rights and fundamental freedoms as recognised in the Charter of the United Nations, the Universal Declaration of Human Rights and international human rights law.*

and

> Article 34: Indigenous peoples have the right to promote, develop and maintain their institutional structures and their distinctive customs, spirituality, traditions, procedures, practices and, in some cases where they exist, juridical systems or customs, *in accordance with international human rights standards.*

and

> Article 40: Indigenous peoples have the right to access to, and prompt decision through just and fair procedures for the resolution of conflicts and disputes with States or other parties, as well as to effective remedies for all infringements of their individual and collective rights. Such a decision shall give due consideration to the customs, traditions, rules and legal systems of the Indigenous peoples concerned *and international human rights.*

So, those who self-identify as Indigenous have human rights, as well as an additional category of rights that specifically addresses their circumstances as Indigenous peoples. Yet, as indicated, this recognition is bound by the parameters of international human rights law. The term "Indigenous human rights," rather than simply "Indigenous rights," is therefore appropriate as the encompassing term.

Likewise, the concept "Indigenous," though now ubiquitous, needs to be understood as a "quintessentially modern phenomenon" that has actively been used only for the last few decades to describe a particular category of human society (Niezen 2003). Another reason Indigeneity is modern is because of the fundamental and complex ways in which this identity is tied to human rights, emerging from the social justice potential of the human rights movement, so that much of its moral infrastructure is coconstitutive. According to Merlan: "This is partly because, as Maybury-Lewis asserts, Indigenous peoples are defined as much by their relations with the state as by any intrinsic characteristics that they may possess" (2009b: 305). This was recognized by the United Nations when the former UN Special Rapporteur (and anthropologist) Stavenhagen stated: "Indigenousness, independently of biological or cultural continuity, frequently is the outcome of governmental policies imposed from above and from the outside" (cited in Merlan 2009b: 305). This is the issue that Brown identifies as the "regulatory dimension of identity based rights," such that rights are never deployed freely but always within a discursive frame (2000: 232).

And although this discursive frame in this Indigenous context may be described as "a balancing act; holding in one hand the principles of equality or equity, and in the other the principle of difference . . . because Indigenous rights encompass both categories [citizenship rights and distinct Indigenous rights]" (Dodson, cited in the *National Human Rights Consultation Report* 2009: 206–207), the balance falls in favor of liberal democratic values. As Kymlicka notes: "When Indigenous peoples from establishing states sought to internationalise their struggles, they were not primarily seeking to transcend the inherent constraints of liberal democratic political values . . . it was not contested by Indigenous advocates during the UN negotiations" (2009: 324). These constraints on the recognition of Indigenous difference or their "distinct rights" were the catalyst compelling this research to return to these human rights foundations. The question thus becomes: What are the limits on the tolerance of difference within this Indigenous human rights discourse? I am cautious, however, about placing all the emphasis on state-centered logics of Indigenous identity and rights; room has to be left for alternative political visions that the UN DRIP, and universal human rights, does not embody but may well foster (see Hale 2009: 323). Nevertheless, a critical interrogation of the normative principles that are embodied within the human rights discourse emerged as a crucial exercise.

Rendering Visible the Tacit

Human rights do not belong to humans, rights constitute the subject of modernity.

Douzinas 2007: 107

The normative principles within human rights can be found to embody many Anglo key cultural concepts (per Wierzbicka 1997), so that human rights are not taken for granted by Anangu. With few exceptions, the Anangu I have been working with first heard of the idea of "universal human rights" through discussions with me. They are very familiar with Anangu rights and responsibilities toward their own families and land. However, rights as individuals, as against the state, and as against each other as individual citizens are different kinds of rights. Such universal rights cut across the asymmetries and hierarchies of kinship, gender, and age: they challenge deeply held notions of relational personhood. Although these ontological struggles between cultural conceptions of rights are real, an activist anthropologist also has to query and explore the exclusion of Anangu from this language of universal human rights and as its embodiment in English. The English rights language is the language of state power; it is intrinsic to governmentality. By uncovering where this language and its concepts do their work, we can gain a clearer sense of the logics of political power.

The use of euphemisms and glosses abounds in this sphere of human rights within the policy and politics of Aboriginal Australia. Perhaps the most common gloss, and one that has gained the most traction across the spectrum, is the apparently neutral vocabulary of "good (corporate) governance." Yet, as will be discussed in Chapters 2 and 6, this concept embodies many core human rights principles. Such euphemisms, which include "shared responsibility agreements" in Indigenous policy, speak to our ambivalence about calling out and naming aspects of human rights. Introducing the term "human rights" into a debate tends to be perceived as politicizing the issue or as advocacy; it's too ideological or too partisan. This dancing around the use of the human rights label happens across the spectrum; from Aboriginal NGOs, to government policy and service providers, to academics and public commentators. By exploring the consequences of this denial and effacement of the work of human rights we are closer to understanding, legitimating, and validating some core principles of human rights and thus also reclaiming certain spheres of human rights practice that have been marginalized. Conversely, we are also able to locate the domesticating and reformative work of human rights. Revealing the work of the rights discourse, given that it is so often tacit within Australia and given that it has its tentacles across the spectrum of remote Aboriginal policy, is the detective work of this book.

On the other hand, how can Aboriginal people be expected to "claim their rights" when they don't even know what human rights are and what constitutes them? For although Englund can be sceptical, indeed deeply cynical, about the local disabling effect of human rights training in Malawi among the poorest people, there is very limited comparable "training" in remote areas of Aboriginal Australia (2006). So from Englund's *Prisoners of Freedom: Human Rights and the African Poor*, we learn lessons on how not to translate the rights discourse into "poor translations for poor people" and how not to further entrench the local, regional, and introduced relations of power through differential access to this discourse (2006: 47–69). In Australia, as this book will trace, this discourse of rights as political advocacy has such limited legitimacy as to be invisible to those who need it most. Limited legitimacy had led to limited visibility.

Personhood Embodied in Human Rights (via Liberal Mobilities)

Merry observed that "we know relatively little about how individuals in various social and cultural contexts come to see themselves in terms of human rights" (2006a: 3). This is the core question pursued in this ethnographic treatment of human rights because, as Merry also observed, asking this question allows us to eschew the relativist/universalist debate that early distracted ethnographers from engaging with this secular global discourse and to instead focus on "the social processes of human rights implementation and resistance" (Merry 2006a: 39).

Although the history of anthropology's ambivalent relationship with human rights has been well traced (see especially Goodale 2009: 18–39), it is useful to briefly specify this ambivalence in the Australian context as it plays out in ontological terms. This is because it seems to me that the differences in forms of personhood between Aboriginal people and the Western conception of the "human rights holder" has been one of the core reasons for this reticence to engage. In Australianist anthropology, drawing the distinctions between the sociocentric or relational Aboriginal person and the egocentric liberal Western individual has been a preoccupation, and these ontological differences have become essentialist and not as useful as they once were (as discussed in more detail in Chapter 4).

If we want to consider how an Anangu person becomes a "human rights holder," we have to first unpack the elements that specify this type of personhood. As Brown points out, the individual is "liberalism's unit of analysis" and, with "its primary project [of] maximising individual freedom," its antithesis is "culture's provision of the coherence and continuity of groups—an antithesis that positions liberal principles and culture as mutual antagonists" (2006: 21). By opening the discussion between these "antagonists" we can more clearly begin to articulate the challenges for Anangu in being or becoming this person and also the points and places of co-optation or vernacularization (to borrow Merry's 2006a term) when they do. This is the work of "behavioral change programs" and therapeutic interventions, discussed in Chapter 5.

The rights discourse anchors the modern moral social imaginary in Australia. At the risk of oversimplifying this imaginary, core elements of it can begin to be understood in terms of what Walzer has identified as the "four mobilities" that underpin liberalism: geographic, social, marital, and political.[10] As Walzer states, these mobilities "represent the enactment of liberty" (1990: 12). We can remind ourselves that these mobilities and the metaphor of movement, as an ever-emerging modernity, can be directly found to underpin many of the articles of the UDHR. The first three mobilities—geographic, social, and marital—disrupt family life. The liberal ideal of disconnecting and untethering enduring relationships, people from place, from history, and from connections to a past is an intrinsic modality of liberalism. This voluntary association (see especially in Articles 18 and 20) has implications for the geographic and social mobilities, as the disruption of the Aboriginal connection to place as ties to land, community, and family. Embodying these mobilities also implies the shift to independent values that are not "cultural" or circumscribing. As Walzer reiterates: "Liberalism, as the language of individual rights—voluntary association, pluralism, toleration, separation, privacy, free speech, the career open to talents, and so on—is simply inescapable" (1990: 14). Discussion of the ways in which these four liberal mobilities are circulating and mobilizing new forms of personhood are threaded throughout this book.

Another key plank on which a human rights–based ontology is founded is the moral emotion of empathy. The development of empathy for others, for strangers, beyond the family group, the clan, or language group is essential for the norms of pluralism and toleration to gain ground. Hunt describes how

the emotional qualities of empathy began to become a political project, leading to notions of equality, when the novel and newspapers first emerged during the eighteenth century (2007).[11] Thus, empathy is a necessary precursor to
imagining a shared equality. This metanarrative can be juxtaposed with the
endosociality of small communities and large families, whereas on the other
hand the Anangu diaspora also speaks to the shift to embrace a larger region
and develop this "stranger sociability" (per Goankar and Povinelli 2003). Indeed, the power of the stranger and the therapeutic technologies, discussed in
Chapters 4 and 5, actively encourage not only empathy for others but also an
emergent agentic and intentional independent self.

This intentional subject as agentic citizen has to operate in all spheres, not
only in interpersonal terms but also politically. As Ranciere argues, being part
of a political community is more than the technicality of citizenship, as the
correct subject of human rights has to be the political actor (2004). Ranciere's
concept of "political subjectivization" is in the same conceptual realm as
Merry's notion that rights have to emerge in the local vernacular, that is, the
rights holder is necessarily a publicly political citizen who has internalized a
particular political agency (Merry 2006a; Ranciere 2004). The implications
this has for Anangu are explored in Chapter 6.

The abiding relationship within the human rights discourse with secularism, rationality, and human agency also attempts to disrupt and challenge
historical attachments that are understood as preordained or divine. In
Anangu terms, such preordained attachments are also structured through
kinship terms, because although settlement has compelled many changes to
Anangu social life, the relational identity that is coextensive with family has
not been so readily displaced. Kinship remains the central organizing principle in social reproduction (see Myers 1986: 159–218 for a detailed analysis
of this kinship system). Anangu are born into a sociocentric web of signification framed by, in anthropological terms, the subsection system whereby
every Anangu person is assigned through the patriline one of eight subsections. Each of these subsection categories, which include the kin terms found
as names in this book, such as Nakamarra and Tjakamarra, is further marked
linguistically for female (n-) and male (tj-). A person is allocated a skin name
at birth based on the skin of his or her parents, so that these are not optional
categories of association. This nomenclature operates as a system that enables
the replacement of individuals within categories, especially important in ceremonial contexts. The fact that social reproduction is not about the person but

about his or her role as certain kin acts both to anonymize individual persons and to structure their relational responsibilities. The multiple and ramifying effects of this public, rather than private, kinship are explored in diverse contexts throughout this book.

Indeed, the concept of family, as an embodiment Aboriginal kinship, is one of the most contested sites both within the realms of human rights and women's rights. For Anangu, the family embodies the values of collective rights, and it is the Aboriginal family that is most threatened by the neoliberal rendering of rights as separatist and individualist. This is perhaps most pronounced in legal contexts, where the individual person becomes the legal subject, most commonly as a "victim" or as a "perpetrator." The unintended consequences of these legal labels, as they shape policies, laws, and programs, are explored in Chapters 2, 4, and 5 because, as for women globally, it is also within the family that Anangu women are most at risk of physical violence and coercive control.

Asmarom Legesse usefully reminds us that human rights are cultural constructs, as he states:

> If Africans were the sole authors of the UDHR, they might have ranked the rights of communities above those of individuals, and they might have used a cultural idiom fundamentally different from the language in which the ideas are now formulated. (1980: 129, in Donnelly 1982: 311)

As the following chapter examines the translation of the UDHR as an intercultural dialogue, resonances can be found between Pintupi-Luritja cultural priorities and those as identified by Legesse for Africans. Although the cultural idioms structuring human rights have become an essential normative element of the modern condition, Legesse reminds us of the contingency of this discourse and that universality in the abstract is an illusion. And so this book explores local cultures of human rights through the ways in which the discourse is inserted, co-opted, and rejected or modified in several communities. As such, this book could in some ways be read as an analysis of the struggles with, and the strained and selective emergence of, forms of modern neoliberalism in remote central Australia.

Paradoxes Inherent in Indigenous Human Rights

As is now well understood in political philosophy, human rights act through paradox. For instance: "Are human rights an effective defence tool against corruption or are they the ideological gloss for an emerging empire?" (Douzinas 2007: 7). Human rights can be, and are, both. This book explores the many unintended consequences of human rights that could also be understood in terms of their paradoxes. For Anangu, this emerges at the many intersections with the legal system, whether in terms of property [land] rights or the rights of Anangu women to be free from violence; their identities lock them into specific rights remedies.

The intersection of the human rights discourse with intimate subjectivities in institutionalized legal contexts has been examined by Merry, specifically in relation to gender violence (Merry 2003, 2006b). A core question she asks is, "How does a person come to understand his or her problems in terms of rights?" (2003: 343). As I also asked this question in the legal contexts that enforced women's right to be free from violence, for instance, what emerged for many Anangu women is that these "rights" were part of the problem. As the protective regimes enforce freedom from violence via the mandatory sentencing and mandatory reporting laws, she is labeled a victim and identified by her subordination. I ask: Has the legal system become another perpetrator?

In the central Australian context, these paradoxes are often expressed through the tensions best exemplified by the communitarian critique of liberalism, led initially by Marx and Engels. As Marx realized, universally distributed rights function not only as power but also as deprivation: "Rights differentially empower different social groups, depending on their ability to enact the power that a right potentially entails" (Brown 2000: 232). Marginal and subordinated groups thus struggle to access and enact their rights. As Brown reiterates:

> Countless critics have pointed out, [that] the more social resources and the less social vulnerability one brings to the exercise of a right, the more power that exercise will reap, whether that right is sexual freedom, private property, speech or abortion. (2000: 232)

Such are the paradoxes of human rights that in the neocolonial Australian context, rights concepts can act as another form of assimilation via their sponsoring of an agentic market-driven individualism through punitive measures that enforce the right to work and school attendance, for instance. However, rights also aim to enfranchise the Aboriginal citizen as a political actor in the right to vote and be an active citizen. Each chapter in this book reveals and explores a paradox. In the following chapter, for instance, the implications of translating of the UDHR into the local language of Pintupi-Luritja are interrogated beyond the usual sunny formulations. The act of translating the discourse of human rights into the local vernacular is not an innocent one. Embedded in the introduced language of English is the politics of colonialism, and so the potential for this intercultural encounter to act as another mechanism for assimilation, another tool of conversion, is real—and not dissimilar perhaps to the Bible translation into the local vernacular, but this time of a secular kind. After all, that imperialism had to be a transformative ideology was an early principle of statecraft (per Hobson 1938).

Substantive Rights versus Formal Rights

Indigenous difference is not just any kind of difference: it is a colonial one. It is not only a "different inequality"; it is also a "different difference."

Hage 2012: 409

The way in which the major Australian political parties engage with the issue of formal and substantive rights tends to be one of the markers most clearly distinguishing between them as political parties. For instance, according to the then Liberal Coalition Treasurer Joe Hockey: "Striving to achieve equality is not the role of the government" (Hockey 2014), as he made plain the Conservative government's attachment to a minimum of formal or technical rights. This approach calls to mind the old joke: "What is the definition of a liberal? Someone who believes all the bad things in the world stem from accidents" (Farmer 2003: 7). Farmer is alluding to the machineries of global capitalism and neoliberalism and the resulting marginality of the vulnerable through what he refers to as "structural violence."

On the other hand, the rhetoric of the Labor Party is the "fair go," as they distinguish between equity and equality. With a focus on social outcomes as well as economic outcomes, they are more likely to sponsor services that are enabling of equity, such as community legal services, women's shelters, public high schools, and so on. This is an acknowledgment that the socially vulnerable or disenfranchised need assistance in accessing their rights. That community organizations that offer social services are accorded funding depending on the model of rights that the government chooses to endorse clearly leaves the community sector precarious. The significant majority of services that Indigenous Australians access are perched in this sector, leaving them permanently vulnerable. The issues that this Indigenous sector has are also compounded, however. As Santos states: "People have the right to be equal whenever difference makes them inferior, but they also have the right to be different whenever equality jeopardizes their identity" (2002: 57). The "Closing the Gap" policy campaign, discussed further in Chapter 2, which aims for statistical equality between Indigenous Australians and the mainstream on a diverse range of measures, is a blunt instrument in this complex domain. In very remote areas, for instance, the indices of quality of life often conflict with the moral and political objectives of statistical equality.

In some "background notes" prepared by the National Directorate for the 1967 constitutional referendum, this idea of enabling substantive rights for Indigenous Australians was elaborated:

> In view of the special disadvantages of lack of capital, education and "know-how" suffered by the Aborigines, the well-known principle of justice that "it is as unjust to treat unequals equally as to treat equals unequally" is a strong argument for special legislation to enable Aborigines to overcome their disadvantages. (Attwood and Markus 1997: 48)

Hugman, for example, argues that human rights without social justice means that inequality bars the most disadvantaged from claiming their rights (2013). The principle of equality is basic to a Marxian theory of rights, that ideally the society cannot be a class society such that significant socioeconomic inequalities have to be eliminated so that everyone will have roughly the same opportunities to use his or her formal rights, such as the right to free speech.

Tim Wilson, a Human Rights Commissioner appointed by the Abbott Liberal coalition government in 2014, gave what could also be understood as another interpretation of formal rights, expressing them as "traditional human rights":

> To keep them sacrosanct human rights are few—such as freedom of speech, association, movement, worship, freedom from arbitrary detention, equality before the law and property rights—and rarely come into conflict when individuals exercise them. By comparison, the socialist approach was about using human rights as an instrument to ensure democratic participation. They saw human rights as a means to advance objectives and, like all aspects of socialism, the individual came second. (Wilson 2014)

Brian Burdekin, the first Human Rights Commissioner (who served from 1986 to 1994), by contrast felt the need to respond to Wilson's approach, illustrated in the previously mentioned and other articles, and his claim that these rights were "traditional" ones and that "in the second half of the 20th century the rise of international human rights law has perverted and distorted our understanding of where our rights come from." Burdekin reminded us that:

> All human rights are "universal" and equally important. . . . Disaggregating rights into sub-categories misconstrues the UDHR's purpose. Freedom of expression is important. However, the Commissioner also bears a heavy responsibility to ensure the rights of the most vulnerable are protected. (*Sydney Morning Herald*, December 24, 2013)

The implications of Wilson's, and the Liberal Coalition government's, regressive focus on civil and political rights, marginalizing the other rights that appear in same foundational UDHR, the economic, social, and cultural rights (Articles 22–27), does not bode well for an active consideration by the same government of the rights contained within the UN Declaration on the Rights of Indigenous Peoples. As so-called third-generation rights, they are even further removed from the "traditional rights" espoused as "sacrosanct" by Wilson. As Wilson continued:

> Australia and other Anglosphere nations were built on a liberal approach. Yet many international treaties are infused with the objectives of the socialist tradition . . . they saw human rights as a means to advance objectives . . . Human rights are not the same as social justice. Human rights are about uncompromisingly protecting the autonomy of the individual. (Wilson 2014)

Although Wilson may claim such statements as fact, this is a particular ideological position. Human rights activists and organizations across the globe, bolstered by statements from the United Nations, variously use all elements of the UDHR as a platform to agitate for social change and governmental reform. Stating that human rights is not the same as social justice fails to connect with this global phenomenon, ignoring the fact that social justice movements gain their leverage from the language and institutions of human rights. Unfortunately, Wilson's approach also seeks to reduce possibilities for the language of human rights to act as a generative tool for moral change and to unsettle and challenge the established relations of power.

Not a Ledger Approach

Taking a systematic ledger approach to human rights, in relation to particular policies and programs or in terms of an adding up of costs and benefits with a tally against the activation, dismissal, or recasting of certain rights, is not the purpose of this book. This is one of the roles of the Australian Human Rights Commission and their annual reporting, some of which can be found in the Social Justice Reports. Nor is this book going to drill down critiquing or evaluating specific Indigenous policies and approaches; there are other anthropological texts that have done just this (notably Sullivan 2011; Sutton 2009; Altman and Hinkson 2007; Dillon and Westbury 2007). The Australian Indigenous policy environment is notoriously volatile. Yet, in the last decade, what can be found to be a constant, across the political spectrum, is the attachment of responsibilities to citizenship for Indigenous citizens. Focusing on the governmentality of this responsibilization discourse, at once diffuse and specific, as a neoliberal rendering of human rights allows a broader view. By refusing to be drawn into focusing on the language of policy, so too any critique can avoid being framed solely by the state and its fickle policy debates.

This is because if the debate is circumscribed by the existing tool kit that the state offers up in its discourse, which includes terms such as "inequality" and used to include "self-determination," then failure of Aboriginal policies and programs is the only outcome (see also Hage 2012). This anthropological relationship with government has been described as a "complex symbiotic dependency" (Hinkson 2010: 5). Not only does the language and discourse of human rights offer potential to reframe and reexamine the seemingly intractable issues and long-standing debates that remote Indigenous inequality poses to a contemporary social ethic, but many of the foundational elements of this discourse can be found in the operations of government policy. Yet, as this book will explore, they are rarely explicitly articulated.

However, one particular policy intervention brought the spotlight on the issues of Indigenous human rights in the Northern Territory (NT). As the "elephant in the room" that enters at various points in the following chapters, the Northern Territory Emergency Response (NTER) of 2007 will briefly be overviewed here.[12] The federal government intervention into the Northern Territory in 2007, referred to as the NTER, was triggered by widespread allegations of child sexual abuse as catalogued in the Report of the Northern Territory Board of Enquiry into the Protection of Aboriginal Children from Sexual Abuse, or the *Ampe Akelyerenmane Meke Mekarle*, "Little Children Are Sacred Report" (Northern Territory Board 2007). A raft of extreme measures were implemented that, as Hinkson notes, taken together constituted a governmental intervention unmatched by any other policy declaration in

Indigenous affairs in the last forty years (2007: 1). Arguably, had the Parliamentary Committee on Human Rights been operating in 2007, then the NTER could not have been implemented or, at the very least, this process of scrutiny would have slowed the passing of the NTER legislation.

The raft of policy interventions, far broader than the protection of children and infringing many fundamental rights, included universal social security income management, acquisition of the seventy-three "prescribed" (remote and town camp) communities through leases, abolishing the Community Development Employment Program (CDEP), and punitive measures for parents who did not ensure their children's school attendance, for instance. Indeed, to pass the three proposed bills as legislation, the Racial Discrimination Act of 1975 had to be suspended (Behrendt 2007: 19). The NTER catalyzed a focus on the issue of Indigenous "rights" in the Northern Territory (Davis 2007) while the Central Land Council also undertook its own research to provide a grassroots response to government (for instance 2007, 2008; see also Concerned Australians 2010).

The NTER also galvanized and polarized politicomoral anthropological and broader debate (Altman and Hinkson 2007; Langton 2007).[13] A core element of this debate was the extent of the disciplines' complicity in acting as academic commentator to these "horrible conditions" (per Langton 2007: 2), rather than as activist scholars attempting to change the status quo, partly because we talk among others in the discipline rather than engage in public debate. Marcia Langton, one of the very few Indigenous social anthropologists in the academy, and who routinely engages in public debate, noted that:

> There is the risk that our work assists, paradoxically, in the creation of identities of victimhood through our descriptions of their suffering [and] the epistemological flaws and fallacies that are ever-present because of the very humanism and relativism of our discipline. (2010: 93)

Is a Rapprochement Possible between Culture and Rights?

In many ways this book is a conversation that moves between and reflects on local values and norms and the norms and values that underpin human rights. In this comparative project, this conversation does not isolate "culture" as something performed on special occasions, such as ceremony; rather, it also includes the everyday intersubjective practices. A UN Development Program report, "Cultural Liberty in Today's Diverse World" (UNDP 2004) states:

Neither cultural freedom nor respect for diversity should be confused with the defence of tradition; the central issue in cultural liberty is the capability of people to live as they would choose, with adequate opportunity to consider other options. (cited in Cowan 2006: 14, UNDP 2004: 4)

This book contributes to the local and regional debate about what these other options might entail and the challenges to engaging with them in terms that engage with intersectional and structural disadvantage, as well as different cultural and socioeconomic priorities. The Australian Human Rights and Equal Opportunity Commission (now the Human Rights Commission) stated that the exercise of "self-determination is central to the achievement of a number of goals including . . . our own justice systems, having control over our own lives . . . being subject to our own laws . . . [and] recognition of customary law" (AHREOC 2003: 9-10).[14] However, they make no mention of how these differing justice systems, as systems of cultural practice, can be reconciled when, for instance, an enduring element of customary law in some remote regions is "payback," or *ngapartji ngapartji kuwarriku* in Pintupi-Luritja. This issue of payback is explored in Chapter 3 in ways that recognize that "local communities often conceive of social justice in quite different terms from human rights activists" (Merry 2006a: 1). The label of "lateral violence" is now applied by external observers to analyze and name this subordinating behavior of "payback" (see AHRC 2011b: 8).

Santos, as an activist human rights philosopher, has attempted to reimagine human rights in multicultural terms to decenter their hegemonic regulatory functions and instead to inscribe a "mestiza" conception of human rights that is emancipatory (2002). This call is, in part, a recognition of the "false universalisms" of human rights claims while at the same time wanting to grasp the possibilities that the human rights language offers. Such a "cross-cultural" discussion recognizes that all cultures have different versions of human dignity and fundamentally wrestles with finding this rapprochement. Thus, when Alison Anderson, a Pintupi-Lurijta woman and member of the NT Parliament (from 2005 to 2016) beseeched me to "do anthropology differently," a fundamental element of her concern was that this conversation be reciprocal. I interpreted this to mean that local conceptions of human dignity also be found and offered as equivalences to the "global standard," for instance. And further, taking a lead from collaborative anthropologist Elaine Lawless, that the ethnographic project be dialogical where interpretive differences are negotiated between myself as anthropologist and Anangu (1992).

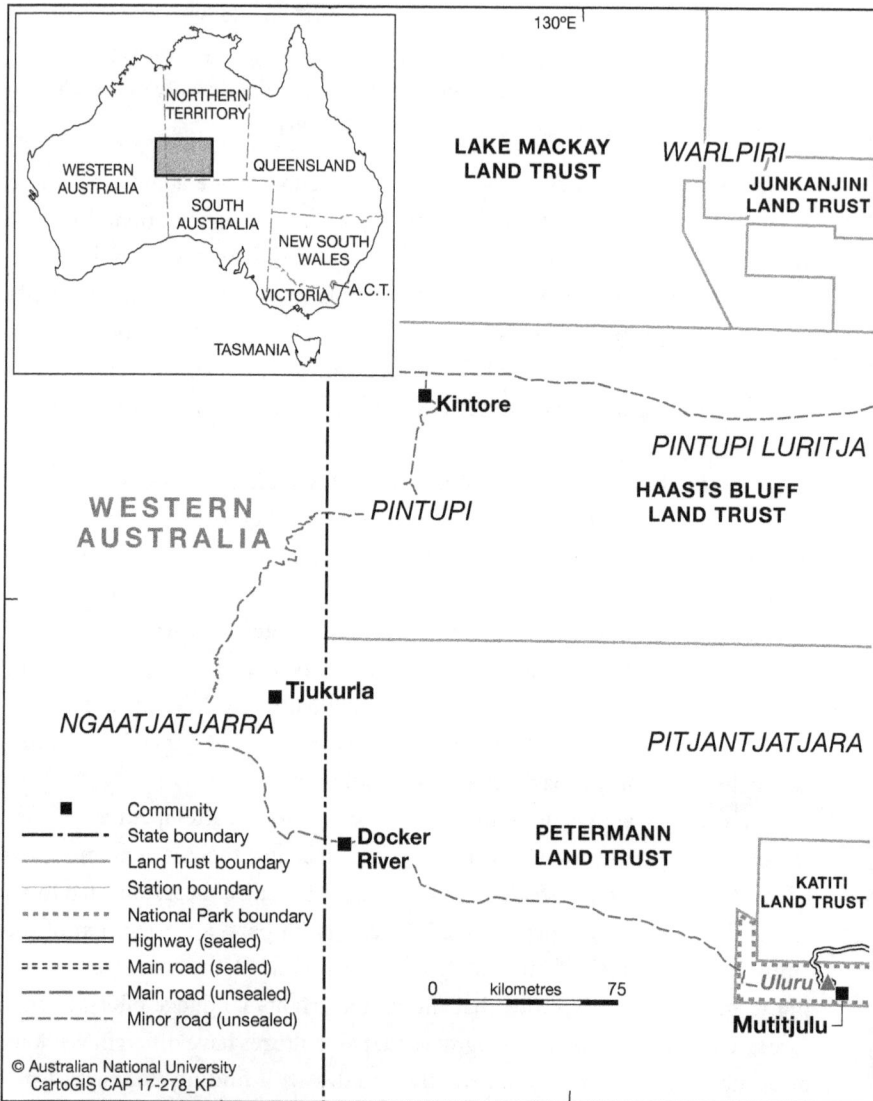

MAP. Central Australian languages with some relevant communities and Alice Springs as the regional center.

Source: CartoGIS Services, ANU College of Asia and the Pacific, The Australian National University.

Such a dialogical approach is undertaken with the realization that "such writing is always a form of political participation" (Hage 2012: 408).

Nevertheless, this is still fundamentally a work of anthropology, and my positioning as a non-Indigenous nonmember of the community presents

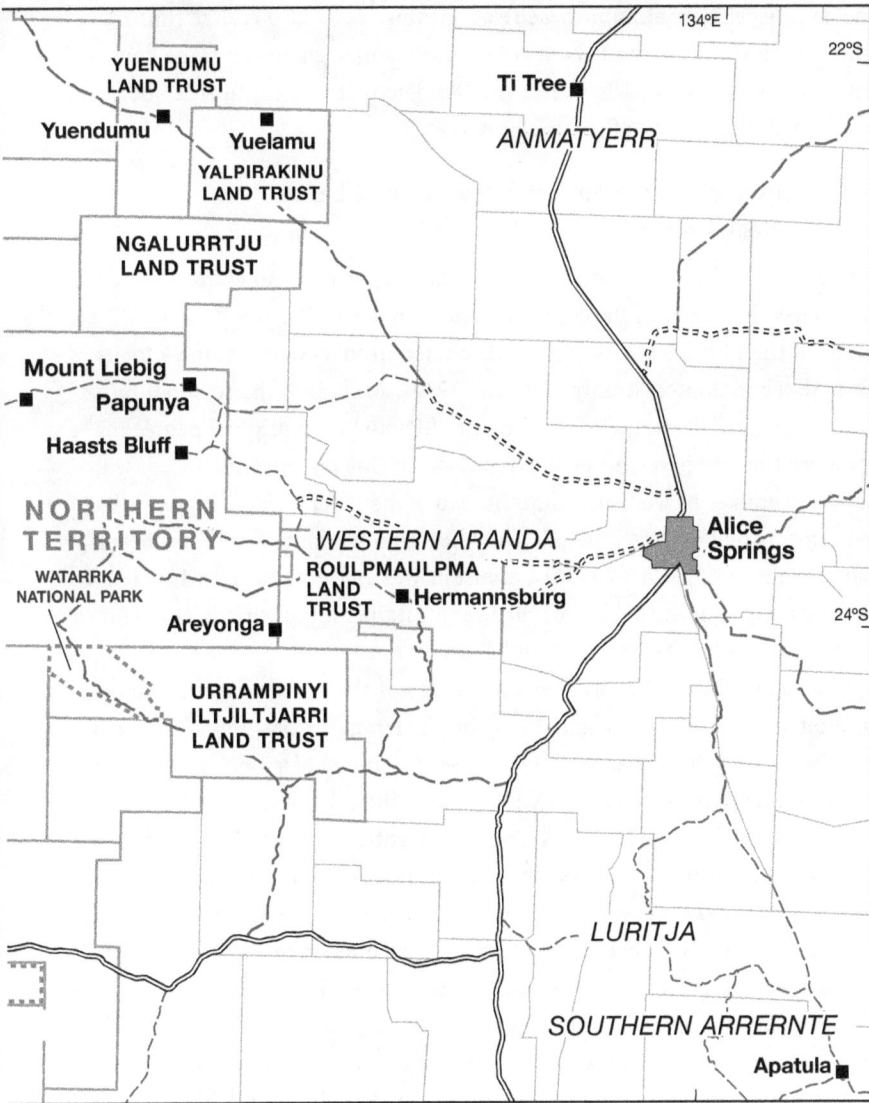

ethical challenges. The fact that, in many contexts, individuals did not wish to be named (but instead asked that I use their skin names), though they were interested in their perspectives being heard, also speaks to the closeness of the community and of the intimacy of much of the subject matter. Ultimately, I have deep attachments with many of the Anangu who shared their perspectives about particular issues and in doing so shared aspects of their lives with me, and I seek to maintain these relationships. Yet, I also realize that subsequent analysis of many of these conversations may challenge some community members, even as I have returned to discuss the ideas in this book and confirmed the veracity of particular quotes.

The Places and Their People: Papunya, Mount Liebig, and the Haasts Bluff Land Trust

These are small places that, like many others in very remote areas, were the last to feel the effects of the colonial frontier in Australia. The Western Desert lands of the Pintupi-Luritja people discussed in this book became a focus of non-Aboriginal interest only from the 1930s. Excluding the regional hub of Alice Springs, 230 kilometers to the east of Papunya, Aboriginal people make up more than 80 percent of the population of this region, which is classified as "very remote" by the Australian Bureau of Statistics (ABS). Huge swaths of land in this region were scheduled as Aboriginal Land (under the Aboriginal Land Rights [NT] Act of 1976) because it was marginal to non-Indigenous interests and thus available with little contest, including what is now known as the Haasts Bluff Aboriginal Land Trust.

Although this region was on the fringes of the violence of this colonial frontier, mainly due to the land being on the fringes of pastoralism, I was reminded that its effects were still felt as I read a eulogy of a much respected recently deceased senior man, Billy Stockman. The brief biography, Blu-Tacked to the wall of the local Papunya Tjupi Art Centre, recalled that he became a lifetime resident of this region (the communities of Haasts Bluff, then Papunya) when, in 1928, he was carried south as a baby with his remaining family as they fled from what became known as "the Coniston massacre."[15] After his mother was murdered by the police, he was raised by his Aunty, as he was one of many Warlpiri- and Anmatyerr-speaking people who sought refuge at what was then the Lutheran missionary outpost of Haasts Bluff. One of his daughters, Punata, is now a community leader with grandchildren of her own. Although this violent legacy is within living memory, there are few memorials to the violence of this colonial frontier. It is a reminder of the recency of colonial intervention in this region.

This history is also a reminder that the Northern Territory is deeply polarized. Of its current population of just over 200,000 people, nearly one-third are Aboriginal, compared to between 1 and 4 percent in other Australian states and territories. One of the outcomes of this relatively high Aboriginal population is, as Sanders notes, a distinctive division among the settler population that he defines in terms of the "moralists" and the "opportunists." He states that, whereas the former are in the Northern Territory because they want to "do good," the latter are there to "make good" in their careers and business (2007: 64–65). As Sanders further points out, this division is also mirrored politically between those focused on improving the socioeconomic conditions of Aboriginal people and those focused on developing the north. Another outcome of this division is that the language of rights is even further on the periphery in this jurisdiction. As a former colleague from the Central Land Council (CLC) joked to me about this research: "Save the rights talk for down south, where it means something."

Papunya has gained renown as the crucible for the Western Desert art movement from the 1970s (Bardon and Bardon 2004; Johnson 2010); it has led some of the most radical politics against the Northern Territory government (discussed further in Chapter 6) and is the community of Alison Anderson, one of the first Aboriginal members of Parliament from Central Australia. The Warumpi Band, the first Aboriginal rock-and-roll band to record a CD, also emerged from Papunya. Their song, "Jailanguru Pakarnu" ("Out from Jail") was the first rock song in an Aboriginal language (Luritja) and released by the Warumpi Band in 1983.[16] Against this dynamic background, however, Papunya has had a turbulent history. Unlike the other three communities on the Land Trust, it was established in the late 1950s during the deeply paternalistic policy period of "assimilation" as a "training institution." According to the policy materials of that period, several of the aims were to provide welfare services fitted to their needs and to their stage of social development; to provide the means whereby training may be given, particularly to children and adolescents; and to introduce the general concept of "work" as a worthwhile aim in life.

The effects of permanent settlement of a nomadic people was deeply disaffecting. The historian Dick Kimber summed up the sentiment surrounding this policy era in the region: "The [assimilation] Policy and its implementation both west of Papunya and at Papunya can best be summarised as a white disaster, an Aboriginal tragedy" (1981: 23), which included a high mortality rate among the newly arrived Pintupi, much of which was blamed on sorcery and related antagonisms (Myers 1976; Kimber 1981). The official medical point of view was that "more disastrous (than fighting and adjustment to rations) were the infections, largely pneumonia or viral (measles), that destroyed more than half the population, which came with low levels of immunity to close contact with reservoirs of disease" (Kimber 1981: 26). Of the seventy-two people who came into Papunya in 1963 and 1964, twenty-nine had died by August 1964 (Nathan and Japanangka 1983: 79–80).

Geoffrey Bardon, who was credited with catalyzing the Western Desert art movement while he was a schoolteacher at Papunya, observed in the early 1970s:

> Many of the whites were not only extremely hostile towards the Aboriginals but showed what I thought pathological psychotic tendencies, as a measure of their dislike . . . quite unconcerned with the most abusive and degrading behaviour they might exhibit towards the Aboriginal people, and they appeared to exult in the contempt and hatred they showed. (Bardon and Bardon 2004: 8)

The Aboriginal residents needed permission to leave the settlement while they were at that time also segregated from the non-Aboriginal residents, other than when Aboriginal men undertook the garbage collection (see also Batty 2011). As Bardon continued, "The racism, the casual paternalism and self-righteousness of the white man's law were all of a pattern with heavy drinking and an intellectual dishonesty" (2004: 6). The introduction of alcohol to Aboriginal people in the NT, which occurred in the same period as voting enfranchisement in 1964, was devastating until the community, in fact all Aboriginal Land, chose to introduce restrictions from 1979 (D'Abbs 1990). Although alcohol is still an issue with "grog running" (illegal trafficking in alcohol) from Alice Springs, there are also other illicit drugs coming into the community, including marijuana (ganja) and methamphetamines, such as "ice."

Although I use the term "community" in this book to refer to these places, as this is the most common referent, they are more accurately referred to as settlements (Newman et al. 2008). The concept of community assumes a shared affinity or a communal "consciousness of kind" (Gusfield 1975: 34), and this was far from the case when these places were first established. Different family groups speaking different languages were compelled to live side by side, drawing out old animosities that led to physical violence and sorcery during the early establishment of Papunya, for instance. With the passing of the Aboriginal Land Rights (Northern Territory) Act of 1976, the residents of Papunya, and other government and mission settlements in the Northern Territory who wished, were enabled to leave these places and return to their customary lands. What became referred to as "the outstation [or homelands] movement" was closely tied to the policy period of self-determination (see Peterson and Myers 2016). After Anangu exercised their choice to either remain in Papunya and surrounds or returned to their lands further west, the places were, however, reconfigured to take on some elements of a "community" (Holcombe 1998, 2004b).

Though I often refer only to Papunya, this community is the regional hub, and there is continual movement of family members among all four communities: Papunya, Mount Liebig (Amunturrngu), Haasts Bluff (Ikuntji), and Kintore (Walungurru) on the Land Trust. One of the reasons Papunya has developed as a hub community is because it is located at the crossroads to communities further west, Mount Liebig and Kintore; and the Warlpiri communities to north, Yuendemu and Yuelemu (Mount Allen). There is considerable circular mobility among these neighboring communities. The population of Papunya and its approximately six surrounding outstations was, according to the ABS Quickstats in 2011: 455 people (including forty-one non-Indigenous people), with a median age of twenty-three. There were 215 males and 241 females. The trend from 2001 indicates that the population is increasing by about one-third every five years. This region covers almost 8,000 square kilometers and includes over a dozen small family outstations or homelands.

It is within this context, briefly drawn, that I have attempted to engage with human rights ideas so that they could be "translated into local terms and situated within local contexts of power and meaning" (per Merry 2006). At the same time, local contexts are exposed to global cultures, and so this is an ethnographic study of a global reform movement through the prism of Central Australian politics and policies. This book aims to illuminate the multiplicity of dimensions in which the discourse of human rights manifests in diverse social, legal, and political contexts. Some of these contingencies and contradictions are revealed in the following poem by Hodder-Watts (Aboriginal activist, spoken word artist, and at that time the CLC media officer).

"Missed the Call" by Steve Hodder-Watts

(portion of a poem spoken at international Human Rights Day 2013 in Alice Springs)[17]

> Let us continue 2 die on grog, keeps us hit with the job network cattle prods, demands we "go get a job," but we turn the white door but can't seem 2 pop the Andrew Bolt[18] lock.

Now we see Conservative blacks who get stacked on the poster boy podium,
   praised as champions 4 having a go at 'em, pointing fingers too, refuse
   2 help us up,
tell 'em "get stuffed, stand up on your own 2 feet,"
just echo & repeat the mainstream bleat that keeps culture & identity tied behind our backs, while the right-wing black trackers apologise & justify the
   hate we used 2 attack,
so we keep going around the 1950's greyhound track, chasing the mechanical
   Abbott[19] with hopeless odds,
now the bets are off since we lost Mandawuy,[20] Mandela, 1 of them mel-
   low blackfellas, ignoring the fact that we get jailed more here than in
   Apartheid,
it was Cane Toad Joh[21] who showed them the ropes & it exists today,
on the streets, in the schools and out the front of bottle shops
but look behind the walls & see the prison rates escalate & so we Missed The
   Call 4 Freedom again as Justice falls.

The Book Structure

My pragmatic practice-oriented approach is juxtaposed with the abstracted
legal instrumentalist nature of the rights regime. As Santos has stated, we have
enough theories of rights; we need to develop "a theory of context" (1996). This
book draws on empirical data to develop such a theory of context through
an exploration of the ways in which this discourse of human rights is active,
albeit often implicit, in diverse locations, institutions, organizations, programs, and policies in ways that are "indirect, fragmented and diffuse" (Levitt
and Merry 2011: 88). These include, through the work of NGOs, such as the
women's NGO Waltja Tjutangku Palyapayi and the Central Land Council
(Chapter 3); via articulations with the legal system in relation to gender violence (Chapter 4); through what are known as "behavioral change programs"
(in Chapter 5); in the gloss's euphemisms for "good governance" (Chapter 6); and so on. In articulating this diverse work of rights, the ethnographic
approach draws from a practice-oriented approach recognizing, like Ortner
(2005) and Wardlow (2006), that subjectivity is the basis of agency, where an
individual has a "specifically cultural and historical consciousness" (Ortner
2005: 34).

This book is divided into four parts. The first part, Chapter 1, opens a dialogue with the concepts of rights as the Universal Declaration of Human

Rights is translated into the local vernacular of Pintupi-Luritja. The semantic properties of English and possible equivalent Anangu concepts are juxtaposed in the translation context, and the limitations and possibilities of the universal human rights discourse are (re)imagined. The dialogical properties of the Declaration are almost limitless, as the concepts embodied within it range across key cultural concepts embodied within Western liberal discourse. This chapter then sets up the core challenges and possibilities of the local uptake of this discourse, as well as its limitations.

With a focus on gender relations, Chapters 2 and 3 examine some of the intersections among social, economic, and cultural rights and Anangu forms of sociality. The multiple ways that gender is relationally reproduced through gender-segregated patterns of work and key elements of ceremony as an ongoing customary practice are explored. The issue of gender became a greater focus than initially anticipated, principally because of the ramifications of the range of gender-segregated social practices that (re)produce gender as a power relation. Gender equality is not a concept readily applied or embraced across contexts. Instead, practices of complementarity resonate with less individualistic notions that more readily embrace the collective. Yet, there are emergent practices to be found in a consideration of independent values and the increase in mobility across a wider region and other liberal values, notably among the Anangu diaspora and those who travel for work in Aboriginal organizations and representative bodies.

Chapter 4 explores the intersections among legal rights, local perceptions of social justice, and gender violence. Spousal or intimate partner violence exposes multiple sites of articulation with formal rights via the legal system at the same time as revealing, often in contradistinction, Anangu responsibilities in customary terms. Anangu women's interactions with and responses to the legal system, including the police, reflect contradictory and competing discourses between family and the state system. The formal legal system representing Aboriginal people has instrumentalized women as the "victims" and men as the "perpetrators" through the extensive range of mandatory reporting and sentencing laws. This chapter specifically elaborates the ways that rights that "entail some specification of our suffering, injury or inequality lock us into the identity defined by our subordination" (Brown 2000: 232). Chapter 6 examines several therapeutic interventions, including the Cross Borders Indigenous Family Violence Program, that aim to change the status of the "perpetrator" to an empathizer, whereas the women's shelter outreach service aims to alter the subjectivity of their clients from a "victim" to an actor. These individuating programs and services attempt to locate and develop the self that would prefer to identify as independent rather than interdependent and also to be purposive and in control. Although not explicitly using the language of rights, they articulate closely with the framework and concepts that underpin human rights.

Chapter 6, on civil and political rights, explores the ways in which the tension in political rights plays out between the regulatory dimensions of these rights for Anangu as citizens—in terms of rights as entailments as this unfolds via the responsibilization discourse—and their emancipatory potential. In doing so, I explore the question of whether there is room to expand the political imagination to incorporate alternative terms and modalities.

Thus, the bulk of this book is a reverse of the structure of the UDHR—which has the first-generation rights, the civil and political rights up front (the first twenty-one articles), whereas economic, social, and cultural rights (as Articles 22 through 29) are at the end of the document. The final chapter, 7, returns to the sites where human rights and Indigenous human rights took their shape and continue to evolve—to the UN Headquarters in New York City and to Geneva. The key question explored in this penultimate chapter is whether and how the Indigenous human rights discourse, at this international level, circulates to these remote places of central Australia, where arguably they are most needed. Chapter 7 also explores the performative aspects of these UN sites as a "public audit ritual" (per Cowan 2014), while at the same time realizing the circumscribing of Indigenous human rights.

I am acutely mindful that this book can provide only a partial perspective. As a guest of the landowners and community members with whom I worked, I have been granted considerable trust from them in their relationship with me, and the mutual respect that has evolved requires that I remain accountable. Among the reasons for this trust are the long-term relationships developed over more than two decades. In terms of my own self-location, I moved to Alice Springs as a fresh-faced twenty-two-year-old direct from an undergraduate degree in social anthropology from the University of Sydney to work for the Central Land Council (CLC). In four years at the CLC, while I worked across remote central Australia, I spent considerable periods in the Haasts Bluff Land Trust region (where Papunya and Mount Liebig are located). This work entailed taking instructions from Anangu traditional owners ("TOs"), as they are termed under the Aboriginal Land Rights Act, on issues such as exploration license applications and undertaking the associated work of "traditional owner identifications" (or TOIDs, as they are known) to ensure the right decision-making group would attend various development meetings. The incorrigible Elsey Gory Nampitjinpa, who passed away on September 15, 2014, became my dear friend and classificatory mother-in-law when she endowed me with the skin Napurrula on one of my early visits to Mount Liebig (Amunturrngu). I subsequently returned to this place to undertake PhD field research in the mid-1990s, and over the years I have continued to work in central Australia or maintained contact with Anangu friends. However, the vast distances from the east coast of Australia, where I have now lived for over a decade, to central Australia challenge these ongoing connections, although they have been revitalized by the fieldwork visits undertaken for this research.

Chapter 1

The Act of Translation

Emancipatory Potential and Apocryphal Revelations

The study of language use, enhanced by ethnographic witnessing, opens up a possibility of considering *how* human rights might actually be universal.

Hastrup 2001, in Englund 2006: 47

I N LATE 2009 THE UNITED NATIONS proudly noted that, according to the Guinness Book of World Records, the Universal Declaration of Human Rights (UDHR) was the most translated document in the world, at that stage clocking up 370 translations.[1] Since then, there have been approximately 100 more translated versions added to the UN website. The Pintupi-Lurijta version was, as far as I can ascertain, the 464th translation, going on line in October 2015.[2] It was also the first translated version in an Australian Indigenous language. Why has it taken this long for the Declaration to be translated into an Australian language? One of the reasons for this was that, according to linguist Jane Simpson, who called attention to this gap on the sixtieth anniversary of the Declaration in 2008: "Translating it would not be easy" (Simpson 2008). Although this was somewhat of a throwaway comment on an informal blogging site, it is useful to recall here because, though the product of a translated version is of intrinsic value in itself, just as valuable is the translation process as an anthropological project. The fact of intercultural complexity, as revealed in the dialogical processes of interpretation, is deeply revealing. As Pitarch, discussing the translation of the Declaration into the Mayan language Tzeltal, indicates:

In the case of translation between European languages—which share a history of moral and European ideas derived from Christianity and the

Enlightenment—the difference is hardly perceptible . . . In contrast, between more distant languages and cultures, the linguistic translation implies an intercultural translation. (2008: 91)

In the translation context, the semantic properties of English and possible equivalent Anangu concepts are juxtaposed, and the limitations and possibilities of the universal human rights discourse are imagined. The dialogical properties of the Declaration are almost limitless—as the concepts embodied within it range across "Anglo key cultural concepts" (per Wierzbicka 1997) such as "freedom," "conscience," "reason," "equality," and the concept of "rights" itself, as well as other deeply held cultural constructs, including private property, freedom of information, the rule of law, and the notion of "social order." Although this chapter draws extensively on this idea of language embodying "key cultural concepts," I prefer to preface the idea with the term "English" rather than "Anglo." This recognizes that the English language, rather than the racialized category Anglo, has been the vehicle for a global cultural movement (see Pennycook 1994, 1998; Rafael 1988).[3]

The discussions held with the Anangu translators, as these revealed competing points of anchorage between Anangu conceptions of personhood and English conceptions, were as of much analytical interest as the final translated outcome (see Appendix). Nevertheless, although there are some distinctive and closely held Anangu values that do butt up against key English cultural values, the point of elaborating them is not to render them as secondary or as culturally relative lesser versions of the "universal." Rather, it is to acknowledge the limitations of this universal rights discourse and to develop or build on other areas of possibility. In doing so we begin to imagine a local culture of human rights even at the same time as it is clear that the state (in this case notably the Northern Territory government) is deeply dismissive of many rights fundamentals such as those embodied in the rule of law, as outlined in Articles 6 to 11. As will be discussed, these are the apocryphal revelations of this chapter's title.

This chapter examines the translation process, taking on Merry's challenge that there is a critical need for conceptual clarification of culture in human rights practice (2006a: 11). This process of translation and dialogue has actively exposed many of these assumptions while drawing out specific Anangu interpretations and thus local priorities that challenge these assumptions and indeed operate as valid in their stead. This then opens the conversation to an emergent multicultural conception of human rights (per Santos 2002).

It was important, nonetheless, that the final translation remained true to the moral and political principles espoused in the Declaration; otherwise we were simply on our own tangent and creating another "Kalgaringi" or "Barunga" statement. This was challenging in many ways as the dry legal and instrumentalist language is, frankly, somewhat repellent. And there are a number of Articles that are not immediately relevant for many remote living Anangu, but this is not to say that in the future this may not change. Indeed, in this vein the translated version might also be regarded as a first-generation draft, just as the translated Luritja version of the Bible is updated as language and experience change.[4] As a result, the two translators, the linguist (Ken Hansen) and I, simultaneously had our eyes on the present context and making the ideas as locally relevant as possible, while also considering alternative future contexts and the possible educational value of the norm-making instrument: its emancipatory potential. During the many translation sessions when we worked on various drafts, there was a real sense that the Anangu translators, principally Lance Macdonald and Sheila Joyce Dixon, were part of a global conversation. In this conversation we discussed the historical evolution of "rights" and their pluralist and inclusive ideology and imagined the many other groups that have also translated the Declaration and their diverse contexts. Yet, the first concerted translation came after more than a year of fieldwork visits, as initial discussions focused only on core concepts and principles.

The need for a concerted translation of the thirty Articles of the Universal Declaration of Human Rights and the Preamble emerged when it became clear that very few of the Anangu whom I was working with, including community leaders and trained translators, had heard the words "universal human rights." This language was not available to these, and presumably other, Aboriginal people in remote communities. And although I am far from suggesting or advocating a simple equation of translation equals emancipation, it seems to me that this almost universal lack of awareness (via lack of dissemination) of this language is symptomatic of the state's attitude to human rights. It is the regulatory dimensions, which principally entail responsibilities, that are the focus of government attention under the gloss of "good governance." As a result, the possibility of Anangu engaging across the whole spectrum of rights has not been enabled, as the title of the Land Rights News piece about this translation project: "Translating Rights for All," suggests. This same news piece goes on to state: "Unless you know about your rights, how can you speak up for them and also think about them and what they might mean for you?" (*Land Rights News* 2015: 9). The last section of this chapter articulates several of the more explicitly local renderings of a range of Articles and what they mean for Anangu, or at least how they were interpreted by the translators as locally meaningful.

I readily acknowledge that "it is an established fact in Translation Studies . . . that if a dozen translators tackle the same poem [or document], they will produce a dozen different versions" (Bassnett in Englund 2006: 60). Yet beneath the variations, Bassnett observes, ought to exist an "invariant core" that is common to all translations of a single work. Although I hope the translation team (Macdonald, Dixon, Holcombe, and Hansen) have found that invariant core, as this is an intercultural dialogue it can only be approximate as issues of commensurability are foregrounded.

This chapter is fundamentally a methodological one, as it explores the dialogical work of this translation as a socially situated practice. This concept of dialogue is useful, as it seems to me that one of the core properties of the Declaration is its potential as a point of conversation. Such a focus aligns with postcolonial theorists who, as Bassnett and Trivedi point out, now perceive the extent to which translation of texts such as the Bible was a one-way process and foundational to colonization. So as one recognizes this, translation projects can now offer a "reciprocal process of exchange" (Bassnett and Trivedi 2002: 5). Nevertheless, being a nonlinguist, though with a long-term familiarity with the language, when I first began this project I underestimated the complexity of the translation task, thinking of it as an end in itself. Perhaps in the vein of Englund's critique of the African Malawian translation of the Declaration:

> Many activists and officers in both government and NGOs shared the usual lay person's idea of translation as a straightforward matter of explaining an issue expressed in one language in the words of another. Any native speaker with sufficient knowledge of English would qualify for the task, an attitude that accounts for activists' failure to see the relevance of lexicographical research before embarking on translating a new discourse. (2006: 55)

It was with this possible criticism in mind that, after the first translated draft was finally completed, I then engaged the linguist Ken Hansen (for instance, Hansen and Hansen 1992) and began the process again.[5] We used the draft I had developed with MacDonald and Dixon as the basis, in what could be regarded as an accumulative endeavor, while continuing to work with Lance Macdonald in Papunya. Hansen's key issue in the translation concerned its communicability, and he wanted to ensure that all Anangu, no matter how elderly or possibly indifferent, could understand and make sense of it. For instance, I was keen to keep some English words in there, such as "freedom," because these are useful and indeed powerful words to know. However, his response to this particular word was: "some fellow *putu kulilpayi*" [can't hear: haven't heard of that word], to the nodding agreement of Macdonald. Likewise, our first translated renderings had, according to Hansen, followed an English logic of grammar and thus of ideas flow. (This was in part due to Macdonald's experience in court translation and the expectations of the lawyers in that context.) The final version more overtly subjectivized many of the dry generalized human rights concepts with localized sentiment and values than our earlier translation had done. Hansen, rather like the translation of the Bible he also undertook as a Lutheran linguist in 1981, with a revision in 2005, was able to infiltrate the "full innerness of the other's spirituality" (Hill 2002: 77). Hansen's empathy actively enabled an intersubjective encounter. The process was thus an intercultural interpretive exercise and an exercise in possible conversion, this time of the secular kind.

Implications of Translation

The act of translation of a new (English) discourse into the local vernacular is not an innocent one. As I have begun to suggest, embedded in the introduced language of English was the justifying logics of early colonialism. The language of English brought with it a radical rupture to the Aboriginal self in their *becoming* Aboriginal through the gaze and the controlling effects of the colonizers (see Rafael 1988; Pennycook 1998). As Bassnett and Trivedi state:

> The notion of the colony as a copy of the translation of the great European Original inevitably involves a value judgement that ranks the translation in a lesser position in the literary hierarchy. The colony, by this definition, is therefore less than its coloniser, its original. (2002: 4)

As they point out, this metaphor of the colony as a translation, as a copy of the original elsewhere on the map, is now recognized. Although the implications this has for Australia, as for other settler colonies, are different from those that have been decolonized, such as India and the Philippines, the point is that it was the original inhabitants whose language (and cultures) were rendered lesser. In many parts of Australia, Aboriginal people were actively discouraged from speaking their mother tongues (Trigger 1992; Harris 2013) and Standard Australian English has become established as the language of the powerful. The deep and abiding monolingualism of Australian governments has consolidated this pattern. And the policy history of bilingualism in Aboriginal schools has been volatile (Caffery, McConvell, and Simpson 2009); indeed, it is no longer funded by government in the Northern Territory.[6] Estimates of the numbers of languages at contact have ranged from 250 to 650, depending on the criteria used for language definition (Yallop 1982: 27). Nevertheless, there is wide agreement that of the over 250 languages, now only around 120 languages are still spoken, and of these about thirteen can be considered strong (Marmion, Obata, and Troy 2014). With over 2,000 speakers, it would be expected that Pintupi-Luritja is among this group.[7]

The introduction of new concepts can affect change on a range of levels, including ontological, as new ideas are inserted into local contexts. In the initial drafting of the Declaration, before the expertise of Lutheran linguist Ken Hansen, I suspected that Anangu were maintaining a "relative autonomy" (per Morphy and Morphy 2013) in a form of diglossia. As Spolsky and Irvine (1982) argued, in a now classic essay, the extent to which literacy in the local vernacular becomes embedded in daily life, as opposed to literacy in the standard language (in this case English), may also be reflective of readiness to culturally assimilate. Alternatively, code switching, word borrowing (such as using Aboriginal English), and acceptance of literacy in the standard or dominant language rather than the vernacular may suggest resistance to assimilation in an attempt to maintain cultural integrity (Spolsky and Irvine 1982: 77). Although I am not investigating the local functions of literacy, the ways in which literacy has been utilized have implications for the translation process of the human rights language. Similarly to the Ngaanyatjarra (another Western Desert language group), literacy tends to be associated with early exposure to Christian literacy practices, so that literate adults also tend to identify as Christian (Kral 2012: 58). The ramifications of this set of associations, English = literacy = Christianity, cannot be elaborated here; suffice it to realize that this history of literacy has been dominated by Christian missionary work. As Nampitjinpa, in her mid-forties, stated, when she was growing up in Papunya the only reading matter in their house was the Bible, first in English form and then the translated version.

Englund's *Prisoners of Freedom: Human Rights and the African Poor* details how the local language of Malawi, Chichewa, was regarded by human rights activists, just as it was by government and transnational NGOs, to be "a language of deprivation, rather than the language of opportunity" (2006). The human rights discourse as a translation into the national language became a one-way relation of power. If the particular rights concept did not find a local resonance or meaningful translation, it was not because the local sociopolitical context found it irrelevant; rather, they were understood as lacking in sophistication. The parallels with Australian Indigenous languages may not be so stark, but, as indicated, bilingual education is not supported in the NT and very few non-Aboriginal staff who work in remote communities have a speaking knowledge, or in some cases any knowledge, of the local language. Indeed, several police officers who were posted to Papunya in 2013–2014—though they undertook "cross-cultural training for an afternoon"—told me that they were not informed of the name of the local language group. According to the Australian Bureau of Statistics (ABS 2011), however, more than 85 percent of the population of Papunya speak an Aboriginal language (as their first language). Many speak more than one Aboriginal language. And although I undertook Pintupi-Luritja language courses in the mid-1990s through the Institute of Aboriginal Development (IAD) in Alice Springs, they have not offered such courses for some years. So in this political context, any formal or informal engagement with Aboriginal languages constitutes both political and practical recognition.

Thus, although I am deeply conscious of the larger political and social context of the ongoing colonial project, there is no denying the agency of the Anangu translators as they effectively rendered the Declaration into a social artifact. This concept of "documents as social artefacts [as they] gather new meanings [when] they are read and used by diverse subjects" is a hopeful element in this translation as both product and also as process (Riles 2001, in Englund 2006: 63). Macdonald, as a regionally renowned translator, was constantly alert to the fact that the translation was going to be associated with him, as fundamentally his work. His social embeddedness kept him alert to the possible diverse readings of his translations. In this sense, this global document has become not only localized but also deeply personalized, as will be discussed in relation to decisions he made about what specific Luritja concepts to include or exclude. Likewise, however, the issue of the limited

formal literacy of many Pintupi-Luritja as first language speakers also has implications for the uptake of the Declaration. A Pintupi-Luritja speaker who
has difficulty reading English likewise is not going to be especially literate in
his or her own language. As a result, it seems essential to have this translated
version read on local radio such as the Central Australian Aboriginal Media
Association (CAAMA) or National Indigenous TV (NITV) if Anangu are to
have access to it.[8]

The Word of God and the Word of Human Rights

The translation of universal human rights principles into literate form is not
unlike the exegesis of the Bible: a moral engagement in a broader field of unequal relations of power. Any attempt at translation and finding comparable
glosses of human rights concepts and terms finds precedent in the Lutheran
translation of their religious texts into local vernaculars, for which there is a
far deeper history (see Henson 1994; Hill 2002). The concerted mission work
that developed over many generations started from 1877 in Hermannsburg
(known then as the Finke River Mission), not far to the southeast of Papunya.
From there began the process of Christian mission expansion further into
neighboring areas of central Australia (Green 2012: 159; Hill 2002). Though
clearly on very different scales, there are parallels between the translation
projects of the word of God and that of human rights. Whereas the aim of
the Bible and hymn translations into local vernaculars has the overt aim of
Christian conversion, introducing the universal human rights language is
also potentially reformative as another element in conversion to a modernity. The Universal Declaration of Human Rights could be considered along
the lines of a "humanist" or secular Bible (per Grayling 2013) in its aim of
global reach.

In central Australia "saving souls" became, as well, "saving bodies," due
to the long period of drought, and "converting" Aborigines from "primitive,"
nomadic savages to "useful citizens" (Trudinger 2004: 31–32). The Lutherans
were effectively performing the work of the state. They attempted to develop a
new civil society incorporating education, employment, and training projects
in the newly settled space of the mission.

The "Christian is an individual-in-relation-to-God" (Dumont 1986:
30) has a ready parallel with the individual as a human-rights holder—as
against the state and as against other individuals as citizens. It appeared
that the Lutherans were attempting to develop both ontologies as modern

characteristics of their flock. And likewise, the ideology that the Lutheran missionaries were to act as "a human being among human beings," according to Hill, places mission intent squarely in the Enlightenment tradition (2002: 76). As Hill examines, this sense of sympathetic insight was entirely due to the empathy toward language and the possibilities this enabled for listening; although he is drawing on the mission work of Carl Strehlow at Hermannsburg, this Lutheran tradition traveled. As he continues:

> Of course this listening, this acceptance was . . . never entirely disinterested. The task in the long run was to show the pagan tribe their way from the folk lives that had affinities with the Old Testament, and to lead them to the New Testament . . . [this] subjective encounter was conducive to relationship, and overall enhanced by an interest in listening *in the others tongue*, and by a practiced ability to hear their song, when song meant everything: the full innerness of the other's spirituality. (Hill 2002: 77; italics in original)

Becoming deeply familiar with the local vernacular was thus fundamental to Lutheran mission work.[9] After all, as Saussure stated, "In the lives of individuals and societies, language is a factor of greater importance than anything else" (1959: 7). The Lutheran mechanisms for entering into this language and co-opting foundational concepts for new explanatory and spiritual purposes has incited much anthropological and linguistic reflection in central Australia. Green observed that "in these early days of missionary contact, much attention was paid to the controversial question of whether or not Aboriginal people believed in a 'high God' or a 'supreme being.' The corollary of this was a search for terms in the local vocabularies that could be used for the purpose of translating religious texts" (2012: 160). This led to the borrowing or cooption of the complex Arandic concept *Altyerre* (glossed as "the Dreaming") for the Christian God.[10] Interestingly, no parallel co-optation of the *Altyerre* equivalent, the Luritja *Tjukurrpa*, has been made in their much later translated version of the Bible. The Luritja term for God is *Katutja* ("pertaining to above"; *katu* is the noun "above"), whereas God's holy spirit is *katutjaku kurrunpa* (the spirit above). This rendering is literal; there is no sense of a semantic equivalent, even though the Dreaming (*Altyerre* or *Tjukurrpa*) does convey the idea of "eternal," which was apparently why it was co-opted by the early Lutherans at Hermannsburg (Green 2012: 160).

In these later Bible translations in Papunya (from the 1970s), when there was already a familiarity with the concept of the Christian God, Hansen, for instance, was more amenable to being led by the Anangu translators to finding the nearest equivalent terms, rather than imposing external interpretations onto local vernacular concepts. It was in this vein that in my discussions of how to translate the title of the Declaration, suggesting that it could be described in terms of a "big law," I provocatively asked Macdonald about using this term *Tjukurrpa* as a possible descriptor. He responded with: "*Tjukurrpa* is part of law, but there's lots of *Tjukurrpa* in our law category. It's a sacred one; we can't use it lightly. Might be women's Dreaming, might be men's." Thus, this complex category was again to remain outside of the realm of co-optation, and it appears in the translation only in relation to the right to practice culture, in Article 27.

The human rights discourse has a deep theological strain—though the focus is usually on its secular narrative. The historical convergences between Christianity and the discourse of rights are already suggested by the theological missive of Article 1 of the Declaration (which also leads the International Bill of Rights): "All human beings are endowed with reason and conscience and *should act towards one another in a spirit of brotherhood.*" The semantics of this phrase corresponds to the core Christian tenet: "Do unto others as you would have them do unto you"[11] or "Love thy neighbor."[12] Indeed this first phrase was co-opted by civil human rights NGO Amnesty International Australia (AIA) in their Faces of Hope Exhibition (2000). The painting by the Australian artist Reg Mombassa (now depicted on AIA fund-raising cards) depicts a white man in a suit and tie holding up his right hand in a two-finger peace salute, with what appears to be seeping blood from his presumably denailed hand. A sacrificial tear drops from his right eye. With a golden halo floating above his head, he stands in front of an idealized urban setting of rolling fields, and his bubble speech reads: "Do unto others as you would have them do unto you." This presupposes a shared universal moral order that shuns ideas of retribution; the "eye for an eye" system of justice that characterizes Aboriginal practices of "payback" (retributive violence), for instance. Thus, when investigating the insertion of rights ideas into the local vernacular, clearly distinguishing between a Christian action or the action of a human rights holder is not straightforward and indeed in some contexts may be false (see Witte and Green 2011; Wolterstorff 2011).[13]

Recognizing this close relationship between the human rights and Christian discourses is thus not a radical move, and the Lutherans perhaps more than other Christian faiths recognized this. As the Lutheran Church stated formally in relation to human rights, "Although the human rights movement has secular origins, 'justice' and 'right' are concepts with a biblical basis . . . Rights are the Creator's gifts to his creatures. The right to life, property, and honour are protected by the Ten Commandments" (Doctrinal Statements 2001). And in this program of mission work in the central Australian frontier Trudinger states:

> The white man had irreversibly taken the nation and the land . . . Much of the urgency in the missionary ventures . . . was compounded by the knowledge that the ruthlessness and severity of the European encounter with the Australian Aborigines meant their death and possible extinction would follow any long term failure of this conversion project. (2004: 41)

Such a "conversion project," however, assumed a unilinear displacement of Aboriginal cultural predispositions, such as relational ontologies, with the individualistic Christian doctrine. We now know that no such ready displacement occurred in Hermannsburg (Austin-Broos 1996; Henson 1994) or elsewhere (Rose 1985; Wilkins 1995). Rather, processes of syncretism that reveal porosity and melding are the more practical outcomes. This can be observed at any funeral service in the Pintupi-Luritja region, where traditional mourning practices of hair cutting and wailing through the night (notably among the older generation) occur alongside the Christian organization of the funeral service with the black and white attire, hymns, eulogies, and plastic flowers (see also Wilkins 1995). The point here is that one can surmise similar processes in the selective adoption of human rights ideology, some of which might already overlap with Christian theology.

The Rights Discourse as Embodying Key Words

The tendency to mistake "Anglo English" as the human norm (per Wierzbicka 1997; Pennycook 1998) can be found in the human rights discourse, principally because this rights discourse embodies key words and it claims to be universal. Wierzbicka was not the first to coin this "key words" concept, but she does elaborate its import at length, as words that are particularly important and revealing of a particular culture's values and preoccupations (1997: 15). For my purposes this key words concept assists in focusing on the particular values embedded in human rights language. This language has a deep history, which coalesced in a concerted way during the seventeenth century with the philosopher John Locke as a founding father and his focus on the rights to liberty, as the first firm statement of the ideas of Western liberalism and a symptom of the growing individualism of Anglo culture. Such individualism as can be seen during the same period in the work of Descartes—making the cogito, the thought of the individual thinker, take the place of authority as the foundation of all knowledge: "I think, therefore I am" (see Raphael 1965: 2). Locke's three principle "natural rights" are the rights to life, liberty, and property. He defines the right to "liberty" as the right to be left free to do as one pleases, to be free from interference of any kind. This concept of liberty has been described as a "negative" concept, the absence of interference, and it has become a marker of classic liberalism. This emphasis on individualism as an underpinning paradigm of the rights discourse has implications for Aboriginal engagement with it and by extension their engagement with the state and its program of modernity.

The intentional agentic citizen is thus the correct subject of human rights, technically referred to as the human rights holder. How does language provide clues as to how such a subject is made, indeed presupposed? There has been considerable criticism in the critical rights literature about the apparently socially disembedded character of this subject and the denial of structural disadvantage that it speaks to (Douzinas 2007; Brown 2000). This asocial, egocentric subject personified in the myth of the "self-made man" can be contrasted with the relational sociocentric character of Aboriginal personhood. Thus, to interrogate the assumptions embedded in the Declaration is also to interrogate the foundations of the secular modern person. Can this rights-bearer accommodate the ideals of the relational spiritual Anangu person?

There is a vast anthropological literature on this relational or sociocentric person, for instance Strathern (1988), da Cunha (2009), Smith (2012), while in central Australia more specifically, Aboriginal identity has been articulated by Myers as being deeply relational (1986; see also 1988). As Smith, however, recently explored, this dividual: individual, or sociocentric: egocentric distinction is now so well established in the anthropological literature that its explanatory capacity has been largely negated (2012: 50, see also Wardlow 2006). Nevertheless, although we might now be uncomfortable in appearing to stereotype a classical Aboriginal personhood in opposition to the Western "standard," it is worthwhile briefly revisiting this early ethnographic subject if we are to reconsider this distinction in terms of a continuum rather than a dichotomy. All persons are both dividual and individual to some degree (Englund and Leach 2000). Such a continuum operates situationally or as context specific in its acknowledgment that Anangu lives are dynamic and inevitably invested to varying degrees in programs of the state.

In this vein it is useful to revisit Myers's (1986) early ethnography, as this analyzed the Anangu person as extending outward from a spiritual identity that derived from the preexisting Dreaming or *Tjukurrpa*. This fundamentally spiritual dimension of the "self" asserted a fluid relationship between oneself and persons, objects, or places. Maffie's ethnoepistemological concept of a "pluriverse," rather than the modern scientific singular "universe," usefully frames this Indigenous ontology (2008). Thus, Anangu identity was found to be fundamentally coextensive with persons and things beyond the physical person (see Myers 1986: 109). Yet this classical rendering of Anangu selfhood as derived from the *Tjukurrpa*, as Myers witnessed in discussions with old men in the late 1970s and early 1980s, is not so readily the norm in the twenty-first century. Since settlement, very few Anangu have been born on their familial estates. Rather, Alice Springs hospital is the norm. As a result, such foundational attachments are no longer a core means of establishing selfhood. Instead, as new contingent forms of identity emerge, so too new vocabularies are required to negotiate them. The language of human rights is potentially among them.

Nevertheless, the relational identity that is coextensive with family has not been so readily displaced. Kinship remains the central organizing principle in social life, referred to by Sutton (2001) as "public kinship." This type of kinship can be contrasted to the "private kinship" in certain Western societies and as espoused in accountable transparent corporate governance processes. Aboriginal public kinship also underpins the "domestic moral economy" of demand sharing (Peterson 1993, 2013). Another aspect of this public kinship system is that it effectively anonymizes persons as actors, as they are fulfilling socially preexisting roles via the structures of kin classification (the subsection system) that all Anangu are born into (see Myers 1986: 180–218). The social reproduction that is established by categories of relationships with sets of kin concomitantly sets up rights and responsibilities between different kin that are also asymmetrical and gendered. "Equality" is not a term readily applied to some of these relationships. For instance, the rights a mother-in-law has over a daughter-in-law, as well as respectful avoidance relationships between mother-in-law and son-in-law, are established patterns of appropriate behavior. Yet, changes in such relationships are perhaps inevitable in the relatively close confines of a settled context. Modifications to the "icy formality of the elaborated structures of kin classification" (Myers 1986: 159) also appear to be emerging as negotiable and less formal under the routines and pressures of settlement.

Juxtaposing Anangu Key Words

Some of the Anangu key words have been juxtaposed with and given as translated equivalents to the English key words that appear in the Declaration.[14] Whereas in English there is one word that provides a descriptor for a complex set of concepts, such as "dignity," for instance, in Luritja a set of practices had to be elaborated for the context of the same or similar concept to be rendered meaningful. As a result, there was very little direct one-to-one translation of concepts. Instead, there was a range of contexts that can be imagined where particular social practices are enacted.

The concept *Waltja*, though it is often glossed as the English word for "family"[15] as indicated earlier, is a foundational one for Anangu. As a deeply multivalent synonym, it is a far more encapsulating concept than even the extended cognatic "family" would suggest. Myers states that "the term *waltja* specifies a sense of belonging together or shared identity. It is used to refer to 1) possessions, 2) 'kin,' 3) one's own/my own, 4) a wider sense of belonging, and 5) oneself, as in the phrases 'he did it himself' or 'she is sitting by herself'" (1986: 109; see also Hansen and Hansen 1992: 163–164). *Waltja* appears fifteen times throughout the translations, including as an inclusive form in contexts that aim to convey a sense of inclusion; "to treat others like family." As Wierzbicka indicates, "Frequency is not everything, but it is important and revealing" (1997: 15). The idea of encouraging the trusting of strangers, as actively incorporating them into ones' sphere of ready sociality, can be imagined as "family" acts as a metaphor for inclusion and shared identity, in this case as fellow human beings. This significant leap in the embrace of the new stranger sociability (per Goankar and Povinelli 2003) is intrinsic to the moral order of a market economy and the modern mark of toleration. However, not all of those within this inclusive net of family are treated equally. There is decided inequality within Anangu families, between ages and genders, that needs to be bracketed for this metaphor to do its rights work.

In discussing possible equivalent concepts for the English word "free" with Nakamarra, one possible equivalent she gave was *waltjangku*—belonging to family:

> You are free to fit into that relationship; you are free if you belong, if you know who you are then you know who you belong to, are connected to—grandparents are important. If you know family you are free. If you don't have family you are nothing, like an empty cup.

According to Nakamarra's perspective, you are free if you belong and know your identity. Nakamarra is using her own cross-cultural understanding of this concept of "freedom," as she perceives it is valued in non-Aboriginal society by providing her own equally valued cultural equivalent.

This concept *Waltja*, along with several other key words, was used for the definition of human rights we developed for the glossary of terms. The first Article says: "All human beings are born free and equal in dignity and rights. They are endowed with reason and conscience and should act towards one another in a spirit of brotherhood." The back translation of this Article from the Luritja reads:

> All people, Aboriginal and non-Aboriginal, those overseas, are all sitting down equal and this includes Aboriginal people.[16] All can learn and think well. All the many different people are living together well, as though they are all family. All together we are one spirit.

This first Article—which appears in all the international Conventions on Human Rights, including the Convention on Civil and Political Rights and the Convention on Economic, Social and Cultural Rights—encompasses many English key words.

Translating "Right"

Wierzbicka defines three general categories of the use of "right" in English: moral, intellectual, and conversational. She leaves aside trying to categorize the "right" of human rights, referring to this sense of "right" as a "countable noun" (2006: 62). Nevertheless, although she doesn't explicitly address the concept of "rights" within human rights, Wierzbicka's general thesis is relevant. She examines in detail how deeply pervasive this word has become within our cultural lexicon "as if 'rightness' were a phenomenon 'out there'"

(2006: 63). She provides the example of an entry on "right action" in *The Oxford Companion to Philosophy*: "No subject is more central to moral philosophy or ethics than that of right and wrong action" (2006: 62). Yet, Wierzbicka argues that this is a problem restricted to Anglo moral philosophy, as "many languages don't have words like the English right and wrong (or for that matter duty and ought). They all however, have equivalents of good and bad, and they also have equivalents of true (though not of false)" (2006: 63). This is also true of the Luritja language.

In discussions with four bilingual Anangu, including Macdonald, all of whom speak Luritja as a first language, a range of interpretations and explications were offered for this concept of "right." Each person was provided with the definition of this concept, as well as the others discussed later on, from the *Essential Oxford English Dictionary* (2010: 257). The adjective "morally good; in accordance with justice; proper; correct; true" seemed to resonate most with Anangu, rather than the noun: "what is just; something one is entitled to." Indeed, this concept of entitlement is very context specific for Anangu, specifically as it operates in relation to behavior toward certain categories of kin. The concept of "rights," as embodied in the human rights discourse as entitlements *and* responsibilities, emerged only across the full context of the translated Declaration. The discussions around developing a definition of human rights were also informed by other translations and conceptualized as a combination of terms, similar to the Mayan Tzotzil of "doing what my heart wants" and "respecting the decisions of other people" (Manago and Greenfield 2011: 23).[17] However, as the heart is not the metaphorical seat of emotions for Luritja, as it is for the Tzotzil or indeed most English as first language speakers, this analogy had to be rethought. Instead, the final definition of "human rights" was rendered as "*Tjutakulampa ngaranyi liipula nyinanytjaku mingarrtjuwiya, kalypakalypa tjungurringkula walytjarringula nyinanytjaku. Pina yalytjurarringkula kaangkurrinytjaku.*" The back-translation of this was:

> All of us should be equal. Being peaceful, reconciled and without spite we should be living together all as family. We should be kind to people with respect and understanding.

This last sentence is literally "open ears equals open minds." So, indeed, the ears are the metaphorical seat of emotions and the intersubjective.

The translation equivalents that I received from Nakamarra and Nungurrayi for "morally right" were *tjukarurru kulintja palya* (literally, "straight hearing good" and further explicated as "the right way of thinking"). *Tju-karurru nintirringkula palyarntjaku*, literally "straight learning and making good," can be explicated as "right way of learning and doing." As these translations show, two different people gave two interpretations. Both translations incorporate verbs—about thinking or doing the right thing. The noun *tjukarurru* means something that is morally right and truthful in this context. But, of course, what is this right thing? Who is it "right" for? Unless the bundle of "rights" as a countable noun (Wierzbicka 2006: 62) is normatively understood and thus experienced in its sociopolitical context, this translation has very limited meaning. It is in the process of explicating each specific Article, or each specific category of "rights," that the conversation can be started about the "right way of thinking, or of learning and doing" according to this human rights doctrine. What this attempted translation does begin to tell us is that there is a pattern to the Luritja theory of knowledge, and it hinges on listening, social interaction, and a particular endosociality.

The attempted translation of the concepts of "reason" and "conscience"—as all human beings are endowed with these qualities according to the rights discourse—is also revealing. "Reason" (as a verb) was translated as *kulintjaku kulitjatjarra* ("to listen and to understand"), *kulirra yilta yilta* ("listening true") or *kulintjatjarra* ("understood"), and *kulintja tiinatjarra kanyini* ("they listened/had good sense and really cared"). "Conscience" was variously translated as *kulintjaku kulini tjapintjaku* ("to listen and to listen and ask") and *kulirra tjungungku wangkanyi* ("listening and talking together").

To Listen Is, Metaphorically, to Think

The consistent use of the verb "to listen," as indicated in the various idiom parts of *kulini*, is of note. As this key word is used to translate "reason," "conscience," and "right," it suggests that a foundational process in doing the "right thing" is first to listen. Indeed, this concept, as various idiom parts, appears twenty-nine times in the final translation. As Myers explains, "In the [Anangu] view, the concepts 'thinking,' 'understanding' and 'hearing' are expressed by a single term—*kulininpa*, which means literally 'to hear'" (1986: 107). The metaphorical organ of thought is the ear. Evans and Wilkins have found that this polysemy is, in fact, found across all Australian languages as they all recruit verbs of cognition like "think" and "know" from "hear" (2000). They demonstrate how this auditory cognition is clearly at odds with the universalizing "visualist" Indo-European methods of expression: "I have seen," "I know"' (2000: 549). Evans and Wilkins remind us of the "close link between the role of literacy in privileging sight as opposed to hearing, which assumes a greater dominance in a purely oral culture" (2000: 585). This concept "listen" can be found in more than fifty idiom parts of *kulini/kulinu* in the *Pintupi/Luritja Dictionary* (Hansen and Hansen 1992: 32).

This focus on sensory modalities, from aural perception to cognition, reveals the intersubjectivity of Anangu cognition. The anthropology of the senses is relevant here, notably the Howes volume (1991).[18]

The "Rights" Word: Liipula

Liipula is probably one of the most obvious introduced words with a direct genealogy to human rights principles. This Aboriginal English concept derives from "level," to make level or even. And it was offered as a translation for the equality and nondiscrimination concepts. Like a high percentage of terms that Aboriginal people use, this is a synonym that has a different range of meanings depending on the context. According to Hansen, "We often expect words that have been borrowed to have the same range of components of meaning as English, but this not the case" (personal communication 2015). As he continued: "In the early days, *liipula* was used in the sense of *kintilpa*— three people hunting together and walking abreast—as they were level in a straight line." He further indicated that it can also still be used as *liipula wati kutjarra ngaranyi*—"two men are the same height," or kids running a race and coming in equally first. These expressions and early usages from the 1970s had no moral or normative content.

Hansen indicated that in later years this borrowed word has come to take on more meanings, such as equality. He stated that people have heard of the idea of equality of different races, as in the expression *liipula latju nyinanyi*, "we sit down level." This statement was overheard by Hansen, which he understood as implying from the context in which he heard it: "Walpala [whitefella] are no better than us." When I discussed the usage of this term with Macdonald, he indicated that although today it is used for the idea of equality, its more routine usage is numeric such as for the football score or if two cars arrived somewhere at the same time, for instance. This concept was also put to use in translating the title of the Universal Declaration of Human Rights: *Yara Tina Ngaatjanya Yananguku Tjukarurrulpayi Liipula Nyinanytjaku Mingarrtjuwiya.* This is back-translated as: "This important story is to ensure that people can live correctly as equals and without spite" (literally, "sitting down together").

The broader discussions with several Anangu around the idea of non-discrimination or equality were also revealing. One translation of the "discrimination" concept with Nungurrayi was, "*Anangu ngatjarri, ngumpu, palurru tjingurru ngurrpa, tjingurru rama, kuunyi palunga nintintjaku tjukarurrungku lipulangku palyantjaku.*" The back-translation for this is, "People strangers, disabled, they might be ignorant or inexperienced, they might be mad, but be sorry [for them] and clever, morally correct and ensure equality." This attempt at explication—though note that strangers (*ngatjarri*) are discriminated against—elides more than it reveals, however. It doesn't engage with the asymmetrical ceremonial and kinship structures, which are challenged by such notions of equality and indeed in treating others—those strangers like family—as translated in other contexts of inclusion. As Pitarch also found for the Mayan Tzeltal:

> There is no exact equivalent for the word fraternal, used in the original Declaration in the sense of affection between equals: siblings are older or younger siblings, never equal; a hierarchy shapes their relationship. In the same way, husband and wife are unequal, and this is what makes them need each other. This asymmetry also explains why not all human beings possess the same respect or, in this context the same rights. (2008: 97)[19]

The gender asymmetry between spouses, in particular, is discussed in the following two chapters in terms of complementarity. The implication that equality is sameness in certain contexts such as in male–female relationships is deeply unappealing to female Anangu I have spoken with. Nevertheless, it clearly depends in which contexts one is discussing gender relations. In many contemporary contexts, such as equal pay, for instance, there is little debate that equity is appropriate. However, in terms of the age hierarchy, Macdonald described it this way:

> When that young one is born they've got nothing. Old man, old lady they've got the knowledge. The oldest is more important in our culture. The baby crawling around is nothing, once they get into ceremonial business he's crossing the line to become more respected. Babies are *ramarama* [unknowing].

The concept *ngaparrtji ngaparrtji*—used widely in the Western Desert—is also often used in this contemporary sense of balance and equity of outcome. The dictionary definition of this concept as a noun is "in return; in exchange," as a reciprocal gift (Hansen and Hansen 1992: 81). This term has been widely appropriated by non-Aboriginal people and also Aboriginal people working cross culturally. The theatre production company Bighart in particular—with the theatre piece of the same name and also a website dedicated to language learning—understand the concept as: "I give you something: you give me something." (Palmer 2010). The work of this company draws inspiration from contacts primarily in the Pitjantatjarra region that incorporate the iconic natural and spiritual feature of Uluru (Ayers Rock). In the Pintupi-Luritja region not far to the north, however, this concept has the additional meaning of payback, or retributive violence. As Macdonald stated: "If someone has wronged you, then you need to square up. You have done damage here, so you will have it done in return there." He provided the example: *Ngapartjirra yua Yanangu wakani kutturungu punganyi*, translated as "payback with a spear or stick." As a result of this term's association with violence, Macdonald suggested that it was not appropriate for use in a document that advocates nonviolence. For this group of Western Desert language speakers, the concept can incorporate the sweet-hearted reciprocity that others in the Western Desert language block understand, but it also has this other meaning. Capturing such idiomatic nuances is essential in localizing the Declaration, such that, conversely, for Pitjantjatjarra speakers this concept of *ngaparrjti* could be useful in evoking the concept of equity and by implication equality.

Freedom

When Hansen saw the English word "freedom" in the draft we were reworking (the one I had earlier developed with Macdonald and Dixon), he suggested to Macdonald, "Some fellow *putu kulilpayi* [can't hear [that word]." However, in the early stages of the translation, as we discussed this word "freedom," two of the translations provided were vernacularized versions of the English word via word borrowing, *pirrku* and *pryitum* (note that there is no 'f' in Luritja). As Wierzbicka indicates, many languages, including the European languages Russian and Polish, don't have equivalents for the English concept of "freedom"; nor does Japanese (see 1997: 139, 152). Likewise, neither does the Indigenous Mayan language of Tzeltal (Pitarch 2008) and likewise Luritja. That historically specific contexts also construct the culturally specific can clearly be seen in this concept of "freedom" (see Wierzbicka 1997: 125–153).

As Hansen stated: "Nobody uses [the word] freedom, that English has no meaning here. Even people who know some English, they still don't know that word." Macdonald agreed. And so we deleted the word "freedom" from the final translation. As an English key word, this foundational concept appears twenty-one times in the Declaration, in contexts such as fundamental freedoms, rights and freedoms, freedom of information, freedom of association, freedom of religion, and so on. Because of the ubiquity of this word it seemed important to specify it, by enabling it to be woven into context with the local vernacular. In this vein, in an attempt to avoid this translation gap, an earlier draft of Article 2 did include "freedom." The English original reads: "Everyone is entitled to the rights and freedoms set forth in this Declaration without distinction of any kind . . . "This was initially drafted as *Tjutakulampa ngaranyi* freedom *tjukarurru wangka ngangka tjakultjunutja* with the following free translation: "This straight message is proclaiming that everyone has freedom." However, in the interests of communicability, following Hansen's advice, we deleted the word, so that the final back-translation of this first redrafted sentence now reads: "The talk here on this paper is for everybody to take notice of and live according to." Nevertheless, it could be anticipated that any future revisions may well incorporate this English word as a more overt intercultural political statement.

One might imagine that the idea of freedom is to be found in the negative, associated with the all too common experience of Anangu men's imprisonment. However, this does not seem to be the case either. Rather, the routine expression heard, taken from the Warumpi Band song: *Ngayulu kuwarri tjiilanguru pakarnu*, is translated as, "Today I'm getting out of jail" [*pakarnu* is "arose"].

However, less locally, the term "freedom" is utilized by urban Aboriginal activists from the Northern Territory and across Australia in terms of freedom from the controls of the colonial state. One of the most reknowned usages was in the 1965 "Freedom Ride" led by Charles Perkins, an Arrernte man from Alice Springs who was also the first Indigenous Australian to gain a university degree in 1966 (from the University of Sydney). More recently, "Freedom Summits" have been held in Alice Springs several times over the past several years, drawing Indigenous leaders from across Australia. These summits have been held to protest the government polices such as the Northern Territory Emergency Response for 2007 (NTER). As the front page of the *National Indigenous Times* reads: "We need to reclaim the Aboriginal rights struggle . . . because all our issues can be addressed through reclaiming th[is] . . . struggle" (NIT 2014). So this concept may yet gain traction as a distinctly political one, as rights against the state. Yet, to date it has not done so in remote areas. The Aboriginal people attending the summit were predominantly urban Aboriginal leaders and activists from across Australia. There were very few people from remote Northern Territory communities, though they are the ones most directly and disproportionately affected by the coercive polices that were being rallied against. Indeed, this issue of the agentic citizen claiming human rights as political project is one of the paradoxes of human rights in this very remote context.

Intentional Vagueness and Respect Registers

The linguist Barry Alpher states:

> A common feature of respectful speech is a certain amount of intentional vagueness. It is as if the message of the utterance becomes to an extent less important than the nature of the social relationship that the speaker is trying to maintain or establish with the person spoken to. (1993: 99)

This intentional vagueness in speech is difficult to manage in a proscriptive and normative document such as the Declaration. One of the reasons for this is that in an oral culture how the text sounds is fundamental. As each draft Article was repeated verbally many times, it seemed (to me at least) that we were coproducing lyrics or spoken word poetry. I often found myself encouraging Macdonald to be more overt and direct with the language, as I was content driven. And while I usually had limited success, there was some in the form of an affirmative refrain that ends twenty-three of the thirty Articles, discussed in the following paragraph.

The Luritja key word *tjinguru*, translated as "maybe," embodies both vagueness and respect. As it is impolite to refuse a request outright, this word is ubiquitous. Myers indicates that a refusal of a request could be perceived as a denial of a relationship (1986). This was one of the first Luritja words I learned, and it is far more common than "yes" or "no." It appears in the translation fifteen times. This language of indeterminacy added to the burden that this abstract document already faced, as we attempted to render these ideas as literally as possible. For instance, Article 27, the first part of which concerns the freedom to participate in the cultural life of the community, was largely interpreted by Macdonald as the right to practice ceremony. As I suggested words that I understood were forms of public ceremony such as *pulapa*, *tulku*, or *inma*, Hansen translated their conversation: "If he puts those words down he feels that he'll be accused of saying too much." And so Macdonald was very circumspect with how culture (as inferring ceremony) was defined, so that no terms at all were included in his concern about the politics of offense. Yet, many terms such as *inma* are widely used in intercultural contexts, and the word *tulku* was used as a translation for the book of hymns: *Tulku Yinkapay-itjarra*. The definition of this term in the dictionary reads: "songs of the social corroboree women and children permitted" (Hansen and Hansen 1992: 132). This circumspection hints not only at Macdonald's awareness of the dynamism of language and the responsibilities of the speaker to a broad and changing audience but also to his possible range of avoidance relationships and avoiding shame.

Civil and Political Rights: Apocryphal Revelations and the Rule of Law

The first half of the Declaration specifies civil and political rights, while civil rights also encompass legal rights. Political rights deal with the fundamentals of a liberal democracy, such as the right to vote and a range of freedoms: of association, of movement, of speech, and so on. Articles 6 to 11 of the Declaration outline the foundational elements of what is commonly referred to as "the rule of law." According to Carothers, the idea of "the rule of law" is legal bedrock, and it is "defined as a system in which the laws are public knowledge, are clear in meaning, and apply equally to everyone. . . . the relationship between the rule of law and liberal democracy is profound" (1998: 96). The rule of law concept includes the right to be presumed innocent until proven guilty, the right to a fair and public trial, equal treatment before the law, and not being subjected to arbitrary arrest, for instance. These principles evoke a sense of entitlement to justice for the dominant mainstream, and, indeed, they are generally understood as practiced by the Australian legal system. However, within the jurisdiction of the Northern Territory, where almost 30 percent of the population is Aboriginal, this is not the case. Although there has always been a deep history of Indigenous exclusion from the rights of citizenship as an essential element in establishing the sovereign nation (per Agamben 1998, 2005), since 2007 with the introduction of the Northern Territory Emergency Response (NTER) and subsequent mandatory sentencing regimes, this has been compounded for Aboriginal citizens of the Northern Territory.

The extensive suite of laws that actively counter the rule of law include the range of mandatory sentencing laws for violent offenses that severely limit the discretion of magistrates, paperless arrest laws where police can detain a person without charge for four hours, public order offense laws, and the associated increase in fines and penalties for loitering, begging, and so on (NAAJA and CAALAS 2013). These laws all directly target Aboriginal people, often when they are visiting the major centers of Darwin and Alice Springs, in what has been described as a police state (NAAJA 2014). The Northern Territory has developed a culture of incarceration in the governing of the Indigenous population through criminalization. Since these laws were introduced the Northern Territory prison population has had the highest annual recorded increase and is five times higher than the national average, with 86 percent of prisoners being Indigenous (ABS 2013). In relation to the new paperless arrest laws, for instance, this governing through crime

> allows police to impose punishment without anyone deciding whether that person is innocent or guilty. But there is a reason why police have to bring cases to court: only courts can decide guilt and innocence and impose punishment. (NAAJA and CAALAS 2014, NAAJA 2014)

It is in this context that the apocryphal nature of the rule of law as practice was revealed. Rather than this translation potentially acting as emancipatory and enabling for Anangu who may read the translation and thus gain some understanding about the operations of the legal system, these Articles on civil (legal) rights were rendered cruelly contingent—on Aboriginality. Though ideas such as "one is innocent until proven guilty" are widely circulated as being true in the mainstream, for Aboriginal people this legal precept is of doubtful truth. In many of the legal contexts within which Anangu find themselves it has limited legitimacy. Translating these Articles was confronting and necessitated a discussion of the sociolegal and political context as this revealed the radical distortion of the rule of law by the state, in this case the Northern Territory government. Although Carothers names the rule of law as "legal bedrock," he also recognizes "the fundamental problem of leaders who refuse to be ruled by the law" (1998: 96).

Thus, one is urged to enquire how Anangu could give this legal system any value, when it instead appears to confirm their marginality, subordination, and routine criminalization. Yet, the legal utopia as revealed in human rights has to nonetheless be acknowledged as a base standard if the state is to be held accountable; if this state of exception (per Agamben 2005) is to be challenged. As Santos suggests, we should "not reduce realism to what exists" (2007: 35). Nonetheless, these were difficult conversations, even given that most of Macdonald's professional interpreting practice has been in the legal context of the courts. The first translation gap to be addressed was "the law." Which law is it that "all are equal before"? And that "all must be recognised as a person before"? This dialogue confronts the incommensurability of talking about "the law" in generalized abstract terms. And even though we focused on non-Aboriginal law, excluding customary law from the discussion, which one? Although many non-Indigenous people may understand in general terms the idea of "the rule of law" as nonarbitrary or politicized, this philosophical principle is profoundly abstract. So we specified the most common contact points between Aboriginal people and the law—how they *should* work. For instance, the translation of Article 7, on equality before the law, is back-translated from the Luritja as:

> There is an important law that is for everyone, everywhere that should be obeyed and followed correctly. And this law is showing us that no one should be discriminated against. That law is for all people . . .

Aboriginal people, men in particular, are the majority court users in the Northern Territory. Rates of recidivism are high, as are shorter sentences, which means that routine exposure to jail is high and incarceration is normalized.[20] Nevertheless, a survey conducted in the north of the Northern Territory, among Yolngu speakers, found that "over 95% of Yolngu surveyed were unable to correctly identify the meaning of 30 commonly used English legal terms" (ARDS 2008: 21–22). The translation gap in this area of legal semantics appears incommensurable, not only because the theories of knowledge required by Anangu or Yolngu to negotiate them are largely inaccessible, but so too are their experiences of discrimination (sometimes referred to as racial profiling) incomparable with that of the mainstream.

Economic, Social, and Cultural Rights

These rights, outlined in the second half of the Declaration, lay out some of the key principles for a limited cultural pluralism or the possibilities for a progressive multicultural conception of human rights, in some contrast to the formal lack of legal pluralism. The limits that have been pushed in this translation context include forms of education because if "parents have the prior rights to choose the forms of education" (Article 27: 3), then Macdonald and Dixon thought it should be specified as the right to bilingual education. If marriage is to be consensual then the age should also be raised to eighteen, according to Macdonald (Article 16). And also in Article 16, if the family is "the fundamental unit," then this also includes the wider family (*walytja tjutatarra matupurra*). And, indeed, given the very high rates of child removals from Aboriginal families in the Northern Territory (discussed further in Chapter 4), then it needed to be specified that "the Government and police can't reject or take no notice of you in the law; Government workers should be there for you and be kind."

One of the accusations leveled at human rights by Marx, and by Marxist philosophers, is their fetishization of private property rights and the subsequent commodification of social relations. For Marx, the contingency of rights could most clearly be found in property rights such that: "the social structure we call rights arises out of the need to lubricate property exchange" (Hargaden 2013; see also Brenkert 1986). Although I have no argument with this, the interest for Anangu was a reading of Article 17 on property rights that focused on the "in association with others" or collective property rights. The back-translation into English reads that:

> You can buy your own block of land with money . . . The country of Aboriginal people does not belong to one person or one family member. Aboriginal peoples' country is for all the family. If one person wants to build a house or something on this land then they have to ask correctly.

The form of property rights that Anangu in the Haasts Bluff Land Trust have is inalienable freehold title under the Aboriginal Land Rights Act (NT) 1976. As discussed in the Introduction, land rights were a high-water mark in the Indigenous recognition struggle. However, consecutive conservative governments have queried the economic rationality of such collective title (Reeves 1998).[21] Indeed, Human Rights Commissioner Tim Wilson (appointed by the Abbott government) stated in a speech to the Australian Libertarian Society, quoting Tibor Machan, that "correctly identifying private property is 'the social precondition of the possibility of a personally guided moral life.'" As Wilson continued: "In the absence of property rights individuals are essentially debilitated in their capacity to demonstrate generosity to others. All charity rests upon property. If people do not own anything, then they can never give anything to others in need" (Wilson 2015). This rather singular statement seems to align wealth creation, in the form of property, with an ethic of generosity. Yet, the "compassion deficit" that the wealthy have been found to have confounds this relationship, as poorer people routinely give proportionally more of their income than wealthier people, if US research can be transferred to the Australian context (see Piff et al. 2010).

Tjintalingka, or the federal government agency Centrelink, which manages the unemployment benefits and other government transfers, was the pivotal word in the "right to social security" of Article 22. This "welfare state" can be contrasted with non-Western countries, such as those in Africa, where, as Englund points out: "If 'social security' has any meaning at all in countries like Malawi and Zambia, [it] denotes in the first place, kin relations and other non-state structures" (2006: 58). In Australia the right to social security has become a polarizing one, referred to by critics as "passive welfare" (Pearson 2000). Increasingly, however, leaders within Aboriginal communities are also voicing their concerns about the high rates of unemployment when there are work opportunities available. It was in this vein that Article 22 was translated, as the back-translation indicates:

> It's OK for a person who is getting money from Centrelink to go and get into real work and stay with that job. When a person is searching for work Centrelink should give them money, without stopping it, because they are still looking around for work.

This attempt to balance entitlement with responsibility is a move away from the attitude embodied in the euphemism of "sit-down money" (unemployment benefits). Such a translation is an acknowledgment by Macdonald—as translator and community leader—that the responsibilization discourse is making its mark in this remote place.

Versions of Human Dignity

One of the fundamental concepts undergirding human rights is the concept of the "individual possessing an absolute and irreducible dignity that must be protected from society, the state, or other forms of hierarchies" (Santos 2002: 44–45). Yet, if we take as a given, as Santos does, that all cultures have different versions of human dignity, then Anangu forms of dignity must also be introduced into this dialogue. In Article 22, the "rights indispensable for his dignity and the free development of his personality" was interpreted as:

> Aboriginal people gather with their relatives as they think about and con-
> tinually learn about the Dreaming, following instruction. The Government
> shouldn't interrupt that or talk against it. It's good for Aboriginal people to
> be together with their Dreamings and the Government should not be boss
> for that.

Identity and dignity are coupled here, as ceremony (including annual "men's
business") is one of the very few areas that the government does not intervene
in. As Englund also observed in Malawi: "The free development of personality
is not necessarily a positive achievement in a cultural setting in which people
gain their dignity not as mutually independent individuals but by attending
to their social relationships" (2006: 58).

As we discussed how this concept might be rendered for Anangu if we
were to define it in a glossary of terms, Macdonald then proceeded to outline
other local practices as constitutive of dignity. The first definition provided
was, as translated back from Luritja: "The one who is boss of his country
has the dreaming story and the name for that person is Kurtungulu. They
should be taken notice of." The second gloss was translated as: "The younger
women should be kind to and care for their grandmothers and learn about
their Dreamings." And the final gloss, which added intergenerational balance and gender equity, was, "Younger men should listen carefully and in a
concentrated way to their grandfathers and learn and follow their teaching
so that they can be like their grandfathers with good thinking." All of these
practices are ideal traditional embodiments of how dignity is earned and carried as a relational exchange worthy of respect. It is worth noting that one of
the definitions of "dignity" from the *Australian English Dictionary*, "sense of
self-importance or person or high official position" (1999: 152–153), has no
equivalent gloss in the Luritja translations.

Human Rights as Emancipatory Script in Rendering Visible the Tacit

The emancipatory potential of human rights is only possible if opportunity
is provided to learn about the embodied principles of equality and non-
discrimination to unsettle the nexus of established power within and beyond
the community. Challenging the monolingualism of the Declaration is a central element in developing a "critical consciousness," to borrow Freire's concept (1970).

In late 2013, about one-third of the way through the research in Papunya, as I realized how invisible the human rights language was in the communities I was working in, I received an email circular informing me that the Abbott federal government had ceased all funding for human rights education. Such funding had been a core plank of the Human Rights Framework that operated, briefly, instead of a National Bill of Rights (Commonwealth Government 2010). Such educational opportunities to learn about human rights had, however, never reached this remote area, at least not through such formal channels, even while this Framework had "education as the centrepiece." Then Human Rights Commission President Catherine Branson stated in 2011:

> Human rights education . . . is about building a culture of respect for human rights. It is not only about providing knowledge about human rights and the mechanisms that protect them, but also about imparting the skills needed to promote, defend and apply human rights in daily life. Human rights are best protected when they are embedded in the way we think and therefore in the ways we act. As was rightly observed as long ago as 1944, if we don't believe in human rights then no law, no charter, no parliament and no court will save them. (Australian Human Rights Commission 2011a)

One of the issues Branson highlights is enabling substantive rights, which is assisted by active acquired knowledge; as this issue became part of our dialogue, Macdonald developed a refrain that concludes twenty-three of thirty Articles. This reads: *Wangka ngaangku ngananan̄anya tjakultjunanyi rapa ngaranytjaku kutjupa tjuta nguwanpa*. In back-translation, this states: "This talk is indicating to us that we should stand up and be confident and strong like other people." The only time this refrain was altered was for Article 3, which advocates the no violence message as the sentiment "stand up and be active" (which is literal), was not what one wants in a message of peace, according to Macdonald.

As Santos suggests: "The true beginning of this [human rights] dialogue is a moment of discontent with one's own culture, a sense that it does not provide satisfactory answers to some of one's queries, perplexities or expectations" (2002: 55). Exposing such discontent was most apparent in relation to the issue of violence in Article 3, which is rather abstract: "Everyone has the right to life, liberty and security of person." The attempt at finding commensurability became, at the same time, "mediating a moral co-presence"

(Povinelli 2001: 327). Because, as will be further discussed in the following chapters, various forms of violence including gender violence are very significant social issues, it was felt that this needed to be specified. Thus, the translation from Luritja became:

> Everybody everywhere should live correctly [implies "morally"]. Men and women should not swear and fight with each other. Men should not hurt women and children. One should not kill a person or sorcerise and kill them. They should care for and look after them.
>
> This talk is indicating to us that we all have to heed this message well.

And so this abstract universal right begins to be specified as locally relevant, and in doing so other commensurable concerns and issues are raised. As Bassnett and Trivedi state, "Students of translation almost all start out with the assumption that something will be lost in translation, that the text will be diminished and rendered inferior. They rarely consider that there might be a process of gain" (2002: 4). Drawing on Freire's notion of "naming" assists in framing this process of gain. In this translation the gain was in the dialogical exercise that effectively necessitated the naming or renaming of the world. It generated new ways to do this (per Freire 1993) as it became a shared process of enquiry. In *Pedagogy of the Oppressed*, Freire secularizes religious metaphors, and his treatment of "naming" as a dialogical process derives from the model of naming in Genesis. According to Gottlieb and La Belle: "For Freire, as for Adam and Eve, the act of naming calls forth the possibility of a new reality . . . to speak the word that they would become" (1990: 9). As Freire articulates his utopia: "To speak a true word is to transform the world . . . to exist, humanely, is to name the world, to change it. Once named, the world in its turn returns to the namers as a problem and requires of them a new naming" (1993: 69). This then becomes a generative practice. Indeed, Derrida's view that texts cannot be the object of definitive interpretations, but that there are multiple possible readings and silences or exclusions rings true in this context (see Luke 2000: 452).

Conclusions

In the lives of individuals and societies, language is a factor of greater importance than any other. That linguistics should continue to be the prerogative of a few specialists would be unthinkable.

Saussure 1966: 7

This chapter has offered ethnographic insight into the ways in which the global language of human rights is understood locally. By rendering visible the tacit I have sought to reveal human rights in terms of locally normative cultural concepts. The constraints, limitations, and possibilities have begun to be specified. Many of the core concepts are not readily rendered into Luritja theories of knowledge and ideology. Yet, this is not to suggest that there are not closely held equivalents or that the concepts embedded in this language of rights are not useful. As new contingent forms of identity emerge, so too, new vocabularies are required to negotiate them.

Although very few Anangu had heard the words "universal human rights," due to very little exposure of these concepts, with this exposure comes the risk of a colonization of consciousness (similar to the translation of the Bible into Luritja), this time of the secular kind. Is this close exposure to these principles, through their rendering into the local vernacular, yet another path to assimilation? Do the modernist and potentially assimilatory effects of this discourse counter the capacity of this global instrument to operate as an emancipatory script (per Santos 2002)? Such a script ideally enfranchises the marginalized. Either way, enfranchisement also implies a form of assimilation. And although the dominant discourse espoused by the state has consistently favored Standard Australian English, many missionaries, such as the Lutherans in central Australia, learned local languages as an essential mechanism for conversion. As Sapir noted, "Vocabulary is a very sensitive index of the culture of a people and changes of the meaning, loss of old words, the creation and borrowing of new ones are all dependent on the history of culture itself" (1985: 27).

Rafael found that "for the [Philippine] Tagalogs, translation was a process less of internalising colonial-Christian conventions than of evading their totalising grip by repeatedly marking the differences between their language and interests and those of the Spaniards" (1988: 213).

This resonates with the case of the Luritja, where the process of close engagement with the text also became a deeply considered exercise in the performance of difference; as the translators are culturally embedded, so too were their translations.

However, a key element of the vernacularization of human rights in local social settings is getting the balance right between making the UDHR locally meaningful and relevant *as well as* ensuring the integrity of the core principles. This was very challenging. Our discussions focused on the Declaration as a moral and a political document in equal measure and the conversations are ongoing.

The language of human rights, in many ways, has embedded within it a tacit contract of citizenship, as human rights underpins both state and citizen power relations. Perhaps it is inevitable that this project of translation can be read as part of a larger political project, as Michael Ghillar Anderson argues: "Learn his game, understand how he fights us, understand and learn his system so that we can undermine him" (Freedom Movement Forum 2015). And I suggest further: "learn his game," at least to hold him to account. Therefore, this translation becomes a potential tool for a more equitable engagement.

Chapter 2

Engendering Social and Cultural Rights

The Indigenous women of CSW [Commission on the Status of Women] are calling for support for the positive aspects of their traditional cultures and to leave behind the aspects that are detrimental to the rights of Indigenous women.

UN Commission on the Status of Women 2013

THIS DISCOURSE OF REIFYING AND INSTRUMENTALIZING CULTURE, as though those living it can stand outside it and pick and choose what they seek to maintain in the name of rights, poses a core conundrum that this book seeks to explore. Although local conceptions of social justice will not necessarily align with the universalist principles in the rights canon, this call "for support" needs to be read as a call for a conversation between competing discourses and regimes of value. When young Anangu women say, "Women's rights! That's a rubbish idea," when they are first introduced to the concept, or when senior women prefer to talk of balance and ideas of complementarity, rather than sameness or equality, is this "unfreedom" (to borrow Sen's term [1999])? One avenue to approaching this conundrum is to consider the universality of human rights:

> not as a vernacular of cultural prescription but as a language of moral empowerment. Its role is not in defining the content of culture but in trying to enfranchise all agents so that they can freely shape that content. (Ignatieff 2001: 73)

Such an approach also recognizes that the subjective lived content of culture shifts, accommodates, and adjusts to new experiences, choices, and possibilities. The intersubjective is a permeable landscape, and universal concepts, such as human rights, can take hold only when they are encountered within local and particular contexts. As Tsing suggests, universals are a relational condition emerging through friction (2005). Indeed, Eleanor Roosevelt (who chaired the drafting committee for the Universal Declaration of Human Rights) recognized this at the outset, as she stated, "Where after all do human rights begin? In small places, close to home" (1958).

The concept of "gender" is often conflated with the concept of "woman." However, as Hodgson reminds us, "gender" is analytically much broader and more useful. To understand the meaning and practices of being a "woman," we must also understand the meaning and practices of being a "man" (2011: 4). This chapter will explore the relationality of gender; of the condition of making and being an Anangu "woman" or "man," with an acknowledged skew toward the multiple subject positions of woman making. The family is one of these core sites and one of the most contested sites within the realms of both human rights and women's rights. For Anangu, the family embodies the values of collective rights, and it is the Aboriginal family that is most threatened by the neoliberal rendering of rights as separatist and individualist. Yet, as for women globally, it is also within the family that Anangu women are most at risk of physical violence and coercive control (per Stark 2007). The gendered sociality of work practices will also be explored as sites that are revealed as reinforcing the status quo of gendered roles and responsibilities.

This chapter begins the discussion on women's rights as human rights by recalling the contested history between early feminism and the Indigenous civil rights movement within Australia. The contested ground between these early movements will be explored to expose the competing priorities and to illustrate how, in the urban context at least, this divide has narrowed. This discussion, partly historical, then enables a consideration of the tensions between collectivist and individualist approaches to women's rights. By making explicit the usually unnamed and taken for granted, new conversations can be started on the ways in which human rights as a global discourse is both mobilized imaginatively and acts as a mobility to break down geographies and localities that bind, as ideas of equality, individualistic agency, and voluntary association are inserted into local places. By exploring where the principles of human rights are operating in nongovernment organizations (NGOs), such as the women's NGO Waltja Tjutangku Palyapayi and the Central Land Council (CLC), the work of human rights is revealed. The language of rights is, however, rarely explicit. Glosses or synonyms for human rights are to be found in this context of NGO work, as in most others, the most common gloss being "good (corporate) governance."

In the NGO context, "good governance" does two kinds of work: it acts to cloak the work of particular human rights principles and render them politically benign while the same time appealing to a particular pragmatic sensibility. The concept of good governance connotes an active lineal process (toward the "good") that is grounded in material conditions, rather than some abstract notion of human rights. The use of such glosses is not necessarily intentional in NGOs or in government policy and programs, but rather it seems that there is a discomfort or uncertainty about naming particular practices as deriving from human rights principles. Principles such as equity, equality, and non-discrimination are part of the public discourse, so their human rights roots are taken for granted and backgrounded. Nevertheless, as will be discussed in Chapter 6, the "good governance" policy agenda can also act as a form of political doublespeak concealing assimilationist neoliberal ideals through a functional approach to Indigenous programs and service delivery that is domesticating and regulatory. In the current conservative political context, arguably "good governance" is a euphemism for certain human rights. Yet, how can one not want good governance?

This chapter, and the following chapter, can deal only tangentially with economic rights.[1] However, in the human rights discourse, economic rights are bundled with social and cultural rights, so economic rights are considered briefly in recognition of these interconnections and overlaps. For instance, the coupling of economic and social rights is most clearly articulated within the development discourse, which is making its way into central Australia most recently via the CLC's Community Development Unit. This development approach actively inserts notions of good governance where practices of accountability and responsibilization are introduced through "participatory planning," so that some core principles of human rights nevertheless become legitimated. This discussion continues the exploration of what domains of rights have been privileged in human rights work.

Recent texts on issues of social justice, such as *Coercive Reconciliation* (Altman and Hinkson 2007), that notably responded to and engaged with the Northern Territory Emergency Response (NTER) focused on the violations of the collective rights of Aboriginal people, such as the rights to land, to culture, to development, and to self-determination. Absent was any discussion on the specific rights of Aboriginal women to be free from violence. Calma's chapter in this text, "Tackling Child Abuse and Inequality," specified that if the government were taking a human-rights based approach to protecting children, as the stated impetus of the NTER, then they must establish protective programs and policies that support families (Calma 2007: 274).[2] Although I concur with this finding, and Calma is importantly attempting to reassert the primacy of family in the policy context, the focus of social justice research and analysis in Indigenous policy has consistently been on the Aboriginal social collective. The intersections among this collective, those individuals who comprise it, and policy interaction have been marginalized, most notably the tensions between family and gender. Likewise, as Cass observes in her analysis of Aboriginal citizenship rights to welfare: "It is remarkable that so little of the Australian Indigenous citizenship literature places gender within the analytical frame" (2005: 97).

Although this consistent submergence of the rights of Aboriginal women to the rights of the collective is a response to the systemic marginalization of all Aboriginal peoples, as the colonized first peoples, it is time to move beyond this impasse. We must acknowledge and engage with the local effects of the global rights discourse and the possibilities and limitations this discourse offers to both collective and individual rights.

The current trend by the conservative Australian government, and its UK and Canadian allies, is to sponsor a historically regressive and narrow interpretation of rights, as those that are principally associated with first-generation civil and political rights. So, although the current government is operating through only one reading and interpretation of human rights, it is of course the dominant reading at play and the most powerful. Perhaps the most archetypal liberal view was articulated by Margaret Thatcher in 1987 when she proclaimed that "there is no such thing as society. There are individual men and women, and there are families" (in Clarke 2005: 51). Thatcher's understanding of the "family" was a nuclear family limited to mum, dad, child one, and child two. They are a small, isolated, independent, self-serving, and mobile group with minimal reference to a community of shared interests that might be sentimental or political. Minimal attachments equal minimum society and maximum mobility dictated by the labor market.

Liberal Mobilities and Communitarian Critique

Revisiting the communitarian critique of liberalism, which situates the human as fundamentally social, offers a rereading of the rights discourse as this approach realizes the limitations of a rights-based conception focused on the individual. This approach also queries social justice as a straightforward equation of equal access (Dietz 1987: 12), as espoused in the "Closing the Gap" policy approach. As Walzer has argued: "The communitarian critique of liberalism . . . is a consistently intermittent feature of liberal politics and social organisation" (1990: 6). As a social and political philosophy, communitarianism "emphasises the importance of community [as immediate social relations] in the functioning of political life . . . and in understanding human identity and well-being" (Etzioni 2013: 1). Although Marx may have been an early critic of liberalism with his vision of the individual as intrinsically social, later philosophers such as Charles Taylor, Michael Sandel, and Michael Walzer (cited earlier) engaged with communitarianism as a corrective to the stronger liberal doctrines, such as libertarianism, which embraces an atomized notion of individual identity, and the excessive individualism promoted by politicians such as Thatcher (see Taylor 1985; Sandel 1998; Etzioni 2015). I introduce communitarian philosophy here to decenter neoliberalism, offering a pragmatic corrective, even while acknowledging that liberal theory embodies many foundational contemporary social, and rights-based, ethics. A key one of these is voluntary association, which, according to Walzer, even communitarians rarely advocate curtailing (1990: 22).

Voluntary association is at the center of liberalism, as liberalism is fundamentally "a theory of relationship" that understands voluntariness as the right of rupture or withdrawal from any relationship: marital, religious, political, and so on (Walzer 1990: 21). Walzer's framing of voluntary association in terms of "liberal mobilities" illuminates a range of social rights. He identifies four of them: geographic mobility, social mobility, marital mobility, and political mobility (1990: 11–12). A consideration in particular of the first three mobilities, the geographic, the social, and the marital sheds light on the local challenges, limitations, and possibilities to the uptake of such voluntary associations in remote central Australia. As a metaphor for movement, this language of mobilities allows us to explore the tensions between the endosociality of the Anangu community that bind and embed and from which individuals strain to go beyond. Conceptually this approach can, in some ways, be further exemplified by considering Fred Myers's ethnographic conception of the constant tension within this endosociality, between autonomy and relatedness (of and between) individuals and groups (1986: 159–179) or, as he also refers to it, as "relatedness and differentiation" (1986: 159). However, such autonomy or differentiation is within socially defined limits as constitutive of social reproduction and, as a result, is usually momentary, whereas the liberal rhetoric of voluntary association and separation that oppose (the family and) relatedness enters as the modern language of autonomy. In this schema, such voluntary association and separation become more than momentary, however. They are consolidated as the geographic and social mobilities that draw out and begin to shape liberal individuals are inserted in remote places and emerge in the Anangu diaspora that can be found most frequently in Alice Springs. These global structural tensions between communitarianism and liberalism can also be partly understood through Tonnies's much earlier concepts of *Gemeinschaft* ("community") and *Gesellschaft* ("society") as a global theory of social change and the move toward independent values (Tonnies 2001; see also Greenfield 2009; Manago and Greenfield 2011).

Multiple Intersecting Sites of Discrimination and the "Audit Culture"

Every March at the UN Headquarters in New York, the UN Commission on the Status of Women holds an annual two-week meeting. The priority theme for 2013 was "the elimination and prevention of all forms of violence against women and girls." To mark International Women's Day on March 8, "the Indigenous women of CSW57" put out a press release, "Indigenous Women Unite to Speak out about Violence," which stated:

> Indigenous women are . . . often over-represented in areas of vulnerability including poverty, disability, remoteness and caring responsibilities and consequently suffer from intersectional discrimination, which must be holistically addressed. (UN Commission on the Status of Women 2013)

Similar to Indigenous women globally, Anangu women confront multiple forms of discrimination on the basis of sex, race/ethnicity, language, and culture (religion is, however, rarely one of these). In some contexts, like Indigenous women elsewhere, they may be labeled as "third-class citizens" because of their inferior status in relation to men *and* in relation to non-Indigenous people (UN Briefing Note Gender and Indigenous Issues 2010). It is not possible, however, to locate disaggregated data specifically on Indigenous women at a global level.[3] In relation to violence against Indigenous women and girls, for instance, "There is almost no disaggregated data and few reports on violence against Indigenous women and girls in most jurisdictions" (UN Permanent Forum on Indigenous Issues 2012:5). Australia, along with other colonized states such as New Zealand and Canada, is an exception to this with a concerted focus on data gathering about Indigenous peoples.

At the 2012 launch of *Human Rights Indicators: A Guide to Measurement and Implementation*, the UN Deputy High Commissioner stated, "If you don't count it, it won't count."[4] As Navi Pillay was stressing the importance of monitoring and evaluation work, she stated, "Policy management, human rights and statistical systems are closely interrelated and thus need to be in tune with each other for promoting the well-being of people" (UN Human Rights Office of the High Commissioner, 2012: Foreword). Nevertheless, this Foreword by Pillay is cautionary: "Devising policy is not a norm or value-neutral exercise . . . most importantly we should not forget that behind every piece of statistical data are human beings who were born free and equal in dignity and rights." And so when thinking through the value and uses of statistical data, not only is Pillay's cautionary reminder useful but, as Merry states, "Numerical measures produce a world knowable without the detailed particulars of context and history" (2011: 84).

This "audit culture" (per Power 1999; Strathern 2000) is very active in Australia, and under the rubric of "closing the [statistical] gap" between Indigenous and non-Indigenous Australians a range of social, economic, and other factors across all states and territories provides "key indicators" or "trends in national outcomes for Aboriginal and Torres Strait Islander peoples." The Council of Australia Governments (COAG) has targets and six headline indicators: postsecondary education, household and individual income, disability and chronic disease, substantiated child abuse and neglect, family and community violence, and imprisonment and juvenile detention. Although one might perceive this focus on such social vulnerabilities as a sign that the government is taking these issues seriously, we also have to be alert to the possibility that some aspects of these "indicators" may be a case of "where humans are involved, more data sometimes yield less truth" (United Nations Human Rights Office of the High Commissioner 2012: 4). For instance, the data on imprisonment rates appear to indicate that Indigenous people are becoming more criminal and less law abiding, when in reality the legal parameters that define criminality have shifted in many jurisdictions, such as the Northern Territory, to capture and criminalize both preexisting and variant activities (as discussed in Chapters 4 and 6).

This language of constraint, adversity, and poverty also acts to reify, victimize, and essentialize Indigenous women and Indigenous peoples generally. The topics of the majority of these headline indicators are unfortunate as indicators of deficit, and, if we draw on the language of the UN "human rights indicators," they also suggest a violation approach in terms of negative human rights, in a murky shifting of blame onto the Aboriginal population and away from the state as duty bearer. Taylor, referring to the earlier but similar headline indicators from the 2005 *Overcoming Indigenous Disadvantage Report* observed that "the framework is constructed around a very explicit and causal model of Indigenous disadvantage highlighting the domestic settings of child rearing and the interactions between family and schooling" (2008: 114). Taylor and others in the Australian context (see Martin et al. 2002) have pointed out that Indigenous Australians, especially those living remotely, often have very different indices of quality of life that conflict with the moral and political objectives of statistical equality. Needless to say, those Indigenous Australians most representative of these "indicators of disadvantage" are those least likely to be engaged by government to formulate alternative indicators.

Nevertheless, in the Kimberley region of Western Australia, the Yawuru people have recently taken the matter of developing indicators into their own hands. Using a collaborative participatory approach with an external researcher, they developed "culturally relevant indicators of Indigenous wellbeing" (Yap and Yu 2016b). In an acknowledgment of the power of data, this project actively sought to reposition "from the ground up" the type of data gathered so that indices of quality of life reflected Indigenous interests and priorities (see also Yap and Yu 2016a). As a local Aboriginal leader, Peter Yu, stated in a foreword to the report:

> The findings of the Yawuru wellbeing survey will be a critical analytical tool in Yawuru decision making regarding investment for social and cultural development into the future and to determine the success of Yawuru native title rights. (Yap and Yu 2016a: 15)

Indeed, this issue of how data are used, what data consist of, and who controls them has recently been framed in terms of Indigenous data sovereignty (Kukutai and Taylor 2016). Thus, government-derived indicators of deficit are a very limited tool, and they are not the sole author of Anangu women and their families.

The Family as "the Fundamental Group Unit of Society"

The call for support of women's rights, by the UN Commission on the Status of Women, can be read as a call for a conversation between the sometimes competing discourses and regimes of value. The question of articulating these possible differences and convergences, and starting this conversation in terms of Aboriginal women's gendered social lives and capacities, must begin with their experiences within their family. According to the Universal Declaration of Human Rights:

> The family is the natural and fundamental group unit of society and is entitled to protection by society and the state. *Article 16(3)*

Yet, this "family" is also the place where gender violence overwhelmingly occurs and where structural gendered inequalities become normalized. Likewise, the configuration of an Aboriginal family as naturally consisting of a male and female partnership is at odds with familial groupings of women, such as widows who choose not to remarry and intergenerational groupings of women, where men are sporadic residents.[5] This notion of women's rights as human rights—as though they are *not* the same—may at first glance appear like a tautology, as human rights claim universality and men and women are both human. Eleanor Roosevelt, who chaired the committee that drafted the UDHR in the mid-1940s, also went to considerable trouble to ensure that the terms "human beings" and "everyone" were used, rather than "all men are born free and equal," for instance. Yet, the Declaration was drafted before the days of inclusive language guidelines, and there is considerable slippage between the apparent inclusiveness of the use of "everyone" and the characteristic "his" throughout many of the thirty Articles. Gender biases start creeping into the Declaration by Article 10, because although "everyone is entitled . . . to a fair and public hearing," this specifies "his rights" concerning "charges against him." Article 12 discusses "his privacy, family, home," Article 13 "his country," Article 17 "his property," and so on (see Bell 1992: 347).

As such, the idea that universal human rights also incorporates the rights of women has been open to question. We know, in practice anyway, that "women are discriminated against in all the world's countries and the grounds for this distinction is often seen as far more natural, inevitable and benign than other grounds for distinction that human rights declarations prohibit—such as race, religion or political opinion" (Okin 1998: 33). It is necessary to rethink human rights to address many important women's rights because, as liberal feminist and political philosopher Okin points out, the power that male household heads wielded during the development of human rights became an intrinsic element of them.

These rights at the household level are not equally shared among its members. Inequitable relations of power exist within households. As "the family" has been made the "natural'" social unit within the human rights discourse, the rights violations of women that take place *within* this sphere have been invisible. It is in this private domestic sphere that great numbers of the world's women live most (in some cases, virtually all) of their lives, and in which vast numbers of violations of women's human rights take place (Okin 1998: 36). A significant field of ethnography, by female anthropologists, has explored this gendered distinction whereby the social practices of females tend to be in the private and domestic spheres, while male social practices are in public and political spheres, in particular the work of Sherry Ortner (1974) and Michelle Rosaldo (1974). So this structural pattern, as a global cultural tendency, has effectively been replicated in the Universal Declaration of Human Rights. As a result, the civil and political rights have been privileged in human rights work. These public rights are monopolized by men in many countries, as rights against the state. In contrast to these public civic rights, men did not fear violations in the domestic sphere of the home. However, "by far the greatest violence against women occurs in the private non-governmental sphere" (Charlesworth 1994: 72). So as the family is regarded as the fundamental social unit and should be protected by the state—as men have historically controlled the state and in most states still do—this family unit has been inviolable. The "private rights violations" that take place within the home have, until very recently, been simply labeled as culturally sanctioned private matters (Charlesworth 1994; Okin 1998).

Although the right to be free from violence is now understood fundamentally as a right that the state has to legally ensure, as a legal criminal offense, this is a very recent development. Indeed, reporting domestic and family violence is now mandatory in many Australian states and territories, including the Northern Territory, effectively criminalizing those who do not report such violence. This indicates that societal attitudes have not yet caught up with the discourse of women's rights. In the Northern Territory, mandatory reporting laws were introduced in 2007, and although these laws appear to be appropriately supportive of Aboriginal women's universal right to be free from violence, similarly for other Australian women, the impact of these laws cannot be understood in isolation from other intersecting laws, such as those that affect the protection of children who are potentially impacted by such violence. Paradoxically, these laws—as they work in concert with the range of other laws that have a disproportionate effect on the Aboriginal population—can also be understood as part of a broader sweep of practices of the neoliberal state and the system of social insecurity (per Wacquant 2010). The state's role in attempting to mandate Aboriginal women's freedom from violence and the interactions of these laws with Anangu social rights, as these also need to be understood as collective familial rights, will be discussed in Chapter 4.

Feminist legal scholars variously argue that the continuing and rising influence of cultural or religious justifications for women's inequality is one reason it is so significant for women's rights to be recognized as human rights (Okin 1998; Bunch 1990, 2009; Charlesworth 1994). Feminist scholars have little truck with discrimination and violence against women that is labeled as "cultural" or "religious." The key question they ask is, "Who benefits from such discrimination?" Clearly, in posing this rhetorical question, the antici-pated answer is "not women." Feminist political theorists, however, argue that the ideals embodied in human rights rest on a distinctly masculine version of the person as an independent, self-interested economic being. How can wom-en's human rights assist in working toward another outcome if the liberal ideals of human rights are so firmly masculinist? As Dietz further expounds:

> While liberal ideals have been efficacious in overturning restrictions on women as individuals, liberal theory does not provide the language or concepts to help us understand the various kinds of human interdependence which are part of the life of both families and polities. (Shanley, in Dietz 1987: 6)

Such a feminist vision of interdependence could align more comfortably with both the communitarian critique of liberalism (per Walzer 1990) and an Anangu critique—rather than a more specifically gendered one. In this con-text of the intersections of Anangu women's human rights and the collective rights of Aboriginal peoples, the type of personhood that feminists, such as Dietz, critique defines not only a masculinity but, for our purposes, a specifi-cally modern and Western one. In locating human rights as relevant and use-ful for Anangu women we need to be alert to this double bind that the rights discourse specifies, as this is both masculinist *as well as* positing the liberal individual. As a Briefing Note on "Gender and Indigenous Peoples" specifies:

Indigenous women's claim for a conception of women's human rights predicated on collective rights challenges both the conventional human rights paradigm and mainstream conceptions of women's human rights, which posit the individual as the only subject of human rights . . . Indigenous women's claims represent more than an extension of the existing human rights framework: they require an overhaul of underlying assumptions starting with the notion that collective rights threaten, rather than complement individual rights. (United Nations Office of the Special Advisor on Gender Issues 2010: 2)

These limitations need to be recognized. There needs to be a rapprochement of individual and collective rights through a focus on the right to development and self-determination within the domains of social and cultural rights. The work of these so-called second-generation rights are reflected in the social and economic rights work of NGOs, underpinned by the central premise of enabling agency, as this can be individual and collective. Indeed, the work of the NGO Waltja Tjutangku Palyapayi is premised on working through families, with women as the key drivers.

Shifting Feminist Politics

The charge of ethnocentrism that has been applied to "Western feminism" (not generally international feminism) by non-Western scholars needs addressing. Mohanty, in particular, was deeply critical of the ongoing colonial affects that this discourse—where the "Third World woman" had become a singular subject (1988). She is ignorant, poor, uneducated, tradition bound, religious, domesticated, family oriented, victimized, and so on. Mohanty suggests that this is contrasted to the self-representation of Western women as educated, modern and having control over their bodies and sexualities and "freedom" to make their own decisions (Mohanty 1988: 65). This discourse, she argues, is implicitly hierarchical—in its relationship with the "Other"—as scholars take it on themselves, as part of their own political project, to lift the Third World woman out of her dire situation. Indeed, the global practices of audit culture, discussed earlier, encourage this Othering.

A parallel discourse by Australian Indigenous female academics during this same period—the 1970s and 1980s—was also emerging that opposed the ideology of feminism as an elite Western position. Patricia (Pat) O'Shane (Australia's first Indigenous magistrate) asked, "Is there any relevance in the Women's Movement for Aboriginal Women?" (1976, in Sawer 1995). She found that "sexist attitudes did not wipe out whole tribes of our people, sexist attitudes are not slowly killing our people—racism did and continues to do so" (in Sawer 1995: 79). As I subsequently revisited my 1989 anthropology honours thesis about urban Aboriginal women in Sydney it seemed like a time capsule, embodying the political and ideological landscape of that time.[6] As it drew on the autobiographies of Aboriginal women from NSW, such as Tucker (1977), Langford (1988), and Bandler (1989), it was clear at that time that notions of feminism or women's rights were dismissed as secondary to promoting the shared interests of Aboriginal people's rights. The recognition of the shared struggle against colonization, where women had to support their men and thus their families, was both the rhetoric and lived reality in these women's lives.

A defining moment that revealed this colonial gender politic and galvanized discussion about a previously invisible reality to the wider public was the publication of Dianne Bell and Topsy Nelson Napurrula's provocative article: "Speaking about Rape Is Everyone's Business" (Bell and Nelson 1989) from their joint work in central Australia. The publication provoked some very strong responses from urban Indigenous female academics and non-Indigenous academics alike. Indigenous academic Huggins responded: "It is our business how we deal with rape and we have done so for the last 202 years quite well," and "we dispute the central proposition that rape is 'everyone's business.' What this reflects is white imperialism of others' cultures which are theirs to appropriate, criticise and castigate" (Huggins et al. 1991: 506). We can recognize that the relations of power between Indigenous and non-Indigenous women were deeply unequal; they were not "sistas" (though Bell and Nelson were, respectively, non-Indigenous and Indigenous). At that time the Indigenous politic was, "We are women and men together who have suffered grave injustices by the white invaders. We have all suffered" (Huggins et al. 1991: 506). And so the rights of the "Indigenous collective" trumped the rights of the individuals within that collective. Likewise, Indigenous academic Moreton-Robinson argued that the:

> Bell-Huggins debate [was] an example of the use of the "traditional" versus "contemporary" Indigenous woman binary in public discourse . . . illuminat[ing] its continuing relationship to the subject position middle-class white woman. (2000: 91)

The field of Indigenous women's scholarship in Australia has since expanded significantly and, in the case of Moreton-Robinson, shifted to one of accommodation, as she states: "Indigenous and feminist scholars share an understanding that their respective production of knowledge is a site of constant struggle against normative patriarchal conceptual frameworks" (2013: 331; see also St Denis 2007).

At that time, as Bell noted in her reply in the letters to the editor, those critical responses did not address the substantive issue that "intraracial rape" was deeply pervasive and that ignoring it by silencing it "kill[s] women" (Bell 1991). In the year 2000, almost twenty years after this debate, the Australian Government Attorney Generals Department established the Central Australian Aboriginal Family Legal Unit (CAAFLU) in Alice Springs—a service principally for female victims of family violence. The service charter emblazoned on the front of their pamphlet and on their website reads *Domestic Violence: It's Everybody's Business.*

It was also from the 1980s that two publications were commissioned with very different findings that variously articulated these contested values and political priorities. These were *Women's Business: Report of the Aboriginal Women's Taskforce* (Daylight and Johnson 1986) and *Aboriginal Women and Violence* (Bolger 1991). The *Women's Business* report by Aboriginal women Daylight and Johnson could be read as a barometer of public awareness and political ideology for that period. This publication focused on the sexual violence of the ongoing frontier of interracial rape: "Since colonisation many Aboriginal women have suffered physical and sexual abuse at the hands of white men . . . the topic of rape is taboo for Aboriginal women. They will not speak about their own rape" (1986: 66). However, they also write that "since working for the Aboriginal Women's Task Force I have become aware of a very fast growing proportion of Aboriginal men rapists. This is something that is very frightening and an area that should be looked at in the future" (1986: 65). With our current awareness of intraracial sexual and family violence, this issue of the number of Aboriginal male rapists as being "fast growing" reveals instead a nascent public awareness that gained more traction with Bolger's text, which was the first of its kind and the first with a focus on the Northern Territory (1991).

Bolger cites a national survey conducted for the Australian government Office of the Status of Women, which found that although 85 percent of people considered that domestic violence was a serious issue and that the perpetrators were mainly men, they did not think that it was a crime (1991: 5). One-third of the people surveyed believed that domestic violence was a private matter to be handled within the family, and more than a quarter said that they would ignore the situation if they found out that a neighbor was beating his wife. It appeared that the silencing and denial by Aboriginal people of intra-Aboriginal violence at that time was also reflected more broadly in a society of violence against all women.

Domestic violence being commonly viewed as a "private matter" recalls to mind an incident when I was working at the Central Land Council (CLC) in Alice Springs in my first professional job in the early 1990s. At that stage the CLC office backed onto the Charles Creek town-camp, and there would often be traffic from the camp through the grounds of the office and sometimes even inside, to use the washroom. From the vantage point of my office window I recall seeing a young Aboriginal woman obviously in distress from what appeared to be a bashing; she looked bruised and teary. She was walking through the grounds and appeared to be heading for the pay phone at the service station across the road. I mentioned this to another colleague, who replied, "that's probably [. . .]; happens all the time." At the time, although I recall being taken aback by this complacency, the fact that I am more shocked at this memory now than I was when it happened speaks strongly to the shift in public sentiment about such violence. I remember explicitly thinking about how intrusive it might appear were I to somehow intervene; it did seem to be her business. Yet today I wouldn't think twice about offering support (as I suspect would that colleague). This shift in public consciousness is the work of realizing women's rights as human rights. As the non-Aboriginal public legitimate this discourse, so too does this relational gaze, to borrow a concept from Cowlishaw (2004), begin to have positive rather than negative effects as witnesses refuse to remain bystanders.

The Work of NGO Waltja Tjutangku Palyapayi ("Doing Good Work for Families")

We are a caring organisation. The principles we promote are Aboriginal—we see family as the foundation of Aboriginal identity and Waltja works with the family. We avoid the problems of social work in the cities where clients are seen only as individuals. Here they are recognised as embedded in their families. And we don't give up and see the family as the problem and remove them [youth] from it.

Senior staff member, July 16, 2015

Although the structure of the contemporary Anangu family may be much more complex, diffuse, multigenerational, and matricentric than could possibly be imagined by the ideals articulated in human rights, it is indeed a "fundamental group unit" of Anangu society. However, the ways in which this family contests and butts up against liberal norms of private kinship (per Sutton 2001) in its inward-looking endosociality, is an ongoing challenge to the state. Exploring the work of one NGO, who works specifically with remote Aboriginal families, offers insight into the possibilities and limits of the human rights discourse and the ways in which it has been co-opted and customized. In exploring the operations of this NGO through the lens of women's human rights I am mindful of Levitt and Merry's statement that "rights and culture are changing all the time and are not oppositional" (2011: 99). At the same time I am cautious about critiquing this, or indeed any NGO, as this potentially plays into government and broader public commentary that is invariably critical of Aboriginal organizations (see also Englund 2006). All Aboriginal NGOs, including the CLC, are under routine government and public scrutiny, and the practices of accountability and reporting for public funds are intense (Moran and Elvin 2009).

The Aboriginal NGO Waltja Tjutangku Palyapayi (which I will refer to as Waltja, as others do), roughly translated as "Doing Good Work for Families," is based in Alice Springs with a regional focus on remote communities and these community residents as they visit town. Its regional footprint is extensive, working across communities in nine different language groups, including Pintupi-Luritja. Indeed, the website indicates they range across 90,000 square kilometers.[7] The name derives from the Pintupi-Luritja language, and there has been a consistent presence in the Papunya region since the organization's inception in 1991, as it was initially established as the Central Australian Family Resource Centre (FRC) with funding from the Labor Keating federal government. Its early role was to assist families in the areas of advocacy, development of family services, information provision, education and training, and needs identification. When this funding was withdrawn in 1997 (and reallocated to youth-specific service providers) by the conservative Howard coalition, FRC members and constituents sought to continue operating. They located other funding avenues, incorporating as an aboriginal association and adopting a new constitution.[8]

The language of the organization is at once one of deficit and of empowerment. It was established "in recognition of the severe sickness, poverty, helplessness and distress . . . as a result of dispossession . . . cultural disintegration and social and economic marginalisation" (per the constitution), while on the other hand it seeks to change this through "self-management and self-determination; to Facilitate community participation in the planning, management provision and evaluation of community based services; to secure the provision of training, employment and related programs; And to represent the views of . . . families, from children to the elderly."[9] These, and other very broad aims, attempt to refocus service delivery from a centralized to a localized model and from an externally assessed needs basis to a demand-driven approach. The broader public discourse of rights has acted as a framework against which to build the organization, rather than an overt platform from which it was launched. As a non-Aboriginal long-term staff member stated:

> Waltja developed as a pragmatic organisation. The principles they [directors] work on seemed to them as self-evident and became the principles for action. While the directors had very little exposure to human rights ideas as abstract principles, they just know—if it's not fair they feel it. (field notes July 16, 2015)

Over the years the Waltja programs supported by government and philanthropy have waxed and waned. They've included aged care and disability, support for young people to address personal issues, homelessness, access to education and career options via the Reconnect and Family Mental Health programs, money management, young mothers' support, and so on. Whether any or all of these programs can be run is dependent on the success or otherwise of funding applications, while the mix of funding has increasingly diversified. Not all programs are run in all communities, and, as this is a busy marketplace, there is competition for scarce resources. A diverse range of NGOs will be successful in gaining funding to run the same program, such as the Money Story, but in a different set of communities to that of Waltja even though they might be run in the region where Waltja runs other programs. And although, to a very significant extent, the success of the organization is dependent on accessing grants, as a staff member stated, "We've learnt not to take projects that don't fit with our values" (see also Lawrence 2006: 431).

There is both the expectation and the appearance that the organization delivers more than it does or indeed can possibly do, given the constant struggle for funding. As Lawrence stated: "Waltja's aspirations are necessarily large in scale, but constrained by the same conditions that the Aboriginal communities struggle with" (2006: 437). Many of the programs are based on one-off funding for a single program—such as a "return to country" walk over a week that drew in elderly women and youth or to hold workshops for the disabled and elderly. Yet, according to staff, these sorts of programs are strongly advocated for by the directors. Unlike these other organizations that compete for the same funding, such as Mission Australia and Lutheran Community Care, Waltja does, however, focus solely on delivering programs in remote Aboriginal communities. Indeed, they received an Indigenous Governance Award (through the NGO Reconciliation Australia) in 2014. As the chair of the judging committee stated: "Waltja is difficult to fault in its governance, it's one of the best organisations I have encountered, the best in Australia."[10] All Waltja directors are Aboriginal women who have to be from the remote communities that the organization serves. There are five executive directors and seven directors on the board. The whole board meets at least three times a year, whereas the executive directors meet four times a year. According to the website, the directors are "responsible for setting direction and making decisions about projects and programs . . . policies and priorities." As I enquired about the role of the directors in the organization, I was informed:

> They shape us! At the same time the fact that our funding comes from competitive tendering to government and philanthropics means that we can't do whatever we want, but we've developed a strong commitment for compliance and fiscal responsibility. (field notes July 16, 2015)

The directors are chosen on the basis that they have made a "big contribution to the community and [are] recognised for their leadership, either paid or voluntary in the community," according to an early version of the website. Most of the women have had long-term involvement with the organization, some since the start-up, and have significant roles in their communities, such as shire councillors. This engagement of these community-based women, the regular meetings in Alice Springs, and opportunities to attend forums and conferences beyond Alice Springs effectively counter the marginality of remote geography. In actively supporting mobility for these women beyond their communities, Waltja is also sponsoring them as individuals. As Irene Nangala, a long-term Waltja director, stated, "I got strong from listening to other people, and it made me really proud . . . talking up for other people, not only for my family or Kintore [home community] but for Aboriginal people everywhere." Another director stated: "We like going to meetings for Waltja . . . we learn a lot when we are together . . . I feel proud to support all the ladies and to help Sharijn [the manager] and the other staff." This theme of coming in for meetings and learning from each other and the staff emerged from the on-line profiles of all of the directors. For them, Waltja is an underpinning element in their life projects, because although there may not be Waltja programs active in the directors' own communities, they are still active with the organization.

Waltja directors have undertaken training in governance and finance, either formally and/or as side-by-side mentoring at executive meetings. In 2014 they requested and received training in community mediation (supported by a regional development grant from the Northern Territory government). In 2011 Waltja's Future Leaders project (with the support of a philanthropic foundation) enabled Waltja directors to mentor and up-skill younger women in the areas of governance and leadership. A two-day workshop was held in Alice Springs, in conjunction with Waltja's Annual General Meeting, with participation from fifty-one women from across the age spectrum. As such, engagement with Waltja is an avenue to mobility and indeed one of the few opportunities for women enabling this. This broadening of opportunity and politicization was observed as: "Waltja members appreciate the opportunities to learn leadership and governance skills through their management committee membership and through Waltja workshops. However, they want this training to be available also for others in their communities" (Lawrence 2006: 435). As a director stated:

> I would like to see other training at our communities . . . like how to run a meeting and how to talk to Government people to help our community . . . [Now] we can run our own meeting and speak up for our place, maybe also talk to Government people for help. It is a really good thing, what we are learning. It is good for people to be able to speak up for their communities. (in Lawrence 2006: 435)

Asserting women's rights to education and employment has also been a defining feature of the organization, and Waltja became a registered training organization (RTO) in 1999. This was in recognition of the fact that women leaders in remote communities spend a lot of their time in meetings and voluntary work to maintain essential community services that urban dwellers take for granted. Community health clinics, schools, child care services, and stores all have community management committees (Lawrence 2006: 425). These committees tend "to lock Aboriginal community members into volunteering without the clear pathways or skills development towards assuming . . . paid roles [which] are almost universally held by non-Indigenous people from elsewhere" (in Lawrence 2006: 425). None of the skills and local governance knowledge of community members, especially women, is formally recognized or accredited. However, although Waltja delivered some training, such as the "training *nintirringtjaku*" initiative, and undertook research on training needs, registration as an RTO ceased in 2011, as simply remaining compliant with the RTO administration cost $70,000 annually, and they couldn't continue to source these funds.

"Waltja culture" is another initiative from the directors that focuses on the intergenerational transfer of knowledge through enabling opportunities for older women to share their knowledge with young women and girls through "grandmother's stories."[11] The Waltja chairperson, April Martin, stated that "women are strong with their culture and knowledge, with the language and with ceremonies as well as teaching the young ones—leading the way." As a judge from the Indigenous Governance Awards (IGA) stated, "Culture is at the very core of what Waltja does. It responds to the needs of its community by being inclusive and doing things the Waltja way" (IGA judge).[12] Interestingly, one of the few areas that Waltja has not to date worked in is family and domestic violence. As I enquired about what seemed to be a significant service gap, given Waltja's primary concern with women's issues and the lack of a women's specific support agency in the region where they predominantly work, such as the NPY Women's Council,[13] a senior non-Aboriginal staff member responded:

> The board has not directed us to pursue this area of work. My feeling is that the directors are vulnerable—they already have a high profile as Waltja directors and get requests for resources as it is. They have little very authority beyond their Waltja role. [Like any role] it does not translate across the community. I have the sense that DV [domestic violence] is such a fraught issue that they are loath to engage with it. (field notes July 16, 2015)

And, as we discussed the history of women's advocacy in the region of Waltja's footprint, I reflected on the role of the broader political context in, arguably, stifling this advocacy. Much of Waltja's region overlaps with the CLC region, while the NPY Women's Council grew out of the support of the Pitjantjatjarra Council (Pit Council) which, like the CLC, operates as a land council though under different legislation and in neighboring South Australia. As a result, the NPY Women's Council emerged with the support of the Pit Council, which was a strong women's advocate. No comparable support was forthcoming from the male-dominated CLC. As a staff anthropologist for the CLC in the early 1990s I do, however, recall discussion at the annual Women's Law and Culture meetings about establishing a women's council to represent women's interests along the same vein as the NPY women's council.[14] Likewise, there was also consideration of a woman's representative body at several full council meetings of the CLC that I attended (as a women's anthropologist) in the early 1990s. And, for a period of time, a women's meeting operated alongside the full council meeting, though it did not become an influential decision-making body. However, this dichotomy between men's and women's decision making did not evolve into any formal structure in recognition of the principles of gender equity, and today it is still the case that there are very few women on the CLC full council. No formal gender-based power-sharing arrangement ever evolved.

In light of the lack of representation of Aboriginal women's issues in this Northern Territory region of central Australia, Waltja filled the void to some extent. Nevertheless, the focus of Waltja is on families, of which women are a core part, rather than on women as individuals. This focus on families is an explicit focus on collective rights, though it may not be expressed in those terms. The blurring between process and outcome can be seen as the women directors become part of the development of the organization and are provided opportunity for further education, training, and travel. It is this process of sponsoring each woman's agency in the organization that bridges individual rights and collective rights. This individual agency is tempered, as the Waltja directors whom I spoke with were extremely conscious that their family-oriented approach differs significantly from that of the NPY Women's Council, who are individual women focused notably in their advocacy on domestic and family violence. As will be discussed further in the following chapter, the NPY Women's Council explicitly uses the individualist language of women's human rights.

To borrow one of Levitt and Merry's three forms of local NGO human rights vernacularization, Waltja's style of rights engagement relies on the "imaginative space created by women's human rights rather than the discourse of rights itself" (Levitt and Merry 2011: 91). As the global discourse of rights provides the backdrop to Waltja's advocacy work, the push for equal access to services and opportunity draws in Aboriginal women to the front and center of the organization. Yet, although they are actively working from the multiple sites that comprise Aboriginal families, their process work as singular human rights holders, though essential in achieving Waltja's goals, is directed at the end-point of the family.

The Role of Women in Development and the CLC's Community Development Unit

The role of women in development has gained significant international attention in the last decade, with the United Nations Development Program (UNDP) funding a major initiative on women's empowerment though UN Women.[15] Along with widespread recognition that gender equality and women's empowerment are necessary to achieve the Millenium Development Goals (see also Nussbaum 2000), there is evidence to suggest that women are often the drivers of change and the innovators within communities. If they are encouraged and enabled, then the whole community benefits. There is also the aphoristic rule of thumb that if you give a woman $1, then 80 cents of it will be spent on her family, notably her children. Men, on the other hand, if given the same amount, will spend 30 cents on their families and the bulk of it on themselves. These global development discourses have found their way to central Australia through the work of the Central Land Council's (CLC) Community Development Unit, established in 2005 (see also Campbell and Hunt 2012: Roche and Ensor 2014).

By establishing this unit, the CLC are rewriting how they do business with their constituents with an explicit focus on gender equity and an inclusive notion of community. This "development" work is being driven by the significant income stream from the community lease monies from the Northern Territory Emergency Response (NTER) five-year leases to the affected communities, and monies from land use agreements and affected area payments, such as from mining agreements on Aboriginal Freehold Land (CLC 2012: 4). The participatory approach to managing these monies derives from the paradigms of gender equity and encouragement of the future-oriented process of responsibilization. As a "thoroughly modern concept," responsibility in the sense of accountability to others is embodied in all modern governance structures, no matter how local (Hage and Eckersley 2012: 3–5).

Very few organizations have operated in this development field in remote Australia, and all levels of government have applied a needs-based approach through a passive service delivery model.[16] Although the CLC approach signals a compelling alternative to the infantilizing welfarist model, in their inclusive and participatory demand-driven approach, it is underwritten by a move beyond the atomistic family to the civic community in an explicit encouragement and facilitation of Anangu engagement with a "responsible" subjectivity. This new approach is a significant departure from the way the CLC has operated since it was established in 1976. In the past, such monies were automatically allocated to individual "traditional owners" (TOs) as those who had "primary spiritual responsibility" for specific *Tjukurrpa* (Dreamings) on the potentially affected tracts of land, as identified by social anthropologists under the Aboriginal Land Rights Act NT (1976). This was regardless of whether they resided in the affected community or still had any cultural or customary land management interest in the land the money derived from. They were not required to be accountable for these monies, so such monies usually enabled "big men" to shore up their networks of relatedness (the term "Toyota Dreaming" was coined to cynically describe the most common spending outlet).[17] The development paradigm attempts to change this model from individual TO-based to community-based interests, so including those who are long-term residents and women. This inclusive approach attempts to challenge the centrality of family through the encouragement of a civil society or a community of shared interests beyond kin. Although this collectivist approach also follows the principles of self-determination, it is conspicuously not fostering customary concepts of family but rather broader contemporary and pragmatic notions of community. This is in acknowledgment of the inegalitarian decision making that has typified local governance processes.

Male community leaders were initially, and in some cases still are, significantly more resistant to allocating monies to community purpose than the women. It was these "big men" who had the most to gain personally from their greater control over these resources as royalty streams for them and for their families (see Holcombe 2005: Langton 2008). The community purpose approach benefits women, as they now have a legitimate voice in decision making, and their choices tend to engage with the community of shared interests and children's education. For instance, school excursions and church renovations are popular projects.

As an evolving model of contemporary governance, the third stage of the six-stage community development consultation process is, "The group talks about the main areas they want to work on to make life better now and for the kids and grandkids in the future" (CLC Community Development News Summer 2013). Although the previous approach of royalty distribution was immediate cash disbursement or written checks, this new approach takes considerably more time. At a full council meeting in 2012, the vote was unanimous: that no community could put more than 50 percent of their monies toward personal cash. And if the lease monies are for more than $A1 million, then the maximum that could be allocated is $500,000 (field notes April 21, 2013). The fact that the full council of the CLC is dominated by men—in 2015 there were approximately sixteen women on the ninety-member full council—suggests that this was an extraordinary result. This gender inequity can be contrasted with the Community Development Units' active encouragement of gender balance in each community committee established to decide the allocation of the funding. Interestingly the two regions (of the nine) from where the majority of CLC delegates/executive women are elected are also where the largest towns are—Alice Springs and Tennant Creek. In several of the regions, including the Western Region that incorporates Papunya and Mount Liebig, there are no female delegates or executive members, at the time of writing.

On the wall of the new Papunya Store (a community-owned corporation) the CLC has pinned up a large pictorial poster outlining what was purchased from the NTER community lease monies in 2014/15. These include monies allocated to a music and video project (recall the Warumpi Band history), the purchase of two coaster buses and a minibus, monies to upgrade the football and softball ovals' grandstand and seating, the purchase of two community vehicles (Toyota troop carriers), each allocated for church and culture uses. Possibly the biggest allocation is upgrading the football and softball ovals. Australian Rules Football (AFL, Australian Football League) is enormously popular and singularly played by men, as softball is an Anangu women's sport. The transparency of the notification of this resource allocation also signaled the accountability of those on the committee that decided this distribution.

Rather like the "good governance" that Waltja has been awarded for practicing, so too the CLC has a growing focus on governance, which seems to have emerged from or been catalyzed by this development work. As part of the Aboriginal Peak Organisations of the Northern Territory (APO NT), the CLC were instrumental in holding what was called the "Strong Aboriginal Governance Summit" in 2013, in the desert township of Tennant Creek.

As is the standard process at most significant Aboriginal meetings, for a period, the men and women separated into gender-segregated groups and discussed their respective concerns about "law and culture" at the Summit (APO NT 2013: 16–19). According to the *Strong Aboriginal Governance Report* that was an account of the event, at the women's meeting gender equity emerged as an issue that women were concerned about in all representative community and regional contexts. It was advocated that, for CLC representation, "when there are two positions for CLC delegates, one of the positions should go to a woman. [And] all organisations . . . should create strategies to encourage more women to run for board elections" (APO NT 2013: 19). This perspective clearly mirrors wider public discourse and the increasing concerns about affirmative action from political parties to the workplace, which will be discussed further in the following chapter.[18]

One attendee asserted her aspiration of: "women and men—equal together" (APO NT 2013: 19). This gender segregation of separate meetings, however, continues to be an indicator that women feel freer to speak and participate publically in a homosocial context.[19] My experience of observing meetings in Papunya and Mount Liebig has not found such a strict protocol. Rather, the public performance of gender is entirely dependent on the content of the meeting. For instance, in the monthly "community safety" meetings that are hosted by the police in Papunya, Anangu women are very active spokespeople.

At the international level, in less than two generations there has been a transformation in the recognition by most states, led by the United Nations and a plethora of NGOs, that gender equality and economic development are inextricably linked. There is an ever-increasing number of publications, sponsored by global agencies such as the World Bank Group, with aspirational titles such as *Voice and Agency: Empowering Women and Girls for Shared Prosperity* (2014). This field of gender development has been deeply informed by the work of Sen and Nussbaum, who focused attention on the ways in which "social norms" intersect with development paradigms. This development work, however, tends to focus on states with minimal or no social welfare structures. Indeed, within the rights discourse there is an acknowledgment that these so-called second-generation rights, though they are to be realized "through national effort and international cooperation" (UDHR Article 22), are recognized as contingent on the resources of each state. As part of a wealthy developed nation, Aboriginal citizens, as with others, have access to both social security and forms of employment. For Aboriginal Australians this access to social security, via citizenship rights, became an entitlement from the 1960s, and for those in remote areas the types of employment options are, again, circumscribed as certain types of work more highly valued than others. Work roles, paid and unpaid, are also deeply gendered. Access to both is, however, unevenly distributed through various forms of structural inequality, and access to social security is increasingly conditional via various "work for the dole" (unemployment benefits) schemes, specifically since mid-2015 the Community Development Program (see Jordon and Fowkes 2016).

Ongoing Dual Socioeconomic Systems?

Although two generations have passed since Hamilton, Bell, and Myers variously asserted the homosociality of Aboriginal male–female gender relations, it is useful to briefly revisit this early ethnographic literature on the gendered socioeconomic roles of Anangu men and women (Myers 1986; Bell 1983; Hamilton 1980). Neither these nor earlier ethnographers (Kaberry 1939; Berndt 1970; White 1978) found equality between men and women. It was widely acknowledged that gender relations were complementary and interdependent and that in their own spheres of ritual, the customary economy and child rearing, women generally had considerable autonomy. And although I am open to Bell's argument that the patriarchal structures of colonization, such as the "patrilineal descent group" of the Aboriginal Land Rights Act,[20] have (among other imposed patriarchal structures) altered this dynamic to the detriment of Aboriginal women, we can't be too hasty in making generalizations given the complex interplay between increased possibilities for mobility and independence for all Anangu from the local binds of commitment to place and family. And we would be ignoring the early ethnographic evidence, as Bern states, "The ideological representation of inter-gender relations is concerned with the primacy of the male in reproducing the conditions of life" (1979: 125). The underpinning centrality of male ritual along with male domination of the public sphere are still true today, though marriage exchange is no longer especially active with "love" marriages more common, at least in the Papunya region.

The change postsettlement in the economies of women and men has, in practice, freed women from subsistence work. Independently from their spouses, women undertake paid employment and receive various government social security transfers, such as child endowment money ("baby money"), unemployment benefits ("sit down money"), and old age or disability pensions. Thus, although the structural dichotomy of women's and men's "traditional" economies no longer operates as the predominant pattern, women

today can still be economically independent, just as they were to a significant extent prior to settlement (see Hamilton 1980).[21] And, likewise, there is
a propensity for men and women to work in very different fields, so that the
daily gender segregation is still a marked tendency. The significant majority
of Anangu men work outside, in manual or labor-intensive work for the regional shire, in packing shelves in the store, and in work as land-care rangers.[22] Women work inside dwellings, in areas such as teaching and child care,
clerical work for Centrelink and the shire, and on the store cash registers. As
I observed this daily gendered work segregation to a male community leader
he was shocked that he had never noticed it but agreed on reflection that it is
marked: "*Yuwa, yilta!*" (Yes, it's true!). Such an unnoticed dichotomy suggests
that the lack of flexibility in these roles transfers itself to other social domains,
as Nakamarra(2) comments:

> Nakamarra(2): But I think Aboriginal men should be encouraged to work in
> those places [school, child care] 'cause they're the fathers of the kids, the
> uncles and grandfathers. 'Cause in our culture men don't really look after
> the kids, it's the woman's job all the time.
> SH: And what do you think about that?
> Nakamarra(2): I think it's terrible [laughing]. (field notes July 13, 2015)

There are exceptions to these gendered work roles, and in Papunya there are
a few individuals who defy this trend. The regional shire president (who happens to be from Papunya) has his own office and computer, while the male
and female Anangu team who work for the Northern Territory government
in child protection both have offices and computers. Interestingly, he is from
the neighboring Warlpiri community to the north, having married a local Luritja woman. There is also a middle-aged couple who work together in the Art
Centre (preparing canvases, taking photos, writing the *Tjukurrpa* stories, and
so on), though Nampitjinpa(2) does the computer entries. Of note, her mother
Nungurrayi is one of the two child protection workers, and an exceptional intergenerational pattern has emerged: when Nungurrayi was younger she also
worked alongside her now deceased spouse, both as health workers. As I was
discussing the rarity of such shared work roles (especially a couple in the same
work space), Nakamarra(1) recalled, however, that when Papunya was first established in the late 1960s, men and women both worked in the kitchen, in the
bakery and butchery, and that her spouse worked on the store cash register in

the 1980s. But as Nakamarra(2) said now, "You wouldn't see an Aboriginal man working a cash register in any desert community or a woman collecting the rubbish [in the council truck]."

To some extent this place is now reflective as a microcosm of the broader Australian employment environment (but with considerably less diversity) in terms of gendered employment fields.[23] But there are several interrelated intersubjective factors that compound this work homosociality. If you were to work with the opposite sex all day, one risk is encountering your mother-in-law/son-in-law or another avoidance relationship. This concern is active in the Art Centre, which women have effectively co-opted, painting there daily. Without specific spaces for men and women, men paint at their homes with concerns over avoidance cited as the reason. Yet, the history of the Western Desert art movement began with men (see Johnson 2010, 2015; Bardon and Bardon 2004). Likewise, the requirement for an Ochre Card (a police clearance for working with children), which came into effect in 2010, makes it difficult for men to work in the school, child-care center, and with youth, as any criminal record makes it difficult to obtain one. Nevertheless, although this requirement makes it more difficult for men now, very few men were working in this caring sector prior to the Ochre Card system. The point here is the considerable evidence that ongoing work gender segregation is constraining and that increased egalitarianism in employment roles is one of the foundational and catalytic pathways to gender equality and shifting the balance of power in the home (Greenfield 2009; Sen 1999).

Yet, as Nakamarra(2) indicated earlier with her disdain of the "woman's job" of child care, maintaining gender segregation in the workplace is not the aspiration of her daughter. As we were discussing employment options for women, Nakamarra's(2) teenage daughter (in year 7 at school in Alice Springs) stated that ever since she was five years old she's wanted to be a policewoman. I respond, "That's a good job and well paid, joining the police force, and Sue [the local policewoman] is a good role model—you should tell her." And her mother responds, "She has, many times." Mothers' encouragement of such agency and gender egalitarianism, amid social change, is important given the centrality of mothers in socializing the next generation (Manago and Greenfield 2011: 3). Yet, the role of primary carer can actively discourage young women from pursuing a career, as they receive "family payments" as a welfare entitlement until the child is aged five (as do non-Aboriginal mothers).

Nakamarra(2) suggested that this can act as a disincentive, leaving the young mother homebound. Yet, she also commented that it didn't have that effect on her, that she soon returned to work. However, this is not the case for the significant majority; although the young mother might be relatively financially independent, her singular role has become that of mother. As Nussbaum articulates the welfarist argument: "Peoples' preferences are shaped by the sheer fact of existing endowments . . . as habituation shapes desire and aspiration" (2000: 143). Young women's options are thus circumscribed by the status quo and the relative ease of slipping into the position of full-time young mother. However, as will be discussed in the following chapter, motherhood is a singularly important aspiration for many young Anangu women.

Nakamarra(2) was not the only community leader thinking about the democratization of gender relations within the family. As Nungurrayi discussed her shared work–life balance with her (now deceased) spouse, she stated, "We worked together in the clinic, and we worked together at home, but I did more than he did at home," whereas Sid Anderson stated,

> Anderson: People got to think that woman can cook things, and men sometimes cook things too you know—got to work both ways instead of having violence you know, getting violent over a woman not cooking. 'Cause sometimes the woman might be tired for cooking too, you know.
> SH: So those old-fashioned roles are an issue?
> Anderson: Yeah, yeah.

In discussing this theme of sharing domestic chores with Nampitjinpa in Alice Springs, she responds to my comment that "I see some young men bossing around their grandmothers, while they wait in their cars and she shops for them at the store":

> Nampitjinpa: My kids [three boys], they grow up no bossing around, they're all good boys.
> SH: You reckon your boys are not going to be like their [violent] dad?
> Nampitjinpa: No, they're just soft and gentle kids. Tjapanangka cook his own feed; they all like cooking, they love cooking. (field notes July 10, 2014)

In an unpublished report on violence for the Ngaanyatjarra Council across the border in Western Australia, Brooks and Shaw found, in relation to the husband and wife unit:

In the "classical" model of life, the man undeniably has the superior rights, and can exert control (incorporating violence) in relation to his wife's behaviour that she cannot reciprocally exercise (although in this as in other matters, there are always exceptions to the rule!). However, in the normal run of events, he does not aggressively assert this superior position, and in fact it is not normally apparent . . . The state of affairs continues even through mild forms of disruption and argument; and it is only when the disruption is serious enough for sanctions to be invoked that the potential inequality in the relationship becomes manifest. (2003: 19)

Within this schema it seems apparent that men have rights over women that women do not have over men. Nakamarra(1), a middle-aged woman, discussed this circumscribing of women's autonomy more widely: "'Cause [his] family is watching me, you see, that other family watches you 'cause every time you make a [wrong] move they get upset." That the relationship is more than the couple has multiple ramifications; marriage is as much about his family as it is about the relationship between the partners.

Conclusions

This chapter has attempted a rapprochement between the classical conceptions of individual rights and collective rights by recalling Walzer's early observation that, in fact, there has always been a tension between these two conceptions of rights because the human is a fundamentally social being. Furthermore, the limitations of liberal theory in enabling us to understand the various kinds of human interdependence, which are part of the life of both families and polities, were articulated to more fully and appropriately locate this collective. Case studies of the sociocultural and economic rights work of two central Australian NGOs, Waltja and the CLC, offered insight into local practices as these organizations channel the right to development and self-determination. This chapter explored the mobilizing mechanisms that several NGOs use to activate human rights.

The family as the fundamental social unit in human rights discourse has an ironic effect for Anangu women, as it does for other Indigenous women. On the one hand respecting and acknowledging the centrality for women on the family in their lives has to be foregrounded in the name of collective rights, while at the same time working through the fact that, as for many of the world's women, the family is also the place where women are often at their most vulnerable. The framers of human rights had male household heads in mind, so within the human rights discourse the rights violations of women that take place *within* this sphere have been invisible until relatively recently. The "discovery" of this intraracial violence was traced for Australian Indigenous women alongside the gradual embrace by Indigenous female academics of forms of feminism. Yet, as will be discussed further in the following chapter, the precepts of feminism are on the margins in remote areas, such as the Pintupi-Luritja region. The relationality of gender and the homosociality of much Anangu activity has multiple and limiting implications for notions of gender equality.

Chapter 3

"Stop Whinging and Get on with It"
The Shifting Contours of Gender Equality (and Equity)

THIS CHAPTER CONTINUES THE EXPLORATION of the contested contours of complementarity and equality through the lens of gender. It does this by exploring the multiple ways in which gender as a relational practice is manifest in a range of social contexts that assert homosociality, or gender segregation. The social ramifications of the ceremonial practices of "men's business" are explored as a paradigmatic location for making gender. Likewise, the Aboriginal English term "women's business" also captures a range of practices beyond the ceremonial to include female sexuality and reproductive rights. Whereas the previous chapter traced some of the global debate regarding the relevance of feminism to non-Western women (including Indigenous women), this chapter begins to specify a regional and local perspective as mediated through notions of gender complementarity, rather than equality. However, the very relationality of gender also plays a central role in reproducing forms of internalized sexism as a species of internalized oppression. Although the applicability of the concept of feminism is challenged, there is a range of indicators of social transformation where these social practices of gender segregation are being modified and adapted, notably in the changing relations of reproduction. The final sections of this chapter will examine the social and ontological structures that mediate violence and that have become known as "family violence."

Would You Call Yourself a Feminist?

"Stop whinging and get on with it . . . don't make it front page news" declared Julie Bishop, the only female cabinet minister in the conservative Abbott government, as a response to how women should manage sexism (Waters 2014). Such a statement, emerging from a positon of power and privilege, dismisses the intersectional forms of discrimination (racial, economic, geographic, educational, and so on), that women as members of marginalized groups face. It also reveals a form of internalized sexism in the acceptance of the established distributions of power. Such a statement is also a reminder that the conservative Liberal coalition government's approach to rights such as gender equality are, in practice, formal rather than substantive.[1] Unlike the Labor Party, they do not have an affirmative action program that enables women the same opportunity as men to enter Parliament. Nevertheless, though the Abbott government may not be leading by example, others at a local level are. As discussed previously, the CLCs Community Development Unit actively fosters gender equity in their committees, and the Local Government Authorities (LGA) Australia-wide have a proactive approach to substantive rights. The LGA have gender equity targets expressed through their 50/50 Vision: Councils for Gender Equity Program (Australian Local Government Association). This seems to be bearing some fruit in the MacDonnell shire that operates over the Papunya region, as five of the twelve elected Aboriginal councillors are women, whereas on the local shire boards (now referred to as authorities) in Papunya and Mount Liebig, for instance, are approximately a fifty-fifty gender split. Although this equity of representation is only one aspect of gender equality, these actions speak to the larger political forces that have begun to penetrate remote communities.

For Australian Indigenous academics working and researching in this area of Indigenous women's rights, there appears to be consensus that "Indigenous feminism differs to white feminisms" (Davis 2007: 20). There are several reasons for this, including the concern for both the collective and the individual rights of women, as this is compounded with intersectional discrimination. As Indigenous legal academic Megan Davis states: "The problems concerning Indigenous women were overshadowed by the problems facing Indigenous people, which in reality equated to problems facing Indigenous men" (2012: 4; see also Davis 2009 and Behrendt 2009). Indigenous women have been forgotten. Davis provides a range of examples of this skew toward the state's focus on Indigenous men, such as the Royal Commission into Aboriginal Deaths in Custody. This Commission, established in 1987 following national outrage over the number of Aboriginal deaths in police custody, failed to address Aboriginal women's issues, such as alcohol-related homicide. Of the ninety-nine deaths that were investigated, only eleven were women, and not one of the final 339 recommendations made were with specific reference to Aboriginal women (Davis 2012: 4; Kerley and Cunneen 1995: 532). This invisibility of Indigenous women's issues in Australia has ongoing implications, and clearly Davis and others wish to claim some ground in feminizing the debate. However, if the notion of Indigenous feminism has any relevant application for Anangu women, then pluralism is also needed in this context, as it is for non-Indigenous women. This need for pluralism recognizes the diversity of Indigenous women's experiences Australia-wide and, in this context, hinges on the formation of Anangu gender identity. The African American feminist bell hooks defines feminism as "a movement to end sexism, sexist exploitation and oppression" (2000: viii). I find hooks's definition compelling, as it recognizes that:

> The movement is not about being anti-male . . . the problem is sexism. And that clarity helps us remember that all of us, female and male, have been socialised from birth to accept sexist thought and action. As a consequence, females can be just as sexist as men. And while that does not excuse or justify male domination, it does mean that it would be naïve and wrongminded for feminist thinkers to see the movement as simplistically being for women against men. (2000: viii–ix)

This reminder of the relationality of gender roles also allows for an intersubjective reading of gendered practices. Although I can attempt to capture something of the multiplicity of Anangu women's perspective and experience, it is, as always, only partial. As a nascent field of research in remote Australia, calling on Indigenous feminisms from elsewhere is informative in developing a language that is potentially relevant. As feminist anthropologist Hernandez-Castillo quotes an Indigenous Mexican woman:

> Indigenous feminism is to me part of a principle—women develop and make revolution to *construct themselves as independent persons who* become a *community that can give to others without forgetting about themselves.* (2010: 539; my emphasis)

As Hernandez-Castillo continues: "In many cases these Indigenous women's struggles for more just relations between men and women are based on definitions of personhood that transcend Western individualism" (2010: 540). As I asked an Aboriginal staff member of Relationships Australia in Alice Springs if she would call herself a feminist, she responded, "It's interesting, I don't think I am, but I'm strong in myself and for Aboriginal women and Aboriginal people" (field notes July 9, 2014). When I mentioned that thinking about Anangu gender relations in terms of complementarity and interdependence rather than equality and sameness might be appropriate, the Northern Territory Aboriginal MP Alison Anderson responded: "I like that, that seems a good way to think about it . . . applying ideas of male/female equality is not straightforward for us." The normative idea that Anangu men and women have the same rights and are thus equal appears, at this stage, to equate to the idea that they are the same, indeed that their roles are interchangeable. As one young woman stated in relation to the notion of men and women being "equal": "That's a rubbish idea *kuya ngaanpa*" (no good for Anangu). I had just interviewed her equally young spouse who was undertaking the month-long prevention of family violence program—as a mandated program for violence against her. She had accompanied him to the neighboring community for the month-long program. During our discussion, she also indicated to me that she had sought support and assistance by fleeing to the clinic when he assaulted her for the first time. From the clinic she called the police, so she is not without agency.

Nampitjinpa, who moved to Alice Springs after leaving her violent partner, stated: "I reckon women are the strongest. Because, it used to be men strong before, but now that they keep coming to town drinking, they gone down. You see a lot of women on the community they talk up, which is good" (field notes July 10, 2014). Such are the nascent beginnings of the appropriation of elements of gender equality that are expanding into more contexts, including in women-only organizations, such as the NPY Women's Council. Nevertheless, pragmatically, the context is all. As a non-Aboriginal CAAFLU lawyer articulated:

> I don't think that the concept of feminism is relevant for Aboriginal women in the same way as it is for me. As a white middle-class woman I worry for equal pay for equal work and access to child care. But, for Aboriginal women, they have such different issues; they might want to get a job in the first place. They are still working on basic bodily autonomy, such as not being hit for not cooking dinner. I acknowledge that a lot of the issues that I rail against come from a position of privilege, whereas many Aboriginal women are still looking for bodily autonomy, integrity, and dignity—the minimum human rights standards. (field notes July 7, 2014)

Hodgson, working with African Maasai women, found that "the key principle should be *complementarity* of gender. Many Maasai women are seeking equality in terms of rights [access to jobs, health care, education, and so
on], but not necessarily roles" (2011: 156). So this is not equality in terms of
sameness of social responsibility—which is what the young Anangu woman
seemed so repulsed by. Indeed, this suggested that interchangeability of male–
female roles also resonates with the larger discourse of equality expressed in
the governmentality of "closing the gap" between Aboriginal people and the
mainstream. Just as this policy discourse radically seeks to impose a homo-
geneity of "outcomes," so too it is essential to recognize that it is legitimate
for the equality concept to embrace some cultural specificity. Any argument
for an Indigenous feminism has to be set against the broader reality that "the
primary harm [abusive] men inflict is political . . . and reflects the deprivation
of rights and resources that are critical to personhood and citizenship" (Stark
2007:5). I have bracketed Stark's focus on violence as coercive control, as his
argument more broadly resonates with and indeed mirrors the dominant and
normative patriarchal structures that are evident in many contexts, including
Pintupi-Luritja communities. As will be discussed in the following section,
men's initiation focuses on developing and maintaining equality between
men, from which females and noninitiates are actively excluded (Myers 1986:
229). As a core site for making gender, the roles and responsibilities between
men and women are actively developed as inegalitarian and asymmetrical
cultural constructs that actively contest any blanket notion of gender equality.

An Outside Story of "Men's Business" and Human Rights

There are serious constraints and limitations on what can be written about
male initiation, also referred to as "men's business."[2] This term is itself indica-
tive that any consideration that I, as a female anthropologist, would give to
it would cause offense to Anangu. So this discussion is necessarily circumscribed as an "outside story" in Aboriginal English. However, it is such a core
aspect of male, and female, identity making that it consequently impacts
on and intersects with multiple domains of community life, notably gender
inequality. The import of "men's business" (entailing ritual instruction and
physical ordeals) prior to colonization maintained not only the cosmologi-
cal order but also marriage relationships and the geographical certainty of
resource access over a wide area, thus reining in uncertainty (Myers 1986:
228–233). Rather, like the issue of Aboriginal family violence, consideration

of the effect of "men's business" on the family, women, and the physical and mental health of the initiates themselves, was off limits or invisible until relatively recently (see for instance ABC 7.30 Report 2014 and ABC The Drum 2014). Male initiation has tended to be essentialized as "high-culture" and unassailable (see Berndt and Berndt 1999). When (male) anthropologists have described "Aboriginal religion," the complexities of male initiation have been central and understood in terms of "world creative powers" (Maddock 1984; Charlesworth et al. 1984; Stanner 1965, 1966).

Men's business is practiced annually in the region for boys from the communities of the Haasts Bluff Land Trust over the summer period. Although it is inappropriate to discuss any details of the ceremonies, considering the social ramifications of these ceremonies is less off limits. The rituals are embedded in the relational ontology of the initiates and a deeply formative element in their identities as Pintupi-Luritja men. Myers states:

> The cult is a corporation of *all* initated men, contrasting itself to women and children. This cult and its songs, the most dangerous and sacred possessions of men, are considered the true markers of male identity. To reveal them to the uninitiated is punishable by violent death. (Myers 1986: 228–229; see also White 1975; Tonkinson 1991)

The Aboriginal English term "no room" and *pika ngurlu* (it's frightening, literally "sick with fear") are used to avoid discussion among the uninitated (see also Anthony and Chapman 2008). A feminist psychological understanding of initation rite societies is that they promote a defensive masculinity (also termed hypermasculinity) where the prominent themes of female avoidance, a division of labor, and exclusion of women from men's ritual knowledge accord with male sex-role resolution theory (see Quinn and Luttrell 2004).[3] As Myers states:

> The main process of initiation begins . . . when a boy is "seized" (*witirnu*) . . . taken to a camp that is removed from women, from uninitiated males . . . At his disappearance, his "close" relatives . . . wail as they would at a death, because they have "lost their boy." (1986: 229)

This separation from the maternal caregivers, from women who were the formative influences in the boy's early life, is "a rejection of those qualities or tendencies within their selves that are understood as feminine" (Quinn and

Luttrell 2004: 505). Feminine qualities such as nurturance and dependency are pitted against the idealized masculinst qualities of freedom and autonomy. As Myers found, establishing equality and a wider sociality among initiated men underpins this formation of masculinity (1986: 229). This equality among men is dependent, however, on promoting inequality with, via difference from, women as they are actively excluded from the ritual psychosocial development of maturing males. However, the concept discussed earlier of complementarity also emerges at this powerfully formative site, as these ceremonies cannot be conducted without the support of the female relatives of the initiates. Women's various kinship roles from grandmothers to sisters of the initiates provide the relational basis for their gender identity. As Napanangka elaborates:

We are behind men, but we also have our own powers, and we draw power from our menfolk, like our brothers, and uncles, fathers, grandfathers, sons, and grandsons; by being closely related to them we get power. Like, I'm at a certain level because my father was a senior Tingarri law man. . . . so when people, when men look at me, they don't see me just as a woman, they see the daughter of that Tingarri . . . That's how we gain our power, through our menfolk. So, when the men do their work in their side, their power comes off to us, and when we do work on women's side well, our strength gains them respect through their womenfolk who are leaders in the ceremony. So, we give each other power by doing our roles. (field notes February 5, 2016)

White's description of Anangu women, drawing on her central Australian ethnography, as "junior partners" fits with Napanangka's schema above (White 1978). As she elaborates: "Women accept this junior role secure in the knowledge that they alone can create new human life in the bodily sense, but that men validate their senior status by claiming for themselves the sole power to create spiritual life" (1978: 36). It seems to me that the patriarchal basis of Anangu religious cosmology has parallels with that of Catholicism, where the key spiritual office bearers (God, Jesus, the pope, priests, abbots) are all men. For instance, the possibility of the pope (Greek for "pappas" or "daddy") being a female is inconceivable for devout Catholics. In the Roman Catholic Church the theological sanction against priests and other spiritual office bearers from marrying is also a reminder of women as the worldly "Other." The preordained logic of both religious systems, Anangu and Catholic, appears to leave little room for innovation. Nevertheless, as an oral culture, the content of Anangu ritual tradition is inclined to dynamism, though the practitioners may not acknowledge this (Wild 1987; Sutton 1987; Holcombe 1997, 2004b). To return to men's business, although there have been significant social changes with settlement, such as greater freedom over choice of marriage partners (even though arranging marriages is structurally a core aspect of men's ceremony), the foundational role of men's business in constructing gender relations remains.

Parents also have less control over their sons' post–men's business, and this also transfers to the issue of continued formal schooling. A trend has developed whereby some of the boys on their return from the ceremonial camp are of the understanding that, as they are now "men" or *watis*, they no longer need to attend school. Ensuring that this formal education remains relevant for these young *watis* is extremely challenging. Likewise, the schoolteachers struggle to recognize that these new *watis* are not like non-Indigenous boys: they have experienced a major life-changing ritual. This is indicated by angry comments made by Nakamarra, a former schoolteacher herself, who said that the (non-Indigenous) teachers don't treat the young *watis* with the respect that they now deserve. On the other hand, the acting school principle has a different perspective: "They take out the thirteen-year-olds to make them men, and now they won't come to school—maybe they've reached grade 3 and they're fourteen. [They say] 'we're now men—we're too cool to go to school'" (field notes March 8, 2013). Nevertheless, a senior male community leader did recognize this disengagement from school as a result of men's business and stated that consideration should turn to waiting until the next initiates are older and had finished school, suggesting the ages of 17 or 18. However, he also noted that "it's a regional issue—not just [this community] who would have to change this." As Myers notes, "Autarky is prohibited: a group should not initiate its own people" (1986: 177). As such, it is not the sole decision of one community, for instance, to make this change to the age of initiates but also those other communities who participate in the initiations. However, according to Nakamarra, this issue has been addressed by a community to the southeast: "They wait until the boys are 18. There is concern over the school issue there. I'd like to change the age—for the boys to be older—but the *kungkas* [women] have no say in it. The men have the right."

This issue of adolescent "adults" is also reflected in the relatively high incidence of adolescent pregnancies, where these boys take a "wife," and as a result there are twelve- and thirteen-year-old girls pregnant. Paralleling this is the significant demographic shift in the drop in the age in which men are starting families. Curran indicates that in 1970s Yuendemu, similarly to Papunya or Mount Liebig, men would have to wait until they were in their thirties and had passed through a secondary stage of initiation before they could form a public partnership with females who were often about fifteen years younger than them. As a result the men are having children fifteen years earlier than they were only a few decades ago and with females of a similar age (Curran 2011: 47).

When discussing the role and value of male initiation today with an Aboriginal staff member of the Ngaanyatjarra, Pitjantjatjara, and Yankunytjatjara (NPY) Women's Council, she asked in turn:

> Where is the benefit from these [ceremonies] that is supportive of women, that helps and loves women and families? There seems to be no translation from these ceremonies into family life; no impact on keeping the families safe . . . How can that ceremony help men to be modern loving fathers, family men? Does it just encourage them to be more frustrated and angry? (field notes July 12, 2013; see also Langton 2008)

The physical implications of making men or *watis* through the ceremonial stages is not seen as a human rights violation in the broader discourse, even though many of the initiates are children under the age of sixteen. To even suggest such a thing would draw ire, even fury, as this is one of the few areas where Aboriginal people remain, largely, out of the purview of government intervention. Rather, the practice is strongly advocated as a cultural and religious right. The process of seclusion in the bush that takes place over several weeks or months is nevertheless an ordeal, and the participants have little, if any, choice in the matter. Interestingly, one could undertake a limited comparison on physical grounds between men's initiation and the female genital cutting (clitoridectomy) that occurs in some African states.[4] This practice, also referred to by activists opposing it as female genital mutilation (FGM), is widely condemned by human rights activists, notably in the name of women's and children's rights (see also Levitt and Merry 2011: 84–85). However, no such comparison has ever been made between these ritual gender-making practices in Africa and Australia. What might this say about broader perceptions of gender hegemony, where women and girls are represented as the powerless victims, unlike the men and boys? Might this lack of public discourse also suggest, or even reconfirm, the primacy of the male as the essential re-producer of culture, whereas women's cultural practices are fundamentally secondary and thus expendable to modernity and rights?

Male initiation can thus be understood as a powerful reiteration of male Aboriginal identity, reinforcing regional relationships and knowledge networks. Whether elements of this socialization are in keeping with state-sponsored notions of gender equality, individual dignity, family formation, and access to a mainstream education are questions that are relevant to consider today, as some Anangu are. There is a nascent awareness of conflicting values. Yet, at the same time, the Indigenous right to "culture" is often galvanized at this intersection, and male initiation is often charged as emblematic of ongoing cultural tradition and essential for identity and well-being (Peterson 2000; Curran 2011). For instance, central Australian Aboriginal human rights advocate Rosie Kunoth-Monks stated:

> What was important to her [Alyawarr] people was Lore and Culture and so the educational attainment that mattered to them was being delivered right now by "the Red Ochre Men" . . . they emptied Arlparra High School last Thursday of all boys that should be in "business" camp and they made no apologies about it. (Bagnall 2015)

Where does the regionally renowned transgender person Starlady fit into this strongly dichotomous gender schema? One might expect a negative reception for her in the desert. Yet just the opposite is the case. She has been employed as a youth worker in this region for some years and is extremely popular with an active Facebook page (2,482 "friends" and counting). In a TED Talk she discussed how she found acceptance in the desert, as was paraphrased: "The transgender woman who grew up identifying as a gay man says that she has never felt more like herself than with the world's most ancient people in outback Australia."[5] According to her blog: "Currently she is delivering hair-dressing training throughout the central deserts and is developing several long-term projects including several salons, youth based magazines, health promotion, sexual health education and working with the Sista girl/GLBTI Indigenous communities."[6] As Sammy Butcher stated:

> It's really good to see someone like that. Is it a man or a woman? But they are still a human being, and it's good to accept them; good to learn about different people. Though in the old days . . . mmm. (field notes March 2013)

This overt recognition of a change from the attitudes of the past is juxtaposed with the nonetheless still active hypermasculinity that is sponsored by men's initiation, where men are not preexistent but are made. Yet, in her work with youth, Starlady actively reengages the new young *watis* who have dropped out of school postinitiation by giving them crazy hairstyles in her work teaching hairdressing. Such contradictory accommodations to modernity signal the complexity of the work of the rights discourse and the high value it places on tolerance and respect for human diversity.[7]

It is revealing to return to the UDHR and Article 27, the first section of which states: "Everyone has the right to freely participate in the cultural life of the community." The import of these gendered cultural domains is apparent as witnessed through the back-translation of this section of the Article, which reads:

> People in one place or area should learn about their own Dreamings. And it's good for them to gather together with other men, while others, the work boss, Government or the police, should not prevent that. They should leave them alone without scolding them. Aboriginal women should learn more about their own Dreamings and should gather together and follow their Grand-mother's Dreaming.

I commented to the translator, Lance Macdonald, on the rather directive phrasing of the interpretation of "culture" in this article, as it alludes to men's and women's ceremony, to which he replied, "It [attending to men's and women's business] is compulsory as far we're concerned." I commented on his choice of specifying women as well as men, and he responded: "Sometimes their husbands might keep them from going to women's ceremony [saying] 'stay and cook for me.'" Hence, it has to be reiterated that they also have to be free to participate in local terms.

Anangu women, similarly to other Aboriginal women in central Australia, also have a distinctive gendered ceremonial life, elements of which actively exclude men (Berndt 1965; Hamilton 1980; Payne 1989; Dussart 2000; Poirier 1992). And, as discussed, they are important participants in men's business. The Central Land Council (CLC) recognized many years ago, however, that women required external support to maintain their more gender-specific ceremonial life and visit women's specific sites and perform ceremonies. This was principally due to men's monopoly of vehicles. Since 1993 the CLC have sponsored "women's law and culture" meetings as annual events where Aboriginal women from across the Northern Territory, with a focus on central Australia, gather at different women's sacred sites for five days to perform their gendered ritual corpus (see also Holcombe 1997, 2004b). These events have become distinctive, and it is unlikely that such large groups of women (up to several hundred), without children on site, would have been possible precolonization. It is usually older women, the grandmothers as senior "law women," who attend these events. And, although there may be local elements of support for these events, it is not comparable to the community-wide mobilization that occurs to facilitate men's business. The external support that women need to continue these large gatherings is telling.

Family and Children: Identity and the Changing Relations of Reproduction

The homosociality of gender relations, as one of the outcomes of the ritualization of masculinity, is also to be found in the social practices surrounding pregnancy and childbirth (Kaberry 1939; Hamilton 1980; Merlan 1992). Indeed, anything to do with women's sexuality is labeled "women's business." Napanangka explains that this was pragmatic: when Anangu were naked, women would remove themselves from the camp during menstruation "as proper," and to respect everyone's privacy childbirth would take place away from the camp, including away from men and children. She also stated that there are women's *Tjukurrpa* that detail segregation at such times. From a men's perspective, there is also ethnographic evidence in the desert region that suggests that during men's business, men were instructed that aspects of women's sexuality, such as menstrual blood and the blood of childbirth, would contaminate masculinity (Berndt and Berndt 1999: 184–185; Kaberry 1939: 238–239). It is possible that this deep psychological undercurrent remains and explains, in part, the overt delicacy about even discussing pregnancy in the presence of men, as this remains a taboo topic for Anangu, especially for the older generation. The distinctiveness of these gendered fields of practice have remained to a significant extent and been transferred to contemporary contexts, although this too is changing. According to a female obstetrician at the Alice Springs public hospital (a staff member of many years), they encourage the fathers-to-be to accompany their spouse into the delivery room, but:

> It's very rare for those men from the bush [remote communities] accompanying their partners to also go into the delivery room. Maybe a handful a

year [do] . . . But that's more than it was twenty years ago; it was unheard of then . . .[8] And when they come into town [as the support person], they often don't even come into the antenatal appointment with them . . . they'll stay outside. You say to them, if they do come into the room, "Are you going to be at the birth?" And they just smile. And I say, "You know you're welcome." (field notes July 9, 2014)

As I discussed this issue of Anangu men now coming into the delivery room, Napanangka, as a senior woman, stated that she would never encourage it, but that:

Yeah, it happens now because at the beginning [when] they weren't going to the hospital it was the same—like when a woman goes away in seclusion—going away to hospital was similar to that. But then when young men and girls went away to boarding school [in major towns and cities] and fell in love, they know the hospitals, that they have rules and it's not segregated any more. 'Cause it's a whitefella environment. (field notes May 12, 2016)

Likewise, Cowlishaw's observation that "women commonly deny they are pregnant. . . . such matters are not discussed openly" (1982: 497) is also less strict. For instance, Napanangka stated, with some disdain, that her nephew (from a large WA community) posted an ultrasound photo of his forthcoming baby on Facebook to "congratulations!" while she indicated that the Aunty [his sister] said that "she can't wait to hold the baby!" Another reason Napanangka was rather mortified about this exchange was the way in which the avoidance relationship between siblings was also modified.

The perspective of this same obstetrician is that Aboriginal women "absolutely value motherhood as a central element in their lives; motherhood defines them." Although the average age of an Indigenous mother across the Northern Territory for the first birth is twenty-five (five years younger than a non-Indigenous woman in the NT), in the Alice Springs and Barkly (desert) regions the first-time mother is more likely to be under twenty than anywhere else in the NT. The fertility rate in the youngest age group (less than twenty years of age) was over four times higher for Indigenous women compared with non-Indigenous women of the same age: 81.6 and 17.8 births per 1,000 women respectively (Thompson 2014). Nevertheless, although we might acknowledge the aspiration of motherhood as valid, we can also realize the link between these youthful fertility rates with low educational attainments (Biddle 2013).[9] The relationship between education and greater female sexual autonomy is now widely understood as a global development issue (World Bank Group 2014: 43). In this central Australian region it is compounded, however, as males typically have a lower educational attainment than females, which is, as discussed earlier, partly due to young age of the male initiates in the region. Nevertheless, Aboriginal women and girls also avail themselves of medical terminations, and the average number of births does not far outstrip non-Indigenous women, being 2.2 children for Indigenous women, and 1.9 for non-Indigenous (Thompson 2014). This suggests an element of control over reproduction. As the obstetrician also observed, the female relatives of the pubertal girls are themselves active in seeking contraception for them, which she indicated has also become more effective; as a result, pregnancy rates have dropped.

There has been significant change since the feminist Marian Sawer stated: "The demand for abortion rights was seen as particularly irrelevant by Aboriginal women who were more concerned with racial survival and stopping forced sterilisation" (Sawer 1995: 78–79). Although this argument may have been less relevant in remote Australia, the ready ability for young women, notably underage pregnant girls, to access a termination is now widely understood as appropriate. Access to terminations is a fundamental element in women's rights to ensure reproductive choices that, in this context, also has wider repercussions. The obstetrician further stated: "The elderly [female] relatives know all about the value of an abortion as being as much in their interests as their young relatives," as it often becomes their responsibility to look after the child. However, she also commented:

> For an underage girl [under 16] to have a termination the consent of both parents is required, and she needs to have seen two doctors and have said that she wants the termination to both of them. Lots of mothers voice concern about the father's consent side in relation to issues of payback for them and the girl, such that they were not looking out for her, so that the mother of the girl often doesn't want him to know . . . This aspect of the legislation is outdated and not relevant to Aboriginal families . . . They will say they don't live with him or don't know where he is. The consent of one parent should be enough, and in reality we ask if the other parent has consented, and we have to rely on the verbal of the mother for the father [because we don't have the resources to locate him]. (field notes May 12, 2016)

Another reason such legislation is not relevant to Aboriginal families is that it doesn't accord with the homosociality that defines gendered sexuality. It is not the father's business but the responsibility of her female relatives. With arranged marriages and polygamy now uncommon for Anangu, the male relatives also have a less formal role in the lives of their young female relatives. Relationships for love, or "love marriages" that develop at school are increasingly standard. While translating Article 16 of the UDHR on "the right to marry and found a family," Lance Macdonald stated:

> In daily life, we might use the expression *yunytjurringkula kungka mantjirra* [literally, to take a female for love or to fall in love with a female]. But if you wrote that in this UDHR, Anangu would all laugh if you said you could grab someone for love, because it sounds cheeky.

Yet, this increasing acceptance of independent consent, rather than arranged marriage, is becoming the norm as a relationship becomes a voluntary association.[10] Nevertheless, there are still concerns about choosing a partner of the appropriate kinship category, especially by older relatives. In the Pintupi-Luritja region there are three options for choosing the correct skin for a "right-way" marriage, which all derive from within the generational moiety an individual was born into, as the eight skin (subsection) categories are divided into two moiety groups. The relationships within and between skin groups are therefore predefined, and forming relationships outside of these moiety categories is generally frowned upon. Such "wrong skin" relationships are a source of discontent and shame for the older relatives of the person(s) involved in them, in particular the parents, and can lead to "payback" violence. And, as will be discussed in the following chapter, once children are involved a couple rarely separates, though separation can and does occur.

Physical Violence as a Form of Social Regulation

There is ample global ethnographic evidence that all societies have used and still use violence as a form of social regulation. Whether violence is understood as domestic and private or as systematic and sanctioned by the state, it still occurs in myriad forms. Yet, there has been denial when violence as a precolonial form of Aboriginal social regulation was asserted as normative (see Wunderstiz 2010; Cripps and Taylor 2009). Various forms of violence were a normative means to maintain the status quo of small group life prior to settlement (White 1978; Tonkinson 1988; Brooks and Shaw 2003; Clendinnen 2003). The historian Clendinnen, for instance, writes:

> The Australians tended to exogamy, usually finding their wives outside their own group. That is rarely healthy for women, so being removed from the protection of their kin. But on the evidence we have, even kinsfolk did not intervene in husbands' brutality. Wives under sexual assault might scream for their husband, but Boladeree, husband of the girl clubbed by Baneelon [Benelong] in the display of "justice," which so shocked [Governor] Phillip, was a silent onlooker during the attack, despite his evident tenderness for the victim. Note too, that the victim did not cry out. She only tried to shield her head. Given such silences, I think we have to assume *a compelling shared understanding of a net-work of rights, liberties and infringements simply invisible to us.* (2003: 165; emphasis mine)

It is this "network of rights, liberties and infringements" that will be briefly explored here and in more detail in the following chapter. A report by social anthropologists Brooks and Shaw commissioned by the Ngaanyatjarra Council (in WA), *Men, Conflict and Violence in the Ngaanyatjarra Region* (2003), analyzes the key cultural concept, *Nganyirri*, which translates as "fierce" or "savage," and in this context can mean "explosive violence." This is also a Pintupi-Luritja concept—in the Hansens' dictionary, "a person who physically hurts others; one who always wants to fight; known locally as a 'cheeky bugger'" (Hansen and Hansen 1992: 80). Brooks indicates that this characteristic had a functional role in maintaining order in classical Ngaanyatjarra conditions: a great premium was placed on quickly resolving conflicts, and a *nganyirri* outburst is expected to be followed quickly by the restoration of calm. However, the authors indicate that if this behavior was functional in the classical past, it no longer is now and represents one of the areas requiring interventions (2003: 5). This report also details the role of scapegoating, payback, and sorcery—as these social techniques were understood as minimizing intergroup conflict.

Myers's perspective was somewhat different, as he asserted that Pintupi "violence is not focused on domination or control over others. Indeed, Pintupi ethnopsychology ordinarily interprets 'anger' as a response to a rejection of relatedness" (1988: 595). Whereas this may explain certain drivers, the outcome of physical harm is nonetheless the same. Likewise, this does not account for men's more routine use of violence than women and the change in the nature of violence as a result of access to alcohol and other addictive substances. The term "family violence" is, according to Memmott and his coauthors, an umbrella term that encompasses violence perpetrated by and against a range of family members, as it describes how violence reverberates throughout the community (see also APO NT 2014). As a result it also includes spousal or intimate partner violence, and it embraces the dynamic social nature of violence, whereby one form of violence can transform into or catalyze another category of violence, such as "payback" (Memmott et al. 2006: 8–9).

In the translation of Article 3: "Everyone has the right to life, liberty and security of person," one of the two articles most immediately suggesting interpersonal violence, the concern was to adapt this rather obscure English to the local context. The back-translation of the Luritja reads:

> Everybody everywhere should live morally and correctly. Men and women should not swear and fight with each other. Men should not hurt women and children. One should not kill a person or sorcerise and kill them. They should care for and look after them.

This attempt at finding commensurability is at the same time "mediating a moral co-presence" (per Povinelli 2001: 327). The forms of violence that are not acceptable are outlined, as sorcery is possibly more an issue of concern locally than gender violence for Anangu. It is noteworthy, however, that retributive violence or "payback" was omitted.

"Payback": Ngapartji Ngapartji Kuwarriku (Literally, "Reciprocity via Spear")

A regionally renown form of customary violence is "payback," as it has become referred to in Aboriginal English. As the term implies, this form of violence is underpinned by regaining balance in relationships through locating the offender or perpetrator of a death or near-death incident or rectifying honor between families of "wrong skin" relationships. As Malcolm Frost, a psychologist at the Central Australian Aboriginal [health] Congress, stated in his experience: "Nobody dies for no reason, it's always someone's fault, and the person whose fault it was must be punished" (ABC Radio National 2010).

In only the last fifteen to twenty years, from the period since 1995 when I recall witnessing a payback on the oval at the crowded Kintore Sports carnival, there has been a signifcant shift in both public and legal sentiment toward payback as emblematic of customary law. At that time (1995), a young man had just been released from prison and had returned to face his Anangu punishment. As the clinic staff, the police, and the carnival crowd watched on, he was speared in the leg and then rushed to the clinic. This issue of how to manage this element of customary law as part of a plural legal system has always been a vexed one for government, and there has been a range of enquiries over the years (see Australian Law Reform Commission 1986; Northern Territory Law Reform Committee 2003; the Western Australian Law Reform Commission 2005). Mandatory reporting laws, after the Northern Territory Emergency Response in 2007, have, however, made it illegal to perform payback in a community, and indeed any form of suspected family violence now has to be reported to police. Perhaps it was because of these new laws that in 2012 a young woman who was due to receive payback after a vehicle accident in which her drunken husband (who was the driver) and her baby died (she and her elderly male relative were injured) came to the Papunya police station and, according to the superintendent on duty:

> [She was blamed] as she bought the car out of her own money. She came here to the station and told me, "I have to go for a meeting" [euphemism for payback], and so I also went along. Ninety-nine point nine percent of people don't want it—if they did then it would happen out bush out of sight. Instead [as in this instance] I am informed of it first and so can go along and supervise and regulate it. It went for an hour, an hour and a half. I stayed clear, and the men huddled together to speak amongst themselves, after which time they came over to me and said, "Can we pick up that stick and hit her?" I said, "The badge on my arm says I can't let you do that." They went away again and after further discussion came back and said again, "Can we just punch her?" I replied, "No—you just can't do that." They went away again and talked, and that was the end of it. I figured that if they really wanted to do the payback they would've gone out bush. (field notes July 11, 2013)

He further recalled, when I enquired, that most of the men were not local, suggesting rather that they might have been from the community of the deceased husband's family, from a neighboring language group. So, as this payback did not proceed, it suggests an emergent phenomenon where the state, not the family, becomes the new interlocutor and the new protector (see also Merry 2003). Although this is not the typical scenario, it does suggest a shift in subjectivity toward a new individualism—beyond the family.

Nevertheless, such an awareness is not articulated in the language of human rights. The active engagement with the legal system via the police protective system in this case (re)enforces the right to be free from violence. Likewise, a small cohort of male and female leaders are refusing to participate in payback; either they refuse to attend the event or, if they do, they are not the physical abusers. These community leaders, in positions of power and influence, travel beyond the community and speak publically denouncing violence at such events as the Ingkintja "Stop The Violence" March in late 2010 in Alice Springs, or to the Aboriginal Governance summit (APO NT Governance Report 2013) or most recently the Central Australian Grog (alcohol) Summit (APO NT Grog Report 2013b), reinforcing notions of personal responsibility and bodiliy integrity. Nevertheless, community leaders attempt to lead by example by not participating in the violence, rather than by verbally denouncing it or physically stopping it themselves. Payback is widely accepted in this region. For instance, Nungurrayi described how her son had been in jail for several years for violence against his wife; while he was out on parole he was violent toward her again, so was soon back in prison. She stated, "I'm scared too, 'cause I work for Department of Children and Families, and I might lose my job—that's what I always explain to my daughters and sons. Don't get involved with a fight or with anyone cause I'm working for Department of Children and Families—I don't want to lose my job. I always say that to my daughters; [I] just tell them to mind your own business and go." Thus, Nungurrayi can cite her work role for her lack of participation in contexts of paypack. On the other hand, Nakamarra attributes her lack of support for payback to religious conversion, as she stated, "I don't have room for that [payback] any more since I became a Christian" (field notes 2012). She is, however, also a formally trained schoolteacher so has a relatively high standard of formal education, whereas Sammy Butcher described the practice as "too barbaric now."

Yet, the perspective that "payback should be allowed in certain circumstances provided that it is managed by senior people" is one I also heard. This support is also found among high-profile Aboriginal people, such as MP Karl Hampton, which set him at odds with his own party. As ABC News reported it: "Minister for central Australia and an initiated Warlpiri man . . . Hampton's statement of support for both systems of law may not be the official line, but he has little choice. He has responsibilites to both his family and his heritage, and to the legal system he is part of as a minister" (ABC News on-line 2010).

Tjakamarra articulated the rationality for payback as such:

> Payback helps stop the violence . . . It helps stop people making an enemy of one another. That's where Anangu people always say: "That's where it stops!" No more trouble either side, when the spear enter the leg that makes sure it will be quiet; there won't be trouble any more. And that person who's been speared he could come into that man's or that lady's family. They could come up dinner, drink, or hunting together; they'll be back to family. If they don't give him a spear, they'll be after him until they get him. (field notes 2013)

I follow up by asking Tjakamarra why a passenger who survived a vehicle accident, when she wasn't the driver (alluding to the earlier case where payback of the woman was averted by the police) would nevertheless be blamed and thus sought after for payback. He responded:

> Well, they have to be "paid back" because they were like a *team* traveling, like a group . . . who've been together a long time and always traveled together . . . why the accident now . . . ? Might be blackfella way, *kutatji* [spirit men with malicious intent] way.

And so, someone has to be held to account to assuage this uncertainty between cause and effect. The classical or "traditional" ideal of a spear in the leg for a man and being hit by *nulla-nullas* (heavy fighting sticks/wooden poles) for women, is, however, rarely straightforward to implement and is ideally managed by senior Anangu on the community. The term "bullshit payback" has emerged to cover the violence that young people engage in, as this is often catalyzed by alcohol and might be more widely understood as vigilantism (see also Cripps and Taylor 2009: 59). Although payback is now technically a criminal offense, if the police have no warning about one or if it happens in the bush outside of the community, it does still occur. Not long before my field research began, there was some concern about the extent of injury perpetrated against several women in a payback incident. This concern was voiced by Anangu who chose not to participate in the community event. The catalyst for the payback was the homicide in Alice Springs of a local Anangu woman by her partner, who was found guilty and was serving a three-year jail term. The payback was against several female family members who were also present at, and thus implicated in, the incident, which also involved alcohol. One of the women, in particular, had to be flown to Adelaide hospital in the neighboring state due to the severity of her injuries. Spears were not involved (and are used only for men), but to relieve their grief over the loss of their relative, male and female relatives lined up to exact punishment on the women with *nulla-nullas*. However, one male community leader responded to my comment that I had heard that one of the women was more badly injured than was anticipated:

> No, that payback was wrongly organized. It should have been *kungka* [woman] against *kungka*. This was men against *kungka*. Men hitting *kungka*, that's what white people don't like. I can't hit you. Only my sister can hit you, you know. That's woman against woman.

In the broader Australian context, there is an increasing echoing of intolerance about what has been referred to as lateral violence, also known as intraracial violence, which incorporates gender and family violence, including payback. As Mick Gooda (then Aboriginal and Torres Strait Islander Human Rights Commissioner) stated:

> Lateral violence is a very sensitive topic. When I first raised this issue I was concerned that some would accuse me of airing our dirty laundry in public. The last thing we need is for certain sections of the society to add lateral violence to the litany of dysfunctions associated with Aboriginal and Torres Strait Islander communities. However, I reckon the benefits of speaking out far outweigh the risks of doing nothing. (Australian Human Rights Commission 2011: 8)

The Irony of Complicity

Many of the core elements of Anangu-gendered homosociality have altered little, as "while women have virtual economic autonomy, men monopolise the ritual knowledge on which society is believed to depend" (Cowlishaw 1982: 492). The process of socialization is an essential element in the reproduction of social forms, even as these forms may include the reproduction of particular inequalities. Although this internalization of sexism is not confined to an Aboriginal sociality, as hooks argues, "We are all participants in perpetuating sexism" (2000: ix; see also Becker 2010), the Anangu social practices of gender inequality, via gender-specific ritual and mundane practices of male/female differentiation, have evolved as a densely woven fabric.

This includes early child-rearing practices that also embed the moral bag-
gage of a male-centered ideology and male entitlement (see Bern 1979; Hamilton 1981; Cowlishaw 1982).

According to Bearman and coauthors: "Internalised oppression is the
genus of which internalised sexism is a species" (2009: 13). They further
elaborate: "Internalised oppression consists of oppressive practices that continue to make the rounds even when members of the oppressor group are not
present" (2009: 13). Indeed, Freire understood this phenomenon as "the oppressor is 'housed' within the oppressed" (in Lloyd 1972: 12). Freire's employment of this concept, however, is rather loose, as he is generally referring to
colonial and economic oppression. Franz Fanon, from whom Freire gained
inspiration, also understood this intraracial violence as unifying, as restoring self-confidence and "hoisting them up to the level of the leader" (1961:
51). A rather strong reminder of the cruel and ironic relationship among
gender, violence, and colonization was articulated by Lee Maracle, a native
"CanAmerican" woman:

> If the State won't kill us
> We will have to kill ourselves.
> It is no longer good etiquette to head hunt savages.
> We'll just have to do it ourselves.
> It's not polite to violate "squaws"
> We'll have to find an Indian to oblige us.
> It's poor form to starve an Indian
> We'll have to deprive our young ourselves
> Blinded by niceties and polite liberality
> We can't see our enemy,
> So, we'll just have to kill each other.
>   ("I am woman" 1988, in Smith 2005: 123)

Some might perceive this concept of internalized oppression—which for
Anangu women coalesces at multiple sites—as merely a new method for
"blaming the victim." But if one does not engage with this reproduction of
inequality, we assume an overdetermination of cultural practices and that
they are always unquestioningly followed.[11] Anangu men and women do not
always "accept their assigned position . . . individuals may be creating potentially subversive conflict" (per Cowlishaw 1982: 505), by posting ultrasound
photos of their baby on Facebook or having the new father attend the birth of

his child and be active as a carer. The subordinating practices, such as the hostile sexism of female-to-female violence, must be recognized and conversations held before it can be challenged. For Freire, developing such recognition also creates the possibility of developing alternative ideologies and practices— as those who live them become aware of constraint and limitation. And thus, movements toward transformative justice then become possible (per Coker 2002). Likewise, for bell hooks the development of a critical consciousness is essential if we are to move beyond feminism as a privileged discourse of the highly literate (2000: 5). Reimagining and capturing the "personal is political" battle cry of early feminism seems to me an essential element in a nascent Anangu feminism.

Nevertheless, the role of men in leading change is crucial, as an African observer to the UN Commission on the Status of Women stated:

> Traditions are highly sacrosanct and untouchable where women are concerned. Still, I have seen traditions change through my lifetime. The change was so easy and smooth when the men took the initiative. Change, however, requires a lot of pain and hard work when it is initiated by women. (quoted in Australian Human Rights and Equal Opportunity Commission 2003)

This issue of men leading the charge for gender equality is now widely recognized as an essential element in its realization. Elizabeth Broderick (Human Rights Commission Sex Discrimination Commissioner) established the "Male Champions of Change" organization and strategy for women's equality in leadership positions in work places. Although this focus was on the elite end of town with large corporations as the target for change, many of the principles apply across context in promoting women as leaders (Male Champions of Change 2016). Perhaps the most relevant principle is male public advocacy and support for women. Indeed, there has been a seismic shift in mainstream public discourse about gender discrimination, including gender violence, over the last several years. In the Northern Territory, Charlie King, an Aboriginal man and ABC (public radio) sports broadcaster based in Darwin, founded and leads the "No More [violence]" campaign. This campaign was the first of its kind to reach out to men in remote communities. King states:

> As a community, we need to build a culture where men are the champions of nonviolence, where men can stand up to other men and challenge behaviours and attitudes. This is why we focused on sport as key site for targeting

change. The NO MORE Campaign is a prevention program aimed at changing attitudes about women through awareness raising and direct action. (No
More 2008)

In 2016, King was awarded the Northern Territory Human Rights Award for
this work as an anti–domestic violence campaigner. Earlier that year the chief
of the Australian army, David Morrison, was awarded the Australian of the
Year title for his "commitment to gender equality, diversity and inclusion,"
and in 2015 the Australian of the Year was family violence campaigner Rosie
Batty, whose young son was murdered by his estranged father, her ex-partner
(National Australia Day Council 2016). Many years prior to this, however,
the White Ribbon organization, a male-led campaign to end violence against
women, began in Canada in 1991 with the slogan "stand up and speak out."
The organization UN Women brought this campaign to Australia in 2003,
and one of the messages they advocate is, "It takes a community to prevent
violence." The following chapter will further consider what the implications
of this are for Anangu in several remote communities.

Conclusions

The anthropologist and comparative ethicist Richard Shweder has considered
the idea of whether there is a defensible version of ethical relativism (1990).
He argues that the value of a relativist perspective is not the denial of universals but rather the insistence that to focus exclusively on what is universal is
to miss much of the action, while failing to understand actual moral decision
making (1990: 212). He defines three types of anthropological sense making
of the morality of the "Other": the "universalists" who look through what is
alien in search of deeper similarities, as though strangeness is an illusion; the
"developmentalists" who perceive the history of culture to be a battle between
reason and superstition, science, and ignorance; and the "relativists" who try
to preserve the exotic and alien to defend the legitimacy of diversity and difference (Shweder 1990: 205–206). He argues that the tension between these
interpretations of the "Other's" moral decision making is at the heart of the
anthropological enterprise. I am not specifying my interpretive approach in
terms of one of these analytical frames, but articulating the interpretive possibilities is useful because it brings to the fore our own presuppositions and
interpretative frameworks that are often unconsciously set as the frame of reference. My interpretive approach intersects with and draws on all three types,

depending on the context at hand and, indeed, how much this context may have already been modified by colonization and settlement.

I raise these three interpretative frames as they are also all variously threaded throughout this book, not only in my interpretations but also in some Anangu interpretations of my interpretations. Some, such as Nakamarra and Sammy Butcher themselves, also use the developmentalist frame to critique what they see as outdated practices, such as "payback as too barbaric now" and ideally waiting until the boys are older before they go through "men's business." As a form of reciprocal ethnography, my interpretations are often counterbalanced with Anangu interpretations, enabling readers to make their own assessments in an ongoing dialogue with the different viewpoints offered within these pages. Nevertheless, although there are community leaders who chose to stay away from participating in payback, for instance, as their way of not condoning it, it is ultimately the case that acting as a bystander is also a form of complicity. A coalescence between a majoritarian rejection of violence from within the community has to also be one that is voiced for the local social imaginary to be actively reshaped (per Taylor 2002).

This chapter has explored some of the core social institutions and practices through which Anangu gender relations are produced and reproduced, as these are the social contexts in which and through which ideas and principles of women's human rights jostle for legitimacy. As Davis has articulated: "The goal of self-determination is no longer what is best for the community but rather it becomes more individualised based on capability and functioning: what is she actually able to do and to be?" (2012:10).[12] Such a question can, nevertheless, only begin to be answered from within the frame of reference of the community, as this is the place where women's agency evolves and is manifest.

Chapter 4

"Women Go to the Clinic, and Men Go to Jail"

The Gendered Indigenized Subject of Legal Rights

THIS CHAPTER EXPLORES THE INTERSECTIONS among legal rights, local perceptions of social justice, and gender violence. Spousal or intimate partner violence exposes multiple sites of articulation with formal rights via the legal system while revealing, often in contradistinction, Anangu responsibilities in customary terms. Anangu women's interactions with and responses to the legal system, including the police, speak to contradictory and competing discourses between family/community and the state system. These discourses are not equal. Although there may appear to be choice, as Henrietta Moore argues, there are dominant and subdominant discourses (in Merry 2003). The formal legal system representing Aboriginal people has instrumentalized women as the "victims" and men as the "perpetrators." Although these two legal positions are oppositional, this is often not the case for the couple, who rarely separate. Aboriginal women are known as "noncompliant" and often discouraged from attending court by the prosecutors of domestic violence cases. By exploring the intersubjectivity in these familial encounters, this chapter makes ethnographically visible why Aboriginal women tend to be "bad victims" (per Merry 2003).

The term "gender violence," referring here to violence against a female spouse, derives its impact from women's vulnerability *as women* due to sexual inequality (Stark 2007: 5). A woman's inequality and subordination are reaffirmed every time she is abused, and there is no or limited recourse for changing this pattern. However, the legal system that attempts to intercept this violence and change this pattern is a site for both making gender and for reproducing Aboriginal (male and female) marginality. Anangu women's exposure to gender violence also compels interaction with the child protection system, via the Northern Territory Department of Families and Community Services and the Family Court. Just as the rates of violence against women are higher in the NT than anywhere else in Australia, so too are the rates of removal of their children the highest in the country (Australian Institute of Health and Welfare 2017: 11). Arguably, this is due to the new measures under the Northern Territory Emergency Response from 2007. The interaction of these family and criminal legal systems produces a potential cascade of marginalization for Anangu women, compounding their vulnerability. As Coker and Macquoid argue, "Framing violence against women as a criminal issue, rather than . . . a civil rights, human rights or public health issue, inevitably narrows the framework for understanding the scope, causes, consequences and remedies for violence against women" (2015: 593). Thus, while in the mainstream context criminalizing such violence has been enormously important in validating women's rights, this has had very different effects in Aboriginal communities, as among other "subordinated groups," to use Coker's term. This is because a crime-centered frame focuses on interpersonal, individualist violence, making invisible the ways in which structural inequalities make some women and men more vulnerable to violence and some more likely to use violence (Coker and Macquoid 2015).

Although this legal system has limitations, in this complex social field there are those Anangu women who have managed to engage the criminal legal system for their advantage. As these women take on new identities as rights holders, an interplay emerges between the role of family as protector of women and the state as the new protector. What changes do the women who manage to negotiate and not be marginalized by the system have to make in their lives to effect this identity change? Does the possibility of this engagement by these particular Anangu women reaffirm the paradoxes of rights that "they are entitlements of those who have accepted the established distributions" as law-abiding citizens (Douzinas 2007: 107)? These women are the "good victims" who follow through with the court process and/or the separation from their violent spouse.

When I began this research, I wasn't anticipating a focus on gender violence. Yet, this horribly routine field of experiences kept intruding into conversations with service providers, particularly lawyers, police, and community nurses in our discussions of the application of universal rights to Anangu. This pervasive intrusion of concerns about intraracial gender violence into wider discussions was also driven by public discourse and broader media scrutiny of the endemic levels of violence in communities and, in particular, violence against women. As I began to talk with Anangu women about their experiences of violence, from their partners, from within the broader community, and from their subsequent engagement with the legal system, the question, "How does a person come to understand his or her problems in terms of rights?" posed by Merry (2003) seemed a key one to explore.

Many of these discussions are intimate and revealing, and my trepidation at even raising these issues bears out over my authority to speak about pain and loss that I have not experienced. However, the public readiness to engage in this issue is different from in the 1980s when Bell and Nelson wrote "Speaking about Rape Is Everyone's Business" (1989). Nevertheless, as I now write from the distance of predominantly Anglo and comfortable Canberra, how can I be sure that I don't "compound . . . the hurt by engaging in a sort of 'pornography' in representation" (Jolly 2015: 282)? As I am embedded in geopolitically constituted relations of power I confront (my) privilege and "right to speak" for these women, thereby risking a complicity in (re)constituting the remote Other (see Roof and Wiegman 1995). Although these concerns are not new to anthropology, an activist and ethical method entails confronting them, especially in this site of multiple and intersecting oppressions, because I could be the "self-abnegating intellectual" that Spivak despises and choose to retreat from engaging with this emotively loaded issue, fearing criticism as I make a choice to disengage (1988). However, quarantining violence from an ethnography of human rights seems deeply dishonest, if not impossible. Further, as discussed in the previous chapter, there is a public readiness now to eschew the identity politics where only Indigenous peoples could speak about these issues (see also Austin-Broos 2010:137). So, instead, like Spivak, rather than a "speaking for" I prefer a "speaking to" in which the scholar neither abnegates her discursive role nor presumes an authenticity of the oppressed but still allows for the possibility that a "countersentence" will be produced that may then suggest a new historical narrative (1988: 295–296). To do this I have sought to embrace an ethnographic practice that enables voices that may not usually get heard through a dialogical approach or, as discussed, a form of "reciprocal ethnography" (Lawless 1992). Such an approach reveals multiplicity and nuance, rather than singularity or essentialism.

Although the issue of violence against women emerged as a human rights issue (women's rights as human rights) from the 1980s on the agendas of international NGOs and UN organizations for women (see Cook 1994; Merry 2006a), violence against Indigenous women and girls has only very recently gained a similar focus. This has been led in part by the UN Permanent Forum on Indigenous Issues (UNPFII). Several recent reports highlight the multifaceted nature of this violence: "The systematic violation of [the] collective rights of Indigenous peoples is a major risk factor for gender violence" (UNPFII 2013: 4; and see 2012). These reports argue that although gender violence cannot be separated from the history of discrimination and marginalization of Indigenous peoples as a whole, colonization is understood as a risk factor, rather than the sole cause. This approach speaks to this larger agenda of contextualizing the violence, as well as acknowledging that local norms and practices also play a part in the perpetuation of violent behaviors (see UNPFII 2012: 5). This relatively recent refocusing away from colonization as the sole, or primary, driver of intra-Aboriginal violence allows for a far more nuanced examination of the intersecting relations of power, as these are patriarchal at both the local level and the level of the state. Although it might be too simplistic to say they are mutually reinforcing, patriarchal paradigms do shadow and thus reinvigorate each other, regenerating women's subordination at multiple cross-cutting sites.

One of the difficulties highlighted in these global reports is the problem of getting access to data on the extent of violence against Indigenous women and girls, as data are generally aggregated, rather than specified by group or region. There is also systemic underreporting globally, as in Australia (Willis 2011). Although reporting of domestic and family violence in the Northern Territory (and indeed Australia-wide) is now mandatory, this reporting is predominantly by non-Aboriginal service workers, not by those immediately affected.

"The Prime Function of Rights Is to Construct the Individual Person as a Subject (of Law)"

To think through the quotation in the title above, from Douzinas (2007: 7), we have to begin with first exploring how this compliant subject of law, this "good victim," gets made. How does the ideal individual human rights holder subject, as articulated through the coercive legal system of mandatory reporting, mandatory sentencing, and domestic violence orders, intersect with and relate to the subjectivity of Anangu female personhood? The type of person that embodies a "human rights holder" consciousness identifies with a genealogy of individualism that is mobile and secular, as they are *what* they do, not *who* they are [related to]. The criminal and family legal systems are specifically structured as a discursive social mechanism to produce and reproduce this liberal individual. After all, as Douzinas reminds us, "Rights were the creation of early modern legal systems and constitute the basic building block of Western law" (2007: 9). This legal subject, as it cuts across hierarchy and locality, challenges the classic desert personhood, which is endosocial, asymmetrical, and gendered and for which kinship is still a pervasive, central organizing principle in social life.

The liberal individualism embodied in legal rights also logically opposes the collective rights of Aboriginal peoples. Such collective rights are the assets of families and communities of language speakers and landholders. They are embodied in the relational personhood of Anangu, where the self is necessarily implicated in kinship and exchange (Myers 1986; Peterson 1993; Glaskin 2012). As a recent UN Permanent Forum on Indigenous Issues report states: "The problem of violence against Indigenous women and girls is not only the question of individual human rights but also of the rights of Indigenous peoples and general human rights of women and girls" (UNPFII 2013: 4). Finding an accommodation between Anangu women's right to be free from violence, as a universal right, and her right to coexist with her family via maintaining her spousal relationship, is not countenanced in the mainstream system. Is it appropriate to even suggest such an accommodation? Surely her right to bodily integrity and dignity trumps her rights to family and community. What sort of family and community allows and enables such endemic violence? Although it is not always an either/or equation, Anangu women are often conflicted about engaging with this legal system. It is therefore crucial to articulate the tensions between these often contrasting subjectivities as particular Anangu women move between them and to what affect.

This positioning of Anangu women in relation to the laws that are ostensibly legislated to protect them from gender violence must also be read against the larger subordinating paradigm of ongoing structural oppression that affects them, their male partners, and their families. These laws are not neutral or applied universally in an impartial way.

Agency and Structures of Feeling

Moore's theory of the self, as the location of multiple and potentially contradictory subjectivities, assists in conceptualizing the complex positioning of women who turn to the law in crises of violence (in Merry 2003: 349). For an Aboriginal woman, the contradictions and tensions between the formal legal system as it operates on and for her as an individual "victim" contrasts with her sociocentric subject position among family and community. I take a lead from Merry's question, "How do women take up a position in one discourse rather than another?" (2003: 349). Unlike Merry, however, I have found in this central Australian context that there is some fluidity between these discourses and rarely a clearly demarcated dichotomy. This is principally due to the mandatory sentencing and domestic violence reporting regimes that do not allow women the choice or discretion to take up a position. Rather, they are compelled through the legal system. How they manage within and beyond this system, by actively calling the police themselves, actively seeking a domestic violence order, or separating from their violent spouse, *are* indicators of the uptake of a rights holder position. Yet, this apparent agency is complicated by women's general reluctance to identify as suffering subjects. As discussed in the previous chapter, women's internalization of sexism, as a species of internalized oppression (Bearman, Korobov, and Thorne 2009: 13), confounds any undifferentiated vocabulary of agency.

This concept of "agency" has gained popular currency in the development literature where it is sometimes defined as "empowerment" and articulated through the related concept of "voice." An outcome is that women are enabled to participate in public and private forums without fear of sanction or retribution (Sen 1999: Nussbaum 2000: World Bank Group 2014). In development programs, agency has intrinsic value where the ability to exercise choice and take action is important in its own right. As a "process freedom" it is now accepted as part of mainstream development thinking (World Bank Group 2014: 6.) Like Ortner, I understand subjectivity as the basis of agency, where an individual has a "specifically cultural and historical consciousness" (2005: 34). Drawing on Bourdieu, this consciousness is mediated by the habitus that establishes a range of options and limits for the social actor (in Ortner 2005:33). Yet, although we know that "ideas about personhood and agency are intimately entwined" (Kratz in Wardlow 2006: 7) the privileging of culturally distinctive categorizations of personhood can serve to "logically preclude the possibility of agency, leaving only the enactment of social patterns" (Wardlow 2006: 7). Aboriginal Australian personhood, similarly to the Melanesian personhood articulated by Strathern (1988), is often defined as wholly sociocentric and hence juxtaposed to the egocentric and independent agentic personhood of the West. Such essentialism is reductive and papers over localized responses to the global movements of colonialism and religious conversion (Rafael 1988) and globalization (Thomas 1991; Tsing 2005). Culture is a verb, not a noun.

Although the accepted anthropological approach to conceptualizing desert personhood has been, and still is, in terms of relationality and a tendency toward endosociality, I seek to take an actor-oriented approach.[1] In doing so, I recognize that Anangu are at least partially knowing subjects, "that they have some degree of reflexivity about themselves and their desires" (Ortner 2005: 34). Although Aboriginal women may be partially or wholly knowing agentic or resisting subjects, they are also members of a dominated group, and so an integral part of this analysis also explores "how the condition of subjection is subjectively constructed and experienced, as well as creative ways in which it is—if only episodically—overcome" (Ortner 2005: 34).

I have borrowed the concept "structures of feeling" from Ortner, who in turn borrowed it from the cultural studies and literary theorist Raymond Williams (Ortner 2005: 35). I find the concept especially evocative, as Williams states: "It is as firm and definite as 'structure' suggests, yet it operates in the most delicate and least tangible parts of our activity" (1961: 61). For my purposes, such activity is manifest in the deeply intersubjective field of kin relations where the everyday normative constraints and possibilities on action and agency are both emergent and contested.

The Normativity of Spousal (and Family) Violence

The statistical facts of spousal violence reveal startling figures. In the Northern Territory, almost 3,000 Aboriginal women experienced spousal violence in 2011–2012, compared to almost 300 non-Aboriginal women in the same year (Sharp 2014). On the basis of the Aboriginal population of the Northern Territory being 30 percent of the total, this proportion seems staggering. Or to contextualize it another way, while Aboriginal women in the Northern Territory make up only 0.3 percent of the broader Australian population, they account for 14 percent of female hospitalizations for assault in the entire country (Sharp 2014).

These extremely high figures are correlated with equally disproportionate imprisonment rates for Aboriginal men. In 2013 the number of Aboriginal men in Northern Territory prisons rose by 12 percent, to 86 percent of the prison population (ABS 2013). This increase in incarceration was driven by the new mandatory sentencing regime introduced earlier that year. Half of these men were serving a sentence for acts intended to cause injury, usually referred to as aggravated assault.[2] This sentencing regime applies to "violent offenses," which include "the use, or threatened use, of violence." This new sentencing regime sets out different "levels" of violent offenses subject to mandatory sentences of imprisonment, according to the seriousness of the offense. Some high-level violent offenses attract a mandatory sentence of three or twelve months imprisonment, whereas some low-level violent offenses attract a mandatory sentence of imprisonment but leave the length of the sentence to be decided by the magistrate or judge. The court may have discretion only in "exceptional circumstances" (Sharp 2014),[3] which I'll discuss further in the following chapter.

These statistics appear to speak for themselves as facts about violent actions. Yet, they also reveal the overpolicing of the Indigenous population, where "governing through crime" (per Wacquant 2010) becomes as normalized as the intraracial violence. Twelve percent of the offenses Aboriginal men are incarcerated for are property and traffic related (ABS 2013). As critical criminology has revealed, the Australian legal system has been complicit in establishing and reproducing the Aboriginal "criminal" over the last two centuries to justify sovereignty (Cunneen 2007; Blagg 2008). It is no coincidence that the first rock song recorded in an Aboriginal language was *Jailanguru Pakarnu* ("Out from Jail") by the Warumpi Band (Warumpi Band 1983). The lyrics translated from Luritja read: *Today I just got out of jail / I'm going to Papunya now / I'm going in a hurry for my girl is waiting / I'm going to sit down good—no more fighting / I'm going to leave that jail for good / Today I'll be together with my family.*

Are Anangu women safer, in the short and long term? And is their suffering reduced when their partners are incarcerated? Although these figures don't disaggregate specifically for gender violence, we can assume that the significant majority of the assaults were perpetrated by men against their spouse. A female lawyer for the Central Australian Aboriginal Family Legal Unit (CAAFLU) stated that the generally accepted anecdotal figure is that 90 percent of Aboriginal women have been physically assaulted at some stage in their life and often multiple times. This physical assault is taking place in a broader normative context in which violence is pervasive, so that the justifying logic that women are innocent victims, however, is not so neat. No Aboriginal family is untouched by violence. Although the individual offender is imprisoned for a period, the structures that enabled the violence haven't altered. Such "structures" refer to and are found in the complex interplay between the marginalizing effects of structural violence, in the work of the state, and the intimate local familial structures that are found in kinship networks. Although I am always conscious of these intercultural imbrications, and this book attempts to make sense of this interaction, the immediate focus here is on the broader concept of "family violence" in a focus on instances of physical violence in this intimate field.

"Family violence" is used as an umbrella term to encompass violence perpetrated by and against a range of family members, as it describes how violence reverberates throughout the community (see also APO NT 2014). As a result it also includes spousal or intimate partner violence and embraces the dynamic social nature of violence (Memmott et al. 2006: 8–9). So, while the term "domestic violence" is used in mainstream legal contexts, including "domestic violence orders," which Aboriginal women, and police, now routinely take out against their spouses, it doesn't capture Aboriginal women's experiences of spousal violence, which inevitably implicate other family members, such as in-laws. Likewise, the term "battered women" used in the United States, for instance (see Merry 2003; Stark 2007), does not apply here. It does not allow for women's agency, nor does it reflect the positioning of women within their families.

Although I acknowledge up front that women and children overwhelmingly bear the brunt of family violence (and I focus on violence against women), it nevertheless seems to me that the categories of "female victim" and "male perpetrator" elide far more than they reveal. These categories disarticulate the spousal relationship and contradict the often heard view within the Aboriginal community, especially by older people, that "*kungkas* [young women] always the ones that start it off" (Nakamarra 2014, field notes). We need to get underneath these categories to realize the intersubjectivity of these intimate encounters where the lines of fault and blame are often blurred, even as we know that in central Australia Aboriginal men are routinely convicted of killing their spouses. So, in undertaking this exercise I in no way seek to minimize this stark fact.

What makes women "bad victims" and "noncompliant" within the legal system? Kinship networks and the custody of children are at stake, and it is these structures of feeling that are negotiated when women remain with their spouses even after years of abuse and that restrain certain categories of family

from coming to their aid. Although these structures of feeling are anthropological categories, they are not fixed. Indeed, with settlement they have not
only intensified but become distorted, principally through extremely high
rates of substance abuse, including alcohol, marijuana, and more recently
methamphetamines. When I quoted the figure that "sixty-seven percent of
gender violence incidents are alcohol related" (per Pyne 2012: 5) to the police
officer with whom I was discussing these issues in Papunya, he responded that
this seemed a very low figure. He would have estimated that, in Alice Springs
at least, the figure was closer to 90 percent (field notes April 15, 2015).

In this context of violence, we have to be careful not to use cultural categories to obfuscate the effects of violence, which can be trauma inducing. Psy-
chologists such as Malcolm Frost, who have worked in violence intervention
programs in Alice Springs, remind us of the intergenerational impacts that
can develop from insecure attachment as a child, childhood sexual abuse, and
childhood exposure to domestic violence that are not reflective of "culture"
but rather, he argues, of universal human level processes (Frost 2014). Nevertheless, using psychological categories such as "posttraumatic stress disor-
der" and "insecure attachment" as diagnostic tools can be reductionist or, as
Kleinman has termed, potentially creates "category fallacies" (1987: 452).[4]

The Gendered Legal System

It has been shown that the legal system serves female victims of violence badly, and
this is particularly so for Aboriginal women. The situation is complicated by the desire to
reduce the proportion of Aboriginal men in prison.

Bolger 1991: 95

This statement, made over twenty-five years ago by Audrey Bolger, unfortunately remains valid today and is compounded for women living remotely,
especially in those places where the court does not sit and where there are no
advocacy or police services. Although we know that the proportion of men in
jail has risen significantly, driven by the mandatory sentencing laws and zero-
tolerance policing, the *actual* sentences handed down for aggravated assaults
and manslaughter send contradictory messages to affected families and to the
offender. The routine nature of this intraracial violence is such that the public
discourse likewise sends inconsistent messages.

In 1973 the first Aboriginal organization, the Central Australian Aboriginal Legal Aid Service (CAALAS), was established in Alice Springs. An early
CAALAS director, Aboriginal woman Pat Miller, stated:

There was just no [legal] representation whatsoever. I can recall when I was a child growing up in this town, on Monday mornings on the footpath outside the local courthouse there'd be people, 30–40 strong, picked up for drunkenness, and they'd just go in and plead guilty. The magistrate would give them a week, a fortnight or whatever he chose. (in Faine 1993: 30)

Yet, although CAALAS had an early focus on public drunkenness—a predominantly male issue—when the Department of Public Prosecutions (the DPP) was established in 1991, the role of CAALAS gradually shifted to focus on defending Aboriginal men from prosecution from spousal violence. A decision was made by the CAALAS Board and legal staff that women victims could not be represented by the same legal service—CAALAS—that was defending their male spouse because of conflict of interest. It was not until over twenty years after the establishment of CAALAS, in 1995, that women gained their own specialist legal advocacy service, the Central Australian Women's Legal Service (CAWLS).[5] This was followed in the year 2000 by CAAFLU (the Central Australian Aboriginal Family Legal Unit), which specifically regards itself as a family violence prevention legal service. This twenty-plus-year hiatus in legal representation for women mirrored societal attitudes at the time which, as Bolger indicated, trivialized and underestimated violence against women as domestic rather than being regarded as "real" violence (1991: 71–80). The legal focus was consistently on the rights of the offender via the sympathetic male police and judiciary (Bolger 1991: 83).

Recently, however, there has been an avalanche of policy and regulation in this area. In 2008 and 2009 the NT Domestic and Family Violence Act and the Domestic and Family Violence Regulations (which replaced restraining orders with domestic violence orders) were adopted. They both provide wide-reaching powers to police to register and enforce such orders and to routinely appear in court on behalf of the victim. Also in 2009, the Act was amended to make reporting domestic and family violence mandatory for all adults in the Northern Territory: a bystander who does not report is effectively criminalized. This reporting also reinforces the police as "instruments for the delivery of social policy."[6] The Act states that:

An adult commits an offence if he or she believes on reasonable grounds that either or both of the following circumstances exist: (a) another person has caused, or is likely to cause, harm to someone else with whom the other person is in a domestic relationship, (b) the life or safety of another person (also the victim) is under serious or imminent threat because domestic violence has been, is being or is about to be committed. (Section 124A)

As a CAAFLU lawyer recently stated:

DV [domestic violence] is taken a lot more seriously than it used to be. Not so long ago she [the Aboriginal woman] would front up at the hospital with horrific injuries and tell the hospital what happened. But they wouldn't tell the police, so she would leave, and the cycle would happen all over again. Only since 2009 has the system been on the presumption for the victim's safety. (fieldnotes July 7, 2014)

This change goes partway to explaining the statement in this chapter title: "Women go to the clinic, and men go to jail" made by a senior non-Aboriginal staff member of the local shire in Papunya. However, although this expression may recall the predominant pattern of violence perpetrated against women and the recent mandatory reporting by nurses, it elides the growing and not insignificant proportion of men who also present at the clinic from spousal violence and the growing number of women subsequently incarcerated.

The current NT approach is in line with the "National Plan to Reduce Violence against Women and Their Children," which runs from 2010 to 2022, and the nationwide "No Excuses" campaign. There is, for the first time, an attempt at a standard Australia-wide approach that has begun to filter into public discourse in central Australia, as a news item in the *Centralian Advocate* (Newspaper) reads: "Domestic Violence Will Not Be Tolerated" (August 22, 2014). In late 2013 Alice Springs Northern Territory police established Strikeforce Halberd—a dedicated domestic and family violence police unit—that is also supported by the equally new "Family Safety Framework" that links the relevant agencies, including the Women's Shelter, in a case management approach. Yet, as I'll discuss in relation to a court case for manslaughter, these significant social policies have yet to infiltrate the deeper public consciousness and the sentencing logic of the courts.

The historical disjunct between defense and prosecution in relation to gender violence was strikingly illustrated by Nanette Rogers, whose early work as a defense lawyer for CAALAS motivated her to became Crown prosecutor and coordinator of a victims support unit, which she did for over twelve years in Alice Springs. Rogers gained some renown for an interview she did on the ABC Lateline program in 2006 where she revealed details of the cases that she had dealt with of the violence against women and children that were, by any measure, shocking. Three months later a Board of Enquiry was established that culminated, in mid-2007, with the *Little Children Are Sacred Report*, coauthored by Rex Wild and Pat Anderson, and shortly thereafter by the commonwealth government intervention, the Northern Territory Emergency Response (NTER).

When I asked a current prosecution lawyer, Ruth Morley, her views on the value of sending Aboriginal men to jail, as it seemed to be a cyclical churn given the high recidivism rates, she responded with, "I don't agree with the view expressed to me by defense lawyers that 'She's just as bad as him'; you then lose sight of victims' support" (field notes July 8, 2014). Her point is that this argument disguises the fact that, as Bolger noted in 1991, "No matter who initiated a fight between woman and man, the woman was more likely to be injured or suffer greater harm than the man," as the men are the lethal fighters (1991: 1). The research of Burbank in Numbulwar (1994) and Macknight in Mornington Island (2002) found that although women were active in defending themselves and in initiating both physical and verbal assaults, it was unusual in these Aboriginal communities for an Aboriginal woman to kill her spouse. However, Nanette Rogers observed in 2006 that, in central Australia at least, this was changing. She noted a number of cases, where "young women, maybe [aged] 19 or 20, have stabbed their boyfriends with fatal consequences . . . it's almost like a new breed of young women coming through. Their mothers and grandmothers would not have done that. They would have just been—not a willing victim, but they wouldn't have taken . . . preventative action, if you like, the pre-emptive stabbing" (ABC Lateline 2006).

Some Parameters for Women's Agency

In the previous chapter I explored the history of ethnographic debate in Australia around gender relations in traditional, "classical" society and the arguments for dual social systems, to shed light on contemporary practice. Though the early ethnographers followed different lines of argument, they variously maintained that women were able to assert some autonomy because of their discreet secret gendered ritual domains, referred to in Aboriginal English as "women's business." The domestic economy also encouraged this relative autonomy in a deeply gendered daily routine where the notion of complementarity, rather than equality, was relevant. Yet, as Merlan argued in the late 1980s: "This tendency toward dualism—insistence ideologically and practically upon some degree of male-female separation . . . impeded analysis and understanding of Aboriginal gender relations as a joint production" (1988: 20; see also Holcombe 1997).

Realizing gender as a relational condition is now fundamental and allows for a rereading of women's agency and a focus on shifting subjectivities due to very significant social changes since colonization, settlement, and the introduction of alcohol and other addictive substances. Further, if gender is relational, how are power relations between men and women reproduced? If gender *is* a "joint production," then so too are the patriarchal structures that favor men also reproduced by women's actions, however subconscious, complicit, or dominated they might be. Through a focus on the intersubjectivity of gender as a power relation, I attempt to trace the linkages between subjectivity and power. By subjectivity, like Sherry Ortner, I mean the "ensemble of modes of perception, affect, thought, desire, fear and so forth that animate acting subjects. But I always mean as well, the cultural and social formations that shape, organise, and provoke these modes of affect" (2005: 31). And, like Ortner, my approach is to track back and forth between the examination of such cultural formations and the inner states of acting subjects.

The parameters for Aboriginal women's agency are shifting—but in what ways and specifically for whom? How does the rights discourse operate through the legal system, and what are its effects? As notions of social justice conflict, what are the outcomes for Aboriginal women? Where are the discontinuities within these normative familial practices? As Geertz argues: "It is in these very discontinuities that we shall find some of the primary driving forces of change" (Geertz 1957: 33).

Women in violent relationships with their partners are not only spouses. They are also mothers, sisters, aunties, daughters-in-law, and cousins, and so on, to other male and female kin. These multiple intersecting subjectivities, with their attendant roles and responsibilities, are usually very close to hand. There are no Aboriginal strangers living in communities; those not originally from the community have married into it.[7] Although not all Aboriginal women are in violent relationships, it would be rare for a woman not to have family members or affines affected. How these family members react to such violence, either as a target or as a bystander, is very often a reflection of their subject status as a relative within a kinship network, of male and female. Several examples will illustrate this:

Nakamarra: 'Cause when you see Anangu fighting you can't report that person, 'cause that person might be *nyuntupa waltja* [your family], you know.

SH: So you can't report them? *Nyaaku*? [why] Just 'cause they're your family?

Nakamarra: *Yuwa* [yes]—it's a really, really hard one. *Yuwa.*

SH: But what if that girl was really getting hurt, you know, someone got to
stand in for her and help her.

Nakamarra: *Yuwa.* When I see someone getting hurt, I just report it in. I used
to report and ring the police, and [they would] say, who are you ringing
[about]? [I'd say] You can't have my name, but I'm ringing to catch this
person, not get myself involved. . . . sometimes it's tricky 'cause you don't
want the police coming and grab your sons, your nephew, or your niece
and take them to the police station and arrest them for three years [her
understanding of mandatory sentencing].

Nampitjinpa, a senior woman from the neighboring community of Mount
Liebig, also spoke of the customary responsibility that women have to their
in-laws:

SH: If you saw a *kungka* [woman] being bashed up—like *nyuntupa waltja*
[your family]—would you call the police?

Nampitjinpa(2): *Wiya* [no]. Family can't call the police; men's family side, they
have to call the police. *Kungka* family can't call them; you can't ring to that
police man, you'd be in trouble family way. Family has to do that.

SH: So who has to call for the police?

Nampitjinpa(2): The family of the man's side.

SH: So they have to take responsibility?

Nampitjinpa(2): *Yuwa* [yes]—that's our law, you know, that's Aboriginal ways.
Our ideas.

SH: But what happens then if they don't call? [silence] That's a hard one, eh?

Nampitjinpa(2): *Yuwa* if they don't call—then they'll keep on fighting with
that lady, with that wife.

SH: So what would happen if the *kungka* side family called—would they be
worried about payback—is that the problem?

Nampitjinpa(2): *Yuwa.*

SH: I see, OK. But what would happen if his family is a long way away, he's
living with her family, he might come from Kiwirrkurra, and he's the one
doing the bashing—is it OK then for her family to call?

Nampitjinpa(2): No—*wati* family right—his side, you know—man's side. *Kungka* side *wiya* [no].

This last example of mine was prompted by a discussion held earlier that morning with Nangala (in her late forties) who *had* called the police as her young niece was being assaulted at their family outstation by her spouse from the Western Australian community of Kiwirrkurra (about 250 kilometers away in the neighboring state). She had no qualms about the fact that she was "*kungka* side family." I had first interviewed Nangala in Papunya about six weeks earlier after her spouse had participated in the Cross Borders Indigenous Family Violence Program (as a mandatory element of his parole). When I happened on them both in Mount Liebig and Nangala and I were heading off to talk, as I had asked to interview her again, Tjungurrayi (her spouse) called out to remind her: "Don't forget to call the police." It seemed more than coincidence that Tjungurrayi had recently undertaken this program and that they were both engaging with this alternative message. Although it is true that Nampitjinpa(2) was articulating *ideal* views on appropriate Anangu behavior, the ubiquity of spousal violence as ongoing multiple assaults does suggest that this model is followed more frequently than this alternative of "*kungka* side family." It is not news that women are rarely provided support from their kin to defend them from spousal violence; they themselves don't wish to be implicated in an escalation of violence and wish to keep it a private matter between the couple as far as possible. Nevertheless, discontinuities with and ruptures between these patterns of normative kin behavior do occur, as illustrated here.

When I asked Nangala, during our discussion, why she's stayed with her long-term abusive partner, her response was: "I never thought to leave him, and he's been growing up all the [adopted] kids with me. When I'm away he misses me, even when I'm in Papunya playing cards, he'll ring me." This couple from the same small community are enmeshed in an intense familiarity. She told me sheepishly that they are actually [second] cousins. Such interwoven families make separation extremely difficult; one of them would have to leave the community, a very serious proposition.

This notion of Aboriginal personhood as deeply interdependent with one's spouse was illustrated as I (naïvely) first attempted to translate the concept of the "individual" into Pintupi-Luritja. The smallest person unit I was given was *miitarrara* (literally, "spouse pair")—a husband and wife unit.[8] Nevertheless, when I asked Nangala what she would do if Tjungurrayi hit her again she said, without hesitation, that she would send him to jail again. For her, jail seems to operate as a form of respite; he has been in several times for aggravated assault against her, and part of his parole on this occasion was to undertake the nonviolence program in Papunya. So, after many years, she has managed to negotiate the system—with an increasing awareness that she has the right to do so. The state has become her new protector. And, like other women who have suffered long-term abuse and managed to survive, this outsourcing of responsibility to the state tends to be tolerated, if not actively supported, by family.

Merry found that the "adoption of a rights consciousness requires experiences with the legal system that reinforces this subjectivity" (2003: 344), and this seems to be the case for Nangala as she has found the police and the Women's Shelter in town supportive. Access to alternative advice—such as the counseling at the Women's Shelter in Alice Springs—seems to be one of the few avenues for altering this pattern of kinship obligation. Likewise, accessing an alternative place to live away from the community for a period is essential. It is extremely difficult in a community for women to access a place of respite, not only because of the intrafamilial network but also because of the severe housing shortage. Women's shelters either don't exist in these communities or, as in Papunya, although they have a building, they did not have the support to develop a case-management program, so at the time of this writing it had not been functional for at least its first year.

Customary Marriage Contracts and Rights to Children

Women, notably those from different communities than their spouses, may not report violence not only because they might fear retribution from his family if he were to go to jail but also because they may lose access to their children. Such loss of access may be through paternal customary kinship obligations or through the surveillance operations of the police as they respond to a domestic violence call. First, I discuss with Nampitjinpa(2) the customary approach if the family do not engage with, or are not intervened by, the state:

> SH: I'm wondering about—say, if a *wati* [male] goes to jail—what happens to those kids from that *wati*? If they're from two different communities, say she's from Mount Liebig and he's from Lajamanu, where will those kids go? Can she hang onto them, or do they go to his family side?
>
> Nampitjinpa(2): They have to go to his family.

SH: So does that happen all the time? Say if he passed away—they got to go to his family side again?

Nampitjinpa(2): *Yuwa* [yes]. His family will come and get *pipirri tjuta* [all the kids].

SH: But what about her family—what happens to the mother? Does she see those kids or nothing?

Nampitjinpa(2): Nothing [shakes her head].

SH: So why does that happen?

Nampitjinpa(2): Traditional way.

SH: For *walpela* [whitefella] way that would make the mother too sad to lose her kids—but that mother-in-law takes them?

Nampitjinpa(2): *Yuwa*, mother-in-law.

Based on her prosecution work in central Australia, lawyer Ruth Morley stated, "In my experience, mothers don't own their children, the fathers do; they are the property of the father and his family." Ruth backed up this strong statement by recalling the experiences of several of her female clients (field notes May 16, 2014).[9] As I enquired among Anangu women whose husbands were in jail and whose school-age children have indeed gone to live with their paternal grandmothers, I realized that here was another site of gender inequality that was virtually hidden. This patrilineal bias seemed to be reminiscent of the levirate system that operated in this region, where the widow married her deceased spouse's "brother" to ensure that his local descent group's children remained within the biological patriline (Meggitt 1962). As I discussed this with Nakamarra, she responded with, "It's a tricky one; *yirritji* [before/in the past] it happened all the time, but now not so much." Yet, Napanangka, who was listening to our conversation, also commented: "Sometimes grandmothers don't look after them so well, they get skinny and cry for their mothers. It's really sad." Although it may not be a standard practice today, there were women who have lost ready access to their children, both through this customary system with its patrilineal bias or through the more recent system of mandatory child protection via their removal by the state.

In remote communities, the family court system has yet to make an impression. However, according to Morley, there was an early attempt at informing Aboriginal people in central Australian remote communities about their rights under the family law system. Nevertheless, in an "Indigenous Legal Needs" Report, CAALAS indicates that very few Aboriginal women are pursuing this legal avenue for potentially gaining access to their children. As one Indigenous Legal Service staff member commented, "[Family law] just doesn't fit the realities of Aboriginal clients . . . in remote communities" (in Allison et al. 2012: 90). However, awareness is increasing in urban Alice Springs at least through Relationships Australia, which operates as a service provider within the family law system. In 2010 they developed a "Model of Practice for Mediation with Aboriginal Families in Central Australia" (Ross, Mallard, and Fisher 2010). As a very recent service in this context they assist in mediation over access to children postseparation, and when they are not successful the families are referred to the family court, the magistrates of which visit Alice Springs four times a year. All of the case study examples they provide strongly suggest this pattern of paternal control, over the children, as follows:

> The mediator visited an Aboriginal referred client in jail. The client was incarcerated for murdering his wife. He wanted to mediate with the deceased wife's family to have the children live with his family (mother) and visit him in jail . . . The client wanted [his] mother to advocate on his behalf with the other parties . . . the day of scheduled joint mediation the mediator was contacted by a third party acting on behalf of the deceased family . . . [and] informed of ongoing conflict between the two families. The grieving family informed the mediator that cultural obligations had not yet been met and that it was too soon for them to agree to any request for the children to live with the [paternal] grandmother. The case was referred to the courts. (Ross, Mallard, and Fisher 2010: 44)

The suggestion in this case is that the deceased's family is stalling and resisting this patrilineal customary practice. Another case study example Relationships Australia provides in the "Model of Practice" also suggests this paternal entitlement to the children:

> A couple had separated through severe domestic violence issues and neglect towards their children, the children were taken away [from] the parents and given to the grandfather on the mother's side. The father was sent to jail and the mother ordered to receive professional help. After six to eight months of caring for the children the grandfather contacts the Family Relationship Centre. He asks for assistance to address the violence towards his family members relating to the children not spending time with the father's side of the family. (Ross, Mallard, and Fisher 2010: 47)

While the children are with the mother's kin, the father's kin are attempting to assert their patrilineal rights. The legal system is supportive, however, in enabling the mother's family to push back against these customary expectations.

The widespread European practice of the father's surname being bestowed on his children, rather than the surname of the children's mother, is also a standard practice in central Australia.[10] This paternal namesaking over the child is also paralleled by an equivalent Pintupi-Luritja practice whereby the subsection name ("skin name" in Aboriginal English) is derived from their father's lineage via the patricouple system. This skin name is also commonly incorporated into an individual's full name, such as Tjakamarra/Nakamarra or Tjampitjinpa/Nampitjinpa (marked linguistically *Tj-* male and *N-* female). As Myers states, "Male speakers usually treat a child's subsection as a product of the father . . . in explaining the principles relating to the subsection categories, men usually described which subsections should marry and which subsections are related as father–child pairs" (1986: 186).

Gaining precise figures for the proportion of the involuntary paternal custody of children while the father is incarcerated or after separation is not a straightforward research task, however. And it can't always be assumed that the mother is desperate after losing her children to her mother-in-law's care, as the young mother may feel relieved of the childcare burden. Likewise, there are instances where the mother may not have been an active parent or is a substance abuser and it is in the best interests of the child to be looked after by the father's family. Nevertheless, the patrilineal structure whereby his family, principally his mother, is able to assert authority seems a defining structure of feeling. Yet, as a form of gendered consciousness for Anangu women living in Papunya, for instance, it is rarely expressed interculturally as an issue that the legal system can deal with appropriately.

When I mentioned this tendency toward the patriline having or seeking custody of the children, a non-Aboriginal counselor at the Alice Springs Women's Shelter stated:

> We always ask if we can help with their kids and if they want their kids with them [when they are at the shelter]. But we also assist with the Department of Community and Family Services (DCF). We are there for them, for advice, as the kids are often removed. (field notes July 11, 2014)

Thus, although I found that the issue of the primary customary rights of the patriline to the children was a significant one, it appears to be now secondary to the interventions of the state in child removals, which is from either the mother and/or other family members, including those in the patri-line. Although it appears that the mother rarely seeks formal legal intervention through the family court when the children are in the custody of the father's family in another community, this contrasts with their support seeking if the state takes custody of their children. For instance, Allison and co-authors found that half of the Aboriginal women having issues with child removal by the state had accessed legal support (2012).

Intimate Intersections: Gender Violence and Involuntary Child Removals

According to an Aboriginal Legal Service staff member, "Every time there's a family problem, child protection gets involved" (Allison et al. 2012: 89).[11] This plays out as nearly two-thirds of the notifications received by the Department of Children and Family Services (DCF) are made by government employees, and the majority of these by police. Police notifications comprised 44 percent of all notifications made in 2013–2014. This is attributed to police attendance at domestic and family violence incidents (Northern Territory Government DCF 2014: 11). Yet, because of this police attendance at every reported violent incident, when I quoted this figure of 44 percent to a police officer who has worked in both Papunya and Alice Springs, he stated that in his experience this figure was a significant underestimation. This is because, at every family or domestic violence incident the police attend, they have to specify if children were there and how they were involved, if at all, in the incident(s); thus his suggestion that the police make the majority of notifications for child removal.

Like the legal regimes for domestic and family violence, the Care and Protection of Children Act (2007) is also underpinned by mandatory reporting. There has been a threefold rise in child removals and subsequently in children in "out of home care" since the 2007 Northern Territory Emergency Response (NTER), when this act was legislated (Gibson 2015). As the NTER policy was catalyzed by the high rates of abuse of Aboriginal children, as found in the *Little Children Are Sacred Report* (Wild and Anderson 2007), so too the act targets Aboriginal families. Of the 917 children in "out of home care," 787 are Aboriginal. Likewise, also in 2013–2014, there were 12,936 notifications or phone calls to the child abuse hotline, indicating close surveillance of parenting practices. Nearly two-thirds of these reports are made by government employees (including nurses and teachers), whereas only 16 percent are from community members (Northern Territory Government DCF 2014: 11). Of these notifications, 4,303 were investigated, and 1,685 had a finding that substantiated abuse (Northern Territory Government DCF 2014). Half of these findings of abuse cases are classified as "neglect."

It is possible that the finding of neglect is constituted by exposure to violence and not actual violence to the child. Domestic violence witnessed by a child is listed as a "reportable offense" for child abuse, alongside neglect and psychological harm. Clearly child abuse is a matter that must be taken seriously, and there is considerable research on the intergenerational transmission of trauma and the risk of violence as learned behavior in Australia and internationally among colonized peoples (Menzies 2008; Atkinson 2002: Hunter 1998). However, the current approach severs the relationship between the rights of the child and that of the mother and other carers. As the legal service CAAFLU noted in a Submission to the Enquiry into the Northern Territory Child Protection System: "In any intervention the well-being of the parents (or carers) must also be addressed" (2010).

Rather, like the image of the innocent female victim of violence, so too the image of a defenseless child is the overriding moral imperative in this politics of compassion (Altman and Hinkson 2007). Like the male perpetrators, the child(ren) will be removed and the mothers will remain. As an Aboriginal Legal Aid staff member stated:

> People are frightened . . . of going to the family court because they associate it with DCF [Department of Children and Families]. So if your husband is beating you up and you want to go to the family court and say "I want to have custody of the children," you are scared silly that DCF is going to swan in and say, "oh, dad's beating up the children, that's not in the best interest of the children, you are not protecting the children from dad, we'll take the children or we'll give the children to aunty x or aunty y"—you are much better resolving the issue within your own family group. (in Allison et al. 2012: 91)

Although this lack of support within Aboriginal families for formally reporting their concerns over the care of children operates within the same set of normative parameters as family violence, the fear of state intervention is further intensified in this realm of children. As the mechanism to enforce the child's right to protection is individuated, it necessitates a disembedding from the family. Like the "female victim" of domestic violence, the child who is removed from his or her family becomes a legal entity. Recall that "the prime function of rights is to construct the individual person as a subject (of law)" (Douzinas 2007: 7).

This attempt by the state to construct a postfamilial (post-Aboriginal?) individual, where institutions and state-constructed apparatuses are established to grow, form, and mold the modern person, is tragically reminiscent of the period now referred to as the "stolen generations" (Read 1999). The long Indigenous policy periods of protection followed by assimilation that ran from 1909 to at least 1969 actively removed mainly "half-caste" Aboriginal children from their families to grow up in institutions or be fostered out by non-Indigenous families.[12] In 2008, in a very moving and widely awaited speech, then Prime Minister Kevin Rudd formally apologized to the members of the stolen generations and their families: "To the mothers and the fathers, the brothers and the sisters, for the breaking up of families and communities, we say sorry. . . . For the pain, suffering and hurt of these Stolen Generations, their descendants and for their families left behind, we say sorry" (Parliament of Australia 2008).

Because of this tragically familiar narrative, an Aboriginal staff member of the Department of Children and Families stated: "We don't call it [our work to ensure children's safety] Welfare" (Nungurrayi, field notes 2013). The term "welfare" was widely applied to the government officers of that period who removed Aboriginal children. Yet, we are reminded again that "apparatuses do not care for people" (Beck and Beck-Gernsheim 2002: 129).

According to the 2013–2014 annual Department of Community and Family Report, only 5 percent of notifications come from child protection staff (Northern Territory DCF 2014: 11). This low figure presumably incorporates Aboriginal staff in communities, who are employed under the Remote Aboriginal Family and Community Program (RAFCP), which was established in response to the 2007 NTER. The two male and female Anangu staff, based in Papunya, operate across the four Haasts Bluff Land Trust communities. As Tjampitjinpa stated:

> We slow the process down. We are here so the DCF really have to talk with us; we know the families. We have the notifications here, the forms, but we're not going to fill one in; we don't use them often. We know the families so are at the meeting, but if Protection is there we don't go; that is serious [inferring that the child(ren) will be removed]. (field notes 2013)

Ten percent of Aboriginal women in the Northern Territory in the Indigenous Legal Needs focus groups reported having an issue with child removal in the last two years (that is, prior to 2012). One of the biggest areas within Aboriginal family law is "recovery orders" for children (Allison et al. 2012: 90), as the parents and/or carers will go to court and make representation to have their child(ren) returned to their care. "On the child protection list this month we had 6 families in and 3 were represented. The other parents weren't even present in court" (Gibson and Behrendt 2014: 9). As a counselor from the Alice Springs Women's Shelter Outreach service stated, "On the most basic level the women are not consulted about issues over their children" (field notes July 11, 2014). The CAAFLU submission to the Child Protection Enquiry also argued that "the interventions are disempowering and reactive of flying in [to communities] and flying out" (2010), as a further element in the cascade of interventions "in the name of the child" (Hinkson 2007).

As "neglect" is the most common reason for child notifications, one also has to query how this neglected subject is defined and who defines it. Although I acknowledge that there are cases of severe child abuse, which may include forms of neglect, it also seems clear that there has been a culturalizing of this subjective concept of "neglect" (see also Gibson and Behrendt 2014). As such, there is no tolerance of variant forms of child raising, which include multiattachment parenting and minimal adult supervision, as children are raised by others of their peer group (Shaw 2002; Yeo 2003), as is common practice in many non-Western small-scale societies.

As an extremely complex sociolegal field, this brief discussion can raise these issues only as part of elaborating the intersections between the legal rights of women and their children as forming potentially another site of Anangu women's subordination. The effect of these intersecting protective legal systems can, for some women, compound their marginalization and alienation from the legal system. On one occasion of family violence she might lose her spouse and her children. These paradigms of safety or protection models are profoundly individuated. In this case the rights of the mother are secondary to those of the child.

"Victims Are a Hindrance to Proceedings"

The perception on the part of magistrates and prosecutors that "women are very noncompliant" when they interact with the legal system as it attempts to process their case against their spouse compels the "bad victim" tag. Merry

coined this term for women who are "tracking back and forth across a significant line of identity transformation," as they file charges and then drop them
or fail to appear for restraining order hearings (2003: 345). In Alice Springs,
the police routinely file the domestic violence orders, as the female victims
are rarely present at court. They are regarded as a hindrance to proceedings
by the prosecutors and the police, according to prosecutor Ruth Morley (field
notes May 16, 2014). This is because if they do present at court it is to accompany the defendant (their partner); as Morley states, 95 percent of women will
say, "I want to drop the charges." Defense lawyers have been known to take
advantage of this contact and successfully defend a number of charges relying
on the victim's unwillingness to give evidence against her spouse. This is so
commonplace that the DPP director prepared a memo that was sent to all Aboriginal Legal Aid Services in the Northern Territory stating that the Crown
position on the matter was that their actions—in taking the victim's advice to
drop the charges—came close to a "perversion of the course of justice."

The although these women may refuse to identify as victims for the legal system (just as their families often also refuse to identify them as such), according to a police officer, this is not the case at the time of the violence. As a police
officer from Papunya stated: "At the time [of the violence] virtually every female victim will report; so there is a small window—about four hours—to get
the victim impact statement. This is crucial, and even if they want to with-
draw it, we will carry it through" (field notes May 7, 2014). This statement,
however, needs to be tempered with the evidence of systemic underreporting
of spousal violence (see Willis 2011), which was one of the reasons that mandatory reporting was introduced. As Morley stated, "When you sit down and
ask a woman why [she wants to drop the charges], she will say 'I want him
home because the kids are crying for him; he's a good father when he's sober'"
(field notes May 16, 2014). Although those within the protective legal system
acknowledge that women have their reasons for not obliging their victim status, the disjunct between this need for coercion to ensure women's rights to be
free from violence and the women's own attitude to the violence is excluded
from the legal process, in order for it to proceed.

The often-heard perception from older Anangu that "*kungkas* (women)
always the ones to start it off," that women precipitate the violence, may also
be an outcome of women's increasing self-assertion. The interrelational behaviors of young women who are accused of triggering violent responses may
be a sign of generational change, as discussed in the previous chapter, and as

suggested by Rogers. A trigger may be her frustration at his gendered chauvinist expectations, which have not altered to align with her own increasing assertions of equality, as Nakamarra(2) stated:

> To me, I think men are selfish . . . They don't help you with this and that, and you think "selfish." And women are trying to make their relationship good, and they start, [but] how can they make it good without yelling and screaming at them, and then [they] get hurt. (field notes October 15, 2014)

I asked the men who participated in the Papunya family violence program: "Who do you think is to blame for your violence?" (the options being: your wife, the police, your family, you?). Three of the seven men I interviewed during the early stages of the program attributed blame for their violence to their spouse. Another participant indicated that it was "me and my family." One participant did not really engage with the question but responded with "somebody." The participant who was mandated to attend because of his involvement in a payback (referred to as a "riot" by police) stated that it was "[the other community's] fault" because they traveled to his community for the payback. Only one of the men acknowledged his role: "Everything is me; I started drinking, stole that grog, and got silly." Note, however, that although "silly" may have an Aboriginal English meaning as used here, it nevertheless suggests a lightened sense of responsibility.

This perspective from some Anangu in the community, that women are actually not the victims but, rather, incite the violence that ensues and so are therefore at least partly to blame, is not unaligned with the formal legal system; through the operations of the defense and the court processes and, indeed, through the sentiments of the broader public. For instance, the prevalence of "mitigating circumstances" that the men's defense routinely use mirrors this Aboriginal community perception, as I discuss with Nampitjinpa(2), as she also raises the issue of custody of the children, if he were to go to jail:

> Nampitjinpa(2): Family, the *wati* [male] family would have to look after them—I wouldn't let the little ones stay with the *kungkas* [females]. I would keep them away from her. The father's in jail, you know. Why would I send his kids to you? You're the troublemaker now. You always put him in the jail, all the time.
>
> SH: So the *kungka* puts him in jail?
>
> Nampitjinpa (2): All the time now. Every day, every day.
>
> SH: But was it her fault that he went to jail?

Nampitjinpa (2): Mmm—her fault. And that's why they [family] tell her: "Go to the court [and] tell him to make them drop [the] charge[s] *punganyi*" (hitting/physical violence), you know.

The following case study, or incidence, illustrates how this pattern of gendered blame shifting is replicated within the legal system. It is drawn from the experience of an Anangu woman of my generation who was one of my language teachers during the mid-1990s when I was undertaking my PhD field research. She was killed by her spouse in 2011.

Defense for Provocation: Mitigating Circumstances

Kumanytjayi's spouse was convicted of her manslaughter in March 2012, almost exactly one year after her death.[13] According to the local paper at the time: "Prosecutor Stephen Geary told Justice Southwood that the pair had been drinking alcohol and had had an argument about the woman's infidelity prior to the stabbing" (*Northern Territory News* 2013). The state prosecutor thus introduces what appear to be mitigating circumstances, so-called evidence one might expect the defense team to mention. That they were both drinking and that Kumanytjayi's apparent infidelity is introduced both serve to justify the violence as manslaughter—not as murder. As the local *Centralian Advocate* newspaper reported at the time: "There were signs of a struggle, consistent with other assaults, but there was nothing out of the ordinary" (2012). This statement could perhaps be read as "out of the ordinary for the Aboriginal population," as the headline on page 5 of the *Northern Territory News* reads "Wife Killer Sent to Prison" (in small type at the bottom of the page). In line with CAALAS practice, the defendant was encouraged to plead "guilty," and so his sentence was reduced by 25 percent to a total of three years without parole.

According to the Northern Territory Criminal Code:

> Murder may be reduced to manslaughter if the conduct of the deceased provoked the killing. The provocation generally needs to be of a kind to have actually caused the accused to lose self-control but also to be of the kind that could have induced an ordinary person to have so far lost control as to have formed an intent to kill or cause harm to the deceased. (Section 158 of the Northern Territory Criminal Code)[14]

Reducing this killing to manslaughter was therefore possible, even though, according to the evidence, "The offender said 'I will stab you with a knife,' and he took a black handled knife from his clothing. He held the knife in his right hand and he stabbed the victim once in her inner left thigh. The blade of the knife punctured the victim's femoral artery" (transcript of the Northern Territory Supreme Court February 27, 2013).

The argument for not charging the defendant with murder is also that his violence was not premeditated, but it seems to me that having a knife at the ready would suggest otherwise. Or was weaponry at the ready also "nothing out of the ordinary"? The use of knives in Aboriginal spousal violence, as a readily available household item in central Australia, *is* common, according to Lloyd (2014: 103). But does the ubiquity of this weapon make it a less serious crime? He did plead guilty, after all. This standard practice by the defense team to advise their predominantly male clients to plead "guilty" seems a cynical act. One would have to ask if admitting guilt actually had any bearing on the offender's subjectivity: do the men who plead guilty feel remorse? Or is this lesser sentence also reflective of the limitations of the legal system when faced with Aboriginal clients as reluctant witnesses, so that pressing on for a trial of murder would confront the difficulties of proof.[15] Thus, in many such cases, the only witnesses are other family members, who may be fearful to be involved in these formal legal processes because of the parallel customary law concerns of payback, discussed in the previous chapter.

Stephen Southwood, the presiding judge in this case, provided his usual sentencing logic in an article where he states:

> The punishment must fit both the offense and the offender. A sentencing court must realistically assess the objective seriousness of the crime within its local setting and the court must have regard to the particular subjective circumstances of the offender. (2007: 3)

He also notes that "often Aboriginal offenders are also victims" (2007: 3). Although this statement seems to be an attempt to accommodate for the structural violence of colonization, his sympathy is directed toward Aboriginal men. This morally relativist approach is also thus a deeply gendered one where, as Bolger observed, mainstream law reflects the interests and experiences of men, be they non-Aboriginal or Aboriginal (1991).

This silencing of women and their marginal status within the legal system could be read as a mirrored effect of "bad victim": they don't play their role, so we too will dismiss their status as "victim." The victim was effectively on trial and her victim status found to be illegitimate. This diminishment of violence against Aboriginal women also intersects with the public discourse via the media. This discourse, as the dominant gaze, combines with the instrumentalizing effects of the legal system, such that these mitigating circumstances are readily interpreted as tolerance of violence against women and minimized as trivial and deserving of only minimal or symbolic punishment. These mitigating circumstances—recall that "the pair had been drinking alcohol and had had an argument about the woman's infidelity prior to the stabbing"— suggest that the victim has forfeited her rights; she was found as undeservingly provoking her own demise (see Howe 2002). This partial defense of provocation:

> endorses outmoded attitudes that women are the property of their husbands . . .
> The defense of provocation operates as a "licence" for men to kill their female
> partners who dare to assert their own autonomy by leaving or choosing a new
> partner. (Bradfield, in Fitz-Gibbon 2013: 4)

This standard sentencing practice of taking into account mitigating effects— such as the alcohol consumed and the fact that they were arguing about her infidelity—sends the opposite message to that being fostered and promoted by the Cross Borders Indigenous Family Violence Program. This program strongly reiterates the message that the man needs to "walk away" no matter the supposed provocation: the "jealousing," swearing, drinking, and so on. The offender is taught that he does have options; it need not be inevitable that violence occurs. So the Northern Territory legal system is out of step with the responsibilization discourse that is being actively promoted by its own Department of Corrections through the Cross Borders Program, as will be discussed in the following chapter. Likewise, provocation has been abolished as a partial defense to murder in other jurisdictions, such as Western Australia, Victoria, New Zealand, and so on, in an acknowledgment that it was conceptually flawed. As Fitz-Gibbon states:

> It was designed and implemented in England in the 17th Century by men and
> for men and consequently its current operation in the 21st Century is gender
> biased and upholds notions of male honour that are out of line with current
> community values and expectations of justice. (2013: 2)

Although I am not advocating longer prison sentences for Aboriginal male violent offenders, the research suggests that this formal justice response is symptomatic of a deeply subordinating system that appears to have changed little since Bolger's research over twenty years ago. As the standard sentencing practice accepts provocation as a defense, the state is proscribing a woman's agency in her own death. Even in death she is the bad victim.

Furthermore, the ubiquity of incarceration for Aboriginal men, given that it occurs often and for short periods, such as three years for manslaughter, also diminishes its effect. After violent offenses, traffic and motor vehicle offenses are the second most common type of offense for which offenders receive jail time, notably for driving while disqualified (Pyne 2012: 3). As Blagg states, "The prison cell is considered a normal place for an Aboriginal person . . . that's institutionally ingrained" (in Ting 2011). As very few of the family of the accused appeared at the hearing for this manslaughter case in Alice Springs (notably the daughters were not there), they are disengaged and alienated from the legal process. And as they heard the details only secondhand (the incident occurred in Alice Springs), the daughters whom I have spoken with are not convinced of his guilt and appear to place little or no blame on him. Rather, they are looking forward to his return so that he can assist with caring for his grandchildren and also provide some leverage in regaining the house they lost when he was imprisoned. They have since been moving between neighboring communities and houses.

"You're in a Trapped World": An Anangu Justice Response to Gender Violence

Because of the extremely high incarceration and recidivism rates of Aboriginal men, in the Northern Territory and across Australia, critical criminologists have for some time reflected on alternatives to the system of incarceration. Such alternative approaches coalesce around concepts of restorative and/or transformative justice. Ideally, the concepts underpinning restorative justice attempt to accommodate collective rights and universal legal rights, that is, both the customary rights of and within groups and the rights of the individuals within these groups. Restorative justice is seen as an alternative to retributive justice or the mainstream criminal justice response. As Blagg states: "The concept of restoration refers to the remaking of the status quo through the re-integration of the offender into his/her network of significant others" (Blagg 1998: 6). For many Anangu in the Papunya region, there is little correspondence with the legal system, as it operates fundamentally as a system of incarceration, and their notions of social justice.

The question of an appropriate justice response to this gender violence in Anangu terms, rather than a merely legal response, was raised with eight people: six women in their late thirties and older and two senior community men. I took inspiration from a set of questions that the feminist criminologist Nancarrow had developed (2006: 97) to ascertain the differential priorities between Indigenous and non-Indigenous women, though my questions were asked only of Anangu. They were the most important element in a justice response for men's violence against women:

- Sending a message that violence is wrong (by holding a public meeting, for instance)
- Restoring relationships (between the spouse and/or families)
- Holding men accountable (by sending them to jail)

I asked each person to place these in order of priority. I clarified the definition of "justice" as "restoring a wrong, getting the situation straight again, say if a *wati* and *kungka* have had an argument and it's the *wati* who has hit the *kungka*, then how to manage that." I described "sending a message" as holding a community meeting to reaffirm that violence was wrong, and "holding men accountable" was described as sending them to jail. In Nancarrow's terms the first two options are forms of restorative justice, rather than retributive justice. Both of the senior men and one senior woman prioritized sending a message, then restoring relationships, and finally holding men accountable. Three of the women had "restoring relationships," followed by "sending a message," and finally "holding men accountable." So six of the eight respondents had "holding men accountable by sending them to jail" last. According to one of these senior men, Sammy Butcher, jail should be reserved for murderers, rapists, and child abusers. Commenting on the perspectives of Aboriginal (Warlpiri) MP Bess Price, who supports the zero-tolerance approach of her Country Liberal Party, Butcher stated:

SB: Bess Price was saying that it's good for young people, if they're in trouble they need to go to jail, they're being fed, they get a good bed, [and] they're in the company of family. That's all wrong, that's all wrong. We should be helping young people to stay and sit down with them—the other way around . . . Jail is not the answer. I think I jumped up on the bed [when I first heard this].

SH: You got really angry, did you?

> SB: I did, yeah . . . You're in a trapped world—where people don't want to see
> you outside—they want you inside. (field notes August 22, 2014)

The exceptions to this pattern of putting last "holding men accountable for their violence," as this was explained as jail, were two women who had both been physically abused by their drunken husbands in the last two years, one of whom, Nangala, had a long history with an abusive partner. In Nangala's case, jail has operated as a form of respite, and it seems to be understood by family that he, not her, is the initiator of the violence—specifically when he is drunk. So there is no blame on her for engaging with this state system. Likewise, the other younger woman, Nakamarra(2), who was knifed in her lower leg by her drunken partner, immediately called the police when it occurred in an Alice Springs town camp. Neither of these women was blamed by their partner's family for his subsequent imprisonment. It seems that they were the innocent victims, although this is not so clear-cut for many others. As Nungurrayi explains:

> Sometimes men should go in if he hits his wife, but sometimes it's in self-
> defense. *Kungka* can really hurt her partner if she's really serious. She might
> ask "Why is he hitting me? He might be got someone else," and she hits him
> back. We say, you've got to stop hitting your wife. My husband didn't hit me.
> (field notes 2014)

Although I have only touched on restorative justice here, as Blagg states it should not only mean a restoration to the status quo, as that is also an aspect of the problem that needs to be transformed (1998: 6; see also Cripps and McGlade 2008; Behrendt 2002; Strang and Braithwaite 2002). Using forms of restorative justice for violence against women is strongly contested under the dominant neoliberal paradigm of being "tough on crime," as well as the paradigm of equality of access to the law that women's rights advocates, most feminists, and prosecutors strongly endorse. Furthermore, under the 2007 NTER any reference to customary law in sentencing is no longer possible (via Commonwealth legislation), while the Northern Territory mandatory sentencing regimes further compounded this lack of discretion by the magistrates. Nevertheless, the work of the Cross Borders Indigenous Family Violence Program, which may be imposed as a condition of a suspended or partly suspended sentence, operates as a form of "justice reinvestment" (see Pyne 2012: 8 and Schwarz 2010). Such programs also aim to be transformative in a recognition that incarceration rarely resolves the problem. In the Indigenous context, this increase in punitiveness also must be understood within the broader context of intersecting oppressive systems that operate in the lives of both "victims" and "perpetrators." Embedded in the "tough on crime" rhetoric is thinly concealed racism (see Coker 2002; Coker and Macquoid 2015).

Same but Different: Deterministic Geography

The complexity of applying mandatory forms of mainstream protection models in central Australia is not only compounded by the dispersed, small, and mobile populations. As this region traverses four state borders there has also been "a variance in jurisdictional responses to identical problems" (Fleming and Sarre 2011: 31). The three borders of South Australia, Western Australia, and the Northern Territory are particularly fluid in Anangu terms, as communities of language speakers move between settled communities as they overlap these borders. In an attempt to deal with this fluidity of movement and thus the potential evasion of perpetrators, these three jurisdictions all enacted identical legislation under the Cross-Border Justice Scheme in 2008 and 2009 (see Jamieson 2008; Charles 2009). However, the issue to consider is whether this scheme's overriding purpose to "enhance . . . victim services" per Inspector Gordon (2012) becomes yet another piece of policing law that results in further incarceration of Aboriginal people, predominantly men, and whether it also serves to reduce Anangu women's suffering. According to Charles, its "extensive reach reorders the operations of the criminal justice system" (2009). This is because magistrates who work across this region will be able to aggregate many more criminal files at the same time, potentially increasing the imprisonment rate.

Papunya, and the other communities in the Haasts Bluff Land Trust, is in the northernmost catchment of this Cross Borders region. The new police station in Kintore, near the WA border, is known as a multifunction remote police facility. However, although the Anangu communities of focus here are in this Cross Borders Justice region, and the Cross Borders Indigenous Family Violence Programs are also held there, the Ngaanyatjarra, Pitjantjatjarra, and Yankunyjatjarra (NPY) Women's Council does not operate there. According to one of their fact sheets, they were influental in the establishment of the Cross Borders Justice scheme and have been actively supportive of it since its inception (NPY Women's Council 2010).

The NPY Women's Council Charter against domestic and family violence states:

> All women and children have the right to live their lives safe and free from domestic and family violence and sexual assault. And, this service declares that Aboriginal women and children should be offered the full range of protective measures that women and children can expect elsewhere in Australia. (NPY Womens Council 2011)

This approach, as endorsed and led by senior Anangu women who initiated the Domestic and Family Violence Service in 1994 as part of the work of the broader Council, can find no equivalence in other parts of the Northern Territory. Most of its focus is on communities in northern SA and the east of WA; it operates only in communities in the far south of the Northern Territory. This punitive approach, which seeks the same protective measures for Anangu women as for the mainstream, was well ahead of public sentiment when it was established. Although they may not frame the approach as feminist, it is proactive in prioritizing services for women as individuals, thus as separate from their partners and from their families, if their families are not protective. It appears to contrast with the restorative justice approach that Anangu from Papunya were advocating. When I mentioned the lack of a similar service for women in central Australia to Aboriginal MP from Papunya Alison Anderson, her response was, "We don't want our men in prison." So although there appears to be universal support from non-Aboriginal people for the NPY Women's Council, as an NGO operating through a moral economy of compassion and drawing from the familiar protective models, this is not the case for Aboriginal people. According to an NPY Women's Council staff member in Alice Springs, a non-Aboriginal staff member was:

> kicked out of [the southern NT community of] Mutitjulu; she was blamed for putting sons and grandsons in jail. But we say that the police put the men in jail—they act as the independent umpires, not us. When men complain that the Women's Council are locking men up, as they still do, that's what we say: "It's not us, it's the legal system, the law." (field notes July 12, 2013)

As discussed in the previous chapter, the Guiding Principles of the NPY Women's Council are drawn from social justice, equality, and access to services—especially the police. As a staff member stated, "The issue was that women didn't have the same access to the criminal justice system that other women had, and there was a big skew in keeping Aboriginal men out of jail to the detriment of women victims" (field notes April 15, 2013). Like legal prosecutors, such as Morley, the discourse the NPY Council use is of "female victims" and "male perpetrators." As I mention the relatively recent mandatory reporting of domestic and family violence in the Northern Territory, an NPY Women's Council staff member states:

> We've always had the approach that assumes mandatory reporting; this is nothing new for us . . . and our mandatory reporting threshold is lower, anyway—that came from our board of Anangu women who will report *any* violence. (field notes April 15, 2013)

Although clearly there are strong female community leaders that make up the NPY Women's Council, whether they are representative of women across the region is tested by the underreporting in this region, as in others (see Mullighan Enquiry 2008 for SA; Gordon et al. 2002 for WA; Willis 2011). They also indicate in their 2012–2013 annual report: "Violence against women and children is still a serious issue in the NPY region." As the rates for domestic violence offenses seem comparable across these three states, it suggests that the reporting from within families (ideally the informal mandatory approach has been adopted within families), as the NPY Women's Council indicates, does not (yet) seem to be the standard practice. And that, similarly to the NT, the majority of the reporting is still by the police. So it seems open to question whether this service, which "has always had a strong focus on ensuring the criminal justice system provides women with the necessary protection from domestic and family violence" (NPY Women's Council 2011) has been more successful than regions such as the Haasts Bluff Land trust in the NT that have not had any.

Nevertheless, I cannot in this brief discussion elaborate on the extent of the support, including ongoing case management and community education that women and girls, as part of the NPY Women's Council region, have access, relative to other women in the NT. The NPY Women's Council were also instrumental in supporting the Cross Borders Indigenous Family Violence Program as a community-based offender rehabilitation program. Attendance at this program operates as part of sentencing or parole and, depending on the severity of the violent offense, in the NPY region of WA and SA it can operate as an alternative to jail. As such, there is clearly some support for forms of restorative and transformative justice.

Are these mainstream models of protection, as strongly advocated by the NPY Women's Council and currently all states and territories, the most appropriate for Anangu women given the locally contested context of their application? Finding the balance between keeping men out of jail and with their families, while also ensuring women's and broader community safety, is the conundrum. Because of the multiple and intersecting forms of marginality, including the geopolitical marginality of remoteness, one avenue to change is exposure to this approach of women's rights as human rights—using a less formal approach. As Margaret Smith, NPY Women's Council Chairwoman, articulated:

> Today there are many Anangu and other people living, working and visiting Aboriginal communities who speak up against domestic violence, who say that it is wrong and that there is no place for it . . . I see these people as heroes standing in the gap between victims and perpetrators. Anangu need these heroes because without their presence, perpetrators of domestic violence and child sexual abuse would go unchallenged. (in NPY Council 2010)

Conclusions

According to Douzinas, "The greatest achievement of rights is ontological: the rights contribute to the creation of a human identity. This function precedes and determines their protective role against public (and later private) power" (2007: 7). The multiple and compounding factors that mitigate against this protective role for Anangu women were examined in this chapter in terms of the intersections between contemporary customary structures of feeling and rights that are embodied in the formal legal system. For Anangu women, these legal systems are overwhelmingly coercive as they act *on them* as Aboriginal women but rarely *for them* as individual human rights holders. For the many Anangu women who experience the interface of spousal violence and the legal system, the juridical discourse subjugates them in its attempt to enforce their right to safety. Thus, the legal system rarely equates to the justice system for Anangu women. If, as Carothers states, "The rule of law can be defined as a system in which laws are public knowledge, are clear in meaning and apply equally to everyone" (1998: 96), then it can only be the case that "the rule of law" rarely applies to the Aboriginal population of the Northern Territory, notably, as discussed here, Anangu women.

This chapter has attempted to address the question of whether this legal system of mandatory reporting and mandatory sentencing reduces the

suffering of victims, because the "moral currency of human rights is fundamentally concerned with reducing human suffering . . . and to improve as best
we can the security of ordinary people" (Brown 2004: 452). Yet, it seems to me
that the risk is that the legal system—as it is supposed to enforce basic human
rights—has served rather to replace one kind of suffering (physical) with another: family ostracism, loneliness, and loss of children. Suffering is a deeply
ontological and intersubjective culturally informed phenomenon and cannot
be mitigated by mandatory forms of justice.

Likewise, as violence is a normative label for a culturally subjective experience; until the intimate subjective tolerance for physical pain is rejected
and personal safety via bodily dignity becomes paramount, these sufferings
compound. The individuated notion of a woman's body as demarcating her
"self" and as embodying her integrity and dignity is a fundamentally Western
notion and underpins Western feminism (see Butler 1990; Moore 1994). As a
non-Aboriginal staff member of the NPY Women's Council stated, "What we
find unacceptable, Anangu women more than tolerate. Connection to family
and country are more important, even, at times, more than their own lives"
(field notes April 15, 2013).

The generalization that all women who are involved in physically violent
incidences with their spouse are passive victims that require mandatory intervention by the state does not hold. Women who effectively engage with
this system have to conform to type; they can't be drinkers like their abusive
partners, and they can't be seen by their families as provocateurs or perhaps
even as too assertive. For the system to effectively work for them they must be
passive victims—only becoming agentic when desperate or following through
when the state intervenes. Both their families and the state have to see them as
blameless. If they do not, it is likely that their suffering will compound, without sympathy and with the loss of their spouse and, possibly, their children.

Though the perspective that many young women are not the victims but
rather incite the violence that ensues and are at least partly to blame is the
norm among some senior Anangu community members, this is also the norm
within the legal system—through the operations of the defense, the court
processes via the defense for provocation, and the sentiments of the broader
public. A particular type of femininity is being sponsored by this dominant
paradigm. The blameless women are the nondrinkers, the nonprovocateurs—
those such as Nangala and Nakamarra(2) who call the police as a standard
response against male violence for themselves and, at times, others. They *have*

internalized key elements of this rights-bearing legal subject. These women embody the discontinuities between normative familial practices and the possibility of the legal system as new protector.

The right to protection from assault has changed to an enforceable right, and those who do not help to enforce it are also now potentially criminals. As Merry states: "The meaning of the sphere of family as a private domain secluded from legal scrutiny has changed to one more porous" (2003: 352). The work of the feminist movement in making public what had been domestic and private is a huge step forward. This movement forced the state to treat violence against women like any other form of violence—as a criminal act. However, this very recent and significant legal shift to a crime-centered approach to gender violence has also narrowed the frame for understanding, and thus treating, the causes of violence.

The Aboriginal family has, again, become the key site of exposure to the legal system. In the past this exposure to the system of state protection was via children and the long policy periods that became known as the "stolen generations." Today this legal exposure is far more encompassing. Although a woman's universal right to be free from violence may appear as fundamental and mainstream, its application and its effects are not.

Chapter 5

Therapy Culture and the Intentional Subject

Article 3: Everyone has the right to life, liberty and security of person.

Article 5: No one shall be subjected to torture or to cruel, inhuman or degrading treatment or punishment.

THE FIRST PINTUPI-LURITJA translation of Article 3 was initially translated as:

> *Anangu winkiku ngaranyi kana nyinantjaku*
> (Literally, All people existing alive, sitting/being)
> *Tjukarruru kurrunpa rapa Anangu tjuta nyarantjaku*
> (In the straight or right way with a strong spirit, all the people standing)

And **Article 5** was initially translated as:

> *Wiyalpi ngaranyi krulurrintjaku nganana*
> (Literally, There will be no more cruelty for us)
> *Ananguku tjunungku tjukarruruwanangku*
> (As humans together in a straight way [implies morally])
> *Palyangku kulintjaku*
> (Good way understanding each other)

Reading both the original English and the translated Pintupi-Luritja version to the male participants of the Cross Borders Indigenous Family Violence Program in Papunya, I realized that the core message of the individual's right to be free from violence, to be safe, was so subtle as to be abstract in the extreme, in the versions of these two draft articles. Earlier, I had begun the process of interpreting the Universal Declaration of Human Rights with a husband and wife team, both trained interpreters. Sharing this draft with these violent male offenders seemed a valuable way to begin the human rights conversation with them and to also check the local veracity of the translation. It became clear, however, that if there were to be any value in this language of rights, then it needed to be grounded in this local world where various forms of violence, including spousal violence, are pervasive and where the space for engaging with supportive alternatives to violent behaviors is limited. This male violent offender program, with nine mandated participants, is one of the very few opportunities provided where agents of the state, via staff of State Corrections,[1] articulate over a four-week period the expectations that the state holds toward appropriate individual behavior both in terms of a no-violence message and more broadly. The Anangu male participants were almost uniformly unaware of the content of this modern liberal democratic social contract, as entailing specific rights and responsibilities.

This process of translation serves to frame this chapter's discussion as a dialogue between theory and practice. A first step in bridging this legal instrumentalist discourse of rights is to render its underlying sociomoral principles as locally meaningful. And although this experiment with the men in this group failed—because the antiviolence message was so opaque—it not only compelled a revision of these translations but, more important, it scaled up a sense of perspective on local practice.

Policy interventions labeled as "behavioral change programs" for the perpetrators and the victims of spousal violence are particularly rich locations for observing active attempts by the state and its agents at inscribing this new Aboriginal self. There are several of these operating in Alice Springs, including within the jail, but the focus in this chapter is on the Cross Borders Indigenous Family Violence Program (the Cross Borders Program) that operates in some remote central Australian communities. The other therapeutic intervention of relevance in this field of gender violence is the outreach service offered by the Alice Springs Women's Shelter. As therapeutic technologies, both the Cross Borders Program and the work of the outreach service actively attempt to engage with the inner subjectivities of the participants or clients, as they attempt to question and dismantle the sociocentric "structures of feeling," to use Williams's terminology, that guide or orient Anangu decision making.

These therapeutic technologies aim to foster the responsibilization discourse where individuals are variously created and taught and cajoled to become reflective outward-looking agents free to make choices that change their status from "victim" to actor and from "perpetrator" to empathizer. Indeed, it might be observed that this language of therapy is another gloss for the language of human rights.

This chapter will continue the discussion of the legal processes—including the domestic violence orders and the victims of crime compensation—that work to discourage spousal relationships. As elements in the suite of perpetrator interventions, considering Anangu women's experiences of these mechanisms allows for a rereading of the ways in which the agentic subject and the suffering subject develop.

"Don't Worry, They'll Be Lovely"

My colleague Inge Kral told me, "Don't worry, they'll be lovely," in an attempt to alleviate my ambivalence about working with this new cohort of people—mainly young Aboriginal men who were on parole for aggravated assaults.[2] Although this isn't intended to sound trite, she was, more or less, correct. Six of the seven participant men (there were to be nine) who "shared" stories of violent incidents against their partners, or in two cases ex-partners, were indeed all unfailingly polite to me and in some cases charming, as I participated in the first and final weeks of the four-week remedial violence program as a pro bono independent evaluator and sometime assistant facilitator.

There are several interconnected reasons for this civility; some are personal, as I know some of the men's elderly relatives (some now deceased), and I always attempt to communicate in Luritja, though poorly, so perhaps this gains me some respect. More pragmatically, of course, we were meeting in a highly regulated space and they were all on parole—so presumably the men were also on their best behavior. Yet, statistically, I was also aware that I, like other non-Aboriginal people, am rarely the target of Aboriginal men's aggression. Australia-wide, in 2013–2014, there were no Aboriginal homicides where the victim and the offender were strangers, according to the Productivity Commission (2014), an outcome of Aboriginal endosociality (ABC News 2015).[3] In all my time working with, living with, and visiting people in this region, I had never felt intimidated or in fear for my own safety. Although certain types of violence may be public, such as the spectacle of "payback" as discussed in Chapter 4, violence against a spouse tends to happen, as it does in other "domestic violence" contexts, behind closed doors.

Yet, all of these men (with one exception) were mandated to attend this month-long course because they had committed serious and, in some cases, multiple long-term violence against their partners. What are the state-driven attempts at shifting this cultural complex of family and gender violence that settlement and substance abuse, such as alcohol and *gunja* (marijuana), have exacerbated and that have served to so disorient subjectivity? It seems to me that the most successful methods at shifting this cultural complex of violence are through infiltrating the "structures of feeling," the customary kinship practices.

In the field of research known as desistance studies, Maruna states:

> As is reflected in the well-known aphorisim among offenders that "You reha-bilitate yourself" . . . families, jobs, age, or time cannot change a person who does not want to or make an effort to change. Presumably, individuals make a purposeful decision to marry or find work, and if these bonds sustain desis-tance, *the internal process involved in staying married or continuing to work needs to be understood if we want to understand how individuals can give up crime.* (1999: 5; italics in original)

These internal purposeful decisions are also shaped by complex external fac-tors. This chapter attempts to tease out the interactions between these internal choices and the external constraints as the state attempts to create new sub-jects. The intersecting sociopolitical and economic factors within the Aborig-inal polity and beyond it are in tension with, and challenge, the development of this new intentional self. As discussed in the previous chapter, the agentic self, as this implies choice, is intimately intertwined with personhood. An ex-ploration, rather than critical examination, of the work of these therapeutic programs allows us to consider these intercultural challenges to shed light on the complexities of making a human rights holder in this remote Aboriginal context. The principles of human rights are the framing discourse for these programs and services.

In *Governing the Soul: The Shaping of the Private Self* (1999), Nikolas Rose traces the rise of psychological expertise, and its offshoots, as social tech-nologies to refashion subjectivities. He argues that it is profoundly mislead-ing to imagine that our intimate lives, our feelings, desires, and aspirations are personal and private. Rather, the management of the contemporary self is distinctive, as the personal and subjective capacities of citizens have been incorporated into the scope of aspirations of the state as part of the techniques of administration and regulation. The most obvious manifestation of this state machinery, he argues, is the complex apparatus targeted at the child: the school, the child welfare system, and the education and surveillance of parents. The regulation of our subjective capacities has infiltrated wide and deep into our social existence (1999: 1–2).

The therapeutic technologies of interest to me are what I'll refer to as the "helping technologies," as practiced by those in the field of, but not necessarily holding a degree in, social work and allied fields such as psychology and psychiatry. They are deeply personal therapies that draw from the liberal democratic traditions of personal freedom and autonomy, as the "self" is to be the vehicle through which to achieve these states of being. This concept of "therapy" is nonetheless relatively new, becoming mainstream after the end of World War II (Rose 1999: 217). It calls to mind a self-indulgent sitcom character (Seinfeld perhaps) reclining on a couch as he revels in his daily neurosis with his therapist, in a form of secular confessional. Although this narcissistic obsession with the self might be at the extreme end of this therapy culture, the techniques or "vocabularies of the therapeutic" (per Rose 1999: 218) have expanded far beyond the couch to the repair of the maladaptive and dependent—a repair to the dominant norm. At its most fundamental, the concept of "therapy" applies to a mental health intervention that might be biomedical (prescription drugs) or through the patient talking (in free association), rather than solely the expert clinician. The latter is often referred to as narrative therapy.[4]

Nakamarra describes her new role for the Department of Children and Family Services as "making [Aboriginal] families strong" and "helping with kinship care." She gives her work title as "Aboriginal Therapeutic Counsellor." I enquire as to what she understands "therapy" to mean, and she replies: "*Wampa* [I don't know], I've never heard of it, but I've just started [the job]" (field notes April 14, 2015). This concept of reformative assistance for personal problems from expert strangers is not so readily accommodated in remote central Australia.

One who wished to study social work at La Trobe (an Australian university), for instance, would:

> Make a difference by helping people thrive. With the practical skills and knowledge from a social work course, you can help work towards a socially

just and equitable society. The strong human rights and social justice focus of our accredited course will prepare you for a range of leadership roles . . . You can expect to work in schools, hospitals, community health centers and government departments in the areas of child and family services, counseling, child protection, disability, aging, mental health, refugees and settlement, youth, substance abuse, mediation and rehabilitation. (La Trobe University nd)

Looking at two key examples of behavior change programs or approaches, it becomes clear that although the Aboriginal participants in these therapies have been variously compelled, either through circumstance, such as fleeing a violent partner, or because they are mandated by the criminal legal system, they are not without agency. And here, I depart from Rose's Foucaultian approach, as this prioritizes social structure as marked out by the all-invasive modern state, where the human subject seems merely a pawn, deluded if he or she imagines he or she can act beyond the dominant social convention. Such a state-centric approach leaves no scope for agency, for co-option, resistance, or struggle, or indeed for reimagining interventions. Examining the workings of governmentality on remote frontiers needs to be balanced and nuanced with an ethnographic understanding of how remote Aboriginal societies have evaded capture by the state (per Clastres 1989 and Scott 2009).

Nevertheless, in this context of "colonial encapsulation," to borrow Austin-Broos's term, marginality is not always a choice (2011). Taking a lead from Ortner and Wardlow, my "practice oriented approach attempts to theorise how and why social systems and structures of inequality are reproduced and/or changed through the actions of persons who are importantly shaped by these very systems" (Wardlow 2006: 5; Ortner 2005). Thus, the therapeutic interventions I analyze are not merely instructive reformative avenues for remodeling pliable naïve Anangu subjects. Yet, neither are the private lives of these subjects necessarily ungovernable, as suggested by Peterson (2010: 256). For although, to some extent, I agree with Peterson that changes are required of Aboriginal people in their everyday practices, not just changes of government policy, there are mechanisms emerging that are attempting to refashion these "private lives." Such mechanisms include these therapeutic interventions, as providing opportunity for self-reflection and to consider new forms of autonomy and personal identity.

Models of Therapy in Central Australia

The Aboriginal town camp organization Tangentyere Council in Alice Springs was the first organization that I am aware of in this region to develop a social behavior program. They called it "Sitting Down Good in Alice Springs," as translated from the Mparntwe Arrernte. Established in the early 1990s it was, according to Memmott and his coauthors, conceived and driven by Aboriginal elders to specifically manage what they referred to as antisocial behavior, principally alcohol misuse and associated violence in the town camps. It was planned as a series of integrated subprograms, with "the overall strategy to reduce the incidence of destructive behaviour through information, intervention, negotiation and education" (1993: 49). As I can't locate any follow-up material, such as evaluations, I'm uncertain whether this program was actually run. However, Tangentyere subsequently developed a "family well-being empowerment" program in 1997, which was initiated through concern over the increased number of suicides and attempted suicides in Alice Springs and the surrounding region (Tsey and Every 2000). This course is "premised on the idea that . . . government policies such as the removal of children and communal living on reserves . . . has resulted in a denial of basic human needs to generations of Aboriginal people" (Tsey and Every 2000: 509). The authors indicate that the course places particular emphasis on parenting and relationship skills, with 90 percent of the participants being Aboriginal women working in human services such as education and mental health. Although the catchment of the program seems to be primarily from Alice Springs, several Aboriginal women from Papunya have also undergone this program, as presumably others have from other surrounding communities.

As one course participant stated, "I have now become a new person," while another stated, "Knowing that I too have a right to have my needs met makes a difference" (in Tsey and Every 2000: 509–511). As the evaluation states, "The course aims to empower participants and their families to assume greater control over the conditions influencing their lives" (Tsey and Every 2000: 510). However, they also observe that "programs which aim to empower people . . . can take years and even decades to translate into health outcomes" (2000: 510). The question of whether these sorts of consciousness-raising programs are effective is a complex one, and they have to be seen in context, as one intervention occurring within a broader frame of intersecting relations of power. As one facilitator of the Cross Borders Indigenous Family Violence Program draws my attention to Maslow's hierarchy of needs, she turns the five-level "need hierarchy"—which in this case appears as a pyramid—upside down (1954). The striving for "self-actualization" (the tip) then appears at the bottom, and the basic physiological needs (nutritious food, shelter, sleep, and so on) and safety/security, as the most fundamental and essential, appear at the top. The implication is that until Aboriginal people have these most basic needs met, the challenges to self-actualization are substantial. And although this program does not actively use Maslow's American models of motivation and concepts of self-actualization, in its attempt to be a culturally responsive program, Maslow's approach is one of a range of resources it draws on. The key point this facilitator was making was a pragmatic contextual one: that their Aboriginal clients face a raft of fundamental material challenges that are not accounted for in such models.[5]

Thinking through this question of program effectiveness needs to be applied to violent offender programs and, following Gondolf, it is appropriate to ask this: "What kinds of men are most likely to change their behaviour and under what circumstances?" (1997: 86). Considering this question not only demands an expansion of evaluation conceptualization and notions of success, but it also situates more specifically the need to develop an understanding of the biographies of those Anangu men who are more open to engage with the program messages. Such "responsivity factors" (per Day and Howells 2008: 11) influence the possibility of the uptake of these learnings and principles, just as they would any other human rights holder principles.

Cross Borders Indigenous Family Violence Program

I sat in on the first and final weeks of this four-week group work program that was held in Papunya in 2014.[6] These violent offender rehabilitation programs have been operating in the Cross Borders region, with a focus on the Ngaanyatjarra, Pitjantjatjarra, and Yankunyjatjarra (NPY) lands in SA and WA, since 2007. They follow a tradition of "batterer counseling" programs that first emerged in the United States in the 1970s (Gondolf 1997: 84) and Australia in the early 1990s (Urbis 2013). From 2007 until July 2014 the program has been delivered in remote communities in this Cross Borders region on sixty-three occasions; of these, five have been run in Papunya and four in Kintore. A total of 373 men had completed it at that stage from across the Cross Borders region (Willis and Holcombe 2014: 10–13).

According to the *Men's Program Manual*, the core aim of the program is to reduce the incidence of physical and psychological harm in Aboriginal families and communities of the NPY lands by developing and delivering culturally and linguistically appropriate programs to address issues of family violence, anger management, and substance misuse (Australian Government 2013: 2). To do this, the program draws on two methodologies, the therapeutic and the educational. As the *Manual* states, "The group process is a personal journey" where the balance has to be struck with the participants talking (therapeutic group) and the educational elements of the facilitators talking (educational group). According to the facilitators, this combination of approaches is crucial as men (and increasingly women) learn to desist violent behavior. The assumption is that behavioral change is possible and is beneficial to individuals and the community. But what actually is "behavioral change," and how does this new behavior relate to or intersect with the modern human rights holding individual?

Aboriginal woman Sharon Forrester, from an Alice Springs family, played a major role in developing the *Program Manual* and also facilitated programs. When I interviewed her, she had just finished running a program for women in Warburton (one of the first in response to the increasing number of women assaulting or killing their partners). She stated:

> By default, we use the systems that are already in place—the kinship systems that are hierarchical. But then we take it all away, and everybody has to be equal, even if we have a mother-in-law and daughter-in-law. In the introduction we ensure that the focus is on the individual. We ask them questions— even simple ones that they've never been asked before: "What do *you* like to do?" "What's *your* favourite music?" Often they will answer for each other— say, with the music—"Ah, it's country—she likes country." But she might reply, "No, I don't; I just listen to it 'cause you always do; I like hip-hop." "Ah—that's the music we've heard sometimes on your iPod." And with the men, the same thing—"What's *your* favourite food?" "Ah, that's easy for him—it's KFC," and he answers, "No it's not—I just eat that food 'cause that's where you always go when we go to town." (field notes July 7, 2014)

This reminds us that the intense communality can carry with it the assumption that everyone knows everything about everyone else and that the interests of family will necessarily overlap. And although this might generally be the case, finding these differences, these discrete personal nuances, is essential in locating the kernel of the self that this program aims to develop and work on. This new self that would rather identify as independent, rather than interdependent, is also agentive, purposive, and in control. As Forrester stated, the course aims to "create a commonality of purpose for individuals that live in collective settings" (field notes July 7, 2014). For this program, this "commonality of purpose" is a shared understanding that they will not engage in or tolerate violence.

Nevertheless, they also need to create the individuals to behave in this way. There is an attempt to address this tension between the individual and the collective throughout the course, for although the language of "rights" is not present (other than my verbal input during the Papunya course), its workings are thoroughly embedded in the program. As the program materials note: "All of the discussions take place within the framework of each male [female] taking complete and total responsibility for his [her] actions" (Australian Government 2013: 5). This agentic approach can be seen in the "increasing motivation" section; as they indicate in the *Manual*, we are not telling them, we are helping them be clear about and develop their own position in relation to violence and in relation to their role/participation in family life (Australian Government 2013: 3; emphasis in original).

As one facilitator stated:

The program aims to make significant connections between an individual's thinking, his feelings, and his actions. Behavior change strategies such as this can provide an individual an opportunity for self-assessment. (field notes July 11, 2014)

Attendance at such programs is usually the first time that the participants have had the opportunity to talk about their behavior and to be reflective about its effects on their relationship and with their families. Over the monthlong course, with its group work methods of the therapeutic and the educational, discussion ranges across themes of resilience and maintenance of culture and being what they refer to as "bicultural." As the facilitators attempt to create "a new story" for the participants, they also encourage them to find ways of getting support from others for this new life story in what is potentially, for some, the beginning of a self-consciousness: an awareness of self in context. As one program facilitator stated: "There are some significant changes in some individual cases. There is an overall community change in vocabulary and understanding of behaviour-change programs" (field notes July 11, 2014).

This self-awareness is centrally concerned with "anger management" or anger regulation, because although anger may be a common experience for a vast number of people, its regulation has been observed as a common problem in offender populations (Howells 2008: 21). According to Howells, one of the triggers for anger is the perception of an "is-ought discrepancy": a perceived injustice about how the world is, rather than how it ought to be (2008: 21). In this remote population there is an explicit attempt at politicizing the participant's anger in the discussion of the changes wrought by colonization. Each group develops a time line of colonization and government intervention, prompting discussion of the changes that have occurred within only a few generations, both positive and negative. In this way colonization is introduced as the "background for violence . . . we cannot change the past but understanding things helps us work through bad feelings and put them to rest" (Australian Government 2013: 46). As Day notes: "Therapeutic interventions that address this sense of personal powerlessness, such as cognitive approaches which enable rational thinking and enhance reasoning skills [are] appropriate ways to increase feelings of self-efficacy" (Day, Nakata, and Howells 2008: 93). Likewise, as one facilitator said, "Self-reflexive thinking tools can build a new relationship with the Justice system" (field notes July 11, 2014). It is of note, however, that in this context, where the key concept of the program is that "violence is a choice" (Australian Government 2013: 8), the relatively abstract concept of structural violence is not introduced, as this implies systemic macrolevel inequalities that actively work to constrain Anangu agency. As indicated, there is discussion of the complex (positive and negative) impacts of colonization. Yet, such structural violence reminds one of formal equality—which all Australians have as a liberal technicality—versus substantive equality.[7]

Although the focus of the program is on reducing the incidence of physical violence, the concept of "violence" discussed is broadened to incorporate the many other forms of control and coercion that men exercise over their partners and other family members. Violence is elaborated as also encompassing sexual, verbal, economic, emotional, and spiritual abuse, and so on. This broadening of the concept to other forms of subjugation is now a standard approach in social policy that seems to draw on the influential work of

Evan Stark (2007). For instance, the No to Violence (NTV) Program based in Victoria uses the term "violent and controlling behaviours to cover the wide range of behaviours that violate the right of another person to safety, autonomy and wellbeing" (NTV Manual 13). Nevertheless, it was instances of physical abuse that triggered the men's mandatory attendance at the Cross Borders Program.

As the men typically have low levels of literacy (the men I spoke with had not gone beyond year nine or ten at high school) and English is their second or third language, the focus is on the visual and interactive, and a range of powerful and confronting films were shown daily. These included affirmative films of Aboriginal male role models (especially footballers) and leaders and films about the importance of fatherhood. Other films were confronting, such as *Mad Bastards*, and others were of Aboriginal women sharing their traumatic experiences of surviving spousal violence and subsequent separation.[8] Though the facilitators don't use this term, many of the role plays of the two facilitators and the films viewed resonate with Richard Rorty's notion of a "sentimental education"—which he views as foundational to the development of a human rights culture (1993: 122–123). The development of the emotional qualities of empathy and trust is a key to becoming a "rights holder"—to respecting interpersonal relations with a stranger or a family member and, as a minimum, their bodily integrity. This extending the boundaries of one's world and experiencing the vagaries of a stranger's life—through movies and alternative media—mirrors historically the emergence of the qualities of empathy in the eighteenth century when novels became widely accessible and people were exposed to the lives of others (Hunt 2007). The historian Hunt traces how the novel and newspapers began instilling this empathetic quality beyond limited provincial boundaries. As an essential component in the emergence of human rights, empathy is the precursor to imagining and extending equality, in this case to these participants' partners and families; as they learn to imagine their pain, fear, distress, or humiliation.

Part of the value in this particular program is that it is held in the men's communities and so, ideally, the men return to their partners or families at the end of each day and put into practice, if not discuss, what they have learned. As discussed in the evaluation, there is a clear need to involve partners in the program, as their behaviors can continue to challenge men to maintain their nonviolent responses. Such spousal involvement also draws them into the core messages and possibly makes them more supportive.

There was consistently strong support for a women's program from Anangu, which has since been developed, though, at the time of writing, it had yet to be run in Northern Territory communities. Forrester, the Aboriginal woman who has assisted developing this new program, revised the earlier version of the men's program, which contained Aboriginal English terms that reflected a patriarchal bias that the program was inadvertently perpetuating—so as to appear "culturally appropriate" and put the men at their ease. Terms such as "your woman" have since been replaced with "your partner" and the idea of "being boss for yourself" "has been replaced with "being in control of yourself."

It is when men or women become agents and begin to see themselves as actors that the cyclical or patterned nature of the violence is potentially recognized. The therapeutic technology enables this seeing into and beyond structure and pattern—the realization that one is embedded in a structure of sociopolitical relations. As one program facilitator noted: "By inviting them to look inside, we really then want them to look up" and, by implication, outside of themselves. This becomes an awareness beyond immediacy: beyond "culture," so potentially beyond constraint and normativity. However, in making this intentional subject there is some perversity or risk. For if this new agentic subject has nowhere to go beyond his or her community, that individual is now aware of his or her constraints, and yet the environment has not changed. That person is still unemployed, and, with limited formal education, some have no stable accommodation, the same nonsupportive family. Although a key lesson that the men and women are taught is to "walk away," and this is a key strategy that they will repeat as learned, there are often very few places to walk away to.

This brings us back to the aspirational idea of Forrester's, the Aboriginal female facilitator and clinical manager, mentioned earlier of "creating individuals who live in collective settings." If enough of these people are created, then the ideal is that a modern social imaginary will begin to take root. Charles Taylor describes this ideal modern normative order as the "mutual respect and mutual service of individuals who make up society . . . where security and prosperity are the principle goals" (2002: 96). He continues: "What may start off as theories held by a few people may come to infiltrate the social imaginary" (2002: 106). Although I am drawn to this idea, such new models of behavior need to be scaled up to become normative, and community leaders, male and female, need to model such practices. As Priscilla Collins

(CEO, North Australian Aboriginal Justice Agency) stated: "We've got some really fantastic programs out there but they are very, very minor . . . there's not a lot of those [behavioral change] programs and they're not spread right throughout the Territory and especially in remote communities where they really should be based" (ABC Radio 2014).

Women's Shelter Outreach Service: "The Cup of Tea with Two Sugars Model"

Although the four-week Cross Borders Program that operates in communities is of a different intensity to the sort of counseling that is offered by the Alice Springs Women's Shelter, the end goals of developing individual agency and self-efficacy are the same. One outreach counselor I interviewed described the sessions she held with women: "It might be called 'narrative therapy,' but we think of it as the cup of tea with two sugars model" (field notes July 11, 2014). As suggested, this "model" works at being informal by setting the women at ease over a ubiquitous cup of sweet tea. Although the Women's Shelter has been operating for over thirty years, the Outreach Service—which offers more intensive counseling than is possible at the Shelter and ongoing case management support—was established only in 2010. According to the recent evaluation, the Outreach Service "works to support the individual rights of women and their entitlement to safety and freedom within their lives and culture" (Alice Springs Women's Shelter 2013: 3). The longer-term goal of the Outreach Service is to provide an early intervention model and so reduce the demand on the emergency accommodation. In 2011–2012, 98 percent of the women and children accessing the accommodation were Aboriginal. Half of these women were from houses in the Alice Springs township, and the other half were from town camps in and around Alice Springs (Alice Springs Women's Shelter 2013). Many of those women in these town camps are visitors from regional communities.

According to one counselor, non-Aboriginal women tend to go to a friend's or family's place first after a violent incident, so the shelter is a last resort for them. The intense familiarity of Aboriginal social life discounts this as a possibility for Aboriginal women and the Women's Shelter is often their only option. As discussed in the previous chapter, certain categories of kin may feel restrained from offering the support and sanctuary required, whereas others may not want to be implicated if the violence were to escalate; at any rate, the spouse is likely to know where she has gone, no matter which family household she flees to. Even so, in 2011–2012 the shelter was unable to meet 1,098 requests for accommodation, while 864 women and children were accommodated (Alice Springs Women's Shelter 2013: 6).

Much of the work of the Outreach Service is outside of the office, visiting the women and accompanying them to appointments and advocating on their behalf. As they indicated, only 21 percent of the women interviewed for the evaluation had access to a car they could use safely (Alice Springs Women's Shelter 2013: 4). So even this basic assistance became fundamentally important. The "power of the stranger" has become the third element in intervening and bringing about social change (per Leene and Schuyt 2008). As one counselor stated: "We focus on them as an individual and their particular support networks. Sometimes there is no safe story, no safe zone for them, but we assist them in imagining an alternative; not just the idea that this is all there is for me" (field notes July 11, 2014).

One of the core beneficial aspects of these intimate interventions is often understood as the impartiality of the social worker or the therapist clinician. The fact that he or she is a stranger, an unknown, is also potentially the biggest obstacle for Aboriginal engagement with this or any similar service. This is illustrated by an early attempt at translating the concept of "discrimination," which revealed the general Anangu repulsion to strangers, that they are discriminated against: "*Anangu ngatjarri ngumpu palurru tjingurru ngurrpa tjingurru rama kunyngi palunga nintitjaku tjukarurrungku lipulangku palyantjaku.*" This translates literally as: "People [such as] strangers, disabled, they might be unknowing, they might be mad, [but] be sorry and clever and make it straight and level [morally correct]" (Nungurrayi, field notes March 6, 2013). This reflection of endosociality is a reminder that it takes time to build trust and rapport, as the primary mental health psychologist nurse who works in the Papunya region stated: "A stranger does not work well with Aboriginal people . . . shame manifesting as shyness is like a brick wall" (field notes March 17, 2015).

Talking with strangers about deeply intimate and subjective experiences is a relatively new experience for Anangu. However, by the time Anangu women are talking with counselors from the Women's Shelter, they will have already been interacting with the Service for some time via the accommodation. Nampitjinpa(1), who was one of my two language teachers during my PhD fieldwork in the mid-1990s, talks about her experience at the shelter as we discussed how she managed to leave her long-term violent partner:

SH: But then, eventually, what made you leave? A lot of *kungkas* [women] stay with their violent husbands.

Nampitjinpa(1): You know what made me forget about him? I was sitting down hoping that he was going to get another woman. It was the counselor [who] helped me to.

SH: Where was this place?

Nampitjinpa(1): The Women's Shelter. You know what, that's the only way. Women got to lock themselves up. You women you got to hear me! You got to lock yourself up! [laughs] And listen [to the counselor] and give him a chance to look for another woman, and then you'll get out free now. (field notes July 9, 2014)

Separation and the Assistance of Outsiders

When I discussed the issue of separation with a long-term resident nurse from Papunya, he indicated that, when he first moved there, approximately six years earlier, he was told that Aboriginal couples never separated and was surprised to learn of instances of separation during our discussion, such as Nampitjinpa's. Although it is still unusual for an Aboriginal woman to separate permanently from her partner, typically the father of her children, the practice does seem to be increasing. It is becoming a possibility for women as they gain a wider range of support. However, several factors need to be in place.

Nampitjinpa was prepared to remain in Alice Springs, and although this was ostensibly so that her daughter could attend high school, the location away from his family (her own mother is deceased) is an important consideration in ensuring the ongoing separation and her autonomy. Importantly, she has a reasonably high level of education, and worked as a cleaner in the hostel where she also lived for several years. She recently moved into public housing, which is highly sought after (the waiting list is typically several years). Another factor for successful separation is the preparedness of the woman to see considerably less of her primary school-aged children who, as mentioned, will often be taken by her partner's mother to live with her for extended periods, if not as an ongoing arrangement. This was the case for Nampitjinpa's two younger cousins in Mount Liebig, who she said had "copied" her and left their violent spouses, one of whom was in prison at the time of our discussion, serving a mandatory sentence for aggravated assault against her, now his ex-partner. Nampitjinpa(1) acted as a role model for these younger family members, and when I spoke with them, they readily acknowledged her influence.

However, six months after our first discussions, one of these sisters, Napaltjarri(1) has returned to her partner, whereas the other, Napaltjarri(2), had moved to the neighboring community to care for her elderly grandmother. Napaltjarri(1) said that she is very content to be single; she is not interested in a casual "boyfriend and girlfriend thing and all that jealousy." And although her two primary school-age sons were with their paternal grandmother in Kintore during her ex-partner's incarceration, on his release they are now with him. He has since repartnered and moved to a community to the north with his new partner and their new baby boy. She stated without any apparent sign of grief that they now have three boys to look after, her two and the new one. Her life is now one of relative autonomy working at the Papunya store and with plans to undertake a Certificate in Youth Work.

As we discussed her new path in life, she stated that she doesn't "hang out with married people anymore." I had thought this an interesting comment as I had observed her socializing with another woman, Napanangka, in her twenties, whom I had previously interviewed while her partner was undertaking the Cross Borders Program. I had assumed that Napanangka was still with her partner, as she was when I had first interviewed her. However, as I spoke with her again she told me that he had remained in town after his release from jail, because while they were both in Alice Springs he had physically abused her again. She fled to where her grandmother, who was also visiting town, was staying, and they called the police. The next day they both caught the Bush Bus back to Papunya while he remained and served a mandatory prison sentence. Though he is now released from jail, he has not returned to Papunya; as far as Napanangka is concerned, they are separated.

The factors enabling these separations are remarriage of the male and/or distance between the couples. This distance might be in different communities or the woman being able to seek refuge in a safe location, such as the Women's Shelter, for long enough that he repartners. This physical distance leading to emotional separation seems a key factor, as this encourages the men to transfer their emotional attentions and investment elsewhere. It is now well understood that the risks of a woman being murdered by her estranged partner are highest during separation, as his final act of control (see

Stark 2007). The role of the Women's Shelter takes on more gravitas given this propensity. As Nampitjinpa(1) said after being at the Shelter for almost three months, "You get out free now." This preparation to be nonattached and mobile pertains to a nascent regional diaspora that encompasses Alice Springs as the key node. The Women's Shelter actively enables separation as a possibility for women, by providing a "healing space," as Nampitjinpa(1) referred to it, and a space to reflect and seek independent counsel. As she stated:

> I was strong to myself. First sometimes they [husbands] trick. They trick 'em like this—"Ah, give this number [via the staff to the estranged partner]—I got phone now, at last I got a phone"—[and you call, they say] "Hello, darling, I really love you, I want to keep staying with you, I still love you," and you say from the Women's Shelter, "Hey, don't play jokes with me." And you hang up the phone, and they say "Good night," and I go to the counselor and ask her again: "He's trying to ring me on the phone, and he gave me a phone number," [she says] "He's only trying to make you happy, to look like you got to go back to him." And another day he'll ring you again [and say], "Oh, I really love you, I'm crying my tears, I really love you" [he says] and he's crying. "Hey, why are you crying? You shouldn't be crying for me." You know, and you go back again to that counselor [and] ask her again: "Hey, he's starting to waste his tears on me, why is that?" [They say] "Forget about it, leave him waste his tears," you know, the counselor talk. The next minute, no sound, I ask my son what happened to his [father's] phone [he says] "He chucked it in the water and he went and grabbed another woman now." That's his wife, new one. (field notes July 9, 2014)

This vignette illustrates the ongoing support women who want to separate require, entailing consistency of advice and the security of a place to remain while choices are being made. As Nampitjinpa(1) learned:

> It's like a circle, a round circle like a wheel, and every time that woman she got to write down, she got to think what she got to put in, what she is experiencing that thing about circle pathways, like a diary about her husband . . . Oh, that's the day that he started hitting me, swearing at me you know. That's that circle of violence . . . I learned that from the counselor, I been think, oh yeah, oh yeah—that's what he's doing—that's the circle of violence against the woman. We should be wearing those T-shirts; that's what happening. (field notes July 9, 2014)

As Nampitjinpa(1) learned to critique her intimate experience as a circle of violence, also referred to as the "cycle of violence," she is engaging with a core tool of the therapeutic intervention against family violence. She realizes that she has been caught in this repeating cycle that is visualized as a circle, whereas the men in the Cross Borders Program learn how they can stop the cycle. They learn to "catch it early/to take action to stop getting wild/getting wild/catch it early"—and so on. As Nussbaum states: "Theory has great practical value . . . giving [people] a framework in which to view what is happening to them and a set of concepts with which to criticise abuses that otherwise might have lurked nameless in the background of life" (2000: 36). This educational process enables critical thinking and also hints at a form of conscientization (per Freire 1993) as new forms of self-reflection and assertive independence are generated.

Although the focus of the legal system is on physical violence, the more pervasive form of violence is what Stark refers to as "coercive control," where women are entrapped in personal life through intimidation, isolation, and control (2007: 5). This form of violence against women partly explains the durability of abusive relationships.

The Work of the State in Discouraging Spousal Relationships

Although separation can be the most appropriate course of action for some women, and indeed more women are actively pursuing this autonomy, there are also many more women for whom separation is not what they seek. Nevertheless, there appear to be no state-sponsored mechanisms to support Anangu women and men to have respectful and safe relationships. The Cross Borders Program makes it clear that they are not a program for couples counseling, and the only Aboriginal-specific programs run by Relationships Australia (RA) focus on mediation postseparation in the development of parenting plans (see Ross, Mallard, and Fisher 2010). Yet, as RA indicates on its website, it "provide[s] counselling to individuals, couples and families to enhance, maintain or where necessary, manage changes in their relationships" (Relationships Australia). It would seem that, in the Northern Territory at least, their focus is on the "managing changes" aspects of Anangu relationships, rather than enhancing or maintaining them. Likewise, the recent RA Program—"Aboriginal Building Connections"—developed for Aboriginal women in the Alice Springs jail is for women already separated.[9] As the

Aboriginal woman who assists in the facilitation of this program stated, it concerns "talking about me and looking after myself; being strong in myself. We undertake a range of exercises and activities, to talk through what they did that has contributed to where they are at and goal setting" (field notes July 9, 2014).

As discussed earlier, Anangu women are often blamed by their in-laws for the incarceration of their spouse, and one of the compounding reasons for this is that the women themselves will break the no-contact order aspect of the domestic violence order (DVO) that they sought. Nevertheless, the police now have the mandate to order a DVO that includes as a minimum no violence but may also include no contact.[10] And during this breach of a no-contact order, further violence may occur, and in breaching the order the male partner will go to, or return to, prison. As a CAAFLU lawyer commented, "A DVO is of limited utility when the parties want to be together" (field notes July 7, 2014) and, further, if the female spouse did not fully understand the extent of the order.

The range of mechanisms where the criminal legal system encourages or coerces separation includes, as the most severe, incarceration for the violent spouse and within this system the ongoing implementation of DVOs, so that the female spousal victim is not allowed any physical contact. As Nakamarra(2), in her mid-thirties, recounts her experience:

Nakamarra(2): When [my partner] went into prison, they wanted me to get a DVO against him. But I said I'm not getting a domestic violence order; if I do get that I won't be able to go and visit him in prison, and our daughter won't be able to go and visit. 'Cause that was the best time for us to sit down and talk about our relationship.

SH: And did you get a chance to do that?

Nakamarra(2): Yes, by going and visiting him every weekend. That's how our relationship started building better. I was out at [community] and came into town every weekend to visit him—just to talk about our relationship and how we can change it.

SH: So that made him think differently, hey?

Nakamarra(2): Yes.

SH: Do you think that's unusual? Or do you think other Anangu women do that, too?

Nakamarra(2): That's unusual. 'Cause they always, they—someone else [the
    police] had a DVO against their husband, and when they wanted to go and
    visit him, they were told they can't—'cause of the DVO.
SH: But if he's already in jail, why would you need a DVO?
Nakamarra(2): Yeah, that clicked in my head—he's not going to touch me or
    throw a punch at me. He's in prison. I asked them before. I knew what a
    DVO was.

Nakamarra(2) is still with her partner, who is now out of prison for aggravated assault against her. And although she managed to negotiate the system
and had the resources to regularly visit the prison, this is not the case for
many other young women. As the long-term nurse in Papunya stated:

> If there is an assault, and the partner is taken away and locked up, the female
> may be relieved initially, but then they start to get really lonely. They wait for
> hours by the public pay phones waiting for the call. It took me some time to
> work out what it was, why they were sitting there waiting [by the phones]. So
> in fact they get so lonely that they might even regret the fact that they went to
> the clinic or reported the incident. (field notes March 4, 2014)

I had also noticed the young women monopolizing the public phone boxes for
hours sitting on chairs—as though in their own living room. This was especially noticeable before the advent of mobile telephone coverage in Papunya,
in mid-2014, as I was also queuing up in a futile attempt to call my own family
on the few public phones that were functional.

The if the woman chooses to remain with her incarcerated partner, being able
to visit him in jail is important for maintaining intimacy and trust and, as
already described, working on the relationship to improve it. According to the
Department of Correctional Services website, there are five allocated times
for visiting hours on Saturdays and Sundays, and the arrangements need to be
made over the phone between 1 pm and 3:30 pm on weekdays (Alice Springs
Correctional Centre). However, according to a police officer in Papunya: "One
of the fathers of a new prisoner wanted to visit his son in prison, and I was
surprised when I rang up and found out the only visiting hours are 2 to 4 pm
on a Sunday, and it was the first-in-best-dressed, as they have limited numbers they allow. So what chance does that give family for visiting—especially
[from] out here?" (field notes March 5, 2014).

The system of incarceration can also exacerbate and compound the psychological issues that led to the violence, which, if the couple do not separate, will continue on his (or her) release. According to a long-term Papunya nurse: "Jealousy is probably the biggest cause of problems out here [that] leads to violence" (field notes March 4, 2014). In recognition of this widespread issue, the Cross Borders Program runs a session on jealousy—which they articulate as operating like the cycle of violence and as leading to controling behavior. When I asked Nakamarra(1) about her perspectives on jealous behavior, she stated:

> Nakamarra(1): Why get jealous? It's just nonsense really . . . Like one of the family members, I used to watch her. She used to clean and wash one of our nephew's clothes now, clean blanket, food all the time, supper on the table. She was good, but he said that she was looking at that *wati* [man], this *wati*, [he'd ask] "Why are you at the telephone?" That jealous business, it's got to stop.
>
> SH: And so was he violent towards her or he was emotionally hard?
>
> Nakamarra(1): Violent sometimes when she would shop and have a conversation with one of the *watis*, could be *Walpela* [non-Aboriginal] or Anangu, and comes and takes her home and bash her up, *Yuwa* [yes], mmmm.
>
> SH: So what do you think about the idea of men going to jail for that? A good thing or not such a good thing?
>
> Nakamarra(1): Mmmm—not a good thing, 'cause [of] the worry he takes to the jail—it gets bigger, bigger, bigger. Then he'll go back in and think, "That *kungka* of mine, she's doing this and that with another *wati* without me watching her," and that thought is getting tighter and tighter. That's when they sometimes get mentally ill.
>
> SH: So when he comes back, it gets worse?
>
> Nakamarra(1): *Yuwa* [yes]. So before that happens something must happen, you know—counselling, or something with a different family to *wangkanyi* [talk with him] you know, to not worry about it. It's just silly. (field notes March 5, 2014)

Unfortunately, the short-term nature of most of the mandatory sentencing of men for domestic and family violence—where sentences range from three to twelve months—does not provide for any rehabilitation programs within prison. These men on short-term sentences are cycling through the system too quickly to access programs (see Pyne 2012). This hyperincarceration—where men are in a continuous loop in and out of jail and away from their families and communities—also feeds this insecurity whereby men become alienated from their children and their partners. As this punitive regime is directed at particular communities and groups, it acts to further create community disorganization and instability, as one of the "collateral consequences" of criminalizing spousal violence (per Coker and Macquoid 2015).

Separation and Victims of Crime Compensation

Women (and men) who are the victims of domestic violence are entitled to Victims of Crime Compensation. As a Central Australian Aboriginal Family Legal Unit (CAAFLU) solicitor indicated, "Whenever we see a DVO, we also do an assessment for compensation" (field notes July 7, 2014). As part of a broader set of legal responses to domestic violence, compensation is now seen to represent good practice, as outlined internationally in CEDAW (UN 1979) and Australia-wide in the National Plan to Reduce Violence against Women and Their Children (Australian Government 2011). According to a CAAFLU solicitor, the legal logic is "that the [compensation] money is an acknowledgment by the State that you met with avoidable harm" (field notes July 7, 2014), that the state had a duty to protect you and failed.

The benefits of compensation are understood in policy circles as both practical and symbolic, according to Barrett Meyering (2010). She indicates that the primary objective is to address the financial impact, such as medical costs and loss of income. The restoration of an individual's sense of dignity is stressed by advocates as part of the therapeutic benefit of receiving compensation (2010: 2). For Anangu women, however, there is often some confusion about the purpose of the scheme, or as a CAAFLU solicitor stated: "There is mystery around the processes; it doesn't seem transparent, and certainly not for Aboriginal women" (field notes July 7, 2014). In the Northern Territory, as for several other jurisdictions, the claims are determined by government-appointed assessors or commissioners. Thus, there is no requirement for a hearing; rather the claim is determined "on the papers" (Barrett Meyering 2010: 4). The question of whether the female victims find the process one whereby they regain a sense of dignity is doubtful. It is also of note that the process of undergoing a formal psychiatric assessment aimed solely at assessing the level of injury, which many women have to do, can itself be traumatic (see Forster and Jivan 2005).

The Northern Territory is one of two remaining jurisdictions (the other is Western Australia) where a relationship clause still operates to disallow or reduce a claim by 90 percent when the victim remains in a relationship with the perpetrator. As a CAAFLU solicitor states: "The CVSU [Crime Victims Services Unit] is careful to ensure that the women leave the offending partners and reduce [the claim] by 90 percent if she stays with him. We disagree with this. She has still suffered, so we are trying to show that this is not reasonable. It's victim blaming, saying that you're asking for it" (field notes July 7, 2014). Thus, the compensation process also becomes another legal mechanism that seeks to enforce separation after a violent incident, as I discuss with Nakamarra(2), who indicated that she is still waiting for any compensation. She is aware that when you remain with your partner you are entitled to only a small proportion of the total possible compensable amount, as she states:

> Nakamarra(2): I reckon that's still taking somebody's rights away. 'Cause it's like my body. I'm the one who got hurt and injured 'cause my knee, this one is like this, and the other is like that [showing me]. But for other ladies as well, if you're still living with your partner, you won't be able to get your money. Why is that?
>
> SH: Well, because maybe the state thinks that you're being a willing victim 'cause you're still with the person who injured you; you wouldn't want that to happen again, so you have to separate from them.
>
> Nakamarra(2): Like you wanted it to happen?
>
> SH: Maybe. . . .
>
> Nakamarra(2): But what if you've changed him? (field notes October 15, 2014)

The system operates on the assumption that, if the woman can't assume responsibility by taking a zero-tolerance approach to interpersonal violence, then the state will enforce it in a punitive way. And yet, as Barrett Meyering states: "Such [relationship] clauses fail to recognise the power dynamics of domestic violence relationships and the personal and structural barriers to leaving," as she indicates that this is why most jurisdictions have abolished such clauses (2010: 8). Such clauses also fail to recognize that women, like Nakamarra(2), may also seek to "maintain and enhance" their relationship, to borrow Relationships Australia's term. According to a clinical psychologist who acts as an assessor for domestic violence claims in Alice Springs:

> Psych: It's very middle class to recover from trauma—or to pursue "recovery." These [Aboriginal] women] are very resilient. Though the money is supposed to be for recovery to pay for counseling for physio and so on—to restore themselves to preinjury—I've never known anyone use the money

for that, or to even contemplate that. And those health services are free [for most Aboriginal women] anyway. Or even to buy items for the house—they haven't got a house to buy a new stove for . . . They nearly always say they are going to buy a vehicle.

SH: Do you think they feel validated when they get the payment?

Psych: Yes, that might be the case for the Whitefellas—the big daddy was validating that the experience was awful—but I don't think so for the Aboriginal clients. For them it's just another billabong oasis, another resource to tap. I disagree with this approach of handouts; it's very uncreative and cynical. Just a tick-a-box. I have argued this and also write this at the bottom of the client reports—that they need access to training instead. Sure she needs assistance, and I'd argue strongly for that, but it needs to be in kind; in services, rather than in money or handouts. But that's too hard for the bureaucrats. (field notes July 8, 2014)

Unlike Nakamarra(2), Nampitjinpa did leave her violent partner, and she received enough money to purchase a vehicle, as she says: "And I've still got the car. That car is helping my daughter go to school now." Her experience with the system of claiming compensation, however, was very mixed, as I ask how she felt when she got her compensation:

Nampitjinpa(1): Maybe it's more like office people you know, they want a job, they go and have job, they get big money.

SH: So the bureaucracy, the people who process this?

Nampitjinpa(1): Yeah, those people might be getting rich, not the bashed-up woman. They just want to look at their job, it's really neat, they're working.

SH: That sounds a bit cynical [laughs].

Nampitjinpa(1): Yeah! They sit down at the computer hoping to get good wages and good job just to make us look silly, us woman. You go there [to the psychologist/nurse] and tell our stories about ourselves, maybe show our *guna* [bottom] you know, we got broken here, stabbed there [pointing to body parts] get all the things naked up [undress].

SH: In front of a male?

Nampitjinpa(1): *Wiya* [no], I had a woman. [She tells you to] show that, lift that skirt up.

SH: So you did that?

Nampitjinpa(1): [You're] hoping you'll get big money, but nothing [laughs].

SH: Did you find the experience a bit humiliating?

Nampitjinpa(1): Yeah! And funny.

SH: But did it make you feel recognized that you went through that trauma?

Nampitjinpa(1): Yeah . . . mmmm. Maybe these mob sitting down and doing all this work, when the paper hits Darwin, them mob in Darwin, they make the decision, you know. (field notes July 9, 2014)

Nampitjinpa(1) was particularly frustrated, as she had an injury that she believes was not recognized in her compensation payout. And her anger over this exclusion, and hence the control that she perceived the bureaucracy held over the process, dominated much of our conversation, as she continued:

Nampitjinpa(1): I been show them my head. I . . . got split in my head—my husband been hit me on the head. [They said] no, we don't give money for that . . . They chop the head off! Ah [laughing] No head . . . women get bashed in the head, split open you know, punched in the nose . . .

SH: Mmmm, so it happens to the head all the time?

Nampitjinpa(1): Blokes aim at the woman always on the head and no compensation for the head. And now that woman got to live with that headache for the rest of her life.

SH: And is that what happens to you?

Nampitjinpa(1): Yeah, sometimes I get a headache. . . . I had it [victims of crime compensation], but I didn't get it for the head, they been chop me off . . . They only gave me $5,500. Because they been chop my answer [ignored this aspect of my statement]. So I got money from this side [touching her lower back] but not from my head . . . They not allowed to give you money for the head, it's hidden, your hair is hiding your head [damaged skull], but they don't know what went in . . . nine staple went in.

SH: So it's hidden, but you're a bit outraged by that. It sounds like it's made you cranky?

Nampitjinpa(1): *Yuwa* [yes], made me cranky, right out!

SH: Did other women say the same thing to you? That if they were hit on the head that was ignored? 'Cause if that's what the men always go for . . . ?

Nampitjinpa(1): Yeah. Hey [calling to her classificatory sister], men always go for the head, *panya* [is that right]?

Classificatory Sister: *Yuwa* [Yes]! (field notes July 9, 2014)

As I returned to Nampitjinpa(1) to check the accuracy of these quotes and ask if she wished to add anything, she replied that she is "still cranky" with the process and that she has also lost her sense of smell because of her injuries and that she still has headaches. Nampitjinpa's(1) "resilience," to draw on the psychologist's understanding of the women he has seen, can be found in her stoic attitude and wry humor.

In the Northern Territory, the standard amount awarded for the compensable injury of domestic violence is $7,500 to $10,000—though the maximum is $40,000. According to a CAAFLU solicitor, "The compensation money is spent the day it is received. The average is around $10,000. If there is no ongoing disability, there is a lower amount" (field notes July 7, 2014).

The Subjectivity of the (Physically) Suffering Subject

The suggestion that different peoples, as different cultural grouping of humans, can tolerate more or less pain and suffering than others does not sit easily with the moral foundations of the human rights discourse. How can one even contemplate culturally relative notions of physical pain and suffering when *all* human bodies are constituted of flesh and blood and a central nervous system? After all, we all have the same physical equipment. Yet, a general reluctance to identify as a suffering subject in accord with the expected behavior of a proper legal subject is one of the confounding factors that can affect Anangu women's uptake of the protective legal system. The form of suffering explored in the previous chapter was ontological, focusing on the social and emotional dimensions, but it can also be physical. And at the risk of promoting an environmentally deterministic anthropology, it seems that an element of this refusal stems from a conditioned stoicism as a deeply formative feature of desert personhood. This stoicism is not a quality that can be readily cast off, and its sweep of inclusive effects can include contesting the modern ontology of comfort (Holcombe 2015). A fundamental element of modernity is the focus on the physical comfort and security of the human individual (Chappells and Shove 2004).

Although there is some mythology around Anangu stoicism that non-Aboriginal people living in Aboriginal communities will voice opinion about, the long-time Papunya nurse's experience is that "Anangu resilience to pain is huge; often people just don't show at the clinic." He continued:

> One time a young woman in her late twenties got off the bush bus from Alice Springs with a badly broken leg. It had been broken in town, and I can't imagine how painful it must have been to have been walking on it and sitting for

hours on that bumpy bush bus [three to four hours from Alice Springs]. But this actually happened twice—another time in town she got another broken leg and again returned here to the clinic on the bush bus. Men are not as re-silient to pain as women, but given that the initiates stay out in the bush for six weeks . . . that teaches them resilience to pain. (field notes March 4, 2014)

There is now wide recognition that global self-reported health assessments for Indigenous people, for whom English is not their first language, tend to confound the biomedical data (Sibthorpe, Anderson, and Cunningham 2001), such that, although subjective self-assessments of the health of Indigenous people in remote areas are comparable with those in cities, according to the mainstream survey tools, the objective health indicators state otherwise, that remote Indigenous health is considerably worse. Sibthorpe and her coauthors state: "Arguably concepts of health do not exist as a simple continuum leading to more bio-medical constructions . . . regardless of the acquisition of illness labels both self-care and the consumption of health services may be organised in culturally distinct ways" (2001: 1663).

Multiple ramifications lead from this distinct culturally informed self-care. This conditioned stoicism and pain resilience compounds the social and familial factors that actively discourage women from reporting and/or carry-ing through prosecution of their spouse for domestic violence. Although the normalcy of violence has a contemporary relationship to the normalcy of pain tolerance, and perhaps even to a significant extent this can be found in the ge-nealogy of hardship that was a desert adaptation, recognition of such "adap-tive preferences" (per Nussbaum 2000) risks eliding more than it reveals. The risk is that although this ethnographic insight may account for patterns of behavior, it does little to unsettle the subordinate status of the women who exercise these "preferences." As Scheper-Hughes states: "It is virtually impos-sible to be continually conscious of the state of emergency in which one lives. Sooner or later one makes accommodations to it" (1995: 416). And in making such accommodations the pain and deprivation are not realized as unjust; why suffer pointlessly? (per Nussbaum 2000: 111).

Conclusions

Fundamentally, women and men need the support of their family to be free from violence. The work of the state in attempting to mandate this "freedom" is inevitably only temporary. If she stays with her violent partner and he has not had access to any form of therapy or counseling while in prison (and he needs to be in there for an extended period to access this or any educational programs), then it is highly probable it will start again on his release. As Franklin D. Roosevelt stated many years ago: "In the truest sense freedom cannot be bestowed [or in this case coerced], it must be achieved" (see also Hubbard 1908: 21).[11] These therapeutic interventions are one means of starting the conversation to inculcate this modern achievement of freedom. However, recalling that rights are never deployed "freely" but within a normative context (Brown 2000: 232), in this legal context of perpetrator interventions freedom is where "the normal biography thus becomes the 'elective biography,' the 'reflexive biography,' the 'do-it-yourself biography'" (Beck and Beck-Gernsheim 2002: 3).

As Rorty has articulated: "There is a growing willingness to neglect the question 'what is our nature?' and to substitute the question 'what can we make of ourselves?'" (1993: 115). As he continues, "We are coming to think of ourselves as the flexible protean, self-shaping animal" (1993: 115). The human rights culture is a core one of these "shapes" that modernity encourages us to make. Rorty describes the human rights culture as not only legitimate but as morally superior to cultures that don't practice such principles (1993: 116). Attempting to inculcate these principles in remote communities, however, also immediately confronts the raft of structural inequalities and the structures of feeling within which Anangu are embedded, as these both constrain the development of this "self-shaping" person. Yet, it seems to me that to locate some of this "self-shaping" work we must uncover and work on the "discontinuities," to return to Geertz, the exceptions from the norm. These include the Nampitjinpas(1) who do leave their violent partners and the young cousins who follow her lead, the Nakamarras(2) who reject the standard domestic violence order and continue to visit their estranged partner in prison to work on the relationship, and the Nangalas who seek out the police for themselves and their family. In locating these spaces—these intersections with interventions—we are closer to encouraging the development of spaces for choice making in the human rights mode and so too, to find some of the primary driving forces of change.

Experts in refashioning the "self" attempt to reorient this suffering subject, as Rose states: "The distinctive features of . . . modern knowledge and experts of the psyche have to do with their role in the stimulation of subjectivity, promoting self-inspection and self-consciousness, shaping desires and seeking to maximise intellectual capacities. They are fundamental in the production of individuals 'free to choose'" (1999: 4). This freedom is also underpinned and guided by the liberal logics of mobility (per Walzer 1990). In this case, the women are provided with encouragement to pursue marital and geographic mobilities and thus to pursue voluntary associations—untethered from family or spouse and community. Indeed, the only support from the state is for separation through the domestic violence orders and mandatory imprisonment as both attempt to compel this untethering.

It is overwhelmingly the case that rather than support a healthy spousal relationship or seek to keep families together, the state works their dissolution. As the raft of intersecting laws focus on the individual as victim or as perpetrator, so too the legal treatment of these individuals is a disembedding from family and community. Whether this is cultivated through behavioral change programs and counseling or whether this legal individual is assumed as the subject of rights and protections, the intended outcomes are the same. The paradox of these unintended consequences is that although there are some women, such as Nampitjinpa(1) and her cousins, for whom this is indeed appropriate, and they relish their newfound freedoms, there are as yet many others for whom this form of freedom adds to their suffering.

This therapeutic technology of modern subjecthood has been considered as it operates in the Cross Borders Program and the work of the Women's Shelter. These interventions are actively attempting to refashion the self of these "victims" and "perpetrators" respectively. The role these therapeutic technologies plays in the production of individuals "free to choose" and free to associate offers an insight into the incremental transformation of Anangu subjects into human rights holders.

Chapter 6

Civil and Political Rights

Is There Space for an Aboriginal Politics?

Are you the one that's gonna stand up and be counted?
Are you the one who's gonna be there when we shout it?
Are you the one that's always ready with a helping hand?[1]
                    "Blackfella/Whitefella"

THESE LYRICS, FROM A POPULAR WARUMPI BAND SONG released in 1983, became an anthem for self-determination long before the concept of "reconciliation" became an aspirational rhetoric and metaphor for intercultural justice. One reading of these lyrics is as an overt call for activating civil and political rights in the tradition of an activist human rights vision that advocates and development theorists also understand as the emancipatory potential of human rights. Yet, this song was written by non-Aboriginal man Neil Murray in the heyday of self-determination, and it speaks to his politics, reflected among other progressives from interstate.[2] At that time, Anangu were returning to their homelands in the west, such as Kintore, and establishing outstations along the way from Papunya. As a result, there was perhaps an expectation that this powerful assertion of independence would transfer to other domains, such as governing the newly established independent communities, as they were developed or transferred from the paternalistic Department of Native Affairs or from mission authorities (Peterson and

---

This chapter is dedicated to Tracker Tilmouth (Aboriginal politician, businessman, stirrer, and activist). I expect, however, given the opportunity, that we would have had a robust debate about its contents.

Myers 2016).[3] This optimism hinged on assumed engagement with the contract of citizenship that was articulated in Murray's lyrics.

This chapter traces the ways in which this contract of citizenship has remained largely tacit, until relatively recently. The politics articulated in this song reveal elements of the diverse work of rights; alternately as a rhetorical call to arms for independent political agency against the state *or* as state-centric. Either way, this call has not been widely embraced in these remote places. And though old Aboriginal men might ask, "Where has all that self-determination gone?" (Yolngu Nations Assembly 2012) in reality, self-determination as a social and political movement was never enabled by the state; indeed, as an active political project it would have been threatening to state sovereignty. And so, the agents of the state withdrew from these remote places in a form of negative freedom under the assumption that land rights were all that was required. The entailments of citizenship were never made plain. As Tsing states, "A tree that falls in an empty forest has no voice . . . they must speak in a way an audience can hear . . . my random complaints similarly have no voice" (2007: 38).

The question of what political register will be listened to and who chooses the frame on which the terms are strung begins to illustrate another paradox of Indigenous human rights. This paradox is sharply defined in Aboriginal Australia where the governing of Aboriginal peoples was initially predicated on the denial of citizenship rights. Aboriginal people did not count; there was no point "standing up" as they were not enumerated as part of the Australian population in the census until the referendum of 1967, and voting enfranchisement was inconsistent across the states and territories until earlier that decade as well. Today, however, as part of a global phenomenon, citizenship is the mechanism for neoliberal reform via the paradigms of "good governance" as embodying democracy and elements of human rights (per Hindess 2002). This reformative approach has taken some time to make its way to remote central Australia.

The core questions explored here are: How do the tensions in human rights as political entailments play out between the regulatory dimensions of citizenship and the emancipatory potential of its promise? What are the terms for an efficacious Aboriginal politics with and against the state, and is there room to expand the political imagination to incorporate alternative terms and modalities?

The terms, as framed in the powerful Warumpi band song, resonate with the terms of engagement as outlined in many of the first articles of the Universal Declaration of Human Rights that have been described as the "cornerstone" of human rights and that are notably driven by the individual: "Are *you* the *one*?" Nevertheless, these are terms defined by the state, and, although they may be part of my political consciousness, these principles for action have been less compelling for Anangu. This chapter explores both why this has been the case and what other strategies have been and are employed instead by Anangu, and other Aboriginal people in central Australia, for civil and political action. In locating these spaces of action and, conversely, spaces of conscious *inaction*, there are intersubjective articulations and borrowings between these individualist agentic approaches and collectivist approaches—as suggested by the final lyrics of "Blackfella Whitefella": "Are you the one who understands these family plans?" Such intersubjective articulations will be discussed in terms of a spectrum of exposure to these dominant political ideologies. Anangu mobility from remote communities into Alice Springs and further afield, facilitated by work for Aboriginal organizations on committees and associations, is the major mechanism for the adoption of this dominant form of political consciousness.

The idea that the state recognizes the rights only of the citizen and not of the human being (per Arendt 2003 and Agamben 1998) has a discursive truth to it. Aboriginal people had to be made citizens before they were rendered an acceptable humanity. Yet, this citizen has to comply with certain behavioral norms. In the case for Aboriginal citizenship across Australia, for many Aboriginal and Torres Strait Islander people, it is also framed by the native title act (while in the Northern Territory also by the Aboriginal Land Rights Act of 1976). As Povinelli notes, Aboriginal peoples' new place as native title holders is conditional on them retaining traditional customs *and* these customs not being repugnant to the common law (2002: 153–185). I will not examine these effects of the native title act here, as Povinelli (2002) and others, for example Smith and Morphy (2007), have done this. Rather, my focus is on discourse of governance, which has infiltrated both the native title processes and the administration of the Northern Territory Aboriginal Land Rights Act. Similarly to international postcolonial and developing states, the discourse of "governance" has become the vehicle through which to channel the political moralities of responsibilization, representation, and accountability to remote

Aboriginal communities to develop this citizen. This chapter explores the ways in which this instrumentalist discourse of good (corporate) governance operates in the space of the emancipatory potential of human rights as a poor cousin, operating instead as the authoritarian side of liberalism (Hindess 2002; Lawrence and Gibson 2007).

Shifting Registers: From Monologues to Dialogues

Politics begins when one decides not to represent victims . . . but to be faithful to those events during which victims politically assert themselves.

(Badiou 1985 in Neocosmos 2006: 357)

(Re)configuring Anangu as theoretical agents rather than as passive "subjects" (per Viveiros de Castro 2004) is the work of an expansive politics that refuses the current monological and totalizing political frame as the only reference points. Are there alternatives to the current forms of representational politics that do not serve Aboriginal people well, as neither do (most) Aboriginal voices seek to be "representative"? Although this Aboriginal circumspection about "speaking for others" has been read by some as a lack of unity and political coherence, this notion of representative politics needs to be revisited. Taking the lead from Foucault, who argued against representative politics because of the "indignity of speaking for others" (in Newman 2007: 9), my central contention is that these others should be enabled to speak for themselves and in registers that are plural and localized in "situated struggles" (Neocosmos 2006). In exploring these local struggles, I acknowledge that such writing is a form of political participation (per Hage 2012), and, perhaps ambitiously, I seek to reinscribe alternate political imaginaries in a dialogue that traverses local discussions and experiences with antihegemonic discourses led by internationalist groups, including Indigenous groups and Indigenous feminists.

Exactly how loudly Anangu as minority group interests have to "shout," especially in very remote areas, changes only marginally with each new territory and federal government. This shouting has been amplified by the corporate identities offered by Aboriginal organizations. Indeed, this is one of their key, yet largely unrecognized, values, the mechanisms of which will be explored in terms of collective rights. Increasingly Aboriginal organizations struggle for legitimacy among the plethora of other service provider organizations vying for a slice of the outsourced pie of government social services, as the example in Chapter 2 of the Waltja organization indicates. Yet, Aboriginal people have not been politically inactive in the Northern Territory. As the home of land rights, indeed inalienable freehold title after the Aboriginal Land Rights (NT) Act 1976, there have been and still are powerful political voices, notably driven by the Land Councils and the scaled up "Combined Aboriginal Nations of Central Australia" (CANCA) and more recently the Aboriginal Peak Organisations of the Northern Territory (APO NT). The Barunga Statement in 1988, followed by the Kalkaringi Statement ten years later, adopted the language of Indigenous human rights to assert not only recognition but the inalienability of land and culture. And there has been a raft of submissions responding to government policies and interventions by these and other Aboriginal organizations with titles such as "Is Anyone Listening?" (CANCA 1998). Yet, Anangu such as Sammy Butcher (Deputy Chair of the CLC and former Warumpi band guitarist) have become deeply cynical that any language will be engaged with, as he states: "I went to that CANCA meeting [where the Kalkaringi Statement was signed] . . . See, did anything happen? *Wiya* [No]. All the big leaders were there, and nothing happened. [The] government—*kuya* [rubbish]. All the old men now passed away; that was fifteen to twenty years ago" (field notes 2014).

These attempts at establishing treaties, via such statements and summits, are nevertheless ongoing by various Indigenous groups, as will be discussed in relation to sovereignty. And indeed, in South Australia the Weatherill Labor government announced in late 2016 its intention of entering into treaty negotiations with the Aboriginal citizens of that state (Maher 2016). As Santos suggests, quoting Sartre: "Before it is realised, an idea has a strange resemblance to utopia. Be that as it may, the important fact is not to reduce realism to what exists" (2007: 35). Such public action remains a vital mechanism for worrying the status quo and reminding the mainstream that there are indeed alternative and diverse Indigenous interests.

Although there appears to be increasing scope for this status quo to shift toward greater recognition of certain Indigenous interests, the gaping historical deficit can be understood as a deafness, a refusal to hear. In this deafness of government, we can recognize the modern neoliberal state of assumed "completeness," to borrow Santos's concept (2002, 2007). This completeness iterates the normalcy of the powerful and deviance of the marginal, as Santos states: "If a given culture considers itself complete, it has no interest in entertaining an intercultural dialogue" (2002: 54). Introducing this notion of dialogue is to entertain the possibility of "reciprocal intelligibility" (per Santos 2002) and in doing so to actively challenge the accepted geopolitic that has rendered Anangu voices barely audible. Rose also registers this totalizing power of monologue as a form of closure against engagement (2004: 19). And although this closure may be compounded by the current neoliberal reign, it has a deep history in Australia. As Fletcher stated in the pithily named paper "Trapped in Civil Society," prior to the Second World War and at the time when governments were thinking about assimilating Aboriginal people into white society, the White Australia Policy was still in place, which meant that the communities most likely to influence the shape of civil society were those with Anglo-Celtic origins (1996: 5).

In Australia, this dialogue starts with reinvigorating the concept of "self-determination." This concept has been derisively described as a muted form of sovereignty or as a "white man's dream" (Johns 2011). However, it has to become a political concept that articulates local struggle[s]. In the *Community Guide to the UN Declaration on the Rights of Indigenous Peoples*, the three-part definition they provide of the self-determination concept is evocative, although, unsurprisingly, pursuing sovereignty is not part of the mix: (1) we have the **choice** in determining how our lives are governed and our development paths; (2) we **participate** in decisions that affect our lives; and (3) we have **control** over our lives and future, including our economic, social, and cultural development (Australian Human Rights Commission 2010: 24; bold in original). Self-determination, as Hage states, can't be reduced to only state politics or state policy. It also needs to be argued and understood as "an anti-colonial politics: a politics that is precisely directed at resisting encompassment." If this concept is perceived as only within the domain of state governmental politics, then failure is the only outcome. To continue with Hage's argument:

> The very discourse of a victorious colonialism trying to negatively essentialise self-determination by portraying its crises as an inevitable outcome generated from the mere attempt to live it. Calling for its abandonment becomes portrayed and perceived as the "rational" course of action to take. This works to mystify the fact that it is *also* the pro-colonial course of action to take. (2012: 410)

Coupling the concept of decolonization with self-determination can assist in reimagining an ethical politics that confronts the ongoing colonial project. Although uneasy with the concept of decolonization, as my pragmatic self queries the implication this concept has of a revisionist history, as part of a set of utopian ideals the concept should not be dismissed. Yet any momentum or traction it gains tends to remain on the fringe and marginalized because those who engage the concepts tend to do so with a limited audience in mind; that audience is often other Indigenous academics, rather than those structurally disenfranchised. Locating traction for a compelling alternative politics is not easy. This political imaginary of forms of liberation epistemologies can be found in Australia in the work of Indigenous scholars Rigney (1999), Moreton-Robinson (2003, 2004), and Watson (2005), for instance, and in the work of non-Indigenous anthropologist Rose (2004, 2005). Although these scholars critique and challenge what is, they also attempt to expand the repertoire of possibilities. An issue with these texts, however, is that they are deeply personalized, and in many cases those written by Indigenous scholars are explicitly racialized. For instance, while one could read "Indigenous standpoint theory" (Rigney 1999) as the "personal is political," this approach can also be read as the politics of exclusion.

Collective Rights, Collective Representation, and Aboriginal Organizations

Political rights are important not only for the fulfilment of needs, they are crucial also for the formulation of needs.

Sen in Nussbaum 2000: 96

The "Indigenous sector," as Rowse termed it, that emerged during the policy phase labeled "self-determination" from the 1970s and 1980s is a distinct not-for-profit sector.[4] The establishment of this sector was a recognition that Indigenous organizations provide more than functional service delivery; they also provide core social rights in a liberal democracy and are the vehicle through which a minority citizen group make themselves visible (Rowse 2005). These Indigenous organizations also provided the voice for the formulation of needs, as was explored in relation to the CLC Community Development Unit and the Waltja organization, in Chapter 2. The distinctiveness of this Indigenous sector, however, leaves it open for government to overlook the important role the organizations in this sector play, especially in advocacy and community development. Such roles of Indigenous sector organizations are a key point of difference from mainstream organizations, and as such they tend to fall into the third sector, the civil society sector. This sector encompasses advocacy, community development functions, and forms of local empowerment.

Although representational democracy may not serve the interests of Anangu well, with scale being a core issue, the more localized and regionalized activities of specific Aboriginal organizations can be representative. Arguably, Aboriginal peoples require corporate or collective expression of their identity, their needs, and their interests as compared to most non-Aboriginal peoples, who are recognized as contributors to social and political life simply by going about their normal business. These Aboriginal organizations also uniquely act as intercultural mediators, mediating engagement with the diffuse apparatus of the state. Martin has discussed this in terms of the need for "strategic engagement" in "a recognition that Indigenous people are not living as part of self-producing and reproducing isolates . . . [and that] within the limits imposed by the values of a pluralist society—[they should] have control over the terms of this engagement" (2003: 8–9).

In mid-2010 there were 2,342 registered Indigenous organizations under the Corporation Aboriginal and Torres Strait Islander Act of 2006, generally referred to as the CATSI Act. In addition, there are at least as many Indigenous organizations incorporated under various state regimes and the Corporations Act (2001). The vast majority of these are noncommercial organizations. An estimate of 5,000 organizations in the Indigenous sector is conservative. The roughly one Indigenous not-for-profit organization for every 90 Indigenous Australian citizens illustrates the prominence of communal organizations in Indigenous Australian life. To briefly examine why this is the case in relation to representation, we have to consider customary land tenure and what Peter Sutton has termed the "tension between atomism and collectivism" (1995). Sutton analyzes how this tendency is thrown into relief in land claims (under the Native Title Act of 1993 and the Aboriginal Land Rights Act [NT] of 1976). Such legal processes tend to compel a certain group formation, and atomism is encouraged through government direct resourcing to claimant groups, Australia-wide. He observes, as others have done, the general rule that desert Aboriginal people are the high end of the collectivist scale, whereas coastal people tend more toward the atomistic approach (however, see also Keen 1997, 2004).

These groupings—whether fluid or tending toward patrilineal clan structures—illustrate that families are the fundamental units of social identity as well as local land holding groups. The fundamental unit of the Indigenous polity is the family. Writing of local landholding groups in the Solomon Islands, Scheffler writes: "Though generally conceived as one or another kind of descent group, local groups were also elementary political factions" (1971, in Sutton 1997: 8). Sutton notes in the Australian context that family groupings are more than "factions," as the mechanism of recruitment is largely through parental filiation. These "families of polity" (per Sutton 1997) have played a major role in the flowering of the plethora of Indigenous organizations, particularly in relation to those organizations that arose in relation to service delivery and resource allocation. This issue of kinship as public, where lobbying for resources is not for a politically bipartisan group, brings with it particular issues. Moderating the resource monopoly of "traditional owners," who happen to have preexisting rights via customary law to the land on which the community is situated, is a persistent management issue, as was discussed in Chapter 2 in the new approach of the CLC's Community Development Unit. This issue of inegalitarian resource monopoly, such as in relation to the profits from the community-owned store, was a focus of journalist Russell Skelton's book about this early period of self-determination in Papunya (Skelton 2010). Although the style of the book was sensationalist and anecdotal, one traditional owner, Tjakamarra, commented in passing that "it was good to have this history out in the open, though it may not all be right [correct]."

As Niezen asks, "Is there a way to profit from human rights universalism, to apply an ethical system based ideally upon culture-transcending consensus and knowledge, without compromising distinct cultural identities or shoring up illegitimate elites?" (2003: 27). Aboriginal organizations are the basis of civil society for Aboriginal cultures that in the past had no use for such a structure. They are both drivers of positive social change and manifestations of such social change. This sector is an expression of Aboriginal political identity and allows for locally grounded strategic agency in the evolution of an Aboriginal civil society (see also Dillon and Westbury 2007). Unfortunately, the political dimension (often as conflict between Aboriginal groups) of Aboriginal-controlled organizations has received more public attention than their service delivery functions. This is one of the reasons that their contribution to the Australian not-for-profit sector has been marginalized. These multipurpose resource agencies form important sites around which Indigenous people's values and practices articulate, but also where these values and practices are contested, adapted, and at times transformed (see Martin 2003). Though many of these organizations may have been established in the first instance through the requirements of the state, to serve governmental purpose, they have inevitably come to serve and mediate distinctive Indigenous interests.

Because the Indigenous policy domain is so fluid and volatile, and indeed the only element that can be predicted is its transience, it is inevitable that moves away from reliance on the government-controlled and -initiated sector will build on and reach outward toward the private and philanthropic sectors. Perhaps ironically, in some ways the government is encouraging this, as its "confetti approach to service delivery" (Havnen, 2012) discourages attachment to particular programs. The move toward more responsive locally based enterprises that are independent of the centralizing one-size-fits-all approach and whims of government is exploratory in the arid zone, but has been anticipated in the work of Noel Pearson in the remote rainforest regions of Cape York. In one Haasts Bluff Land Trust community there are nascent plans to engage with philanthropic organizations to leverage the store profits, where according to the enterprising store manager they are formulating a policy to ensure community development (through building visitor accommodation, a youth center and café, a garage, and a community center) in a move away from the majority of store profits going to individuals (field notes November 8, 2012). In communities such as Papunya, the store and the art center (Papunya Tjupi Arts) are the only enterprises. This approach to building a locally responsive civil society through community development initiatives that are relatively independent of government process was preempted by the Central Land Council (CLC). Yet, for such initiatives to gain traction, the concept of "the future" has to be locally articulated and valued.

Non-Aboriginal people tend to have a choice about whether they will use a not-for-profit organization. However, for many Aboriginal people it is the only service choice and practical representative voice available. Aboriginal peoples, particularly in regional and remote areas, depend on their organizations for essential services that, in the case of Papunya, include the Papunya Store and the local job service provider (through the Ngurratjuta Corporation) and a regional office of the CLC.[5] Other Aboriginal organizations based there also include the Papunya Tjupi Art Centre (see Johnson 2010, 2015). Aboriginal organizations that routinely work in Papunya and the other communities of the Haasts Bluff Land Trust include Waltja Tjutangku Palyapayi and the Central Australian Youth Link-Up Service (CAYLUS, as a division of Tangentyere Council).[6] As most of these organizations are registered under the Corporations/Aboriginal and Torres Strait Islander 2006 Act/CATSI

Act) the board members are obliged to undertake "governance training." Although this has been the case for some years, in 2014 under the Conservative Abbott government's Indigenous Advancement Strategy, all Indigenous organizations that receive $500,000 in government funding in one year have to be incorporated under the CATSI Act as the "government . . . mov[es] to further strengthen governance arrangements . . . by supporting robust and accountable corporations" (Scullion 2014).

Corralled by "Good Governance"

This concept of good governance has come to capture an extremely diverse range of activities that attempt to both induce and regulate civil society. The most fundamental element of "good governance" is the public good of accountability. For the small group of Anangu in the communities of Papunya and Mount Liebig who sit on the boards of the various community organizations, including the local Board of the Regional Council, participation in "governance training" is standard fare. As Nakamarra(1) stated: "If you're an important person in the community you have to learn that governance training" (field notes 2013).

At the risk of oversimplifying this now ubiquitous concept of governance, its broad spectrum of application can be located along two axes of intent. At one end, there is the discourse of government as funding provider seeking to ensure compliance to a mainstream standard of accountabilities to government and community leaders to the community, whereas at the other end is the attempt to insert a discourse of legitimacy that attempts to balance local authoritative structures with these accountabilities. Paradoxically, although they may be driven by different values, this multivalent concept of governance is engaged for both ends, reformatory and liberatory. Nonetheless, at its heart, all of the processes and activities corralled under the label of "good governance" speak to the development of the engaged, responsible, and accountable citizen.

According to a media release from the MacDonnell shire, shire President Sid Anderson (of Papunya) stated: "We want local community members to be trained up in governance so that they can speak to other community members about what good governance is" (MacDonnell Shire Council 2014).[7] As you enter the local Papunya shire "Service Delivery Centre," a large shiny red notice reads: "Our Values: We Are—Open/Respectful/Accountable/ Inclusive and Innovative," with an explanation next to each value. Indeed, under the 2011 National Indigenous Reform Agreement, "which frames the task for Closing the Gap on Indigenous disadvantage" one of the seven "building blocks" is "governance and leadership," with the clear assumption that if training is undertaken, then "reform" will be owned:

> Strong leadership is needed to champion and demonstrate ownership of re-
> form . . . Indigenous people need to be engaged in the development of reforms
> that will impact on them. Improved access to capacity building in governance
> and leadership is needed in order for Indigenous people to play a greater role
> in exercising their rights and responsibilities as citizens. (COAG 2011: 7)

Governance training has become one of the core mechanisms for enforcing the "liberal rationality of rule," to borrow Dean's term (2002: 37). This reform represents a particular genealogy of freedom, a "promise to create individuals who do not need to be governed by others, but will govern themselves" (Rose 1996: 45). Australian political culture, like other Western democracies, places great value on freedom. However, as Lawrence Mead observed: "A free society is possible only when the conditions for order have substantially been realised . . . a 'free' political culture is the characteristic, not of a society still close to the state of nature . . . but of one far removed from it by dense, reliable networks of mutual expectations" (Mead 1986: 6, in Dean 2002: 38).

Although the Anangu shire president has a certain obligation to endorse this rule of spreading "mutual expectations," others are more circumspect. As Sammy Butcher stated:

> Well, it's good to get a little bit of advice from the [governance] training you
> get, but the real story is—where's mine—where's my governance? The big story
> I ask is where's mine, where's my governance for me . . . ? I can listen to you,
> but listen to me too. *Ngapartji ngapartji* [reciprocity]. (field notes July 13, 2015)

Likewise, at the 2013 "Strong Aboriginal Governance Summit" in Tennant Creek hosted by the Aboriginal peak organizations of the Northern Territory (APO NT 2013)[8] under the theme of "Who Makes the Decisions? Who Is in Control?," this singular regulatory dimension is challenged. As one of the participants stated: "I did my governance training, but I have my own governance through my culture" (APO NT Report 2013: 6). This struggle between "knowledge as regulation" and "knowledge as emancipation" (Santos 2002: 48) is acute in this site of governance training. Nonetheless, there can be accommodations or, as Christie has framed it, a "co-emergence" of practices (2014). As an Aboriginal woman, Pat Brahm stated at the same summit:

> Good Aboriginal governance means being inclusive, getting consensus, keep-ing your community and people with you. It means men and women together equal. Making strong decisions then doing it! Being responsive and getting things done. Making each other accountable and making sure Government are held accountable. (APO NT Report 2013: 6)

The ubiquity of the governance concept has filtered into celebrating the good corporate Aboriginal citizen in a form of "public audit ritual" (per Cowan 2014) in the biennial Indigenous Community Governance Awards. These awards have been running since 2005 and are managed by the independent not-for-profit organization Reconciliation Australia (primarily funded by the Commonwealth government). They were also a partner on a four-year research linkage project on Indigenous Community Governance[9] (Hunt et al. 2008), aspects of which critically engaged with the governance concept in intercultural terms (notably Morphy 2007, 2008 and Smith 2008). Recently, an Australian Indigenous Governance Institute[10] was established, and the APO NT has also developed an Aboriginal Governance and Management Program (in 2015 they established a "collaborative partnership" together). One of the range of governance definitions provided by the APO NT program is: "Ab-original governance solutions must simultaneously and satisfactorily meet 'mainstream' requirements of government and other funding bodies while remaining culturally legitimate and relevant to the Aboriginal social setting" (APO NT 2016). In relation to this program, CLC Director David Ross stated:

> Governance is not just a matter of service delivery, or organisational compli-ance, or management. It is about the self-determining ability and authority of clans, nations and communities to govern: to decide what you want for your future, to implement your own initiatives. (APO NT 2016)

As Indigenous governance was the theme for the annual 2012 Aboriginal and Torres Strait Islander Social Justice Report (Human Rights Commission 2012), the concept of "governance" was consolidated as a gloss for many core human rights principles. The Report notes that "good governance" has been associated with democracy and civil rights, with transparency, with the rule of law and with efficient public services" and that these are also associated with Western liberal democratic government (Australian Human Rights Commission 2012: 88). Nevertheless, as this report goes on to state that "governance is critical to achieving the aims of Aboriginal and Torres Strait Islander Peoples," hope and aspiration are invested in the governance concept. It is imagined as an amalgam of human rights standards, as "good governance and human rights mutually reinforce each other":

> The international human rights framework is, in its own right, a governance framework for governments and communities. It can be applied internationally, nationally, regionally or to more localised structures to strengthen their foundations. (Social Justice Report 2012: 96)

In the remote Northern Territory community context, Christie pragmatically dismisses the "good governance" discourse and suggests instead that "good-enough governance" is appropriate (2014). This is in response to what he refers to as the "fundamental incommensurability" between "top-down corporate governance and leadership training" and "traditional governance practices" (Christie 2014). Meanwhile, the Indigenous Community Governance Project suggested that instead of talking about "good" governance, it's more useful to talk about "effective" and "legitimate" governance (Hunt et al. 2008).

As this persistence on using glosses for fundamental principles of human rights, in this case "governance," is made visible, then the types of governance labeled "good enough governance" or specified as "effective and legitimate" have come to incorporate the foundational dimensions of a multicultural and, to borrow Santos's terms, a self-consciously "incomplete" human rights. This pluralist approach differs considerably from the governance training sponsored by the Commonwealth government, which focuses instead on the narrow dimensions of upward accountability and representation. As Indigenous organizations are attempting to manipulate the concept and reimagine its purpose, the language of self-determination is central to this recasting and does not appear in the state-sponsored versions where the practices of governance are increasingly directed at individuals.

A Collective of Individuals

Aboriginal public intellectual and lawyer Noel Pearson, in the booklet entitled *Our Right to Take Responsibility* (2000), was one of the first to actively assert the coupling of rights and responsibilities within the Aboriginal policy arena. And although unremarkable today, the implications of this policy shift for the three most recent Liberal Coalition governments is that citizenship, even recent as it is for Aboriginal people, should be undifferentiated; all individuals treated the same, with the implications of structural disadvantage dismissed.[11] This imagined community of citizens becomes a collective of individuals. This is a difficult contradiction to govern in the tension between this collective—"these family plans" (to return to the "Blackfella Whitefella" lyrics), Aboriginal organizations and individuals. On the one hand, they have to take responsibility for others, as well as freely taking responsibility as independent agents for themselves. As Hindess states:

> The liberal ideal may be for the state to rule over, and to rule through, the free activities of autonomous individuals but liberals have traditionally taken the view that substantial parts of humanity do not . . . possess the minimal capacities for autonomous action that would enable them to be governed in this way. (2002: 133)

Developing these liberal capacities as obligatory in "a project of gradually improving subject populations" (Hindess 2002: 133) occurs not only via training in "governance and leadership" but also via other policies. Because although the Australian Indigenous policy environment is slippery, even to the extent of where Indigenous issues are placed within government and departments are regularly restructured, across the political divide there has been a firm trajectory toward embedding the responsibilization discourse in all government policies and programs. The initiative of Shared Responsibility Agreements (SRAs) that emerged in 2004 was the clearest marker of this shift. As then Prime Minister Howard stated on the advent of this policy initiative, "Part of the way out of Indigenous Disadvantage is for local communities to accept personal responsibility for their own actions" (National Nine News, May 31, 2005, in Lawrence and Gibson 2007: 661).

SRAs tied welfare entitlements and discretionary "development" funding to behavioral change. As Sullivan noted: "SRA's resonated well with the public increasingly convinced of Aboriginal irresponsibility with well-intentioned public funds . . . With [the signing of each agreement] the media was invited to celebrate the gift of yet another facility to the native population in return for its promise to be good" (Sullivan 2011: 9). These SRAs were defined by the government as being agreements in which "both governments and Indigenous people have rights and obligations and all must share responsibility" (in Collard et al. 2005: 502). This rhetoric of a diffuse series of government

agencies sharing responsibility in a manner somehow comparable to those remote living Anangu who are the recipients of these services seems awkward,
even as metaphor. Yet, the government is technically the duty bearer. As the
Social Justice report for 2005 stated: "SRAs have the potential to improve or
undermine Aboriginal . . . people's enjoyment of their human rights." As they
point out, it hinges on the communities' participation in their development
and the content (Human Rights Commission 2005). Nonetheless, the concept
of an SRA operates as a form of tied aid.

Wright and Elvin undertook one of the very few "assessments" (their
term) of an SRA in the Northern Territory, in the desert community Ali Curung, to the northeast of Papunya. This was also the first and most comprehensive agreement, as they state: "Most SRAs were single issue agreements,
with a limited number of parties [only] a handful were comprehensive,
covering multiple issues with many parties involved" (2011: 5). Though two
years in preparation, shortly after signing this agreement one of the major
signatories—the Ali Curung Council—no longer existed due to the abolition
of local Government Community Councils under the new centralized system
of regional shires. Thus, the only signatory representing the Aboriginal community (out of seven) no longer existed. According to Wright and Elvin, this
had "a considerable impact on the SRA implementation: due in part to the
transfer of assets and accountabilities" to the new shire (2011: 5). As the establishment of shires was a territory-wide initiative, this situation was presumably replicated in all other communities that signed SRAs. Indeed, none of the
Anangu leaders I spoke with in Papunya could recall the term "Shared Responsibility Agreement," let alone what it comprised. Although the following
Labor government "quietly allowed SRAs to drop out of its policy tool box,"
the "policy settings" of shared responsibility have continued (Sullivan 2011:
33), as can be seen in the 2015 Northern Territory *Homelands Policy: A Shared
Responsibility*.[12] Memorandums of Understanding (MoU) have also become
commonplace, such as the community safety MoU among Papunya, the regional shire, and the local police service. "Safe communities" are another of
the seven building blocks of the National Indigenous Reform Agenda.

The Indigenous Engagement principle outlined in the National Indigenous
Reform Agenda also articulates: "Engagement with Indigenous men, women
and children and communities should be central to the design and delivery of
programs and services" (in Sullivan 2011: 107). The practical implication of
this is that the localized and regionalized Indigenous organizations that have

been established to represent collective interests are marginalized and individuals are foregrounded. However, as a core ingredient in the "effective and legitimate governance" discourse, current Aboriginal leaders, such as Central Land Council Director David Ross, now argue that taking responsibility is coupled with self-determination. As he stated in the 2013 APO NT Aboriginal Governance Summit: "I am very keen that we don't spend all our time and energy talking about what should be delivered by government . . . I am most interested in what you can do for yourselves, how you determine your own futures . . . implement your own initiatives and take **responsibility** for your **decisions** and **actions**" (Ross 2013; bold in original). In throwing out this challenge to the 100-plus Northern Territory Aboriginal participants, though acknowledging the structural disadvantages that have led to some inequalities and the "service rich, but outcome poor" context, Ross was fundamentally advocating a radical cultural shift. In doing so he was rewriting the language of the left, a language that has traditionally not been comfortable with attaching responsibilities with citizenship nor with a concrete approach to promoting these responsibilities (Kymlicka and Norman, in Rowse 1998: 79). That there is still a chasm between this new vision of moral order as "modern social imaginery" (per Taylor 2002) and the daily unfolding of social life is further witnessed in forms of liberal policing.

Surveillance and Public Capture: Coercing Civility

Isolating individual behaviors deemed unacceptable and fining individuals are part of a routine approach for noncompliance with an increasingly diverse range of obligatory behaviors. These range from fining parents for not sending their children to school[13] to fines for driving without a license, not wearing seat belts in cars, driving uninsured, drinking alcohol in the community (a proscribed area), and so on. Although some of these fines may appear to be reasonable, such as those imposed on driving without a licence, the fundamental issue in this remote context is the inevitable capture. In many of these small communities there are now police stations and thus routine surveillance. Three out of the four small communities on the Haasts Bluff Land Trust now have their own permanent police presence. And although there are some positive elements to this, for those most vulnerable within the community, the risk of overpolicing is routine.

Any Aboriginal person who appears in court and is found guilty of a charge is fined a "victims' levy" of $150, as well as facing good behavior bonds and fines for various categories of offense.[14] The pervasiveness of Anangu contact with the criminal legal system via the courts cannot be catalogued here (see Pyne 2012; Pilkington 2009). However, it was noted by one police officer that, ironically, the system of fines was an effective way for the Northern Territory government to recycle Commonwealth social security monies back into the Northern Territory coffers, given the high rates of unemployed.[15] During a court sitting at Papunya that I observed in late 2014, every person convicted had to sign the "victims' levy" form before they left the court. The fines ranged from $100 to $1,600, depending on the offense and what the individual could afford as their CAALAS legal representatives outlined how much each person had on his or her BASICs (social security) card or, if employed, in the bank. For instance, one of the approximately forty cases to be heard in the Papunya Court on that day was as follows:

> Police to an Anangu male: You are charged with driving without a licence, driving unregistered, with no insurance, no child restraint. and no seat belt on one passenger. How do you plead? "Guilty" to each. Roadside breath test was negative. CAALAS defense: He says "she [his child] doesn't listen" when asked why the children are unrestrained and asked to wear a seat belt. He has four priors for unlicensed. The magistrate states: "Dispose by way of fines." CAALAS: "He earns $1,000 fortnightly from the shire work." Magistrate states: "Once you get your license, you will then need to learn the rules." Aggregate of $800. And five times $150 victims' levy. (field notes October 17, 2014)

More than one-third of the offenses that day entailed driving infringements. During a discussion with the magistrate during the break he commented, "It would be good to know why the sentences we hand down seem to make no discernible difference to behavior, as the same people keep appearing before me for the same offenses." The driver of the vehicle, not the passengers who choose not to wear the seat belts, pays these fines, though the driver routinely states that "she been tell me to drive" and/or "he wouldn't put the seat belt on." This suggests that responsibility in this context inheres in relationships and the concomitant lack of the right to tell another person how to behave—"Put your seat belt on!" They have to do so voluntarily, and there have to be adequate seat belts in the vehicle. Likewise, saying "no" to a request for a lift, for instance (even if the potential driver is drunk or doesn't have a license), is often perceived as a rejection of a relationship. And yet even if this punitive approach was to expand the equation of "blame" to incorporate the "humbugging" family member(s) or at least those in the vehicle with the driver, this liberal logic still rests on at least two other assumptions. These are: that all Anangu value money in the same way as the broader capitalist society and thus loathe paying fines, and that there is a stigma to engaging with the criminal and civil legal systems.

Anangu Citizenship, the Right to Vote, and Democratic Representation

They always have that smiley face [on the voting card]. Then we don't see that face again for a couple of years.

Lance Macdonald, Papunya, September 4, 2015

They say that by voting you have a voice, but you don't.

Linda Leichleitner, Papunya, 2014

Disinterest or disaffection in the NT and federal political systems mirrors that of the broader public, where democracy is little more than a media spectacle of sound bites, the fetishism of the opinion polls, and the inevitable ramping-up toward elections, when the politicians actually visit. Yet, while this disaffection is intensified at the federal or Commonwealth level for Aboriginal people because of the tendency to equate democracy solely with majority rule—given that as less than 3 percent of the total Australian population they can never be part of this majority—this is not the case in the Northern Territory. In this regional administrative context, Aboriginal people are almost 30 percent of the population and control more than 50 percent of the land. In the electorate of Namatjira, where the Aboriginal land of the Haasts Bluff Land Trust lies, they are almost 80 percent of the population. Nevertheless, even when proportional representation occurs, disaffection is still the outcome for many.

According to Hill and Alport: "Determining the extent of electoral participation of Aboriginal people in any setting worldwide is notoriously difficult" (2010: 242). However, they also state that it is widely acknowledged that voter turnout is lower among these populations, as is underenrollment. The Australian Electoral Commission notes on its website that "Indigenous Australians are half as likely to enrol to vote. Those that are enrolled are less likely to vote and less likely to fill in their ballot papers correctly." For urban Indigenous activists, failure to vote might be understood as a form of political protest against illegitimate state sovereignty (Mansell 1993, in Hill and Alport 2010: 245). However, such a "protest [non]vote" is not a particularly salient issue in Papunya or Mount Liebig.

As Linda Leichleitner stated, "Some people ask—why am I ticking a box? What name looks good? It's a bit like betting on a horse at the races. A lot of people don't understand the point of it" (field notes 2014). When I asked two Anangu women in their fifties, CP and TP, if they voted, CP stated: "Some people reckon they might get fined," to the nodding agreement of TP. CP, the more senior of the two, had been recently engaged by the Australian Electoral Commission to update the Mount Liebig community electoral roll and has in the past handed out "how to vote" cards. Two sisters in their late twenties, also from Mount Liebig, stated: "We vote for any Labor government; we voted for Kevin Rudd. And if we don't vote we will get a fine. We heard that it was an $8,000 fine for not voting." This issue of being fined if one doesn't vote was raised by all Anangu spoken with, so the sense that they are coerced into this ritual of citizenship, rather than free to vote, is pervasive. Because, while voting is compulsory for all Australian citizens and hence the possibility of a fine (which incidentally is $20),[16] Anangu are routinely fined for noncompliance across a diverse range of civil, legal, and social contexts, as discussed earlier. The punitive nature of the fine, unfortunately, reduces democratic citizenship to yet another obligatory "entitlement." The fact that, according to Hill and Alport, these fines are not strictly enforced in remote Aboriginal communities matters little (2010: 246).

It was not until 1962 that all formal restrictions against enfranchising Aboriginal voters were removed in the Northern Territory, for both territorial and federal elections. Chesterman and Calligan detail the highly exclusory and restrictive electoral regulations that applied to the few potential Aboriginal voters under the 1949 Aboriginal Ordinance Act, followed by the 1957 Welfare Ordinance, where those Aboriginal people defined as "wards" could not vote.[17] They state that in 1961, out of the official Aboriginal population of 17,000 in the Northern Territory, there were only eighty-nine Aboriginal people not declared as "wards," likely those who had served in the Second World War (1997: 172–177; see also Attwood 2003: 131–160). Nevertheless, in 1961 this enfranchisement meant little, as:

> The Chief Electoral Officer was advising state and territory counterparts that the "policy of this Branch in relation to Aborigines, is not to solicit enrolment from persons who are quite incapable of understanding the law and not to enforce the compulsory enrolment or compulsory voting provisions in such cases." (in Chesterman and Calligan 2007:159)

Unlike other citizens, it was not compulsory (that is, not fine inducing) for Aboriginal people to vote until 1983, when the Commonwealth Electoral Act was amended (Sanders 2001: 160). Likewise, it was not until 1979 that the Australian Electoral Commission (AEC) established an Aboriginal and Torres Strait Islander Electoral Information Service, which encouraged enrollment and education about this aspect of citizenship. Nevertheless, there were no evaluations of its efficacy, and the conservative Howard government cut its funding when they came to office in 1996 (Hill and Alport 2010: 249). Thus, voting was reduced to a formal right, rather than a substantive right. It was not until 2010 that another program—the Indigenous Electoral Participation Program—was established. It is worth recalling that, although Aboriginal peoples have been entitled to vote for about fifty years, in regions such as the NT this right has been rendered visible, with sporadic government support, for only about thirty years (see also Sanders 2001).

Although the AEC was initially unmoved about Aboriginal voting rights, for others such as the Minister for Territories Paul Hasluck, enfranchisement was a further step in the direction of assimilation, as he stated in September 1951: "The recent native welfare conference agreed that assimilation is the objective . . . Assimilation means, in practical terms that, in the course of time all persons of Aboriginal birth or part blood in Australia will live like white Australians do" (in Kimber 1981: 21). Prior to the 1950s, this policy had been largely directed at Aboriginal people in more settled areas, leading to the removal of "half-caste" children that became known as "the Stolen Generations" (per Read 1999), while those in remote areas such as the Haasts Bluff Land Trust were under a protectionist regime, and these reserves were understood as "buffer zones" (Hilliard 1968) and "inviolable."

Within two generations of gaining the substantive right to vote, the NT has become unique within Australia in the proportional representation of Aboriginal residents via elected Aboriginal MPs at the territorial parliamentary level. In the unprecedented 2012 NT elections, in three of the four central Australian electorates three sets of Aboriginal candidates ran against each other from across the political spectrum.[18] In the electoral seats of Namatjira (which includes Papunya) and Stuart, all six candidates were Aboriginal people, including two candidates from the First Nations Peoples Party.[19] In this short section I can only touch on the volatile complexity of the formal NT political system, so my focus will be on the Aboriginal MP Alison Anderson who grew up in Haasts Bluff and Papunya and whose first language was Pintupi-Luritja, though she also speaks several other Aboriginal languages.

Anderson was first elected as the "star candidate" in 2005 for the Labor Party as the member for MacDonnell (now known as Namatjira). This result constituted a 30 percent swing against the conservative Country Liberal Party (CLP) sitting member. She was subsequently reelected unopposed in the following 2008 NT election. To date in her more than ten years as a parliamentarian, she has been a member of both major political parties, an Independent, a member of the marginal Palmer United Party (PUP), and in 2015–2016 an Independent again. According to media commentary, her volatile politics are principally driven by her beliefs:

> I left Labor because of the failure of the Strategic Indigenous Housing and Infrastructure Program; then left the CLP because they were trying to destroy Aboriginal organisations and land rights. I left the PUP because we [made] enquiries to help Aboriginal people and didn't get them, and the chaos in the party had become a national disgrace. (NT News November 29, 2014)

These are not the actions of a career politician, though the current leader of the CLP, Adam Giles, stated in the same newspaper article that she has "no political conviction."[20] On the contrary, in discussions with Anderson, she confirmed that her experience has led her to shed any party political allegiance. Instead, she focuses on which party will deliver on her principles. Given that she is an independent, no major political party has been able to do this. As she commented about another Aboriginal MP, Bess Price, who has remained with the CLP government: "She is always going to have to play the card of the CLP and we are going to play the cards of our people who got the CLP elected" (Alice Springs News online May 19, 2014). While commenting on the possibility of amalgamating central Australian electorates as impacting on Anderson's political future, NT academic Gerritsen stated that "Anderson would probably be able to win either seat: She is the only hero blackfellers have got because she ignores the whitefellers. She can campaign wherever she likes" (Alice Springs News online February 9, 2015).

Whether Anderson is called a "rebel with a cause" (Alice Springs News online May 19, 2014), "feisty" (ABC Radio 2011), "mercurial" (Sydney Morning Herald 2014), or as having a "shoot from the lip" approach (NT public servant) (field notes 2015), the point here is that this emergent lack of party political conviction may reveal more than a personal volatility. If Anderson can't seem to find her proper place in the political mainstream, then one key reason is that this system operates through an "economy of abandonment," to loosely borrow Povinelli's concept (2011). The system itself is disenfranchising: the scale of it too large, the bureaucratic processes too removed, and the policies not locally developed. Indeed, the proportional representation of government is far from being replicated in the public service bureaucracy, with only 8 percent of the public service being Aboriginal and less than 2 percent of these being in senior positions, according to Ganter (2011). Ganter found that this was even more "pronounced in Alice Springs, at the periphery of Northern Territory administration," based as it is 1,500 kilometers north in Darwin (2011: 385). Interestingly, she also found, "Every Central Australian [Aboriginal public servant she interviewed] who had left the public service in 2007 had moved into the Indigenous sector" (2011: 387; see also Arabena 2005). This sector is where Aboriginal interests are made visible and are community driven locally and regionally. As the daughter of (now deceased) early local political activist Dick Leichleitner (see Nathan and Japanangka 1983; Wright 1998: 323–325) stated:

> A lot of strong people come out of here [Papunya]. Like Alison Anderson—when you listen to her beliefs and stories, but being a politician they have to tweak it, they have to change to fit. Being an activist is much better. You can be more honest. People say about Aboriginal politicians, "But they've done nothing for us!" But I reckon they get swept up, and then they have to leave and go independent [Alison's experience], and then you get shut out. (Linda Leichleitner field notes 2014)

It seems inevitable, where the needs are so high and apparent, that there will be some disappointment, as two sisters in their late twenties from Mount Liebig stated: "We voted for Alison [Anderson] 'cause she visited and told us that if we voted for her we would get new housing and that the outstations would get fixed. But still nothing" (field notes 2014). Likewise, Sammy Butcher's perspective on the electoral process was, "It's the same cycle, and the promise is always broken. They say one thing and do another" (field notes 2015). For Anderson, at this very local level, although such criticism must be felt directly, the tension between delivering to all constituents and more specifically to family is impossible to bridge. Nevertheless, during Anderson's 2012 election trail it was observed: "It's an election campaign like no one else's: parties, policies and platforms seem to matter little compared to ties that bind" (Alice Springs News-online August 2012).

It seems to me that for Anangu, more significant than proportional representation in parliament, through electing Aboriginal MPs, is the recognition that this system of representative democracy is rather "capitalist parliamentarianism" (per Badiou in Newman 2007: 7), such that those who have the most significant influence in government policy are the most significant taxpayers and contributors to economic development. This necessarily precludes the majority of Aboriginal people in the Northern Territory. Because, although their vote might now count, this neoliberal discourse also necessarily captures Aboriginal MPs and constrains their electoral promises and what they can actually deliver, even though the 2012 election was met with much excitement with headlines such as: "It's a Knockout: How the Aboriginal Vote Won the NT Election" (Langton 2012) and "Aboriginal Voters Vent Their Fury and Change Government" (Graham 2012). For Anangu, this core ritual of democracy has, at this stage, proven itself to be a hollow one. Instead, voting for roles closer to home has far more impact, whether this is for the local bodies (now authorities) of the regional council, for the CLC, or in the past for the Aboriginal and Torres Strait Islander Commission (ATSIC, which has not been replicated; see Sanders 2005) and likewise working for Aboriginal organizations.

Situated Local Struggles

Historically, Papunya has been a site of civil activist action at the forefront of local struggles against particular NT government policies.[21] Anderson's career began as the CEO of the Papunya Community Council in 1985 where she worked for almost fifteen years before being elected to the, then, ATSIC regional council for six years before moving into NT politics, from 2005 until August 2016. Two particular disputes with government are noteworthy, as Anderson recounts the dispute over paying for electricity in Papunya:

> In 1992 PAWA [Power and Water Authority] attempted to introduce service charges for power in remote Aboriginal communities. But they didn't consult with the people. The Authority came into Papunya at 6 o'clock one morning and disconnected all our electricity. We woke up having no power! So, to let PAWA know it was not on, the community decided to go without power for 6 months and this was in the middle of winter, in the desert! We also took

all the kids out of school. PAWA soon realised that the community has to be spoken to and eventually initiated a consultation process. We agreed that we should pay for the use of power and ended up getting the system where we buy power tickets at the shop. (ATSIC Newsroom 2001)[22]

The Northern Territory ombudsman also investigated the issue and recommended that the introduction of the new system be delayed as he found that another community "had been confused over the billing scheme . . . [and that this community should] have the billing arrangement explained to them in a way they could understand" (*The Koori Mail* 1992). Anderson likewise stated, in relation to this strike, "I think one of the main problems with the consultation that goes on is that people [government] don't come and sit down and talk to people in the language that they understand . . . unless people can think and speak in their own language then those doing the consulting are missing out on a lot" (ATSIC Newsroom 2001). Dalton Abbott, another community leader at that time, also stated:

> The issue of the power billing has in a manner been the last straw for us . . . a primary issue for us, the people of Papunya, is to have the ability to affect decisions which have influence over the quality of life we are able to pursue . . . we are the people who have lived the history of Papunya. We are aware who has made all the decisions regarding where we should live and how we should live. (*Koori Mail* July 1, 1992)

During this same period, Anderson and Abbott also led a campaign to boycott the school by keeping the children at home, "as the education system was undeniably failing our children, our community and our future" (*Koori Mail* July 1, 1992). Several years later the Human Rights and Equal Opportunity Commission (HREOC)[23] visited Papunya, as one of two remote central Australian communities on the Bush Talks touring program of information gathering and human rights education. Their attention was focused on local access to education and the fact that only one percent of the regional population aged fifteen years and over attended secondary school, part of the reason being that students have to move to Alice Springs for high school (HREOC 1999: 11). Anderson is one of those very few who did so (as have her children and to schools further afield). Unlike most other Anangu residents during the power dispute that continued over the cold desert winter, Anderson had access to power via a generator, presumably like other council staff. Skelton argued that this fact infers hypocrisy; that "she should be standing shoulder to shoulder with them. It is not freezing in the council offices" (2010: 75). Yet, this mainstream education and the fact that she was not in material poverty, unlike many other Anangu residents, was an enabler for this political consciousness and subsequent activism. As Spivak asks: "Are those who act and struggle mute, as opposed to those who act and speak?" (1988: 275).

The focus at the time from the CLP government and Skelton's later reading was on the failure of these disputes. "As the [school] boycott fizzled" and "the [power] protest dragged on through the freezing winter nights, it lost momentum"; the suggestion is that Anderson and the other community leaders were merely agitators, that their tactics were, according to a CLP minister, "dictating and patronising" to the community members suffering (Skelton 2010: 75–76). Ironically, these "tactics" could be leveled at the government, as being those that catalyzed the resistance. Anderson is clearly less socially vulnerable than many of her Anangu relatives, and the suggestion is that this precludes her from inciting protest on their behalf. Yet, just because they're not the voice agitating for change, this doesn't mean that they don't need it. Perhaps it says instead that they have been long habituated to the absence of reciprocal dialogue (see also Sen in Nussbaum 2000: 139). In the media release from the Papunya community at the time they note: "As we have always stated, we simply wish to negotiate with the minister over the issue of power billing . . . [yet] the minister . . . described our actions as uncooperative and irresponsible" (Papunya Community October 15, 1992, letter). Indeed, this "power struggle" also illustrates that "the presence of power is demonstrated through economic sanctions and the ability to inflict deprivation" (Kolig 1982: 27).

These early disputes were in opposition to the conservative CLP government approach to Indigenous policy, as this government dominated the legislative assembly in the Northern Territory from self-government in 1978 until 2001. The CLP's adversarialism to specific Aboriginal interests was most prominent in its consistently opposing land claims under the Aboriginal Land Rights (Northern Territory) Act 1976 (introduced by the Commonwealth government) in costly court proceedings. This encouraged widespread Aboriginal support for the Labor Party, which was almost guaranteed the Aboriginal vote. As Tracker Tilmouth (activist, businessman, and ex-CLC chairman) observed in 2000: "For the last 20 years we've all voted Labor, they just expected us to vote Labor. It's a plantation mentality" (quoted in *New Matilda* January 24, 2013). This acceptance of the status quo, in this case the marginality of the Northern Territory Labor Party as reflective of Aboriginal marginality, was to change when Anderson was elected in 2005 as a Labor candidate. Yet, as discussed, the volatility of Anderson's party political allegiances suggests that this marginality changed little with the change of government and the establishment of proportional Aboriginal representation, as the parliamentary system has consistently failed "her people." Nevertheless, the role the formal political system plays in this equation of failure is only one element of Anangu disenfranchisement from mainstream politics.

The Citizen Agent and the Scales of Representation

The Rights of man are the rights of those who make something of that inscription.

Ranciere 2004: 303

In this realm of political participation, human rights are most needed by those who are either unaware of their existence or are unwilling, or unable, to be agentic citizens. And although many key elements of human rights are found in the euphemistic language of "good governance," whether "good enough" and self-determining *or* the coercive and instrumentalist governance, both forms rest to varying degrees on the agentic or public citizen. This citizen is not a marginal structurally disadvantaged figure. As Brown reminds us, "The more social resources one has and the less social vulnerability one brings to the exercise of a right, the more power that exercise will reap" (2000: 232).

As Beck and Beck-Gernsheim suggest, "for modern social advantages, one has to do something, to make an active effort. One has to win, know how to assert oneself in the competition for limited resources—and not only once, but day after day" (2002: 3). This consistent theme in an emancipatory politics cannot, however, absolve itself from the paradox of capture. That is, if Anangu maintain their ungovernability (including low rates of employment, education, and training, and a high value placed on family relationships), then given the current "policy settings" the controlling neoliberal hand of government will move in ever more tightly to compel engagement with the structures of enforcement and obligation to conform. That means enforcing the right to work and education, including parents being fined for not sending their children to school and undertaking training for unemployment benefits, for instance.

In a 2005 article, I had considered Anangu mechanisms of disengagement in terms of a "society against the state" (Holcombe 2005). In his 1974 seminal work of this title, Pierre Clastres examined "non-stratified stateless societies in which cultural practices are not only *not* submissive to the State model, but actively subvert it, rendering impossible the very conditions in which coercive power and the State could arise" (Clastres 1989). In analyzing the source of power in stateless societies, Clastres argued that "[hunting and gathering] society is the place where separate power is refused, because the society itself, and not the chief, is the real locus of power" (1989: 154). However, within a generation the arts of the state have become more persuasive and more persistently intrusive via their embedding across Aboriginal organizations and all aspects of service delivery, making this disengagement increasingly difficult to sustain. In the government report series entitled "Key Indicators in Overcoming Indigenous Disadvantage," participation in decision making is identified as a key to self-determination, which in turn they state is a critical part of governance. Participation, they maintain, includes both wanting to participate and feeling that one can (Australian Government 2014: 23). This needs to be recognized as operating in local political contexts, as well as the more formal level of parliamentary politics. When discussing this research with a local shire services manager on one particular community and explaining whom I was primarily talking with and interviewing, she stated:

> The talkers, they're always the same people. They must be 10 percent or less of the local community who are always involved . . . Sid [Anderson] will go around the community with his loud hailer to call people to attend community safety or other meetings, but they don't come. They stay inside their houses. (field notes September 3, 2015)

This place, like other remote communities, is an "Indigenous domain [as] the resident Aboriginal population constitutes the public" (Von Sturmer 1984).[24] And although this "public" is becoming more porous, as discussed, the community is not a flat democracy. As a result, "feeling that one can" participate in local issues is not necessarily the case. It is no coincidence that there are several families that are consistently in the public domain, the Anderson family being one of them. Some families feel that they do not have the right to be assertive in the daily community decision-making context. Indeed, the "right to speak" is highly circumscribed by context, gender, and age (see for instance Christian 2009; Holcombe 2015). And although the CLC community development unit has actively attempted to alter this pattern (as discussed in Chapter 2), all of those on their decision-making committee are the same as on the local shire authority and indeed many of the same Anangu on my interview rounds.

Perhaps an extreme example of representation and the "right to speak" is the recent contesting of this right as asserted by the most prominent Aboriginal human rights activist in central Australia, Rosalie Kunoth-Monks from the Alyawarr homelands of Utopia. She recently won the inaugural (Indigenous) Dr. Mandawuy Yunupingu Human Rights Award, has regularly been a spokesperson against the 2007 NT Emergency Response (NTER) for Amnesty International Australia (AIA) sponsored events, has appeared on the ABC television show *Q&A Program*, and so on. However, it was perhaps her major role in the political documentary *Utopia* (John Pilger 2014) that most incited local Alyawarr concern. Variously cited as a sensationalist polemic or as an exposé of gross inequality and neglect experienced by Aboriginal people—notably from that region as representative of central Australia—this film portrays the Utopia homelands as, ironically, far from utopic. Rather, it is a vision of severe material poverty such as one might see in any developing nation. Since the release of the film a "petition signed by about 60 people, describing themselves as traditional owners of the Utopia homelands, [identifies Kunoth-Monks and two relatives as] 'no longer welcome' on our homelands . . . Under no circumstances has any one person been nominated to speak for or represent us, the Traditional Owners of this area" (Alice Springs News online 2015). This recalls the "indignity of speaking for others"; in this case as these "others" are portrayed in abject poverty and voiceless (Alice Springs News online January 27, 2014). Maintaining the status of generalized Aboriginal victim comes at the cost of disabling the local voices of disenchantment and agency and instead reinscribes their "entrap[ment] in the Aboriginal reality show" as pornographic spectacle (per Langton 2007). As the film depoliticizes the local for the global politics of pity, we can see more clearly the import of Ranciere's argument that human rights need to be used in forms of political subjectivization, in the local vernacular. Yet, this correct subject of rights also has to be recognized externally. As Olga Havnen recently stated at an Aboriginal health conference:

> I am tired of the media and public commentary that is of the view that the only Aboriginal people with intellect and ideas are those with a public profile—profiles which those same media outlets and public commentators

have created. It's another form of risk intolerance—you get the views that you have cultivated and expect. It is a disservice to those who contribute daily at the coal face of service delivery. (NACCHO 2013)

And we might include here at the "coal face of the community." Nevertheless, while these local voices need to be located and enabled, the fact that there are not more of them is nevertheless a conundrum within the wider polity. As Dietz reminds us, "Citizenship must be conceived of as a continuous activity and a good in itself, not as a momentary engagement," such as voting in parliamentary elections (1987: 16). Delving further into the sociocentric forms mediating Anangu personhood assists further in clarifying this tendency to "momentary engagement."

Kuntarringu/Kuntangka: The Dual Moralities of Shame and Respect

Kunta [noun]: shyness; respectful, reticence; reluctance to be involved; has connotation of fearing to make the wrong move which may result in scolding or harm.

Hansen and Hansen 1991: 35

This coupling of shame and respect has implications across a diverse range of sociopolitical contexts and can be a debilitating emotional practice. As the province of a socialized being, shame is the most powerful emotion in Aboriginal life (Stanner 1979; Bauman 2002). It underpins the relationality and interdependence of Anangu personhood. As Bauman states, shame "is a condition to be avoided at all cost . . . shame invokes fear, the 'fear of shame'" (2002: 213). In Pintupi-Luritja, the verb *kuntarringu* is used for both shyness and respect; if you are not reticent you risk not being respectful. Yet, its effect as one of apparent shyness is debilitating in the face of a modernity that demands an active, indeed vocal, citizenry. It has been noted that "radicalism, much to the frustration of urban activists, is frequently disavowed and avoided by what are often called "tradition-oriented Aborigines" (Merlan 2007: 138). This pervasive emotion of shame plays a major role in this lack of radicalism for Anangu, as I discuss its centrality with John Liddle, the Aboriginal manager of the Ingkintja Men's Health Service in Alice Springs:

> JL [discussing the role of Ingkintja]: But what we want to do is give the guys the skills and confidence and maybe this rights stuff, so they can go out and get a job if they want to.
>
> SH: So a lot of it is about building confidence?

JL: Yes. But I don't think a lot of our mob want confidence.

SH: Does that have any relationship to this shame business?

JL: I mean, why? It's built in! We've got to get rid of that shame. I hear it all the time and people do get rid of it, but only when they're drunk. They go from that to that [gesticulating with a hand near the ground to the other over the table].[25] We've got to change that close family stuff—extend those networks.

SH: One of the definitions an Anangu woman [Nakamarra] gave me for "freedom" was "belonging to family." What's your perspective on that?

JL: No, I don't like that idea. 'Cause I reckon that's restricting, myself. (field notes December 11, 2013)

Both within the Aboriginal polity and beyond it, this moral category of "shame" discourages authoritative behavior in anything other than the very specific. Shame can be understood as one of the regulatory social instruments that ensures a dispersal of power (per Clastres 1989). Because, although there are indeed asymmetries within the community, these are both tempered *and* reinforced by the workings of shame. Although there are distinctive power differentials within the community, no one person is absolutely dominant. This ensures the context-specific exercise of power. Indeed, as a gloss for respect and restraint, the quality of shame in some contexts is highly valued as an appropriate humble demeanor, especially by the young to the more senior (see Christie 2010). Shame can operate to reproduce one's place within the social fabric, yet as Liddle suggests it can also be used to explain the reticence to "stepping up." This tension is not ameliorated in the contemporary polity by the "good governance" discourse because, as discussed, the majority evade capture. As Nakamarra further explains the relationship between shame and the families of polity:

Nakamarra: In meetings, like if you see a person is *kuntakunta*, you know, away from the group and not speaking—but he's still part of the meeting and would be connected to that country, such as in a land council meeting, or he's not ready to ask questions or not ready to put his hand up and say, "Oh I know that place, it's my *ngurra* [my country]."

SH: They might miss out?

Nakamarra: They always miss out. Some people who don't have that strong family, like all the people who have grandfathers, fathers, and mothers, they would contribute, but others miss out. You need the strong family.

As I was talking about the idea of having to "speak up for rights and claim them" with two senior community men, Amos Anderson and Sammy Butcher, Amos recalled a recent incident of a visiting television crew. He stated: "Everyone disappeared, *kuntangka* [shamed]," inferring that Anangu did not want to push themselves forward; they want to disappear from public view. As I later handed a photocopy of an article published in the (southern edition) of the *Land Rights News* to Sheila Joyce Dixon, about the UDHR translation that she had assisted with, I noticed a similar response. As she briefly viewed the photo of herself and co-translator Lance Macdonald, she immediately folded it away, muttering sheepishly "*kunta*."

This emotion has a wide range of regulatory aspects that attempt to enforce the intersubjective demeanors of avoidance protocols, such as mother-in-law and son-in-law avoidance and adult sibling avoidance, for instance (see Hiatt 1965; Bauman 2002). As shame results if these appropriate kin behaviors and taboos are neglected, this potentially compounds the risk of public speaking in a large gathering. Nevertheless, although Aboriginal communities are a complex web of largely invisible relationship protocols, the contemporary reality is that in the small settled community these protocols are also daily challenged by continuous proximity and changed spatial arrangements. Now mother-in-law and son-in-law may reside in the same house, so that the avoidance practiced is significantly modified and may involve only lack of eye contact and direct touch. However, although the "icy formality" (per Myers 1986: 159) of many kinship protocols may be tested by the contemporary polity, they are not abandoned.[26]

The fact that the Anangu structures of kin classification, also referred to as the subsection system, are sociocentric rather than egocentric has multiple ramifications for assertive individuation as a human rights holder. Myers has detailed the ways in which "kinship coordinates the complex relations of social reproduction" (see 1986: 180–218), so this theoretical and empirical material need not be repeated here. However, the significance of these sociocentric kinship categories, where each Anangu person is a member of one of eight subsections, operates as a system that enables the replacement of individuals within categories, especially important in ritual contexts, including funerals. Social reproduction is not about the particular individual but about his or her role as a kin relation, effectively anonymizing people. The individual is immersed in and enmeshed by the relational web of signification (see Ortner 2005: 38). Nakamarra's comment that "freedom is belonging to family" could thus also be equated as freedom from shame, or from freedom from the fear of shame. As Bauman states: "Shame can be avoided by the empowering experience of knowing one's proper place in Aboriginal society, of having one's identity embedded in a regional network of kin, socio-cultural practice and mutual recognition" (2002: 206).

When Liddle states that we've got to "extend those networks" and "change that close family stuff," it is in acknowledgment of the challenge in retrieving this individual from this dense familial polity in an effort to encourage "stranger sociability" (Povinelli 2001) and develop a new form of freedom based on individual autonomy. The implications of the practice of this deeply felt intersubjective modality of *kunta* offers insight into the local limitations and challenges of active citizenship across both the instrumental and emancipatory forms of universal human rights. It also suggests that a multicultural human rights will need to better accommodate elements of these family values and relational personhood.

Human Rights as an Emancipatory Script toward a "Critical Consciousness"

To date, I've focused on some core social and structural challenges for Anangu in adopting the consciousness of the citizen agent and on the authoritarian and obligatory functions of coercive liberalism—where human rights operate as a functionality to inculcate a particular civility. That is, the focus has been on exploring what is, rather than imagining what could be. This limited governmental discourse of human rights can offer only regulatory possibilities, even if some of them are the acknowledged public goods of representation and accountability. The discourse of human rights as channeled through citizenship can't be reduced to these functions only. There are other elements in the human rights discourse that act as emancipatory and that challenge the limits of both liberal paradigms and Anangu ontologies. As Santos argues, the potential for human rights as an emancipatory script rests on a cross-cultural dialogue where the incompleteness of human rights has to be recognized in the same measure as that of the local or non-Western culture. In this way (if we can bracket the essentialisms of "culture" that Santos works through) any dialogue is reciprocal, requiring "the production of a collective and participatory knowledge based on equal cognitive and emotional exchanges, a knowledge-as-emancipation rather than a knowledge-as-regulation" (2002: 48).

Countering the domesticating, rather than enfranchising, pedagogy of human rights discourse can be usefully reimagined through engaging Freire's early work with the marginalized and oppressed in terms of the sociopolitics of education (1985). There are parallels with the counterhegemonic methodologies Freire employs with that of Santos (2002, 2006); whether it is literacy education more broadly or more specifically human rights education, the same principles of social democratization apply. Freire's now iconic approach to adult literacy and education actively countered the then standard "banking" approach to learning as a middle-class, individualistic skill acquisition that maintained the status quo and indeed the passivity of the colonized Brazilian peasants with whom he worked.[27] Freire revealed how this form of antidialogical learning, where the students are passive patronized subjects, was far from neutral. Instead, his "pedagogy of the oppressed" charges the student with a critical literacy education where the goals are democratization and radical social change.

This activist and liberatory education was to be achieved through enabling a critical consciousness or "conscientization." This concept has been defined as "the process in which [people], not as recipients, but as knowing subjects, achieve a deepening awareness both of the socio-cultural reality which shapes their lives and of their capacity to transform that reality" (in Lloyd 1972: 5). Developing this critical consciousness "both initiates and supports a process by which people become aware of the contradictions in the social structures and situations in which they live, in order to change such structures or situations" (Lloyd 1972: 5). And as Freire indicates, such knowing implies that when I realize I am oppressed, I know I can transform the concrete situation in which I find myself oppressed; it implies a historical commitment to make changes. As a type of political consciousness this active discursive education is also an anticolonial movement in the vein of Fanon (1961 [2004]).[28]

I readily acknowledge the avowedly utopian philosophy of Freire and the criticism that he himself is patronizing in marking out the poor as in need of help to realize that they are hungry and oppressed. Indeed, it can be countered that "they acquiesce in their oppression because they have no other choice. To offer them hope through conscientization is worse than deceitful. What they need is for people to fight on their side, so they can overthrow the oppressors" (Zachariah 1986, in Ohliger 1995: 8–9). A single Aboriginal activist cannot alone change generations of structural disadvantage and the global capitalist system within which Aboriginal peoples are now embedded. This is clearly an impossible call, notably given the minority status of Aboriginal peoples. And Freire's politically simplistic concepts of "oppressor and oppressed" bracket oppressions within the home and community. Nevertheless, I agree with Gottlieb and La Belle that the development of a critical consciousness "should not be judged for its economic and political effects, but should be viewed as a means for understanding the mechanisms of oppression and for exploring alternatives to make society more just" (1990: 12).

My aim here is to reimagine Freire's dialogical and reflexive approach to informal education by adapting and extending it to more effectively articulate with the human rights discourse so that it becomes a more porous and engaging set of principles for interaction with government, and with family and others locally. It seems to me that the "governance training" is discursively set up as the non-Indigenous expert subject narrating to the patient listening to Indigenous objects (see Freire 1970 [1993]). To continue following Freire's methodological reasoning, rather than the domesticating indoctrination of the "good governance" training, liberation and humanization should be the intent of problem-posing human rights training. In this shared process of enquiry the incompleteness of human rights is not only recognized but reconciled with local dialogue.

An element of this reciprocal approach is to realize the UDHR as constructed knowledge—as a historical document reflective of a particular set of secular philosophies. Such critical engagement can also act as a way of rapprochement to engaging with its deeply abstract form (ironically, Freire was accused of abstract generalized writing). Yet, important for my purposes, his insistence on situating educational activity in the lived experience of participants finds ready parallels with the process of vernacularization in the translation. As discussed in Chapter 1, Freire described this as the process of "naming the world" by reading it, literally though gaining literacy.

In this reciprocal dialogue, discussions would be held about the limitations or incompleteness of human rights and how they can be bolstered or set to one side as local Anangu values are raised as more humane or more relevant. For instance, according to the UDHR, the environment has no rights because no duties can be imposed upon it (Santos 2002: 49).[29] The lack of acknowledgment of the interrelationship between humanity and the environment is a serious void within the UDHR and the two derived conventions. The environment is reduced to property, a form of capital. There is a growing awareness globally that the concept of private land ownership—whether land is owned by corporations, farmers, urban dwellers, or the state—is the major cause of environmental destruction. For instance, in Australia, since colonization approximately 90 percent of native vegetation in the eastern temperate zone has been removed for agriculture, industry, transport, and human habitation. About 50 percent of Australia's rainforests have been cleared, and the proportion of Australia covered by forest or woodland has been reduced by more than one-third (Aretino et al. 2001; see also Bush Heritage Australia).

The liberal focus on and attachment to private property rights and the singular use-value of land is a rejection of the collectively held and avowedly spiritual and familial dimensions that land holds for Anangu as custodians or stewards, rather than as owners. A Luritja translation of Article 17, "Everyone has the right to own property alone or in association with others," recognized the prevalence of the dominant conceptualization of property ownership. As a result, this translation was limited to a modern-built dwelling and politicizing the issue of "property" to make it locally relevant. The back-translation from Luritja of an early version of this Article is as follows:

> Everyone can buy a house with money to own and keep, in the city, town and bush. Aboriginal land is different. It can't be bought with money. It's for all the family and is very sacred to us.

As Santos suggests, for human rights to operate as a counterhegemonic form of globalization, the concepts must be reconceptualized as a progressive form of multiculturalism (2002: 44). In this context, this requires a redefinition of property rights to reflect Indigenous values and land tenure; such as "the land owns us; we don't own the land." That land rights became an almost singular and iconic platform for Indigenous prior rights and recognition should not obscure the ongoing values this land continues to hold, as it is interdependent with identity. Forms of development have to creatively engage with this collective interest.

The type of individuated personhood characterized in the UDHR is often opposed in a binary to the relational Anangu person as revealing rather different predispositions and priorities. Yet, we also know that although these two extremes are useful heuristics, they do not entirely speak to reality. Rather, the ideal forms they represent provide useful points for discussion, if human rights education was ever to be sponsored in remote places. Questions that encourage dialogue might include: How does the Anangu family and kinship system place limits on autonomy and freedom of choice? How do family expectations circumscribe opportunities or indeed encourage illiberal values, such as not coming to the aid of certain family members in crises of violence? On the other hand, what are the positive values of the family and its role in a strong Anangu identity, sense of place, and well-being? A contrastive discussion about the strengths and limitations of Anangu familiarity opens a dialogue with the alternate liberal social mobility of voluntary association. What are the implications of actively engaging with these mobilities— including geographic and marital mobilities (Walzer 1990)? And one might consider other connotations that the social mobility concept suggests, such as economic improvement. Furthermore, what does moving into Alice Springs from the community entail? And what are the risks and benefits of leaving one's abusive partner? Such discussions begin to open up an emancipatory discourse on civil rights that includes discussion about local structural oppressions and local illiberal values.

As Santos suggests: "The true beginning of [such a] dialogue is a moment of discontent with one's own culture, a sense that it does not provide satisfactory answers to some of ones' queries, perplexities or expectations." This educational dialogue, if it were to happen, would create a "self-reflective consciousness of cultural incompleteness . . . as a precondition for a balanced and mutually reinforcing relationship between global competence and local legitimacy" (Santos 2002: 44–55).

The first "human rights advocacy training" program for Indigenous "community leaders and advocates" was in 1990, though the Diplomacy Training Program (DTP) at the University of NSW, with a concerted program developing in 2007 in partnership with the NGO Oxfam Australia.[30] Although this program is "consciousness raising," this can be distinguished from Freire's overtly political socially reformative concept of conscientization. From the materials gleaned there appears to be little problematizing of the discourse; rather it is concerned with "building knowledge of human rights," learning about the international human rights framework, and exploring ways in which to hold governments to account. Terms used for the training materials focus on "capacity building." This educational process is still along the reformative line, without acknowledging the limitations of human rights for Aboriginal people. There is the risk that this program follows the liberal logic of much adult education, as predominantly a creation of the middle classes serving middle-class interests with a focus on individual self-improvement and so subordinating the social justice aim of adult education (see Lloyd 1972: 13). The prerequisite for English and that the programs are held only in towns and cities have largely precluded Aboriginal people from remote communities. Indeed, an evaluation of the program stated that many alumni requested that the program be expanded to remote communities (Kent 2010).

Nonetheless, the program as an educational intervention is clearly powerful for some. A comment from a participant who attended the program held in the Northern Territory town of Katherine stated: "It made me realize just how bad we are being treated—it's not right! We have to try and change it" (Fred Hollows Foundation 2012: 4). Another participant stated, "I have always known that what Aboriginal people are going through now and in the past is wrong and that we have to keep talking and making noise, no matter how small and low we might think we sound" (Fred Hollows Foundation 2012: 4). As this evaluation pointed out: "Although people already possessed a strong sense of 'right' and 'wrong' based on their own experiences of injustice, the . . . training provided an international framework to apply their experiences to resulting in increased confidence to speak out" (Fred Hollows Foundation 2012: 4).

The Diplomacy Training Program appears to be the only human rights training program for Indigenous Australians that has had a consistent presence, though it is dependent on a range of philanthropic funding sources. Shortly after the conservative Abbott government gained office, they ceased funding grants for human rights education, which had been tendered out to NGOs. Such funding had been a core plank of the Human Rights Framework that operated, briefly, instead of a National Bill of Rights. A diverse range of organizations applied for this funding to host workshops and develop educational materials, including the Aboriginal and Torres Strait Islander Healing Foundation. Although the work of these organizations, some hosting only a once-off series of workshops, must be applauded, it seems to me that the missing link for this transformative potential of human rights can be found by moving beyond asserting rights as principally a series of claims, usually against the state. Rather, it lies in enabling political struggles in which human rights crystallize the moral imagination and provide power in political struggles, both in larger terms against the state and in the local normative context, within the family and community (in Neocosmos 2006: 358).

Sovereignty Claims and Counterclaims: Possibilities to Expand the Political Imagination

The UN Declaration on the Rights of Indigenous Peoples rests on the fact of sovereign states, including those that are colonial products such as Australia. The global system of states is the "bricks and mortar of the UN system" (Niezen 2003: 116), and so it is no surprise that the Indigenous rights elite, such as Megan Davis and Les Malezer, realize the futility of the exercise in pursuing an independent sovereign Aboriginal state; it would invalidate the Australian constitution. As Davis states: "We can't maintain a historically adversarial position with the State" (in National Congress of Australia's First Peoples 2013: 50). And thus "self-determination" has become the proxy for sovereignty in international circles (Brown 2007: 173). So, although the pursuit of legal sovereignty for some in Indigenous Australia may have been bracketed, the concept of sovereignty in this version of the debate has perhaps been overdetermined by international law in a pragmatic reading. This hasn't deterred other Indigenous groups, such as "First Nations Asserting Sovereignty" and the "Aboriginal Provisional Government" (who also offer an Aboriginal passport) from asserting their own independent versions.[31] Ironically, as these groups reject the sovereignty of the Australian State and hence the legitimacy of the constitution, they assert their own mirror image, in a striking example of interpellation, as the First Nations Asserting Sovereignty state:

> The only thing we want is our sovereignty recognised, our Law and culture recognised; and by having each Nation map their own country and then negotiating their own Treaty packages will we be able to gain a type of satisfaction in this war of attrition against the colonialists. (Anderson 2015)

The "Act of Sovereign Union between First Nations and Peoples 2013" in Australia mimics the style and structure of UN Declarations in co-opting the language of republics and sovereign embassies (there are four First Nation sovereign states, according to the website). Yet, this Act and its utopian ideologies also represents the unquenched thirst of decolonization in an attempt to assert independence within the given frames of reference (see Brown 2007: 172). Nevertheless, the limitations of co-opting existing statist notions of sovereignty are clear. This radical separatism of "separate nations mapping country" is premised on idealized homogenous and bounded territorial cultural groupings that are not likely to have existed prior to colonization and don't exist in the real diasporic world where Aboriginal people are now embedded among the political economy of the settler colony (see Benhabib 2002).

The Indigenous feminist movement has reimagined this concept of sovereignty beyond the hierarchical inegalitarian and bounded State. The aspirations embedded in the sovereignty concept are too complex and nuanced to be consigned to legal formalities. Aboriginal women academics, Watson, Moreton-Robinson, and Bunda, in the text *Sovereign Subjects*, also critique the way in which sovereignty has been framed within the textual confines of law, policy, and history. As they attempt to "widen the reading of Indigenous sovereignty" by asserting the "black sovereign warrior woman as negotiator, fighter and nurturer" (Bunda 2007: 75–80), they critique the framing as a fundamentally white patriarchal discourse, as they attempt to assert and inscribe alternative embodied sovereignties that cannot be displaced (Moreton-Robinson 2007).

Michael Brown wonders whether, even if (legal) sovereignty were an option, would it provide the most suitable or appropriate set of political structures for Indigenous peoples (2007: 172)? Native American feminist Andrea Smith suggests that in this project of imagination it is helpful to draw on the work of Native women activists who have begun articulating notions of nation and sovereignty that are separate from nation-states. Whereas nation-states are governed through domination and coercion, Indigenous sovereignty and nationhood is predicated on interrelatedness and responsibility. Smith draws on Crystal Ecohawk:

> Sovereignty is an active, living process within this knot of human, material and spiritual relationships bound together by mutual responsibilities and obligations. From that knot of relationships is born our histories, our identity, the traditional ways in which we govern ourselves, our beliefs, our relationship to the land, and how we feed, clothe, house and take care of our families, communities and Nations. (in Smith 2005: 129)

Smith provides an alternative political framework by a feminist community activist group in the United States, described as the dual strategy of "taking power" and "making power":

> It is necessary to engage in oppositional politics to corporate and state power, "taking power." However, if this is the only politics engaged in, then there is

a tendency to replicate the hierarchical structures in our movements. Consequently, it is also important to make power, by creating those structures within Indigenous organisations, movements and communities that model the world that we want to create. (Smith 2005: 130)

Similarly, Patrick Dodson, a Yawuru leader from Western Australia, also stated: "A system that builds on the strength and resilience of Aboriginal people and recognises Indigenous knowledge systems can enable us to navigate our own path through modernity."[32] One means of reinventing local and regional power is through the principle of subsidiarity, the recognition of which "allows for relative autonomy within wider governance systems . . . and recognises that rights are inherently lying at the local level rather than conceded from above" (see Sullivan 2011: 13). A major issue for Aboriginal people at the 2012 Northern Territory elections, which took precedence over the issue of the Northern Territory Emergency Response (NTER), was the amalgamation of the local community government councils into regional shires that occurred without their consent in 2008 (see Sanders 2008; Sanders and Holcombe 2008). This massive scaling up of decision making into the regional shires was tempered when a new government came to power (see Sanders 2012). In this hyperfluid policy environment local decision-making authorities were (re)established at each of the thirteen communities under the MacDonnell Regional Council; as CEO of the MacDonnell Regional Council stated: "Local Boards have always played a part of representing the voice of the community at a grass roots level. The new local Authorities will continue and expand upon this vital role" (MacDonnell Regional Council 2014).

Conclusions

The master's tools will never dismantle the master's house.

Lorde 1984

This chapter has in some ways been a thought exercise in an alternative dialogical politics that is driven by the fact that "equality in Government policy always privileges whiteness" (Tsing 2007: 42), because although the quotation heading this section may be true in part, it is nevertheless essential that Anangu have access to these tools. As part of the diverse work of rights I have sought to not only open a dialogue with the emancipatory potential of the rights discourse, but to refocus this discourse beyond and away from the dominating regulatory and domesticating modes that have come to work their hegemonic script. This script is written in the glosses of good (corporate) governance, shared responsibility and the arrogance of a neoliberal completeness that is resistant to reciprocity and conversation. The current discourse sponsored by the neoliberal state, much of which is embedded in the "good governance" discourse, is coercive, intolerant of pluralism, and dismissive of cultural and Indigenous recognition and any forms of substantive rights in their language of entailment and obligation. As Santos states, "Low intensity human rights act as the other side of low intensity democracy" (2002: 46).

The domestication and co-option of Indigenous organizations to advance the project of the state as they draw Indigenous people into the fold is not a new thing. Rowse noted that the establishment of the Aboriginal and Torres Strait Islander Commission (ATSIC 2005) and other bodies necessarily drew Aboriginal people into structures and processes that they did not devise when this "Indigenous sector" was first developed. Fundamentally, any emancipatory politics that questions the sovereign liberal state is limited by the state (Neocosmos 2006: 366). What I am suggesting here, however, is that we have moved into a new phase where the controls on Aboriginal organizations are ever more tightening—as the entailments of citizenship are becoming mandatory in forms of low-intensity human rights and in the demands of attaching responsibilities with citizenship in the diminishment of the welfare state. As this chapter has revealed, key elements of human rights are found in the euphemistic language of "good governance." Whether "good enough" and self-determining *or* the coercive and instrumentalist governance, both forms rest to varying degrees on the agentic or public citizen. This citizen is not a marginal structurally disadvantaged figure.

And although the potential for the emancipatory value of human rights to be fostered has never been taken up by the government, it is, likewise, barely visible in the NGOs that operate as service providers. There is, however, some optimism that by reclaiming the concept of self-determination it can be remade. David Ross argues, "It is clear . . . that governments have lost their way in Aboriginal Affairs . . . their own governance and implementation capacity is the lowest it has ever been. At the end of the day governments will come and go, but our people will still be here" (Ross 2013). This assertion of government dysfunction then draws in an Aboriginal program of reclamation, a reversal of the stale paradigm.

In the comic science fiction *The Hitchhiker's Guide to the Galaxy*, Arthur Dent attempts to locate the plans that were to demolish his house to make way for a highway bypass. This quote, for me, encapsulates the barriers and challenges for Anangu around accessing the emancipatory discourse of human rights beyond the statist paradigms, and by extension the possibilities for self-determination:

"But the plans were on display . . ."

"On display? I eventually had to go down to the cellar to find them."

"That's the display department."

"With a flashlight."

"Ah, well, the lights had probably gone."

"So had the stairs."

"But look, you found the notice, didn't you?"

"Yes," said Arthur, "Yes I did. It was on display in the bottom of a locked filing cabinet stuck in a disused lavatory with a sign on the door saying 'Beware of the Leopard.'" (Douglas Adams 1979)

Chapter 7

International Human Rights Forums and (East Coast) Indigenous Activism

E ARLIER CHAPTERS EXPLORED THE WORK of several NGOs in central Australia as they articulate at arm's length with the human rights discourse. Although they use many core rights principles, such as gender equity in community issue decision making and principles of good governance, direct engagement with the language and institutions of human rights is a rarity. This intuitive, rather than instrumental, approach can be contrasted to the approach of Indigenous organizations based in urban areas in east coast cities among the majority population, including the Aboriginal Land Councils and Indigenous representative bodies based there. It is also these organizations that routinely engage in international human rights forums, with Indigenous staff traveling to New York City and Geneva, both to Indigenous-specific UN forums as well as to the range of other UN human rights forums. And although participants from Central Australia, and the Northern Territory more generally, do also attend these forums (and this chapter will discuss some examples), they are typically in the cohort of attendees who attend only once. Their roles and reasons for attending are often less about lobbying and more about the experience and scaled-up networking, as will be discussed.

Two of the major international forums at which Indigenous Australian activists and advocates attempt to variously compel and shame the Australian government into action to "transfer international commitments into domestic obligations" (Les Malezer, field notes May 2013) are the UN Permanent Forum on Indigenous Issues (UNPFII) established in 2002 and, since 2011, the four yearly Universal Periodic Reviews (UPRs) in Geneva, which operate through the UN Human Rights Council. The UPR addresses all human rights issues, and, along with refugee issues, Indigenous rights are high on the list of state interventions to Australia. These international forums act as a "higher authority." This concept "account[s] for the way Indigenous peoples have appealed to external powers in order to restrain colonial and national authorities and to have their claims heard" (de Costa 2006: 3). As the core site where the discourse has emerged and flourished, the UN role has been foundational, so mapping the trajectories of the discourse from this site is an essential one. Although the methodology of this chapter has telescopic tendencies, it is also a reflection on the issues that confound the possibilities for the mobilization of this discourse to remote central Australia. Although Niezen "realise[d] the extent to which the international movement of Indigenous peoples was influencing local political behaviour" with the Canadian Cree (2003: preface), I have not observed the same. The rights discourse hovers on the periphery, even as significant principles of the actual content—such as the right to development, to culture, and to free prior informed consent—are intrinsic to the workings of the major Aboriginal organizations in central Australia, such as the Central Land Council. These are, as yet, rarely explicitly tied to a larger global Indigenous politics or indeed to the UN Declaration on the Rights of Indigenous Peoples.

Other than the UNPFII, the other UN body that focuses solely on Indigenous rights is the Expert Mechanism on the Rights of Indigenous Peoples (EMRIP), established in 2008. EMRIP was created by the Human Rights Council as a subsidiary expert mechanism with a specific mandate to provide thematic expertise on the rights of Indigenous peoples to the Council. In 2011, for instance, the Expert Mechanism considered a progress report on its study on indigenous peoples' right to participate in decision making. I will focus on the first two forums, the UNPFII and the UPR, exploring the chasm between the government's abstract instrumentalized human rights rhetoric as a "public audit ritual" (per Cowan 2014) and the attempts by Indigenous civil society organizations to influence and hold to account the government's enactment of its international human rights obligations. In both forums I articulate the UN processes and procedures that at once enable and constrain. In doing so, we witness the irony of the current government (as of this writing) championing of "fundamental freedoms," such as freedom of expression and the role of civil society organizations in maintaining this freedom. This advocacy appears to have very limited influence on government. This was not always the case. Australia was a leading human rights state, at the forefront of history making. The Labor politician Doc Evatt (Dr. Herbert Evatt) led the Australian delegation to the meeting that founded the United Nations in San Francisco in 1945. And in 1948 Evatt was elected President of the General Assembly of the United Nations, during which time he presided over the adoption and proclamation of the Universal Declaration of Human Rights (UDHR). As he reflected at that time:

> It was the first occasion on which the organised community of nations had made a declaration of human rights and fundamental freedoms . . . millions of people, men, women and children from all over the world would turn to it for help, guidance and inspiration. (Evatt Foundation nd)

This triumphalist and optimistic statement is a contrast to the dismissive and derogatory approach of the current government. An Abbott government senator maintained that the people of Australia have said, "We don't care about Treaties"—that the government in its legislation was giving the Australian people what they wanted (Fraser, *The Age Newspaper* February 4, 2015). One might expect such a statement to come from a rogue state. However, here it reflects a complacency that those seated in the comfortable carriage of the mainstream—driven by middle-aged and elderly white male politicians—can afford. Given Australia's lack of a national bill or charter of rights, however, these international forums gain added significance on a range of levels. For instance, the UPR process has been described by a senior public servant of the Department of Foreign Affairs and Trade (DFAT) as "something to hang onto." As he continued: "It is awkward [that the] Human Rights Framework, that was implemented by the Labor Government in 2010, is no longer the policy platform under the current Liberal Coalition Government." As a result, even a recalcitrant state, such as Australia under the coalition government, has to engage with its human rights record in, at least, the international context. Thus, these international human rights mechanisms provide formal opportunities for Indigenous Australians to focus attention on specific concerns in an attempt to shift the public discourse and the "policy settings."

There are two key elements to my investigation of these two UN sites. The first involves tracking the participation of Australian Indigenous representative bodies and NGOs and their insertion of Australian Indigenous rights issues into these forums. How are these issues articulated and represented? What shapes and forms do "interventions" (submissions) have to squeeze into to be included, and what gets left out (to borrow from Cowan 2014: 45)?

How do we make sense of the juxtaposition between the "vaulted rooms and corridors of the Palais des Nations in Geneva" (per Niezen 2003: preface) or, indeed, at the United Nations Headquarters in New York City where the UNPFII is held annually, with the stark material poverty of central Australian community living? The second strand of enquiry will track how and by what mechanisms these ideas are reproduced on return from these international forums and circulated. An understanding of the role of these transnational Indigenous activists and intermediaries enables a tracing of the emerging contours of the Indigenous rights discourse in Australia and theorization of the interface between this global engagement and local appropriation. These UN forums are the sites where these instruments have taken their shape and the resources to "operationalize" them continue to evolve.

Merry (2006b) argues that Indigenous or local intermediaries are crucial to the deployment of human rights discourse. This role is presumably equally important, if not more essential, for the deployment of Indigenous human rights. As Niezen states: "The readiness of Aboriginal leaders to pursue their grievances through legal processes has been more historically constant than might be initially supposed" (2009: 25). In Australia, this history of trans-national engagement predates the emergence of the universal human rights discourse by approximately 100 years, to attempting an audience with the English monarchy of the invading colony. There were petitions to Queen Victoria from as early as 1846 from the inhabitants of Flinders Island off the coast of Tasmania (de Costa 2006: 46) and again to Her Majesty in 1863 from Kulin men in the State of Victoria (Attwood 2003: 15), as well as to later kings from a raft of other Indigenous Australian petitioners. The themes of these early claims have altered little, as they dwelt on Indigenous prior ownership and subsequent dispossession; however, they have gained more nuance and became more circumscribed.

This call to the greater public consciousness found firmer ground with the establishment of the League of Nations, followed by the United Nations (UN) and the emergent language and institutions of human rights. Aboriginal activist Pearl Gibbs was possibly the first to engage with these formalized structures, writing to the League of Nations in 1938 seeking their intervention into the working conditions of the "downtrodden natives of the Northern Territory" on behalf of the Aborigines Progressive Association (Damousi, Rubenstein, and Tomsic 2014: 84; see also de Costa 2006: 71). There has been a consistent presence of Indigenous Australian activists pressing their claims through these forums, including through the International Labor Organization (ILO), since Gibbs. The Working Group on Indigenous Populations (WGIP), established in 1982, drew on the groundbreaking reports by UN Special Rapporteur Martinez-Cobo, who was critical of the limitations of existing human rights instruments for Indigenous peoples, which "were not wholly adequate" and "not fully applied" (in de Costa 2006: 128). The WGIP led the development of the UN DRIP, again with a consistent contingent of Australian Indigenous delegates from the newly emerging Indigenous sector, burgeoning under the self-determination policies of the period.

Although current domestic policies, in relation to both Indigenous rights and human rights, may be in reverse mode (with the language of self-determination and the human rights framework both dropped from the policy tool kit), when I attended the annual two-week UNPFII in New York City in 2010 and in 2013 the significant Australian Indigenous presence at these Forums belied this domestic reality. On both occasions it would be fair to say that the Australian delegation was the largest, as they each time claimed their prime position at the front of the Trusteeship Council Chamber. In 2010, the NSW Land Council, the National Congress of Australia's First Peoples, Amnesty International Australia, and the Australian Human Rights Commission Office of the Aboriginal and Torres Strait Islander Justice Commissioner, among others, sent significant delegations of Indigenous staff. In this global celebration and affirmation of identity politics and networking in hyperdrive, I was very much an outsider.

UN Permanent Forum on Indigenous Issues (UNPFII)

"You have a home at the United Nations." This statement, by the then Secretary-General of the UN Kofi Annan, was made on the establishment of the Permanent Forum on Indigenous Issues in 2002. And as the annual two-week forum opened in 2010, in the iconic General Assembly Hall of the UN Headquarters in New York City, it did seem a powerful moment for cultural diversity with a carnival spectrum of cultural clothing as performance to the flash of multiple cameras (even though there are "no photos" signs). However, this recognition was a long time coming. The circumstances of Indigenous peoples were virtually invisible at the United Nations until the early 1970s. In this short period, Indigenous peoples have made significant inroads toward the recognition of their rights and the acceptance of their legitimate place within the international community. Indigenous peoples are now recognized subjects at international law.[1] The endorsement of the UN Declaration on the Rights of Indigenous Peoples (UN DRIP) by the UN General Assembly in 2007, after twenty years of development, was a significant turning point in this politics of recognition. And, rather like the early work of human rights advocate Doc Evatt, Australia was also a leader in establishing Indigenous rights: "Internationally, Australia is at the forefront of formulating international law concerning the right to self-determination of Indigenous peoples" (Sullivan 1996: 110). Both DFAT and Indigenous representatives were active in the working group that drafted the UN DRIP. And it is primarily this Declaration that Indigenous rights advocates in Australia, as elsewhere, agitate to have adopted in policy approaches and principles in their state's approach to Indigenous affairs. To this end, every second year there is a different theme that focuses on particular articles of the UN DRIP, while every other year is a "review year." In 2010, the theme was "development with culture and identity"—referencing Articles 3 and 32, with 2013 being a review year. Although my focus is not specifically on the content of each annual session, it is worth noting that the theme of 2014 was "good governance."

The referencing back to this multivalent concept, what I have previously referred to as a gloss or euphemism, is a clear recalling of its foundational elements. So it is in this international context that good governance can be named for what it is—a bundle of particular human rights. As Dalee Sambo Dorough, Chairperson of the UNPFII in 2014, articulated the theme:

> The theme of "principles of good governance consistent with the UN Declaration on the Rights of Indigenous People" gave voice to Indigenous legal traditions that emulate and represent good governance. . . . My interest in the use of this theme was to highlight the relevance of transparency; responsiveness; consensus oriented; equity and inclusiveness; effectiveness and efficiency; accountability; participation; consultation and consent; human rights; and the rule of law in order to influence both the high level plenary meeting and the ongoing dialogue concerning the Sustainable Development Goals. (See Dorough 2015)

Indeed, this all-encompassing definition leaves out only cultural particularity, as the "Indigenous legal traditions" that have a "voice" under good governance are those that emulate the liberal human rights tradition. The National Congress also made a YouTube video with, among others, Les Malezer (National Congress Co-Chair at that time) about the work being done at this particular forum (National Congress 2014). And he articulated the Articles that specifically referenced the workings of good governance in the UN DRIP, which he refers to as Articles 3, 4, 5 (which all focus on self-determination) and 6 (the right to a nationality). Finally, he states that there was "also a lot of attention on Article 46 . . . which also says that it has to be implemented in good faith and at the highest levels." Interestingly, the final Article 46 (3) states: "The provisions set forth in this Declaration shall be interpreted in accordance with the principles of justice, democracy, respect for human rights, equality, non-discrimination, good governance and good faith."

The paradox here is that, as both Malezer and Dorough are keen to point out, Indigenous peoples seek to be treated by their states via these "good governance" principles—in relation to free, prior, informed consent required for development on their lands and via the raft of principles given already. But this also assumes that Indigenous groups will also operate under these same principles. As illustrated in Chapters 2 and 6, Aboriginal community leaders' attendance at good governance training is now commonplace in this expectation of dual accountability. As the UNPFII attempts to draw diverse groups of Indigenous peoples into this frame, there is a risk that it will also be read as an attempt to eliminate difference on a global scale (see, for instance, Kymlicka 2007: 7).[2]

There are several key dimensions to the activities of the UNPFII. The first is its role within the UN system, of which there was early criticism. For instance, Alfred and Corntassel (2004) criticized its mandate, stating:

> Given its severe limitations in addressing or acting on the blatant injustices and continuing genocide perpetrated against 370 million Indigenous peoples worldwide, structuring the permanent forum to function solely as an internal report writing and data-gathering agency for state policy circles is tantamount to an act of criminal negligence on the part of the UN. (quoted in Niezen 2009: 20)

Unlike the UPR process, the UNPFII is not an accountability mechanism. It is symbolic and performative for soft advocacy and lobbying between Indigenous peoples and their state. It is enmeshed in and constrained by the system of state sovereignty, which constitutes the bricks and mortar of the UN system. This embeddedness remains a fundamental obstacle for equality at international law as Indigenous people's structures of governance in all states, including postcolonial states, are not recognized. As a result, Indigenous peoples will always be in a fundamentally inequitable position vis-à-vis the states. This is presumably one of the reasons that, as the communications officer at the 2013 UNPFII, Amala Groom stated:

> In Geneva [at EMRIP and the WIPO intergovernmental meetings][3] you've got ambassadors and diplomats—people who are movers and shakers. Here it's essentially an Indigenous forum where they send a few shit kickers in all due respect . . . no [Australian] minister has ever been to the UNPFII. (field notes May 2013)

So perhaps a more important role than soft advocacy within the UNPFII might be its educatory and emancipatory elements through further development of the second wave Indigenism. Networking with Indigenous Peoples Organizations (IPOs) from other countries is clearly important, learning advocacy strategies from other global Indigenous brothers and sisters. As Mick Dodson (then Australian Human Rights Commissioner) stated in relation to his first session at the UN WGIP, which was established to develop the UN DRIP: "I was sitting in a room, 12,000 miles from home, but if I'd closed my eyes I could just about have been in Maningrida or Doomadgee or Flinders Island. The people wore different clothes, spoke in different languages or with different accents, and their homes had different names. But the stories and sufferings were the same" (Dodson 1998: 18–19).

Although Indigenous groups may not have a direct line of political sight to their state at the Forum, it is another opportunity to gather the spotlight of global attention on issues of gross social and environmental injustice and compel a state to take action because of international pressure. The Forum acts as another point of leverage, among the other UN forums.[4] The UNPFII, for instance, is on the annual attendance list for Cultural Survival International, whose work routinely advocates for the principles of the UN DRIP to be the standard of engagement by states. This is also a major aspect of the role of the UN Special Rapporteur on the Situation of Human Rights and Fundamental Freedoms of Indigenous People, who was invited to Australia for the first time in 2009 with a focus on the NT Emergency Response (Anaya 2010: Appendix B). As the Special Rapporteur visits diverse and often remote places across the globe, this scaling up of human rights as a global social practice touches on ever more places.[5]

In 2006, the then Aboriginal and Torres Strait Islander Social Justice Commissioner, Tom Calma, stated:

I see a need for any project on international engagement by Indigenous peoples to create a stronger connection between activities at the international level and engagement with Indigenous communities domestically. This includes through facilitating domestic consultations to inform international participants and to engage with government prior to international dialogues taking place, as well as providing mechanisms for feedback and disseminating information on the outcomes of international deliberations back to Indigenous organisations and communities. (Australian Human Rights and Equal Opportunity Commission 2006)

Circulating the global Indigenous rights discourse back to communities has been an agenda for some time, but what are the mechanisms? The UNPFII is purely an advisory body to the UN Economic and Social Council (ECOSOC), with the sixteen Indigenous members providing expert advice, much of which is in the final annual forum report to ECOSOC that results from the interventions (the papers) the various IPOs submit. This, however, is the only UN Forum that is purpose-built for Indigenous engagement. As a young assistant to Megan Davis (Australian State-elected Expert Permanent Forum Member) shared her experience at the 2012 Forum: "I never felt so elated to be part of something as I did on that Sunday" at the Opening in the General Assembly Hall (Ferguson 2012: 24). As the most important secular ritual of universality, to borrow from Cowan (2014), the international order of the United Nations fulfils this human need to be part of something greater than the sum of its parts: greater than its human components. The scale and complexity of the UN machinery is, itself, awe inspiring for participants.

"Processes of Collective Self-Representation"

This phrase from Niezen (2009: 21) speaks not only to the complexity of engaging with the bureaucratic machinery of the UNPFII but to the corporate identities that Indigenous peoples require to express their citizenship. Indeed, the fact that I was not tagged to any "collective self-representation" was one of the reasons I was an outsider in this context; I wasn't part of a larger delegation. Those participants who have key roles at the Forum are not only staff members of organizations; they are Indigenous staff members of Indigenous organizations. Unlike myself, their selves are part of a collectivity that is formalized in this context. Umbrella organizations—known as Indigenous Peoples Organizations (IPOs)—have to be established for each participating state.[6] There is nothing random about UN process, and my thoughts on the first day were that it was a "bureaucratic circus"; it appears busy and even chaotic, but it is highly orchestrated. This phrase captures the theatrical, the grand, and perhaps the bizarre, as the elaborate dress of diverse Amazonian Indian groups, the Sami, the Peruvian, and so on is juxtaposed with other suit-wearing Indigenous representatives. The Secretariat (of the Indigenous Peoples Centre for Documentation, Research and Information) is the ringmaster, as the complexity behind the scenes belies the smooth stage performance.

Australia established its IPO during the 1990s. According to a media release in 2013, the IPO network is a broad affiliation of Aboriginal and Torres Strait Islander organizations and individuals, who engage with UN mechanisms and frameworks to advocate for the implementation of the Declaration. There are at least eleven Indigenous organizations within this network, though it varies on an annual basis depending on attendance at the Forum.[7] They are predominantly national organizations and include the National Native Title Council, the National Indigenous Higher Education Network, the Office of the Social Justice Commissioner, the National Congress, and so on. An organization cannot make an "intervention"—that is, be listed to speak for a maximum of three minutes and thus be on record—unless this status is approved. The IPO Facebook page is an annual frenzy of activity, with postings of their interventions, "side events," and social activities. On the two occasions I have attended the Forum, the Australian delegation clearly seemed to dominate in terms of numbers. It included not only about twenty-five staff of the IPO organizations but also individuals sponsored by NGOs, such as Oxfam Australia, Amnesty International Australia (AIA), and Global Voices. Many of the staff of the organizations that make up the IPO are core participants who return annually. Les Malezer (National Congress Co-Chair at the 2013 Forum) is one of these. He commented on how the focus at the Permanent Forum, since it was established in 2000 (with the first session in 2002), has changed, stating:

> Initially it was all about lobbying for the UN Declaration [on the Rights of Indigenous Peoples], but since they were successful in 2007—and then the Australian government endorsed it in 2009—we have been a bit lost. So now the focus has shifted to implementation and every second year is now a review year—where recommendations are followed up. (field notes May 2013)

We might consider this shift of focus in terms of "second-wave Indigeneity," a concept borrowed from Barcham, as characterizing the enabling moment in international Indigenous politics, which looks to the future in the wake of the endorsement of the UN Declaration on the Rights of Indigenous Peoples by States (in Venkateswar and Hughes 2011: 1).

Although there are no central Australian organizations routinely in the IPO network, both individuals from central Australia and representatives from central Australian organizations have attended the Permanent Forum over the years. In 2011, the Indigenous media officer from the Central Land Council, Steve Hodder-Watts, attended for the first time. He was sponsored as part of a youth delegation by Oxfam International. Like others sponsored by Oxfam, prior to attending he also participated in a one-week workshop on human rights and UN processes to prepare for the complexity the delegates were to encounter. In the regional *Land Rights News* he noted his skepticism about the value of attending: "The UN is probably seen by some as weak and a bit like a spear with no head," but "he hoped to learn more about the UN processes so he could make other Aboriginal people in central Australia aware of how to use the mechanisms to advocate for their peoples" (*Land Rights News* 2012: 20).

This analogy of a "spear with no head" is a useful one. It speaks to the limitations of this Forum to shift, in a meaningful way, the sociopolitical power relations between Aboriginal Territorians and the two levels of government, the NT government and commonwealth government. As I'll discuss in relation to the UPR process, Australia's federal system places significant limitations on what pressure can be bought to bear by the Commonwealth government on the states and territories (see also Holcombe and Janke 2012).[8] However, the state, as the federal or commonwealth government, is one jurisdiction in international terms.

An ambivalent response about the value of engaging with the UN system was also offered by a senior Aboriginal woman public servant in Alice Springs, who was the NT representative on the National Aboriginal and Torres Strait Islander Women's Alliance (NATSIWA).[9] She stated that:

> They [NATSIWA] wanted an international focus, and we're not ready for that yet. I had the opportunity to go to the UN, but I didn't want to go. We sit under the UN DRIP—but that is not yet relevant here—not when women are sitting under the NTER [NT Emergency Response]. What's the point pushing

an international agenda when people here are so disempowered and disillu-
sioned? (field notes July 9, 2014)

Indeed, the most significant issue of the last ten years that has galvanized Aboriginal interest in these international advocacy processes is the NT Emergency Intervention (NTER) of 2007. A number of delegates from the NT were
sponsored to participate, most notably Barbara Shaw, an Alice Springs town
camp resident who actively campaigned against the NTER and ran as a candidate for the Greens political party. She was sponsored to attend by Amnesty
International Australia, who have run side events about the NTER. The NTER
also catalyzed a visit for the first time from the UN Special Rapporteur, James
Anaya, to the NT in 2009. Anaya's report (2010) was based on a ten-day visit
to Australia—including to town camps in Darwin and Alice Springs and to
several remote communities. Though it focused on a raft of issues Australia-
wide, specific attention was paid to the Northern Territory and the NTER
policies. When Hodder-Watts interviewed Anaya during his visit to an Alice
Springs Town camp, he put forward his "spear with no head" analogy. Anaya's
response was that he "probably agreed in part but it was important to remember that it's not the place for international bodies such as the UN to interfere
but persuade state bodies (nations) to do the right thing" (*Land Rights News*
2012: 20). This diplomatic rhetoric was also apparent in the report, where the
scaled-up legalistic language acted as a disconnect to grounded experience,
as Anaya concluded that "the intervention as currently configured is racially
discriminatory and incompatible with Australia's international human rights
obligations under the Convention to Eliminate Discrimination and other
international instruments." Although these points of law had already been
made (Davis 2007: Human Rights Commission 2008; Social Justice Report
2007), such high-profile confirmation was possibly useful to bolster the Human Rights Commission's case, for instance. However, as Edmunds pointed
out, the report reads as "quite formulaic" (2010: 21), and it is clear that soft
diplomacy leads the response, as the Rapporteurs have to be "invited" by the
state under scrutiny to be scrutinized.

On UNPFII Interventions and Side Events

The strategies to engage with the UN system at the Permanent Forum, as for
the other UN forums, are highly circumscribed. To be able to make an intervention, that is, present a brief paper about an issue that may then make it

into the final report, ECOSOC status is required for each Indigenous Peoples Organization (IPO).[10] Such accreditation is hard to get, as Malezer indicated there are:

> Mountains of paperwork as the states can query it. Russia did so for some of its IPOs, and it can take up to six years. Indigenous groups are querying this formal status requirement, which they argue should instead be based on Indigenous forms of governance—not those designated by the states and the bureaucracy of the UN. (field notes May 2013)

According to Malezer, in 2013, the General Assembly was considering this. Such accreditation also needs to be maintained with reporting every four years. This is seen as an issue of exclusion or elitism fostered by the UN system. Even though this is clearly a hurdle for attendance, it is a largely Indigenous advocacy to ensure a more effective participation by Indigenous peoples in the United Nations and greater attention to issues affecting Indigenous peoples *globally*. In 2012, more than 1,300 delegates from around the world attended (according to the OXFAM 2012 prep materials). As Groom, the communications officer, attending the UNPFII for her fourth time in 2013 stated:

> The aim of the game is either to get your recommendations from the interventions into the final report of the Permanent Forum or to bring media attention to an issue back home, because just saying that you participated in the UN is a big deal. Everyone thinks it bigger than what it is . . . 'cause it looks great on a C.V., on a media release, in the newspapers. White people care about it. (field notes May 2013)

Yet, given that many states send government representatives, although not ministers, to the Forum, it is a formal opportunity for Indigenous delegates to engage with their state. This increasingly became an important strategy for the National Congress, who were writing joint statements with the government in 2013. The value of this has been criticized by some delegates as being too closely embedded with the state. Malezer's rationale for this strategy was that:

> One rule you can apply is that all states lie . . . through what they leave out of their statements. This is the value of joint statements. We involve the Human Rights Commission, so we ensure they [the government/state] are not lying. We insisted in our Joint statement that "they support the Declaration." It's

like being in a fast-moving stream, and by hanging onto them you ensure that
whatever happens to them happens to you. (field notes 2013)

However, given that the National Congress is, as of 2016, no longer funded
by the current conservative government or recognized as an Indigenous representative body, until there is a change of government such joint statements
are unlikely.

During the two weeks of these annual events, there are special forums
daily—termed "side events." These side events are intended to either educate
and "capacity build" participants hosted by an NGO about a particular issue
such as Free Prior Informed Consent, or by particular Indigenous organizations to engage debate and draw attention to a specific local or regional issue.
For instance, in 2013, such side events were held as "Celebrating and Commemorating the Rights of Mother Earth for the Seventh Generation: Sharing Our Vision of the Past, Present and Future Generations," hosted by the
America Indian Law Alliance and Native Children's Survival. Another event
on the same day was "UNDP's Environmental and Social Compliance Review
and Dispute Resolution Process," hosted by the UNDP (UN Development
Program).

Since 2008, as far as I can ascertain, Amnesty International Australia (AIA)
has hosted an annual side event focusing on different aspects of the Northern
Territory Emergency Response (NTER).[11] Barbara Shaw participated in two of
these in 2009 and 2011, and others from the NT-affected communities in the
Utopia Alyawarr region, Richard Downs and Ngarla Kunoth-Monks, also attended in 2011. Unfortunately, at the NTER side event that I attended in 2010
there were no affected Indigenous peoples there; rather they were represented
on the panel by the Indigenous spokespeople of AIA and other Australian Indigenous delegates. Among these were Geoff Scott, the CEO of the NSW Land
Council, who discussed his visit to Ampilatawajt (a community in the Utopia region) and the issue of income management under the NTER (see also
their 2010–2011 annual report: 62–63). The NSW Land Council has an international advocacy and engagement strategy. In 2010, they sent five people to
the UNPFII and three people to the UPR (NSW Land Council Annual Report
2010–2011: 63). This is a significant contrast to the Central Land Council who,
though they routinely have significant sections on "Advocacy and Representation" in their annual reports (those examined from 2010–2015, for instance),
this does not include international advocacy or any mention of the UN DRIP.

In an extraordinary coincidence in 2013, one of the delegates sponsored by an NGO, Global Voices for Youth, was from Papunya. A young man whose father was the resident Lutheran linguist and whose mother was the Luritja translator, Matt Heffernan moved to Alice Springs as a six- to seven-year-old to attend school there. And though as a child he would regularly return to Papunya to visit family, he had never returned there to live. After gaining a university education he now lives in Darwin (the administrative center 1,500 km to the north) and works for the Northern Territory government. He hadn't returned to Papunya for several years and indicated that doesn't have plans to in the short term, though he is active on Facebook with his Anangu family. As we talked about the country of his childhood he reminisced: "It feels like it's another planet—even the landscape is so different—just thinking about it now evokes all the emotions—looking upon the ranges and smelling the air" (field notes May 2013). As part of the condition of his employers for enabling his attendance, he was required to write a paper on Indigenous economic development (his area of expertise) on his return. This may have contributed to further developing a rights-based dialogue with his colleagues in Darwin and further activating his own political life. It did seem ironic, however, that as I was searching for mechanisms for mobilizing this rights discourse at a local level in central Australia, the local that I would find had moved away to pursue a different trajectory. In relation to his visit to the UNPFII, Heffernan stated that:

> I had a lot of preconceptions—I really wanted to come to connect with other Indigenous peoples—which I've done, and I feel so much more enriched now talking with others about their experiences, their struggles. That was essentially why I'm here. My preconceptions were that there'd be more engagement by the Australian government in what gets discussed here. So we [Indigenous Australians] do participate, and we do a lot . . . but I don't see that roll out back in Australia. And especially the ideals around self-determination—it's nonexistent in Australia and mainstream discourse. And while I think it would be very hard to implement any sort of sovereignty or that kind of system—we still need to discuss how we're still a separate people, which still could fit under an Australia government legislation and framework. (field notes May 2013)

Because of the complexity of engaging with these UN processes, there tends to be continuity about attendance. Many of the people who were at the United

Nations when I was there in 2010 were there again in 2013. When I spoke with Les Malezer in 2013, he had been eleven times (see also Hart 2009). Initially I thought perhaps spending two weeks in Manhattan was a bit of a rort, a junket. However, as I began to attend the daily 8 am Australian caucus meetings in the UN food hall area, which are followed by the Pacific caucus[12] meetings (which include Hawaii, New Zealand, and PNG, for instance) until the Forum reconvenes at 10 am, it became clear that the core participants work long hours. They are lobbying, networking, meeting with government staff, writing interventions and media releases, and generally engaging with the highly regulated labyrinthine UN bureaucracy. When I spoke with Amala Groom about the interventions she was working on during the 2013 Forum, she stated:

> AG: Now with the "culture paper," I'm meeting with the Permanent Forum member this afternoon to talk about making our recommendations more specific so that they can be included in the final report.
>
> SH: Is this the portfolio person you met with?
>
> AG: Yes, because it's not just lobbying beforehand and getting it into the final report—you also have to make sure that it's *realistically actionable*. And then once it's in the final report you need to lobby again to see it being implemented . . . Well, all of the recommendations obviously need to be non–nation specific in order for them to be able to move through the UN, otherwise nothing's going to happen, and then when working with the Australian government you just make reference to the international standard and what our international treaty obligations are.
>
> SH: You mean the Universal Declaration of Human Rights?
>
> AG: All of the standards, the eleven [fourteen] conventions and treaties that we're a party to. (field notes May 2013)

Thus, any recommendations within the interventions have to be broad enough and encompassing enough to apply to all Indigenous peoples. As Groom stated in 2013: "The recommendations that they make have to be non–nation specific—as they are directed to UN agencies—otherwise they won't make it into the final report." It effectively is an internal UN process, whereby the governments do not have an obligation to respond, but the UN agencies do because they have the relationship with ECOSOC. This lack of specificity of the UNPFII to country issue reporting contrasts to the targeted procedures of the UPR.

Although the participating states as well as Indigenous NGOs read out "interventions," the aims of the states' interventions and those of Indigenous NGOs are often completely at odds, because, while the states often trumpet their achievements in terms of Indigenous policies, such as improvements to education and health care and so on, the NGOs tend to outline a litany of Indigenous human rights abuses, concerning development without free prior informed consent, forced removal from lands, environmental devastation, and loss of livelihoods. It can be quite emotive. Indeed, until 2012 the states got five minutes to speak, while Indigenous groups got three minutes; from 2013, it became equal time at five minutes each. However, many of the interventions never actually get read out as there are too many; instead they are provided to the Forum members to read after the event.

What is particularly notable is the disconnection between the Australian government's active engagement with these international forums and their inaction domestically. Although the Australian government is supportive of the Indigenous rights agenda at these international forums (the exception to this was the years of the conservative Howard government from 1996–2007), this rarely translates into domestic support. In the 1980s and early 1990s, Mick Dodson admitted: "To be fair I must say that the Australian government has been by far the most co-operative and supportive of any government represented at the Working Group [on Indigenous populations, which developed the UN DRIP]. It is a pity that they don't bring that attitude back on the plane from Geneva" (in Pritchard 1998: 64). Twenty years later this hasn't changed. Nevertheless, although the second wave of strategies to mobilize this message via the Indigenous networks of civil society, such as the Facebook pages and blogs that now galvanize the discourse at this forum, are increasingly sophisticated, ease with this discourse remains with a limited few.

The Universal Periodic Review (UPR)

The UPR mechanism was established in 2006 by the UN Human Rights Council to replace the Human Rights Commission, which had developed as a politicized "naming and shaming" process routinely targeting specific (usually non-Western) countries. The new flatter system ensures that all 192 member states are equally exposed to four yearly scrutinies by all other member states and their civil society organizations. Ban Ki-moon, then UN Secretary-General, claimed that this mechanism "has great potential to promote and protect human rights in the darkest corners of the world" (UN Universal

Periodic Review 2011). In Australia, according to a senior public servant under the current conservative government, the UPR "acts as a de facto framework . . . forcing the Government to engage with human rights" (field notes November 26, 2015). This is significant, even though he also admitted that the UPR is "fundamentally flawed; as it is a political and diplomatic process, it is [nevertheless] valued by most states, which gives it legitimacy." Indeed, Sarah Joseph (Castan Centre for Human Rights Law; see also Joseph 2015) stated that "the UPR process is exposed to more diplomatic skin" than other human rights reporting bodies. As she continued: "The states care about what other states think. The Australian government would rather be bashed by AIA (Amnesty International Australia), than New Zealand" (personal communication December 3, 2015). Although the UPR is one of a range of UN mechanisms whereby each "State has to give an account of itself" (per Butler 2005, in Cowan 2014: 50), the treaty body reporting by contrast is largely administrative and has a much longer turnaround time of two years, rather than the several months of the UPR procedures.[13]

Although the UPR is a site of ritualized diplomacy where states look outward and where weasel words are standard fare, it is also the case that Indigenous advocates take it very seriously. This is because this forum is concerned with lobbying states to ask the difficult questions of their government as the state under review. The UPR provides a systematic and independent (within the limitations of the United Nations) consideration of the strengths and weaknesses in Australia's human rights observance and is regarded by Indigenous advocates as a far more direct opportunity to engage with the UN system, and as a result the Australian government, than the UNPFII. However, as civil society organizations or NGOs don't have a direct audience, and Indigenous human rights is one of many human rights issues addressed, there are fewer Indigenous representatives attending.

Australia has now had two reviews, the first in January 2011 and the second in November 2015. Of note, the first appearance was under a (relatively) progressive Labor government, and the second was under a conservative Liberal Coalition government, which plays a significant role in how seriously the reporting is taken. At the first UPR appearance, fifty-three countries asked Australia about its human rights record and made 145 recommendations for improvement (Australian Human Rights Commission 2012). These covered a wide range of human rights issues, including the treatment of asylum seekers,

Aboriginal and Torres Strait Islander peoples, multiculturalism and racism, and the status of Australia's obligations under international human rights law. Of these 145 recommendations, thirty-five were Indigenous specific.

As a result of this first UPR, Australia also made a number of voluntary commitments during the dialogue, which included: establishing a full-time Race Discrimination Commissioner in the Australian Human Rights Commission (which occurred in 2013) and using those UPR recommendations accepted by the government to inform the development of Australia's National Human Rights Action Plan (which occurred, but is no longer subsequent government policy). Two of the recommendations from states were to amend the Native Title Act of 1993, to remove "strict requirements which can prevent the Aboriginal and Torres Strait Islander peoples from exercising the right to access and control their traditional lands and take part in cultural life," and to implement the UN Declaration on the Rights of Indigenous Peoples into domestic law. This latter recommendation may be standard fare for each country with an Indigenous population and NGOs to push the cause. Nevertheless, it recalls to mind Santos's statement: "The important fact is not to reduce realism to what exists" (2002: 35). Although there may be a utopian element to the agitation behind this lobbying, it is necessary that it occurs in this forum. The UPR Info Report *Beyond Promises* states that the issue of minorities rights, encompassing Indigenous rights, is one of the most-raised issues in the UPR (UPR 2014: 45).

According to Groom, who had also participated in the 2011 UPR process:

AG: The UPR is a great way to review a nation's participation to ensure that they are upholding the nations' human rights obligations back home.

SH: Did you see any value in Australia's first UPR?

AG: Yes, absolutely—so much value in the UPR, it's awesome . . . also the Australian NGO team did the most exceptional job of lobbying—Les Malezer and the fellas from the Human Rights Legal resource centre. Their lobbying was phenomenal, and what ended up happening is, because you have all of the states being reviewed with the same issues, the shadow team— the NGO lobbyers—they just had fact sheets, and they ended up ensuring that the majority of the issues and the questions were put out there, so that the states would deliver those questions verbatim and then make recommendations verbatim. So I see that as really successful. (field notes May 2013)

This process of ensuring that the relevant questions are asked—leading to recommendations for the states under review to improve particular human rights standards—is only the first step. The state then has to implement them. And, although direct outcomes are expected, as each state under review is required to respond to each recommendation, the language is that of slippery diplomacy. McMahon, working with the organization upr-info.org, developed a five-stage action category for implementation, because although many UPR recommendations are issued and accepted, "recommendations are not made equal when it comes to their potential impact on the human rights situation" (in UPR 2014: 20). On the scale of 1 (minimal action) to 5 (specific action), the specific verb leading the recommendation is the telling indicator. As a result, "full implementation" declines from category 1 to category 5. For instance, category 2 recommendations could be "continue advancing," category 3 recommendations are "consider alternative," category 4 "take further steps." The most positive and grounded are the category 5, "which usually cover precise topics, ask for specific actions, and demand certain tangible or measureable outcomes" (UPR 2014: 24–25).

Interestingly, a measureable outcome (in the 5 category) that appeared positive for Australia and was presented as such by the UPR Info Report was the establishment of the Prime Minister's Indigenous Advisory Council in 2013 (UPR 2014: 45). However, this new government-appointed council was established and supported by the conservative government as an alternative to the National Congress, which had been established as the representative body shortly before the first UPR in 2011. The conservative government ceased funding this organization in 2013, as it ceased to formally recognize its role as representative body. So the Australian government's statement at the 2011 UPR that "the National Congress of Australia's First Peoples will provide a central mechanism with which Government, the corporate and community sectors can engage and partner on reform initiatives" did not have any traction with the subsequent government, and thus the UPR had little bearing. Instead, it reveals the volatility of Indigenous policy as none of the recommendations pertaining to Indigenous peoples was implemented, according to the UPR Report of the National Congress (2015). Indeed, only 10 percent of the entire UPR recommendations had been implemented in whole or in part by the second 2015 Review (Australian Human Rights Commission 2015).

As a senior public servant stated in relation to the 2015 review: "Our UPR response reflects the views of government, not civil society. There is a very clear distinction between them. One is government, and the other is civil society organisations" (field notes November 26, 2015). It seems to me that, for Australia at least, the question of "whether the move from 'naming and shaming to cooperation' . . . will improve compliance with the international human rights regime?" (Cowan 2014: 44) has bearing only if the will of the government at the time is amenable. If not, there is ample scope within the UN discourse of harmony, soft governance, and diplomacy for wriggle room. Likewise, given Australia's federal system, as a senior public servant noted there is a "disjunct between the government's response at a federal level and what each state and territory actually does. As a result, the government has to make abstract claims—nothing too specific" (field notes November 26, 2015). This lack of specificity is a significant shortcoming.

Shadowy Elisions and Contradictions

The lobbying by Indigenous civil society organizations happens in the "shadow reporting." According to the website "New Tactics in Human Rights":

> Shadow reports are a method through which NGOs can supplement or provide an alternative point of view to governmental reports that states are required to submit under international treaties. . . . [it is] a report that has been published after or in response to the governmental report. [They] are a unique tool through which NGOs can present opinions of civil society on government action and present it to the United Nations' Committees. . . . The role of civil society [could be described] as the "monitor of monitors," . . . illuminat[ing] what the government has done with respect to what it claims to have achieved. (2009)

As far as I can ascertain the United Nations refers to all NGO submissions in the less political language of "stakeholder reports." The UN Human Rights Council Working Group on the UPR usefully prepares a summary of these stakeholder submissions for each state under review, noting on page one that their summary "does not contain any opinions, views or suggestions on the part of the Office of the United Nations High Commissioner for Human Rights (OHCHR), nor any judgement or determination in relation to specific claims." It is the country-specific content of these documents that sits against and contradicts the formal state responses. These shadow reports set up the limitations of the state reporting and are telling of the inadequacies of the reporting processes. So my interest here is "what is left off the agenda—what cannot be said or cannot be heard in the context of [the UPR] discourses, modalities and processes" (Cowan 2014: 44).

In the second UPR, Australia's "National Report" stated that "since 2009–10 the National Congress has received $29.3 million from the Australia Government to support its operations" (National Report of Australia 2015: 7–8). However, the shadow report from the National Congress countered instead that "in 2013 the Government withheld the financial aid set aside to sustain the role and operations of Congress" (National Congress of Australia's First Peoples 2015: 2). The government in the National Report of the UPR for 2015 fails to mention this or that they are no longer supportive of the organization. Rather, they state that "the establishment of the Prime Minister's Indigenous Advisory Council affirms the high priority Australia gives to Indigenous Affairs" (National Report 2015: 7). These elisions are routine, as the National Report continues: "The Australian Government engages with a range of Indigenous leaders, organisations and communities when designing policies, programs and implementing services that affect Aboriginal and Torres Strait Islander peoples" (National Report 2015: 8). Again the National Congress shadow report strongly counters this: "At no time since [the first UPR of] 2011 has the Australian Government engaged with Congress to follow-up on or implement the recommendations of the UPR in 2011" (National Congress of Australia's First Peoples 2015: 2). Although there has been some criticism of the National Congress, that it does not reflect a broad representative base Australia-wide (as of early 2015 there were 8,241 individual members and 181 member organizations, according to Australia's National Report), as a new organization presumably it takes time to establish broad support. There are challenges to it mobilizing support in remote communities such as Papunya, where very few community leaders I spoke with had heard of the organization.[14] Nevertheless, relative to a twelve-member government-appointed advisory council (which no community members I spoke with had heard of), the National Congress follows democratic and indeed (very) good governance principles (National Congress 2010).[15]

Further, the National Report for the second UPR states: "On 4 March 2015 the Australian Government announced investment of more than $860 million in grants to [Indigenous] front line services" (National Report 2015: 7). However, the submission by NATSILS (the National Aboriginal and Torres Strait Islander Legal Services peak body) again counters this with: "In 2013, the Federal Attorney-Generals' Department announced a cut of $13.34 million from the Indigenous Legal Aid and Policy Reform Program between the 2014–15 and 2016–17 financial years" (NATSILS Submission 2015: 5). Such funding cuts to Indigenous "front-line services" were also a significant focus of a recent senate enquiry into the major restructuring of the Indigenous Affairs Budget (*The Australian* 2016 and Commonwealth of Australia 2016).

Conclusions

"The Declaration now exists, and so do these international forums, so we are obliged to participate" (personal communication with Steve Hodder-Watts 2013). This statement suggests that although there is now a seat at the big table for Indigenous voices, they should not have to be grateful. Rather, maintaining autonomy and distinctiveness within this domain has become another site of struggle, though it may not be articulated as such yet by those who routinely engage with this site.

Those Indigenous Australians who participate, routinely or occasionally, at international forums, such as the UPR in Geneva or the UNPFII in New York, are rarely the marginalized, even though sometimes they may come from remote towns such as Alice Springs. They are the elite who, more often than not, already work in this space and are simply going about their work business through their participation. It is their job to lobby and attempt to progress change on a political and policy level. The exclusivity of the accreditation process through ECOSOC makes it an essential requirement that Indigenous peoples form into corporate groups. These groups are not expressions of corporate identity, such as native title groups; rather they are service provision organizations—such as those IPOs outlined earlier that are recognized by the states—and indeed funded by the state. They are rarely expressions of Indigenous governance, and they are not threatening to sovereignty but circumscribed by it.

Those who participate at these global forums tend to be the urban-educated elites: those who have mastered this rights discourse and who themselves do not practice the locally offending "traditional culture" (Merry 2006).

Bridging the gulf between these sites of practice is a massive challenge in the remote central Australian context. Enabling the circulation of this discourse to these local places, and thus potentially its mobilization, has barely begun in central Australia. And although I am not dismissive of the claim making in this global arena, the work of these international forums, at this stage at least, has not been mobilized or reached into the remote areas of central Australia that are the focus of this book. It is telling that the peak regional Aboriginal advocacy body, the Central Land Council, chooses instead the language of "good governance." At their first full Council meeting for 2016, their newsletter stated that "before the elections [for the new executive team] . . . [a] good governance workshop came first" (Central Land Council 2016). This was where "old and new delegates spent one day learning and teaching each other about good governance." There seems to have been little shift since a CLC policy staff member stated to me in 2012 that they don't have any policies on implementing the UN DRIP because "we don't want to get people's hopes up." Yet, these same staff routinely refer to the UN DRIP in their advocacy work in policy submissions to the government. It does not yet seem to be a comfortable part of the political imaginary in the full council meeting discourse, even as the CLC is at the remote frontline.

The UNPFII is at once a site for pragmatists and also a site for those who dream of social justice and recognition. Those Indigenous advocates who engage with the UN processes long term have also gotten inside the matrix of governmentality and learned the craft to push for reform within the limitations and boundaries of the states. As a core crucible for change, this is the peak of international exposure. It is also a site for those with aspiration who seek inspiration from this scaled-up momentum that is the bearer of hope and social justice.

Niezen states: "While leaders of Indigenous movements gain some stature through their ability to navigate the workings of international organisations and organise themselves through NGOs, much of their wider support comes from representing the concept of 'community,' by 'demonstrating the power of the local'" (in Niezen 2009: 32).

This generalization does not resonate for Indigenous Australian delegates. In contrast, Australia's IPOs have been domesticated, through colonial history and regulation. As one Indigenous member of an IPO attending the UNPFII in 2013 stated:

We don't have the same structures as, say, they do in North America, where they've got this chief that represents these people, and if you look at my people—Wiradjuri NSW— because I'm fifth-generation colonised— compared with the Yolngu [in the remote north of the NT] who still have their structures and where they can say this person speaks for this land. We don't have that, and so we have organizational structures instead. (field notes May 2013)

That Australian Indigenous organizations, as part of the IPO, tend to represent national interests, such as the National Native Title Council, rather than regional Land Councils or more local bodies, offers up a challenge to the possibilities of this rights discourse circulating back in daily discourse other than the urban. They are not small community interest groups representing a specific group over an infringement, though this can happen, in relation to the NTER and the side events sponsored by AIA, but it is not the norm. However, a key element in this second wave Indigenism is, to borrow UN jargon, "operationalizing" the Declaration, and this is increasingly the focus in Australia, with the National Congress hosting what they are calling "Declaration Dialogues" as workshops over a day or more. These workshops, in regional centers and towns, have been described as a major joint project by the Congress and the Australian Human Rights Commission. The first Declaration Dialogue was held in Alice Springs in 2013.

The First Special Rapporteur on Indigenous Issues, Rudolfo Stavenhagen, predicted: "In the coming years . . . the focus of attention of many Indigenous peoples organisations will shift from the international arena to more local concerns" (Stavenhagen 2009: 366). This is evident in the partnership between the Congress and the Australian Human Rights Commission. Brian Wyatt (then Chair of the National Native Title Council) told me at the 2013 UNPFII that "the question is for Aboriginal people; they need to be asked, 'what are you doing?' People may be sceptical of rights, but we can't wait for the state, can't rely on them. We need to recognise rights ourselves"(field notes May 2013).[16] Ultimately, this statement currently speaks to the Indigenous Australians who attend these UN forums and recalls to mind Ranciere's statement: "The Rights of man are the rights of those who make something of that inscription" (2004: 303). Those that attend these forums, routinely and even occasionally, are attempting to build the case for the verification of the power of the inscription (per Ranciere 2004).

Yet, I think that the specialized field of practice of these UN Forums does not circulate to the regions of remote central Australia. But that is not necessarily its orbit; it is at this stage beyond its range. Indeed, engagement with the UN system, as for any UN forum, is likely to remain a specialized field, and it is telling that many of the most prominent Indigenous activists on the international stage are trained as lawyers. A high degree of mainstream education is required to engage meaningfully with the jargon of international law and the associated UN systems.

Conclusion

To be truly visionary we have to root our imagination in our concrete reality while simultaneously imagining possibilities beyond that reality.

bell hooks 2000: 110

THE CONCRETE REALITY EXPLORED IN THIS BOOK is the extensive and diffuse range of regulatory and domesticating dimensions of human rights that underpin a diverse range of government policies, approaches, and programs in a very remote context in central Australia. Many of these dimensions are the acknowledged public goods of accountability, representation, and gender equity. For Anangu citizens of the Northern Territory, the entailments of citizenship are dual edged. Whether explicit or tacit, there has been an ever-increasing mechanistic coupling of rights and duties. The rights discourse is cloaked in the language of responsibility and the associated implications of the free will of the individual in questions of duty, accountability, and morality. By exploring the diverse work of this discourse, the relationship between what constitutes a [human] right and what constitutes a person has been revealed. Imagining possibilities beyond the liberal entailment of personhood is challenging because, as Hage states, "Part of the governmentality that marks the neo-liberal era is . . . a highjacking of the political imagination and the difficulty of thinking of what alternatives exist" (2012: 412). One avenue to locating alternatives is to realize that human rights, like liberalism, are not complete. This book has begun to agitate for alternative understandings of human dignity and more porous human rights that are less dependent on singular renderings of liberal forms of humanity. At the same time, the moral language and social justice potential embodied within human rights has much to offer Anangu. I hope that this book opens up further conversation and dialogue that encourage engagement with it.

The Self-Shaping Person

I have explored the challenges for an Anangu person in understanding his or her problems in terms of rights. As Merry reminds us, "Adopting a human rights subjectivity does not happen quickly or easily. It is a slow process. It means adopting a new sense of self that incorporates rights" (2006: 181). In considering how an Anangu person becomes a "human rights holder" the elements that specify this type of personhood had to first be unpacked. The liberal individual in the pursuit of freedom tends to be set up as the antithesis of culture as a coherent shared identity and group formation. Liberal principles and culture are normatively positioned as mutual antagonists (Brown 2006: 21). By opening the discussion between these "antagonists" we can more clearly articulate the challenges for Anangu in being or becoming this person and also the points and the places of co-optation or vernacularization when they do. This is the work of "behavioral change programs" and therapeutic interventions that were discussed in Chapter 5 and also, in more quotidian contexts, the work of the increasingly pervasive "good governance" project.

Methodologically, this book has taken a dialogical approach to open a discussion between the human rights culture and Anangu cultures. I have begun to trace the complexities entailed in developing the self that identifies as a human rights holder. By doing so, I have also begun to develop a "theory of context," to borrow from Santos, within which this "self" emerges and evolves or is challenged or stifled. This theory properly situated the Anangu person within the relational web of kinship that operates through structures of feeling that "tend to forget that human suffering has an irreducible individual dimension: societies don't suffer, individuals do" (Santos 2002: 49). This context also encompasses the racially divisive Northern Territory sociolegal system and the raft of structural inequalities in which Anangu are embedded, as these also act to variously compel or constrain the development of the self-shaping intentional subject. Intersectionality in this context also illuminated the restraints that identity-based rights impose, that define and demarcate female "victims" from male "perpetrators" in family and domestic violence, for instance.

As an exploration of the regulatory dimensions of rights, each chapter in this book has attempted to work through some of the fundamental paradoxes of human rights, notably that "rights differently empower different social groups, depending upon their ability to enact the power that a right potentially entails" (Brown 2000: 232). In Chapter 4, the category "Anangu woman" was considered as a dual identity as I explored the question of whether "in mobilising the discourse of law, do they enter the ideal space of neo-liberal subject making?" (Speed 2007: 181). That rights are never deployed "freely" but always within a normative context (per Brown 2000: 232) was illustrated in these sociolegal interventions and also, as discussed in Chapter 6, in relation to formal representative democracy that for Anangu has proven to be hollow.

The growing fields of behavioral change programs, as these channel the therapeutic technology of modern subjecthood, were examined as they operate in the Cross Borders Indigenous Family Violence Program and the work of the Alice Springs Women's Shelter. These interventions actively attempt to refashion the self of these "perpetrators" and "victims," respectively. The role these therapeutic technologies play in the production of individuals "free to choose" and free to associate offered an insight into the incremental transformation of Anangu subjects into human rights holders. Such therapeutic technologies attempt to make the personal political both within the Aboriginal polity and within this legal sphere to develop a new form of articulation with the state and among Aboriginal families within the Aboriginal polity.

These therapeutic interventions are one means of starting the conversation to inculcate this modern achievement of freedom. Freedom in this case is where "the normal biography thus becomes the 'elective biography,' the 're-flexive biography,' the 'do-it-yourself biography'" (Beck and Beck-Gernsheim 2002: 3). Such biographies cast off the binding ties of family and community. Such a particular freedom is also underpinned and guided by the liberal logics of mobility (per Walzer 1990). In this case, the female victims of spousal violence are provided with encouragement to pursue geographic and marital mobilities and thus to pursue voluntary associations untethered from (remote) community and family. Indeed, the state actively supports separation through the domestic violence orders and mandatory imprisonment; as the focus is on the protection of the individual, the legal logic attempts to compel this untethering. In Chapters 4 and 5 I have explored how, rather than support a healthy spousal relationship or seek to keep families together, the legal frameworks and government programs facilitate their dissolution. The paradox is that while there are some Anangu women for whom this is indeed appropriate, and they relish their newfound freedoms, including from violence, there are as yet many others for whom this form of freedom adds to their suffering.

In exploring what it means in practice for an Anangu person to become a human rights holder, my embrace of the moral triumphalism of human rights sentiments has been cautious. Although I readily acknowledge that key aspects of the human rights culture are not only legitimate but morally superior to cultural contexts that don't practice such principles (per Rorty 1993), the enveloping normative context within which these principles are deployed or employed has to become the point of conversation. Human rights culture is at the forefront of the modern governmentality of the self-help shape-shifting individual, and, in the current political milieus, it is coupled with a disinvestment in communities and the diminishment of the welfare state. Locating and retrieving positive investments in human rights have been a challenge in this context, where the entailments of citizenship are overwhelmingly punitive and where the responsibilization discourse is deeply dismissive of structural inequality and human diversity. The blind assumption is that once the options for freedom are known then the preferred shape of personhood is the secular mobile individual. Thus, in reality, this "self-shaping" person has an ideal shape. Therefore, it is important to make the human rights culture, indeed as my own culture, more self-conscious, reflective, and porous, rather than taking an oppositional approach that seeks to demonstrate its universal moral superiority.

An Expanding Repertoire

With this study, I have attempted to expand the repertoire of alternative descriptions of human rights, to borrow from Rorty (1989: 40). Doing so critiques liberalism as both cultureless and as a completed culture.[1] The project of modernity, although ever emergent, is imagined as being on a fully accomplished trajectory and so can afford to be deaf and mute to alternatives. This goes to the heart of the fundamentally apolitical and uncontested character of the liberal project of human rights. To contest it is also to begin the call to develop a shared vocabulary that is able to decentralize the individualist focus and consider the possibilities that the influence of a deeply networked family is not all negative.

As this approach aligns with the pursuit of a multicultural conception of human rights, possible alternatives were explored in an attempt to chart political and imaginative mobility beyond current paradigms. To do this, there had to be reciprocal dialogue, which began in Chapter 1. This chapter offered ethnographic insight into the ways in which the global language of human rights is understood locally. By rendering visible the tacit I sought to reveal human rights in terms of locally normative cultural concepts. In doing so the constraints, limitations, and possibilities of the human rights language could begin to be specified. Many of the core concepts are not readily rendered into Luritja theories of knowledge and ideology. Yet, this is not to suggest that there are not comparable equivalents or that the concepts embedded in this language of rights are not useful and indeed essential to know about. As new contingent forms of identity emerge, so too new vocabularies are required to negotiate them. The translation of the Universal Declaration of Human Rights (UDHR) became a central exercise, exposing the fact that very few Anangu had heard the words "universal human rights" due to very little exposure of these concepts. Furthermore, the process of close engagement with the human rights text also became a deeply considered exercise in the performance of difference. As the translators are culturally embedded, so too were their interpretations. Underpinning this program of the vernacularization of human rights in local social settings was finding the balance between making the UDHR locally meaningful and relevant at the same time as ensuring the integrity of the core principles. Directly engaging with the human rights discourse also enabled a clear-sighted view of a range of local perceptions, which include violence as a normative means of dealing with disputes, as well as gender inequality and hierarchies within the community that are underpinned by a patriarchal religion. Such social structures actively challenge gender equality and notions of feminism.

Chapter 2 attempted a rapprochement between the classical conceptions of individual rights and collective rights by elaborating on Walzer's observation that there has always been a tension between these two conceptions of rights, because the human is a fundamentally social being (1990). The limitations of liberal theory in enabling us to understand the various kinds of human interdependence, which are part of the life of both families and polities, was articulated to more fully and appropriately locate this collective. Case studies of the sociocultural and economic rights work of two central Australian NGOs, Walytja and the Central Land Council, offered insight into local practices, as these organizations channel the right to development and to forms of self-determination.

As an active political project, neoliberalism has sought to discredit relativism. Nevertheless, as Englund suggests, "Universalism must continue to give us pause" (2006: 203). That culture is a gap in the Indigenous "policy space" was recognized by a Social Justice Report (Australian Human Rights Commission 2011b: 40). They state, perhaps generously, that "culture is an afterthought in the development [of] policy and programs" (2011b: 40). In relation to an evaluation of the Northern Territory Emergency Response (NTER) undertaken by the Allen Consulting Group, one survey shows that service providers', government business managers' (GBMs), and non-GBMs' responses indicated that local cultural traditions were "never" considered (35 percent), considered "some of the time" (43 percent), or considered "most of the time" (18 percent) (in Concerned Australians Opinion: NTER Evaluation 2011: 3). Exactly what is understood here under the label "culture" is not clear. However, we might assume that it refers principally to Indigenous difference, which includes indifference to certain liberal values. The value of a relativist perspective is not the denial of universals but rather an acknowledgment that universalism cannot be compelled via the denial of difference. As Shweder states, "To focus exclusively on what is universal is to miss much of the action, while failing to understand actual moral decision making" (Shweder 1990: 212).

How to Talk about Absence

As Australia is without a ready human rights narrative, this book has grappled with the issue of how to speak about absence. With barely legitimate frames of reference, the language of human rights is often marginalized, politicized, or rendered as mere ideology. Apart from those who immediately reference the space of human rights—such as staff of Amnesty International Australia or the Australian Human Rights Commission—many key Aboriginal organizations on the frontline, such as the Central Land Council (CLC), are ambivalent about engaging directly with the discourse. A local move beyond "land rights" to this broader frame of reference has been circumspect. As Chapter 2 explored the mobilizing mechanisms that several NGOs use to activate human rights, it was telling that the peak regional Aboriginal advocacy body, the CLC, chooses the language of "good governance." Indeed, it is under the purview of this discourse that the community development approach of the CLC has also, in a somewhat radical move, managed to

incorporate an inclusive nonhierarchical method of distributing local resources in an attempt to move beyond the patrilineal bias of customary forms
of traditional resource distribution. The April 2016 CLC Council News stated
that, at their first full council meeting for the year, "before the elections [for
the new executive team] . . . [a] good governance workshop came first" (Central Land Council, full Council News, April 2016). This was where "old and
new delegates spent one day learning and teaching each other about good governance." There seems to have been little shift since a CLC policy staff member stated to me in 2012 that they don't have any policies on implementing
the UN Declaration on the Rights of Indigenous Peoples (UN DRIP) because
"we don't want to get people's hopes up." Yet, these same staff routinely refer
to the UN DRIP in their advocacy work in policy submissions to government.
It does not yet seem to be a comfortable element in the political imaginary in
the full council meetings. And so the gloss "good governance" has become the
standard phrasing to articulate many of the public goods of human rights, effectively acting to cloak this work of human rights while rendering the rights
work as ideologically benign and thus less contestable.

The uniquely colloquial Australian euphemism of "the fair go," coined by
mainstream public Australian discourse, has a particular contingency in the
Northern Territory.[2] This book has in many ways been concerned with confronting and naming this contingency. When faced with the extensive range
of mandatory sentencing and reporting laws and the zero-tolerance policing that has led to the hyperincarceration that typifies the Northern Territory, even those who are critical of such laws call on this familiar language.
This can be found in reports of the NT Coroner Greg Cavanagh, who has
investigated all of the deaths in custody in the Northern Territory since at
least 2000. He found that the "paperless arrest laws," which led to the most
recent death in custody of Aboriginal man Kumanjayi Langdon in 2015, were
"manifestly unfair" (Cavangh 2015: 32). He elaborates that this is because they
disproportionately targeted Aboriginal people. However, as for his previous
coroner's reports, such as that of the 2012 death in custody of Aboriginal man
Kwementyaye Briscoe in the Alice Springs Watch House, the words "human
rights" and "discrimination" cannot be found (Holcombe 2016). The rule of
law, as articulated in Articles 7 and 11, that "all are equal before the law" and
are "innocent until proven guilty" is apocryphal when applied to many Aboriginal citizens in this jurisdiction. They are not given the benefit of the doubt
because of the lack of discretion that sentencing magistrates have, even if they

proceed to court. This plays out in multiple ways but also in the far fewer re-ferrals from the police and the legal system to the Cross Borders Indigenous Family Violence Program relative to referrals from neighboring South Aus-tralia and Western Australia who do not have such laws. This not only means that Anangu in the NT have less opportunity to avoid incarceration, but they also have less opportunity to break the cyclical pattern of violence though reformative and transformative programs. That family and domestic violence is now understood solely in terms of criminality, rather than in terms of hu-man rights or health or poverty, has led to these very distinctive sociolegal responses.

The euphemisms of a "fair go" and "good governance" and others in their purview through the responsibilization discourse render invisible the work of human rights and tame the emancipatory potential of the rights language for political and advocacy work. On the other hand, when human rights viola-tions are overt, neither are they named. It seems to me that naming and being explicit as to what is demoted, domesticated, or simply denied allows us to call out the poor cousins of human rights. Bolstering the legitimacy of the human rights discourse can begin only when we reveal both the diverse and often hidden work of human rights and, conversely, where human rights abuses are clear.

Harnessing the Emancipatory Social Justice Potential of Human Rights

In 2012 the Australian Human Rights Commission sponsored an on-line site entitled "Rant against Racism," where the public could post their inspirational thoughts. I found the following post especially evocative, as it encapsulated many of the core human rights ideals:

> We will wear no badge, no uniform, no beret. We will remain anonymous except when it matters. There could be one of us, or a thousand of us on that tram, that bus, train or in that crowd. No one will know unless needed. We will leave no one behind. We will abandon no one, to stand alone in fear, in a crowd. This is a personal commitment. This is a silent pledge. I will stand up and I will stand next to the person in silent solidarity. (by Kem, Australian Human Rights Commission 2012).

This is a core plank girding the hope of human rights, the progressive social activist and emancipatory imagining that refuses the complicity of silence.

It speaks to the subtlety of being a human rights holder as a thread of solidarity, a conscientization that is deeply personal. It is where stranger sociability has moved from merely a means of interaction in the market economy to empathy with diverse others in any context. In the unruly world, this individual can be counted on to guard the rights of others, as that person expects his or her rights to be guarded. In this development of an empathetic sensibility, intervention is a method of choice, instead of being a bystander or one who walks away. This is Charles Taylor's modern social imaginary (2002). However, this imaginary is illusory and rendered illegitimate in many public contexts of the Northern Territory because racism has been legalized and become the new governing norm. If a local whitefella or tourist were to see an Aboriginal person being targeted and subsequently detained by the police for one of the many minor misdemeanors that lead to incarceration under the paperless arrest laws, could they and would they call it out? When the work of the state is veiled in the anticrime rhetoric, what scope is there for the implicated bystander public to respond? As the state becomes another perpetrator, they compel the public to be complicit in their wake. This silent scream of complicity has become the majoritarian voice in the NT.

Within an Anangu community there are very different structural issues challenging the development of this social imaginary. Although there are community leaders who choose to stay away from participating in payback as their way of not condoning it, it is ultimately the case that acting as a bystander is also a form of complicity in this context, as in others beyond the community. A coalescence between a majoritarian rejection of violence from within the community has to be one that is also vocalized for the local social imaginary to be reshaped.

This book has attempted to work on imagining what it takes to reshape this voice: to make explicit the voiceless, the implicit, or the dormant and by doing so to expand this domain of the social justice potential of human rights to places where the values and principles have not been made explicit. I have tried to extend the conversation and the dialogue, to reopen the debate on the need for a national bill of rights, just as there is a need for constitutional change to recognize Indigenous Australians as the First Peoples. The language of human rights offers a new lens through which to consider intransigent or "wicked problems," such as the relationship between intersectional disadvantage and certain Anangu cultural practices.

Although this book has attempted to chart alternatives and locate limitations, these also need to be balanced against the raft of moral and social goods
that a contemporary ethic values and that are to be found in the language of
human rights. The language of equality and the intersubjective qualities of
empathy for strangers, voluntary association, and so on are important liberal
values. Anangu need access to this language to make of it what they will. I
am not aware of any educational programs that specify the content of human
rights declarations in remote areas. The translation of the UDHR laid bare the
parameters of personhood that Western modernity accepts in its citizens, thus
enabling Anangu to begin to think about them and what they mean for their
situation. This is because "it is through contingent collaborations that incompatible interests and dispositions can turn into compatible ones, moments of
shared vision and hope" (Englund 2006: 34). One of the tasks of this book has
been to locate local practices that were intersecting with and, at times, explicitly drawing from human rights norms to reveal what it takes for sociomoral
normative practices to change. As Eleanor Roosevelt stated, "Where after all
do human rights begin? In small places, close to home" (1958).

We must uncover and work on the discontinuities, the exceptions from
the norm. These include Anangu who refuse to participate in "payback,"
women who do leave their violent partners and the young cousins who follow
their lead, the women who reject the standard domestic violence order and
continue to visit their estranged partner in prison to work on the relationship,
and the others who seek out the police for themselves and their family. In locating these spaces—these intersections with interventions—we are closer to
encouraging the development of spaces for choice making and so, too, to find
some of the primary driving forces of change.

Women who engage effectively with this system, however, have to conform to type; they can't be drinkers like their abusive partners, and they can't
be seen by their families as provocateurs or perhaps even as too assertive.
For the system to effectively work for them they must be passive victims—
becoming agentic only when desperate or following through when the state
intervenes. Both their families and the state have to see them as blameless. If
they do not, it is likely that their suffering will compound, without sympathy
and with the loss of their spouse and, possibly, their children. The Anangu
community perspective that many young women are actually not the victims but rather incite the violence that ensues and so are therefore at least
partly to blame is the norm. Yet, this is also the norm within the legal system,

through the operations of the defense, the court processes via the defense for provocation, and the sentiments of the broader public. A particular type of femininity is being sponsored by this dominant paradigm of the "(good) victim" in this context. These Anangu women *have* internalized key elements of this rights-bearing legal subject. They embody the discontinuities between normative familial practices and the possibility of the legal system as new protector.

Revealing the multifarious ways in which the language of human rights is, in many ways, also the language of state power also serves to expose this tacit contract of citizenship. Although Chapter 1 was an explicit focus on the intercultural translation between the Anglo English of the UDHR and the Pintupi-Luritja translations, as an anthropological project, the book in its entirety can be more broadly read as a project of translation and thus of revelation. Because of this, it is perhaps inevitable that this translation can be read as part of a political project, as Michael Ghillar Anderson argues: "Learn his game, understand how he fights us, understand and learn his system so that we can undermine him" (Freedom Movement Forum May 7, 2015). And I suggest further: "learn his game" at least to hold him to account. So potentially this translation project becomes a tool for a more equitable engagement.

Chapter 6 was, in some ways a thought exercise in an alternative dialogical politics that was driven by the fact that "equality in Government policy always privileges whiteness" (Tsing 2007: 42). Although many of the regulatory dimensions of human rights—such as the good governance project—can be understood as tools of assimilation, it is nevertheless essential that Anangu have access to these tools. As part of the diverse work of rights I have sought not only to open a dialogue with the emancipatory potential of the rights discourse but to redirect this discourse beyond and away from the dominating regulatory and domesticating modes that have come to work their hegemonic script. This script is written in the euphemisms of good (corporate) governance and shared responsibility though it expresses the arrogance of a neoliberal completeness that is resistant to reciprocity and conversation. The current discourse sponsored by the neoliberal state, much of which is embedded in the "good governance" discourse, is coercive, intolerant of pluralism, dismissive of cultural and Indigenous recognition and any forms of substantive rights in their language of entailment and obligation. As Santos states: "Low intensity human rights act as the other side of low intensity democracy" (2002: 46). And although the potential for the emancipatory value of human rights to be fostered has never been taken up by the government, it is, likewise barely visible in the NGOs that operate as service providers. There is some scope for optimism; by reclaiming the concept of self-determination it can be remade, as David Ross argues: "It is clear . . . that governments have lost their way in Aboriginal Affairs . . . their own governance and implementation capacity is the lowest it has ever been. At the end of the day governments will come and go, but our people will still be here" (Ross 2013).

Although the Australian Human Rights Commission has been hosting annual Human Rights Awards since 1987,[3] under five areas including "enhancing the rights of Indigenous Australians," the establishment of the National Indigenous Human Rights Award in 2014 further specifies, publicizes, and legitimizes the work of human rights. There are three categories for this Award: the Dr. Yunupingu Award for Human Rights, the Eddie Mabo Award for Social Justice, and the Anthony Mundine Award for Courage. The awards were developed by NSW parliamentarian Shaoquett Moselmane, who had two aims in doing so: "To recognise the phenomenal contribution that many First Peoples make to human rights and social justice, and to also recognise the First Peoples rights struggle as Australia's greatest human rights and social justice struggle . . . [which] is ongoing" (Georgatos 2014). The awards have been described as "a signature recognition of the struggle itself" (Georgatos 2014). At the very least, they are a public endorsement of the value of human rights to affect social and political change and presumably energize the work of those in the field. The first recipient of the Dr. Yunupingu Award for Human Rights was Rosalie Kunoth-Monks from Central Australia for her strong opposition of the NTER and advocacy work with Amnesty International Australia, discussed in Chapter 6. That these awards are aimed at Indigenous recipients also speaks to the recognition of an active vocal Indigenous citizenry. As I spoke with Brian Wyatt (then Chair of the National Native Title Council) at the 2013 UN Permanent Forum on Indigenous Issues, this recognition was clear as he asked in turn: "The question is for Aboriginal people—they need to be asked—'What are you doing?' People may be sceptical of rights, but we can't wait for the state, can't rely on them. We need to recognize rights ourselves" (field notes May 2013). This statement recalls to mind Ranciere's premise: "The Rights of man are the rights of those who make something of that inscription" (2004: 303). Those who are award recipients, perhaps like those who attend international UN forums, are attempting to build the case for the verification of the power of the inscription (per Ranciere 2004).

As Hodder-Watts remarked: "The Declaration [on the Rights of Indigenous Peoples] now exists and so do these international forums, so we are obliged to participate" (personal communication 2013). This statement suggests that although there is now a seat at the big table for Indigenous voices, they should not have to be grateful. Rather, maintaining autonomy and distinctiveness within this domain has become another site of struggle, though it may not be articulated as such yet by those who routinely engage with this site. Those Indigenous Australians who participate, routinely or occasionally, at international forums; speak at public events; and work in rights advocacy tend to be the elite who have embodied the discourse. Enabling the circulation of this discourse to these local places, and thus potentially its mobilization, has barely begun in central Australia. And although I am not dismissive of the claim making in global arenas such as the United Nations, the work of these international forums, at this stage at least, has not been mobilized nor has reached into the remote areas of central Australia that are the focus of this book. The level of complexity that needs to be mastered to engage with the UN system is also a reminder that one needs to learn to walk before one can run. Nevertheless, Stavenhagen, the First Special Rapporteur on Indigenous Issues, suggested that: "In the coming years . . . the focus of attention of many Indigenous people's organisations will shift from the international arena to more local concerns" (2009: 366). The Indigenous Human Rights Award is a sign of this shift and perhaps of the emerging conversation to which this book hopes to contribute.

The Universal Declaration of Human Rights in Pintupi–Luritja

*Yara Tina Ngaatjanya Yananguku Tjukarurrulpayi
Liipula Nyinanytjaku Mingarrtjuwiya*

Ngaatja Yurrunpa Riitarripayi

Kaantjala tina (United Nations) nyinanyi yanangu yuwankarraku, pana yurungka parrari nyinapayi tjutaku. Palunya kaantjala ngurrara tjutangku kulini wati, kungka, maru tjuta, tjulkura tjuta, kutjupa tjutatarra liipula nyinanyi, wiya kutjupa tjutangku mingarrtjurringkula kutjupa tjuta pikangku pungkunytjaku. Yuwankarra kalypa kutu nyinanytjaku. Wiya kutjupa tjuta, kutjupa tjutaku mayutjurrinytjaku, yuwankarra liipula nyinanyi.

Kaantjala palunya ngurrara tjutangku kulini pana kutjupa pana kutjupangka palyaya nyinanytjaku kuutawutjutjarra. Palya luwiya tjutangku yananguku ngalkinmankunytjaku yaalytjiyaalytji yara tina ngaangku tjakultjunanyi. Piipa ngaatja ngaranyi Kapamanta ngurrara yuwankarrangku kulira tjukarurru nyinanytjaku. Yalatjingkuya ngaatja kulintjaku, kapamanta kutjupa kutjupangku, kapamanta pana kutjupa yurungka parrari nyinapayi tjutangkutarra.

Kuwarri ngaatja United Nations mantjini, Universal Declaration of Human Rights.

Naampa 1

Nganana maru tjuta, tjulkura tjuta, manta yurungka parrari nyinapayi tjutanya liipulala nyinanyi, nganana yanangu maru tjuta wiya kuyakuya.

This translation was undertaken by Lance Macdonald, Shelia Joyce Dixon (both from Papunya), Sarah Holcombe (ANU), and Ken Hansen. Final version September 2015.

Yuwankarrangkuya palya nintingku kulini. Tjanaya palya kutjupa tjutaku tjukarurru nyinanytjaku, walytja tjuta nguwanpa, mingarrtjuwiya. Tjungungku palyangku kurrunpa kutjungku.

Wangka ngaangku nganananya tjakultjunanyi rapa ngaranytjaku kutjupa tjuta nguwanpa.

Naampa 2

Wangka piipa ngaangka ngaranyi yuwankarrangku kulira palulawana nyinanytjaku. Kutjupa tjutaku wiya mingarrtju nyinanytjaku. Ngurra pana kutjupa ngurraraku wiya mingarrtju nyinanytjaku. Kungkaku watiku wiya mingarrtju nyinanytjaku. Wangka kutjupa wangkapayiku wiya mingarrtju nyinanytjaku. Katutjanya walkulpayi tjutaku tjinguru walkuntja kutjupa tjutaku wiya mingarrtju nyinanytjaku. Kapamanta ngurraraku, kapamanta kutjupa kutjupaku, kapamanta pana kutjupa yurungka parrariku wiya mingarrtju nyinanytjaku.

Wangka ngaangku nganananya tjakultjunanyi rapa ngaranytjaku kutjupa tjuta nguwanpa.

Naampa 3

Pana winkiku ngaranyi nyinanytjaku tjukarurru. Watingku kungkangku wiya warrkira pungkunytjaku. Watingku wiya pungkunytjaku kungka, pipirri. Wiya kutjupa mirri pungkunytjaku, wiya kuyara pungkunytjaku. Yantayantara marangku purinypangkula kanyintjaku,

Wangka ngaangku nganananya tjakultjunanyi kutjupa tjuta nguwanpa palya nyinanytjaku.

Naampa 4

Yanangu tjuta wiya tjiinangku piyuku karrpira kanyintjaku. Mayutju kutjupangku yirriti tjananyaya kanyilpayi pungkula mayutjurringkula katiyinkupayi. Kuwarri yanangu tjutaku wiyalpi yalatji palunya palyantjaku.

Naampa 5

Wiyalpi ngaranyi, nyinyipungkunytjaku yitjipungkunytjaku.

Tjukarurruwanangku pungkunytjawiyangku, palyangku yantantantjaku.

Wiyalpi pungkunytjaku kutjupa kutjupa tjutanya.

Naampa 6

Tjutaku ngaranyi tjukarurrungku luwuwanangku waarrka tjanampa paly-antjaku, yurrkunytjingku, kuutaku mayutjungku kuutaku ngalkinpa tju-tangku. Tjana wiya tjulkuraku kutju tjukarurrungku palyantjaku, yanangu marukutarra tjukarurrungku palyantjaku.

Wangka ngaangku nganananya tjakultjunanyi rapa ngaranytjaku kutjupa tjuta nguwanpa.

Naampa 7

Luwu tina ngaranyi pana kutjupa kutjupa ngurrara tjutaku kulira kaangkur-ringkula wanantjaku. Yalatji luwu ngaangku nganananya nintini, wiya kutju-paku mingarrtju nyinanytjaku. Tjungu ngaranyi kutju kutu luwu palunya kapamantaku, yirrkunytjiku, yanangu maruku, tjulkurakutarra, yurungka parrari nyinapayi tjutakutarra.

Wangka ngaangku nganananya tjakultjunanyi rapa ngaranytjaku kutjupa tjuta nguwanpa.

Naampa 8

Yanangu winkiku ngaranyi tjapintjaku kuutangka,
tjinguru mantjintjaku ngalkinpa luwiya, palumpa wangkanytjaku.

Ngalkinpa nyarrangku, wiyanta kulira wantinytjaku.

Wangka ngaangku nganananya tjakultjunanyi rapa ngaranytjaku kutjupa tjuta nguwanpa.

Naampa 9

Wiya nyuntunya tjarrpatjunkunytjaku tjiilangka, tjukarurru yirrkun-ytjingku luwuwanangku purinypangku kulintjaku luwu katantankutjawi-yangku, waarrka tjukarurru palyantjaku. Kapamanta ngurrarangku wiya payintjaku nyuntunya ngurra walytjanguru.

Wangka ngaangku nganananya tjakultjunanyi rapa ngaranytjaku kutjupa tjuta nguwanpa.

Naampa 10

Yanangu winkiku ngaranyi yalytjura kuutangka tjarrparra kulintjaku.

Kuuta tinangka, wangka walytja kulilpayinya mantjintjaku, matupurra.

Yananguku wangka taanamilalpayinya ngururrpa ngaranytjaku nyun-tupa ngalkinpa.

Wangka ngaangku nganananya tjakultjunanyi rapa ngaranytjaku kutjupa tjuta nguwanpa.

Naampa 11

Maru tjutangku tjulkura tjutangkutarra wiya yurrnyuntjaku, tjapira ngurrira kulintjaku. Kuutaku patara marungku tjulkurangku wiya wangkanytjaku nyakunytjawiyangku. Yara palunya tjukarurruwanangku luwungka mayutju winkingku kulintjaku. Tjinguru yara palunya yilta? Tjinguru wiya?

Wangka ngaangku nganananya tjakultjunanyi rapa ngaranytjaku kutjupa tjuta nguwanpa.

Naampa 12

Wiya nyuntunya tjapira ngaranytjaku, ramantjaku nyuntupa walytja tjutatarra, Waala nyuntupangka wiya tjarrpanytjaku ngatjarri.

Yuuputjungka nyuntupa liita wiya yalytjuranytjaku ngatjarringku tjapintjawiyangku.

Nyuntunya wiya panypurangkunytjaku kutjupangku, ngantingkarringkula parra wangkayinkunytjaku. Tjana nyuntupa kuya tjutanya yalatji palunya palyani

nyuntu tjanampa mantjilku yirrkunytji nyuntupa ngalkinpa ngaranytjaku. Palunya kuuta ngurrarangku tjapira ngurrilku.

Wangka ngaangku nganananya tjakultjunanyi rapa ngaranytjaku kutjupa tjuta nguwanpa.

Naampa 13

Maru tjuta tjulkuratarra yankukitja yunytjurringanyi ngurra kutjupakutu yurungka parrari pana kutjupakutu parra yulytjayinytjaku, kala palya tjanampa yalytjura ngaranyi yankunytjaku ngurra kutjupakutu yunytjurringkula.

Naampa 14

Kutjupangkunta mirri pungkukitjangku pikapikani yilatu yilatu palya nyinanyingka, palya nyuntu yananyi ngurra kutjupakutu, yanangu kutjupa tjutangka nyinanytjaku. Ngulurringkula yankukitja yurungka parrari ngurra palyara nyinakitja, wiyantaya payintjaku ngurra tjanampanguru. Wangka ngaangku tjakultjunanyi nganampa yalytjura pana kutjupangka nyinanytjaku, pikangkamarra.

Wangka ngaangku nganananya tjakultjunanyi rapa ngaranytjaku kutjupa tjuta nguwanpa.

Naampa 15

Nyuntu yunytjurriku yurungka parrari pana kutjupangka rawa nyinakitja, palya nyuntu yankula tjapintjaku palula ngurra palyara nyinakitjangku. Wiyantaya marrkura payintjaku ngurranguru. Tjinguru nyuntu yunytjurriku pana walytjangka kutu nyinanytjaku, yalatji palunya palya. Wiyantaya payintjaku, ngurra walytja nyuntupanguru.

Naampa 16

Wangka ngaatja ngaranyi yuwankarrangku kulintjaku, watingku, kungkangku, pana kutjupa ngurrarangku, Katutjanya walkulpayi tjutangku, kutjupa walkulpayi tjutangku. Tjana palya miita walytja mantjira nyinanytjaku kutjarrapula yunytjurringkula. Palyapula pipirri tjuta kanyira tinantjaku.

Luwu tinangka ngaranyi kungka yukarra wiima miita mantjintjaku yiitiinarringanyingka kutju. Pana winkiku luwu yutitja ngaranyi miitararra pipirritjarra, walytja tjutatarra matupurra, tjukarurrungku Kapamantangku yanga kanyintjaku, kuyangkamarra yantayantantjaku.

Wangka ngaangku nganananya tjakultjunanyi rapa ngaranytjaku kutjupa tjuta nguwanpa.

Naampa 17

Tjutakulampa ngaranyi, pulaaka walytja maningku payimilantjaku yunytjurringkula ngurra walytjangka nyinakitja, waala walytjatjarralpi nyinaku, tjitiyingka ngururrpa, tawunungka, tjaatangka.

Ngurra walytja yanangu maruku wiya palatja yanangu kutjuku, walytjarrinytjaku. Yanangu maruku ngurra walytja winkiku ngaranyi, tjapira tjukarurruwanangku maruku ngurrangka panangka waala palyalkitjangku.

Wangka ngaangku nganananya tjakultjunanyi rapa ngaranytjaku kutjupa tjuta nguwanpa.

Naampa 18

Tjutaku ngaranyi nintirrinytjaku puntura Katutjaku tjukurrpa walkuntjaku tjinguru kutjupaku yunytjurringanyi walkuntjaku. Kala palya kutjupa walkuntjaku, yunytjurringkula. Wiyaya marrkuntjaku walytja tjutangku yanangu nyarra paluru kutjupa wanantjaku yunytju. Yaalytjiyaalytji walkuntjaku palumpa walytjangku kulintjaku.

Wangka ngaangku nganananya tjakultjunanyi rapa ngaranytjaku kutjupa tjuta nguwanpa.

Naampa 19

Maru tjutangku tjulkura tjutangkutarra palya tjapira pungkunytjaku tjukarurru wangkarra pungkunytjaku, kuntarrinytjawiyangku. Kutjupangkunta tjapintjangka palya nyuntu tjakultjunkunytjaku. Nyuntu wangka tjakultjunutja putu kulira palya nyuntu yankula yara kulilkitjangku tjapintjaku. Yaalytjiyaalytji tjukarurru, nyuntu kulilku. Kapamanta pina yalytjura ngaranytjaku kulira ngalya yaluntjaku nyaa nyuntu tjapiningka. Yarrkatjunkunytjawiyangku Kapamantangku yara tjukarurru tjakultjunkunytjaku nyuntulakutu.

Wangka ngaangku nganananya tjakultjunanyi rapa ngaranytjaku kutjupa tjuta nguwanpa.

Naampa 20

Tjutakulampa ngaranyi wangka tina ngaatja. Palya nganana miitingi tinangka tjungurringkunytjaku, tjapintjaku, kulintjaku. Kapamantaku yuuputju ngurrara waarrkana palumpa tjutanya, yanangu maruku mayutju tjutawana tjungurrinytjaku, kulintjaku miitingingka tjukarurrungku. Nyurrangarrimpa yara tjana kulira tjukarurru watjantjaku palyawanangku. Nyurrangarri putu kulira yankula tjungurringkula walytjangkulpi miitingi palyalku, maru tjutawana.

Wangka ngaangku nganananya tjakultjunanyi rapa ngaranytjaku kutjupa tjuta nguwanpa.

Naampa 21

Yanangu tjutangku piipangka yunpa nyakula puutarringkula ngurrtjantjaku kapamanta ngaratjunkukitjangku. Yanangungku palya tjapintjaku kapamanta ngurrara tjutangka waarrkarrikitjangku tjungurringkula.

Putu kulira palya nyuntu yankula kapamanta ngurrara tjapintjaku tjinguru maninguru tjukarurruntjaku, tjinguru kutjupaku nintirrikitjangku.

Wangka ngaangku nganananya tjakultjunanyi rapa ngaranytjaku kutjupa tjuta nguwanpa.

Naampa 22

Yanangu mani tjiintalingkangka mantjilpayingku palya yankula ngur-
rintjaku waarrka yiltangka tjarrparra waarrkarrikitjangku. Yanangungku
waarrkaku ngurriningka tjiintalingkangku manira yungkunytjaku, wiya
mani palumpa marrkuntjaku. Paluru kuwarripa waarrkaku ngurrini.

Yanangu maru tjungurringanyi walytja tjutawana tjukurrpa kulira nintirringkula wanalkitja. Kapamantangku wiya kuyara pungkunytjaku, wiya
marrkuntjaku, palya yananguku tjukurrpangka tjungurringkunytjaku, wiyantaya mayutjurrinytjaku.

Wangka ngaangku nganananya tjakultjunanyi rapa ngaranytjaku kutjupa
tjuta nguwanpa.

Naampa 23

Yanangu tjuta waarrkarringkula tjukarurru mani mantjintjaku, tjulkura tjutangku mani mantjini palunya nguwanpa. Yanangu maru yunytjurringanyi
waarrka palyantjaku tjulkura tjuta nguwanpa. Tjinguru yuuputju tinangka
waarrkarriku. Tjinguru waarrkaku mayutju nyinaku. Tjinguru wanma
yankuku waarrka parra yulytjayinkula palyantjaku. Kala palya yalytjura ti-
nalingku ngaranyi yanangu marungku kulira waarrka mantjintjaku.

Paluru rawa nyinaku mani palya mantjilku tjulkura tjuta nguwanpa,
waarrkangka rawa nyinarra. Nintirringkula kulintjaku yini turayit yunyun
(trade union). Tjana waarrkana tjutaku ngalkinpa ngarapayi. Waarrkanan-
gku putu kulira turayit yunyunangka tjakultjunkunytjaku. Paluru tjana kulira tjukarurrulpayi, tjinguru nyuntupa maniku, tjinguru nyuntupa mayutju
mingarrtju nyinanyingka.

Wangka ngaangku nganananya tjakultjunanyi rapa ngaranytjaku kutjupa
tjuta nguwanpa.

Naampa 24

Waarrkana tjutakulampa ngaranyi. Rawa waarrkangka nyinarra purrkar-
ringkula yunytjurringkula yankunytjaku yalatayi (holiday). Kala palya nyurrangarri yunytju yankunytjaku yalatayi.

Wangka ngaangku nganananya tjakultjunanyi rapa ngaranytjaku kutjupa
tjuta nguwanpa.

Naampa 25

Tjutakulampa ngaranyi miintangkamarra mangarri palyangka nyinanytjaku, mantarra kutjupangka tjarrpanytjaku. Waarrkawiyapaka nyuntu nyinanytjala tjiintalingkangku nyuntunya yantayantalku manitjarrangku nyuntu walytjangku mangarri mantarra payimilantjaku. Piintjina mantjilpayinya, nyumpurringutja tjutanya yalatji palunya nguwanpa tjiintalingkangku tjananya yantayantani.

Yanangu tjutakulampa tjukarurru palyantjaku yuutjupilangka waarrkarripayi tjutangku. Ngaa tjutanyatarra tjukarurru purinypangku yantayantantjaku, kungka pipirri wiimatjarra, pipirri kutjupa tjutatarra tina tjutanya, wiima tjutanya.

Naampa 26

Tjutakulampa ngaranyi puntura nintirringkunytjaku tjulkuraku tjukurrpaku, kuulangka tjarrparra. Nintirringkula yunytjurringkula yankuku kaalitjikutu puntura nintirrinytjaku, pana kutjupaku tjukurrpaku. Palunyatjanu waarrkangka tjarrpakitjangku yankula nintirrinytjaku yunipatjiti (university) tinangka. Maama paapangku nintintjaku yaalytjikutu yiyalku pipirri palumpa kutjarraku. Tjinguru kuula tina kaalitjikutu (college) yiyalku paluru kutjarra miitararrangku ngurrtjaningka.

Kutjupa tjuta yunytjurringanyi maruku tjukurrpa nintirrinytjaku wangka walytja riitarringkula wakantjaku. Palyaya kuultiitji tjapintjaku pipirri tjanampa wangka kutjarraku nintirrinytjaku kuulangka.

Wangka ngaangku nganananya tjakultjunanyi rapa ngaranytjaku kutjupa tjuta nguwanpa.

Naampa 27

Yanangu tjuta, ngurra kutjungka tjukurrpa walytjaku nintirrinytjaku. Palya tjungurrinytjaku wati kutjupa tjutawana, wiyantaya marrkuntjaku waarrkaku mayutjungku, kapamantangku, yirrkunytjingku. Wantinytjakuya payintjawiyangku. Kungka maru tjuta puntura nintirrinytjaku tjukurrpa walytjaku, tjungurringkula wanantjaku kami tjanampa. Wiya marrkuntjaku miitangku.

Kampatjangkatarra palyara purinyarrinytjaku yanangu kutjupa ngurrarangku tjukurrpa yarrkalpayingkamarra mulyatangku. Tjamulu kamilu tjukurrpa tjunkupayi yara wangkarra piipangka. Matupurra ngantitja tjutangku yanga kanyintjaku, pana kutjupa ngurrarangku mulyatangku mantjira walytjarringkupayingkamarra.

Wangka ngaangku nganananya tjakultjunanyi rapa ngaranytjaku kutjupa tjuta nguwanpa.

Naampa 28

Tjutakulampa ngaranyi tjukarurru nyinanytjaku kalypa yulykarra mingarrtjuwiya. Yanangu waarrkangka ngaranyi. Waarrkaku mayutjungku tjukarurru katiyinkunytjaku pungkunytjawiyangku. Yalatji palulamarra yanangu marungku kulintjaku ngalkinpalampa nyinanyi kuutangka waarrkarripayi tjutanya. Yalatji kulila walytja tjuta!

Tjinguru kutjupangku nyuntunya kuyara punganyi nyuntu tjakultjunku yirrkunytjikutu paluru tjana mantjilku nyuntupa luwiya ngalkinpa ngaranytjaku. Matupurra kuulangka tjuta tjarrpanytjaku nintirringkula kulintjaku. Kapamantangku tjukarurrungku yantayantantjaku, mingarrtjuwiyangku.

Piipa ngaangka ngarrinyi wangka tina tjuta. Uwankarrangku kulira palunya tjutaku tjukarurru nyinanytjaku, wiya panypurangkula wantinytjaku.

Naampa 29

Yanangu tjutala kaangkurrinytjaku, ngurra kutjungka nyinarra, yulykarra pungkunytjaku kaangkurringkula pungkunytjaku, mingarrtjuwiyangku. Tjukarurruwanangku yanangu kutjupa tjutawana, maruku tjulkuraku palya kaangkinytji nyinanytjaku. Waala kapamanta ngurrarangku palyara ngaratjunutja wiya yatura kuyantjaku, kapikunu puu, payipi tjutatarra wiya yatura kuyantjaku.

Naampa 30

Piipa ngaangka ngarrinyi wangka tina tjuta. Uwankarrangku kulira yara palya tjutaku tjukarurru nyinanytjaku, wiya panypurangkula wantinytjaku.

Wangka ngaangku nganananya tjakultjunanyi rapa ngaranytjaku kutjupa tjuta nguwanpa.

Notes

Introduction

1. This film (2013) is a true story based on the 1853 autobiography of Solomon Northrup.

2. Britain has a Human Rights Act (1998), rather than a convention or bill of rights. However, the European Convention on Human Rights is also incorporated into British law, and there is public debate in Britain about replacing the act with a bill of rights.

3. Several states and territories, Victoria and the Australian Capital Territory (ACT), have human rights acts. The ACT has the Human Rights Act 2004 (ACT), and Victoria has the Charter of Human Rights and Responsibilities (2006). However, there is no Australia-wide bill of rights under Commonwealth legislation (see Byrnes, Charlesworth, and McKinnon 2009 and Williams 2010). Note that a "bill of rights" is a list of rights that is encompassed in a legal act.

4. This was established by the Human Rights (Parliamentary Scrutiny) Act of 2011.

5. When Australia became a federation in 1901, Indigenous people were excluded from this nation-building moment. There were no Indigenous representatives in the negotiations and processes in the 1890s that led to the development of the modern Australian state (Brennan et al. 2005). The only references to Indigenous peoples in this foundation document concerned their exclusion from the population count and from the powers of the national Parliament. And, likewise, the new constitution made no reference to prior Indigenous occupation and ownership.

6. This contrasts with ethnographic work internationally, notably Terence Turner (1997), Richard Wilson (1997), Sally Engle Merry (2006a) and Mark Goodale (2006, 2009). Niezen explains this "disappointing delay" in the social study of human rights as caused, among other things, "by the quasi-utopian search for ideal justice and the inherently abstract nature of law, in its quest for impartiality" (Niezen 2011).

7. Nevertheless, there has been some consideration of the Indigenous rights discourse by several anthropologists—such as Merlan in several articles and commentaries (2009a, 2009b) and Edmunds (2010). These works outline important conceptual

signposts on the path to critically engaging with this discourse and the challenges of applying it in absolute terms in remote Aboriginal communities. See also Cowlishaw (2007).

8. The mainstream adoption of the term *Indigenous* from the 1980s is both a political category that serves as a bridge to the global and a form of resistance against the centralizing tendencies of the state. This scaling up of identity speaks of difference and solidarity with others elsewhere who also identify as "Indigenous" (see Niezen 2003: 91).

9. However, Phillips's intent is to deessentialize the bounded and homogenizing discourse. She states that her object is a "multiculturalism that dispenses with the reified notions of culture that feed those stereotypes to which so many feminists have objected, yet retains enough robustness to address inequalities between cultural groups; a multiculturalism in which the language of cultural difference no longer gives hostages to fortune or sustenance to racists, but also no longer paralyses normative judgement" (2007: 8).

10. However, Walzer argues that these four mobilities have led to the development of a profoundly unsettled modern society, "where individuals are relatively dissociated and separated from one another—continually in motion, often in solitary and apparently random motion."

11. Because of readily available literature in the eighteenth century, for the first time, considerable numbers of the population in Europe were able to read about and experience other people's lives; ordinary people, women, the poor, the vulnerable, the lives of their servants. The realization that the human condition of suffering, fear, hopes, loss, and so on was shared no matter the socioeconomic, and later the cultural, context was fundamental for recognition of a shared humanity.

12. However, a more detailed discussion of the ways in which the frictions and contradictions of the rights discourse were galvanized by this policy complex can be found in Holcombe (2015).

13. In particular, the diverse essays in *Culture Crisis: Anthropology and Politics in Aboriginal Australia* (Altman and Hinkson 2010) and Dianne Austin-Broos's *A Different Inequality* (2011) provide insight into what developed as a deeply divisive public anthropology (see also Hage 2012).

14. See Australian Human Rights and Equal Opportunity Commission 2003.

15. This massacre claimed the lives of from seventeen, the "official toll" (Cribbin 1984: 75), to thirty-one (the number the board of enquiry found), to 100 Aboriginal men, women, and children, depending on which texts are consulted. Fred Brooks, the non-Aboriginal dingo hunter who was killed by Aboriginal people, would never have been at the same soak with the group of Ngalia Warlpiri if mutual desperation for water and the Aboriginal need for nonnative foods had not been high. The massacre, led by police, was an official reprisal party. The Central Land Council held a seventy-five year commemoration; see Central Land Council 2003.

16. See Warumpi Band 1983.

17. Thanks to Steve for allowing this to be reproduced here.

18. Conservative public commentator.

19. Australian conservative coalition prime minister at that time.

20. Yolngu Aboriginal leader from Arnhem land in the NT.

21. Premier of Queensland who became notorious for corruption and curbing civil liberties—such as public demonstrations.

Chapter 1

1. United Nations Office of the High Commissioner for Human Rights 2010.

2. United Nations Human Rights Office of the High Commissioner for Human Rights. 2015. Universal Declaration of Human Rights: Pintupi-Luritja.

3. Indeed, some of the finest contemporary English literature has emerged from non-Anglo postcolonial states, such as India.

4. Although Pintupi-Luritja is the linguistic term for this language, the speakers refer to it only as Luritja, and so I will also from now on. However, note that there is another Luritja language to the southeast of this language region, which is a different dialect (see Holcombe 2004a).

5. And I gratefully acknowledge a small grant from the Human Rights Innovation Fund of Amnesty International Australia to assist in the travel and accommodation costs of Lance Macdonald and Sheila Joyce Dixon. This enabled me to spend two weeks working with them in my Australian National University (ANU) Canberra office to complete this first draft.

6. However, some Aboriginal communities, such as those in the Warlpiri region, which includes Yuendemu, fund their own programs with monies from mining royalties, known as the WETT Program (the Warlpiri Education and Training Trust).

7. The Report, however, does not specify all of these thirteen languages. Nevertheless, as Warlpiri, Pintupi-Luritja's northern neighbor, is specified and has a similar number of speakers, one might anticipate that it is in the same category.

8. This is being investigated currently.

9. The monumental work of the German missionary Carl Strehlow from 1894–1922 who, among other writings, wrote a seven-volume treatise on Arrernte and Luritja language, ceremonies, customs, and beliefs: *Die Aranda- und Loritja-Stamme in Zentral-Australien.* According to Kenny: "This was the first Australian work that comprehensively recorded oral literature of Australian Indigenous people in their own languages" (in Green 2012: 160).

10. Much has been written about this contentious borrowing; most recently see, for instance, Green (2012).

11. The Gospels of Matthew 7:12 and Luke 6:31.

12. The Gospel of Mark 12:31.

13. Rafael's play on the concept of "equivalences" is useful here: "Conquest and conversion, aside from their primary meanings, may connote the surrender of a person's desires and possession to another: conversion, like conquest, can thus be a process of crossing over into a domain—territorial, emotional, religious, or cultural—of someone else's and claiming it as one's own" (Rafael 1988: ix, in Trudinger 2004: 29).

14. The program of translation may be only as good as the interpretation of the English words as these are then rendered meaningful into Luritja. To this end I referred to the Macquarie English dictionary for the majority of the English meanings.

15. Note the Aboriginal organization *Waltja Tjutangku Palyapayi*, loosely translated as "Doing Good Work for Families."

16. Note that this apparent repetition was intentional, to reiterate Aboriginal inclusion.

17. Tzotzil is a neighboring Indigenous language group to Tzeltal, mentioned earlier.

18. Howes draws from the seminal work of Walter Ong: "Cultures vary greatly in their exploitation of the various senses and the way in which they relate their conceptual apparatus to the various senses. It has been commonplace that the ancient Hebrews and the ancient Greeks differed in the value they set on the auditory. The Hebrews tended to think of understanding as a kind of hearing, whereas the Greeks thought of it more as a kind of seeing, although far less exclusively as seeing than post-Cartesian Western man has tended to do" (in Howes 1991: 26–27).

19. The UDHR was translated from the Spanish into this Indigenous language, so that I can only assume that this term "fraternal" was the Spanish equivalent of "brotherhood."

20. The average sentence is 1.3 years in the Northern Territory, compared to three years nationally (NAAJA 2014)

21. When the NTER was first introduced in 2007, the then Minister for Indigenous Affairs Mal Brough stated that "land rights have locked people into a collective tenure . . . we need to actually recognise that communism didn't work, collectivism didn't work. It doesn't work to say a collective owns it and you don't have anything" (in Hinkson 2007: 6).

Chapter 2

1. Nevertheless, I recognize that "the image of the market as a means of regulating and co-ordinating the activities of numerous actors without direction from a single controlling centre [or directive state] has always played a central role in liberal political thought" (Hindess 2002: 140).

2. Written as then Aboriginal and Torres Strait Islander Social Justice Commissioner of the Human Rights Commission. This commission, however, was then known as the Human Rights and Equal Opportunity Commission.

3. There are of course many reasons for this, one of which is how to define the category "Indigenous" in some states, especially those in Africa and Asia.

4. On July 28, 2014, the UN Human Rights Indicators Manual was launched: "A Best Seller: The Users Manual for Implementation of Human Rights Indicators."

5. Note that the family is specified as "men and women" in Article 16 (1).

6. Entitled *Contextualising Koorie Women: Reserve and Urban Profiles.*

7. Waltja Tjutangku Palyapayi "Service Area" nd.

8. Waltja Tjutangku Palyapayi "History and Origins" nd.

9. Waltja Tjutangku Palyapayi "Constitution" nd.

10. "Australia's Top Aboriginal Organisations Announced" 2014.

11. Waltja Tjutangku Palyapayi "Grandmothers Stories."

12. Waltja Tjutangku Palyapayi "Waltja wins . . . Indigenous Governance Award."

13. The Ngaanyatjarra, Pitjantjatjarra, and Yankunytjajarra Women's Council operates in the land of these language groups in South Australia, Western Australia, and to a limited extent in the south of the Northern Territory. They have a "no tolerance" approach to gender violence.

14. See Holcombe (2004b: 175–177) for an analysis of these contemporary women's law and culture meetings.

15. Some of the material in this section derives from Holcombe 2015.

16. And although I will not specifically be addressing government programs in this chapter, as my focus is on NGOs, the recent shift in welfare reform, from a welfarist model to enforcing a compliance-based job-seeking and training model, has been distinctive. The Community Development Program, which was introduced in mid-2015, is part of a broader policy approach that enforces the mutual responsibility paradigm as an element in citizenship entailments, discussed in Chapter 6 (see Jordan and Fowkes 2016; Kral 2017). The Commonwealth government is the primary funder of employment programs, as the other side of this role is that they also fund Centrelink—the welfare transfers for the unemployed. The Community Development Program (CDP) replaced the long-running Community Development Employment Program (CDEP). Although these programs have the terms "community development" within them, they have never been development programs in the sense that the UNDP would categorize as development.

17. Four-wheel drive vehicles are commonly referred to as Toyotas in reference to the brand of the troop carriers (people movers with bench seats) that are highly sought after.

18. The Australian Labor Party has had an affirmative action for women policy since 1994 and in the twenty-plus years since its implementation, they now have 37.3 percent women at the federal level, relative to the Conservative coalition of 22 percent women, who don't have any such policy.

19. And here I am reminded of Austin Broos's work with the neighboring Arrernte, where she found that "someone who doesn't know" was described as "a woman who takes the floor at a meeting" (1996: 8).

20. See also Rose 1996.

21. Women still use the same methods to hunt and forage for the same foods; rumiya ("sand goanna"), maku ("witchetty grub"), and various bush vegetables are the most common. However, this food gathering is not a daily necessity for survival. Rather, today it is done for enjoyment, including modern understandings of the nutritional value of bush foods, while some Anangu will site the general "well-being" benefits of getting out of the community.

22. However, there has been some success in encouraging women locally to be rangers, but proportionally they are very few. This is not the case south in

Hermannsburg—at Tjuwanpa, or north in Yuendemu—where there have been and are consistently female rangers.

23. See Gender Composition of the Workforce: by Occupation (Workplace Gender Equality Agency April 2015).

Chapter 3

1. Australia's Parliament has 26 percent women, ranking forty-fourth in the world in 2014 (McCann and Wilson 2014: appendix 1).

2. This also includes the use of some common terms used by non-Aboriginal people associated with the the practice.

3. See also Roheim (1974, 1988) and Morton (1988) for anthropological psychoanalytic interpretations of male initiation in central Australia from a male perspective.

4. This also used to occur in some regions in Australia, among other female pubescent physical rites of passage (Berndt and Berndt 1999: 180–187).

5. News.Com.au 2015.

6. Starlady's personal website, retrieved on August 6, 2015, from www.starlady .com.au/about-star-lady/,

7. The Australian Football league (AFL) is the other archetypal domain in which men's masculinity and identity is asserted. Although I acknowledge that in this domain of sport there is some mirroring of the mainstream Australian fetish, in the microcosm of small remote communities this fetish is intensified and the admiration of the physical elevated. The warrior mentality has transferred itself onto the public sports field.

8. Indeed, as I suspect it was for the non-Indigenous mainstream.

9. Biddle indicates that the statistical region of Apatula (that excludes but surrounds Alice Springs) "had the lowest rate of completion [across Indigenous Australia], with less than 5 per cent of those Indigenous males who lived there in 2006 having completed Year 12 in 2011." This was followed closely by Aboriginal females; that is, 4.4 percent of males to 8.6 percent of females completed year 12 (2013: 5–6).

10. Note that formal church weddings or legally binding marriages are not especially common, although they do occur among Anangu who are devout Christians. Rather, the expression "married kangaroo way" is used. Nevertheless, couples once they have children and whether formally or informally married tend to remain life partners.

11. We have to be cautious about using the cultural and political discourse of Fanon's black pathology; the preconscious forces shaping the colonized self, in an unproblematic way as if it were a predetermined ontology and only ever reactionary (see Moten 2008), when, in fact, in Fanon's psychiatry of racial difference he is also deeply interested in the practices of self-making; how black personhood is experienced so that it can be decolonized.

12. Davis draws on the capabilities approach of normative philosopher Martha Nussbaum.

Chapter 4

1. See also Ortner (1996, 2005) and Wardlow (2006).

2. This compares with 20 percent Australia-wide for this form of crime (ABS in Sharp 2014).

3. The mandatory reporting legislation was introduced in late 2009 under the Domestic and Family Violence Act. All adults in the Northern Territory must report abuse that occurs in a domestic relationship *and* has caused *serious physical harm* or where there is a *serious or imminent threat to the life or safety of a person*. This overview from the Department of Health and Families further states, "This is based on the belief that everyone has a responsibility to prevent domestic or family violence and assist victims and their children from violence" (Northern Territory Government Mandatory Reporting Guideline 2015: 2).

4. It is beyond the scope of this chapter to investigate the ways in which clinical instruments devised for Western populations might be engaged for the betterment of the mental health of Aboriginal populations. However, I am alert to the possibility that there are assumptions (as there are in the human rights discourse) of certain forms of personhood that in this case frame diagnosis and subsequent treatment.

5. As prosecution lawyer Ruth Morley stated, "For the first time there was a DV legal service based in Alice Springs" (field notes 2014).

6. A submission from the Northern Territory Police Association for the Kwementyaye Briscoe inquest noted this in Part 7, Division 4 of the Police Administration Act in the Northern Territory (NTPA 2012: 3).

7. Concomitantly, the other effect of this endosociality is, as Napaltjarri said, "There are no boyfriends here."

8. The Hansen's *Dictionary* states that *miita* is a "shameful term" for spouse or mate (1992: 60). However, in my experience this term was commonly used among younger Luritja speakers, and one may surmise a possible connection with the English term "meat" that may have "shameful" connotations. Also note that the *-rarra* is a relator suffix: "pair."

9. Morley discussed the case of a woman who had to give up her four children to her in-laws when her husband died in a car accident. So she suffered the loss of her husband and then the loss of her children. She had to return to her community while her children moved to the community of their paternal grandparents. Although she was allowed to visit them, she was sent back to her community. With this secondary access, according to Morley, she descended into alcoholism. As she stated, she was last heard of in Darwin where she was run over and killed on the road after being intoxicated. "This pattern of losing custody hasn't shifted—it is prevalent to this day."

10. The exception to this is when the mother is a "child" (under the age of consent) and the family won't admit paternity for fear of getting him into trouble with the police. The age of consent in the Northern Territory is sixteen years old.

11. According to Child Protection Australia, the 2015–2016 figures for "children who were the subject of a child protection notification" for children in the NT are

86 children per 1,000. The next highest figures are from NSW, with 28.2 children per 1,000. Likewise, children on "care and protection orders" in the NT are 21.2 per 1,000 children, whereas the jurisdiction with the next highest is again NSW with 12.8 (12.8) children per 1,000 (Australian Institute of Health and Welfare 2017: 11).

12. In 1909 the Aborigines Protection Act gave the Aborigines Protection Board legal sanction to take Aboriginal children from their families. In 1915, an amendment to the Act gave the Board power to remove any child without parental consent and without a court order. In 1995, the Commonwealth Attorney General established a National Inquiry into the Separation of Aboriginal and Torres Strait Islander Children from their Families, to be conducted by the Human Rights and Equal Opportunity Commission (HREOC). The Inquiry report was entitled *Bringing Them Home* (1997).

13. *Kumanytjayi* is a Luritja term of respect and mourning to avoid naming the deceased. All Central Australian languages have equivalent terms.

14. According to NT law for the charge of manslaughter, the maximum penalty is imprisonment for life, but there is no mandatory sentence. The court takes into account the offender's age, circumstances of the offense, prior convictions, and/or other matters. See Sections 158 and 159 of the NT Criminal Code.

15. Personal communication with Paul Burke October 30, 2014.

Chapter 5

1. The program funding is from three states (SA, NT, and WA) and the Commonwealth, whereas the staff are SA public servants through their Department for Correctional Services. Most of the funding, however, comes from the Commonwealth, which the program manager reports to through the SA State Office.

2. She has worked with Aboriginal youth during her long career as schoolteacher and then as a linguistic anthropologist, whereas I had tended to work with women (from their twenties through their eighties) and senior men.

3. However, though violence against non-Aboriginal people is rare, it does happen, and it tends to be the sexual abuse of women by men. An example is the 2012 case of Bruce Impu and two other Aboriginal men who violently raped two European female tourists in Alice Springs (see ABC News 2015).

4. Narrative therapy—as a psychotherapeutic method—was originally developed by Sigmund Freud in the late 1880s, though, as his focus was on the psychosexual, he was not a mainstream clinician. However, his method of dialogue with the patient became standard practice. This was notable in the treatment of soldiers after World War II.

5. Cianci and Gambrel have critiqued Maslow's widely referenced model as driven by individualist forms of motivation underpinned by Western capitalism, rather than a collectivist model (2003).

6. I'd like to acknowledge the invaluable discussions held with Graeme Pearce (the Program Manager and initiator), Sharon Forester (then clinical manager and facilitator), and also several of the program facilitators, including Peter Jagger.

7. As discussed in the Introduction (see also Australian Human Rights Commission 2002: 22).

8. The *Mad Bastards* film (2011), set in northern WA, explores the story of a violent and alienated Aboriginal man who is released from prison and returns to his community and his estranged wife and teenage son to make amends.

9. This was codeveloped with the Central Australian Women's Legal Service (CAWLS) and the Department of Corrections (CBIFVP staff).

10. Three types of orders can be made, which can also be a combination of any of the three. They include (1) full contact and premise access orders, (2) noncontact when intoxicated orders, and (3) nonviolence orders.

11. Elbert Hubbard uses this quotation in his essay on Booker T. Washington in *Little Journeys for 1908*: 21; Franklin D. Roosevelt later used this line on the occasion of the seventy-fourth anniversary of the Emancipation Proclamation on September 22, 1936.

Chapter 6

1. Written by George Rrurrambu and Neil Murray. Lyrics (c) Universal Music Publishing Group. Lyrics Licensed and Provided by LyricFind http://www.lyricfind .com/.

2. In the book of the same name as the song, Murray describes how the song came to him when he was living and working in Papunya in 1982. He is from the state of Victoria on the east coast where the majority population live.

3. As an intrinsic element of the colonial administration Australia-wide, Aboriginal people were compelled to settle in purpose-built enclaves that ranged from places that were controlled by mission authorities, such as nearby Hermannsburg (Ntaria) and initially Haasts Bluff (Ikuntji), to those established by the government, such as Papunya. Such places brought together nomadic peoples from different languages who, though they may have been neighbors, ordinarily would not have resided together for extended periods. The outstation movement allowed these different groups to decentralize and return to living in more traditional family structures on their customary lands. However, such decentralization could occur only where Aboriginal people had land ownership or land title, which was not the case in many other parts of Australia.

4. Some of this section takes inspiration from previous research in Holcombe and Sullivan (2013).

5. Other regional communities, such as Kintore, have their own independent community-controlled health service, Pintupi Homelands Health Service.

6. This council is the advocacy and service delivery agency for the sixteen-plus town camps in Alice Springs, and since it was incorporated in 1979 has also established a diverse range of other functions, including social services, employment and training services, enterprises such as art and construction, and financial services (www.tangentyere.org.au/). CAYLUS states on their website that they take direction from a steering committee made up representatives of Aboriginal organizations and

communities—as listed on the site—with several other organizations such as the Drug and Alcohol Services Association.

7. As will be discussed later in this chapter, the local councils were amalgamated into shires in 2008, and then the name changed to Regional Councils and Local Authorities in 2014. As a result, I am referring to the different structures as they were referred to at the time.

8. This was the third major Aboriginal-run event post-CANCA that I am aware of.

9. This was based at the Centre for Aboriginal Economic Policy Research (CAEPR) at the Australian National University; I was one of the team of approximately ten full- and part-time researchers, including postgraduate students.

10. The Australian Indigenous Governance Institute was established in 2011, after a deliberative process of establishment.

11. Pearson's work does not dismiss the implications of structural disadvantage, though he does not seem to recognize the complex ongoing effects of Aboriginal cultural predispositions as they interact with contemporary issues of substance abuse, welfare transfers, and so on (see Martin 2001).

12. In central Australia, the term "outstations" is more commonly used to refer to these dispersed small family settlements.

13. Senior attendance and truancy officers can issue infringement notices when a parent or child fails to comply with an officer's notices/directions (including the attendance plan) without a reasonable excuse. Parents and guardians can be given a fine of $282, and children over fourteen years of age living independently can be given a fine of $28 (Northern Territory Government Department of Education and Children's Services 2011). This was an element of the School Enrolment and Attendance Measure (SEAM), which I note, on returning to locate this reference, to have ceased on December 31, 2017.

14. The Victims of Crime Assistance Act, Section 61, states that a levy is imposed to provide a source of revenue for the Victims of Crime Compensation Fund, an example of the operations of which were discussed in the previous chapter. Subject to any exceptions prescribed by regulation, a levy is imposed on a person: (a) who is found guilty of an offence but not imprisoned for the offence; or (b) who expiates an offence by paying an amount specified in an infringement notice issued to the person; or (c) against whom an enforcement order is made (3) Subject to any other amount being prescribed by regulation, the levy imposed under subsection (2) (a) on an adult (i) is $200 for an offence following prosecution on indictment; or (ii) is $150 for any other offence; or (b) on a child is $50; or (c) on a body corporate is $1,000. (4) The amount of the levy imposed on a person under subsection (2)(a) must be specified in: (a) the formal record of the finding of guilt and sentence; and (b) the notice of the finding of guilt or sentence given to the person.

15. The victims' levy is interesting, because although there are cases where individual victims do receive compensation from the state, and thus from the Victims of Crime Fund, for having "met with avoidable harm" (as discussed in the previous

chapter in relation to family violence), in the majority of cases where the levy is applied there is no human "victim." Rather, as is the case for traffic offenses discussed earlier, the state is effectively the "victim."

16. Australian Electoral Commission, "nonvoting."

17. This was among many other restrictions, such as the right to drink alcohol and the right to marry a "nonward" (non-Aboriginal person). As Chesterman and Calligan outline: "The Director of Welfare exercised enormous power over wards and could order a ward to be taken into custody or removed to a reserve or institution" (1997: 175).

18. The candidates were Bess Price (Country Liberal Party) against Karl Hampton (Labor) in the electorate of Stuart, Des Rogers (Labor) against Alison Anderson (CLP) and Warren Williams (First Nations Peoples Party) in the electorate of Namatjira, and Barbara Shaw (Greens) against Adam Giles (CLP) in the electorate of Braitling.

19. This party was established in 2011 on the platform of Indigenous sovereignty and local issues such as Northern Territory statehood and opposition to a nuclear waste dump. The official launch in Canberra was underwhelming. At the Northern Territory election they received 2.1 percent of the votes, similar to that of the senate for the federal election. The party was subsequently deregistered by the AEC in 2015 due to lack of members.

20. Adam Giles is the only nonlocal Aboriginal MP; although his electorate is Alice Springs, he is from the eastern state of NSW. All the other Aboriginal MPs have customary ties to land and kin in various parts of the Northern Territory—indeed in their electorates.

21. I'd like to acknowledge Jeff Hulcombe (no relation) for giving me access to his archive of media releases from this period of Papunya's history. Unfortunately, here the focus is only on the power dispute, but the education dispute was also very complex, as was the dispute with the health department during this period.

22. More specifically, Anderson accused the CLP government of "racial discrimination." She argued that "people on welfare could not afford to pay the extra $2,000 a year required to heat and cool desert homes . . . [and] that government employees—teachers, police, and health workers—continued to receive free power and other subsidies as part of their salary packages" (in Skelton 2010: 74).

23. HREOC changed its name to the Human Rights Commission in 2008.

24. Von Sturmer states that "in parts of remote Australia it is possible to talk of Aboriginal domains, areas in which the dominant social life and culture are Aboriginal, where the major languages . . . are Aboriginal, where the dominant religion and world views are Aboriginal; in short where the resident Aboriginal population constitutes the public" (1984: 219).

25. This relationship between substance abuse and "losing shame" has also been drawn by Tjitayi and Lewis (2011: 60).

26. This is also indicated in the discussion in Chapter 2 on intentional vagueness and respect registers.

27. This "banking" approach is the standard unidirectional form of curriculum-based education where the educator makes "deposits" into the educatee—filling the students with information (Freire 1970 [1993]: 56–58)

28. In Brazil, when Freire was writing, literacy was a requirement for voting and thus in some ways for suffrage.

29. Environmental rights are in the realm of so-called third-generation rights, along with the rights of Indigenous peoples.

30. Diplomacy Training Program. The Australian NGO Fred Hollows Foundation has also funded some programs.

31. As they state: "The Aboriginal passport is a document issued by the APG [Aboriginal Provisional Government] as part of its policy of acting sovereignty. The act of presenting an Aboriginal passport on arriving in other countries and when re-entering Australia shows you are committed to the principle that the Aboriginal nation is separate from the Australian nation. Aboriginal people have inherent independent rights, including having a separate passport." The Mohawk Nation in the United States and Canada also offer a First Nations passport (see Simpson 2014).

32. See the Greens Political Party 2015.

Chapter 7

1. The concept "Indigenous peoples" had to be fought for, as the language used of "Indigenous populations" was a term of political containment and control; "populations" are not formally recognized collectives but rather random and assimilable, whereas the term "peoples" has legal implications for political self-determination as a distinct group within a modern nation state (see Thompson 1997: 792). Apparently ensuring the adoption of this term within the Declaration was one of the reasons it took over twenty years to finalize. Indigenous societies were first mentioned in international law in the 1920s (Thompson 1997: 792), and they were the subject of a separate International Labor Organization (ILO) Convention in 1957 entitled "Concerning the Protection and Integration of Indigenous and Other Tribal and Semi-Tribal Populations." Yet members of the Indigenous populations being referred to had little input into the convention, and few if any had developed a self-referential Indigenous identity (Niezen 2003: 4) at that time. This Convention also stressed their protection and future integration into the state in an assimilationist vision.

2. Recall Kymlicka's statement: "Every international declaration and convention on these issues makes the same point—the rights of minorities and Indigenous peoples are an inseparable part of a larger human rights framework and operate within its limits" (2007: 7).

3. WIPO is the World Intellectual Property Organization.

4. There are many UN forums that are leveraged by Indigenous groups, depending on the specific issue at hand. They include the international climate change forums such as the Paris climate change talks, the WIPO (World Intellectual Property Organization) forums in Geneva, and the UN Convention on Biological Diversity Annual Conference of the Parties. These, and other, UN forums have implications

for Indigenous livelihoods, biocultural rights, issues of equitable knowledge management, and so on.

5. In fulfillment of her mandate, the current Special Rapporteur:

> Promotes good practices, including new laws, government programs, and constructive agreements between indigenous peoples and states, to implement international standards concerning the rights of indigenous peoples; Reports on the overall human rights situations of indigenous peoples in selected countries; Addresses specific cases of alleged violations of the rights of indigenous peoples through communications with Governments and others and finally; Conducts or contributes to thematic studies on topics of special importance regarding the promotion and protection of the rights of indigenous peoples. (United Nations Human Rights Office of the High Commissioner nd)

6. The first IPO began with ATSIC (Aboriginal and Torres Strait Islander Commission, which operated from 1990–2005), and when that was abolished by the Howard government, the then Human Rights Commission took over managing and funding this process. The funding is administered by the Aboriginal and Torres Strait Islander Social Justice Commissioner. The funding is of such a limited amount that it is not possible to replicate the level of engagement and support previously provided by ATSIC. The IPO members meet twice annually, with occasional meetings on specific, urgent issues.

7. In 2013 these included National Aboriginal and Torres Strait Islander Women's Alliance Corporation (NATSIWAC), National Native Title Council (NNTC), New South Wales Aboriginal Land Council (NSWALC), Office of the Social Justice Commissioner, First Peoples Disability Network Australia, Foundation for Aboriginal and Islander Research Action (FAIRA), Foundation for Indigenous Recovery and Development Australia (FIRDA), National Aboriginal Cultural Community Health Organisation (NACCHO), National Congress of Australia's First Peoples, National Aboriginal Torres Strait Islander Legal Services (NATSILS), and National Indigenous Higher Education Network (NIHEN).

8. In Holcombe and Janke, we note for instance that the Environment Protection and Biodiversity Conservation Act 1999 (Commonwealth)—which purports to be Australia-wide—is compromised by the federal system, and so the approach to conservation is ad hoc with several states and territories creating their own biological resources acts and regional Indigenous groups their own management processes. The government-commissioned Hawke Inquiry into the Environment Protection and Biodiversity Conservation Act 1999 (Commonwealth) found that "each jurisdiction has different rules and requirements for accessing biological resources" and that the "Nationally Consistent Approach" policy developed in 2000 "should be reinvigorated." Clear parallels can be seen in the approach to human rights.

9. Now known as CAASWA—the Central Australian Strong Women's Alliance. They hosted a dinner and set up a website (no longer active); Elaine Peckham was the founder. She is now no longer aligned with NATSIWA, which was progressing in a different way.

10. I was told in 2013 by Malezer that the Australian government is encouraging Aboriginal organizations to gain this status and wants more to gain accreditations.

11. This advocacy on specific issues, on what AIA refer to as "within country" issues, is a relatively recent, post-2001, shift reflecting AIA's broadened statute to include a focus on economic, social, and cultural rights, so moving beyond their sole focus on civil and political rights.

12. The Pacific caucus within which Australia participates is one of seven Indigenous regions recognized by the United Nations that then develop caucuses. The United Nations operates on only five, but the seven regions are understood as more accurately reflecting Indigenous cultural and political regions.

13. Australia is a party to fourteen international treaties, which include the International Convention on the Elimination of Discrimination (ICERD), the Convention on Civil and Political Rights, and so on.

14. This contrasts with the previous representative body ATSIC, which had local representation.

15. The council has built into it a range of equity-based management structures and an oversighting Ethics Congress; for instance, see page 34 of their Constitution (National Congress 2010).

16. He had been attending since 2006 and was the chairman of the National Native Title Council and joint chair of the IPO with Sandra Craemer. Sadly, he died on October 28, 2015.

Conclusion

1. As Brown states, "Liberalism presumes to master culture by privatising and individualising it . . . it is a basic premise of liberal secularism and liberal universalism that neither culture nor religion are permitted to govern publically; both are tolerated on the condition that they are privately enjoyed" (Brown 2006: 21).

2. The first report by the Australian government to the Universal Periodic Review (UPR) of the UN Human Rights Council noted that "it believes that everyone is entitled to respect and to a fair go. . . . All Australians are responsible for respecting and protecting human rights and ensuring that our commitment to a fair go becomes a reality for all Australians" (Australian Government Attorney-General's Department 2011).

3. It was first established when the commission was known as the Human Rights and Equal Opportunity Commission (HREOC).

References

ABC Lateline. 2006. "Crown Prosecutor Speaks out about Abuse in Central Australia." May 15, 2006. Available at www.abc.net.au/lateline/content/2006/s1639127.htm.

ABC News 2015. "Bruce Impu Sentenced to 18 Years' Prison after Raping Two Backpackers at Gunpoint in Alice Springs." February 24. Rosa Ellen. Available at www.abc.net.au/news/2015-02-24/alice-springs-rapist-bruce-impu-sentenced-to-18-years-prison/6249768).

ABC News on-line. 2010. "Payback: A Violent Difference of Opinion." Eric Tlozek comment December 23. Retrieved on March 3, 2016, from www.abc.net.au/news/2010-12-23/payback-a-violent-difference-of-opinion/1884738.

ABC Radio. 2011. "Feisty Independent Swaps Sides." *The World Today* with Eleanor Hall. September 8. Available at www.abc.net.au/radio/programs/worldtoday/feisty-nt-independent-swaps-sides/2877044.

ABC Radio National. 2010. Radio National Background Briefing. November 14. "Making Violence Men's Business," Chris Bullock. Retrieved on March 3, 2013, from www.abc.net.au/radionational/programs/backgroundbriefing/making-violence-mens-business/2981568#transcript

———. 2014. "Domestic Violence Blitz in Alice Springs Prompts Calls for More Alternatives to Jail." *PM with Mark Colvin*. January 17. Available at www.abc.net.au/pm/content/2013/s3927579.htm.

ABC "7.30 Report." 2014. "Anger in NT Community after Circumcision Rite Ends with Three Boys Airlifted to Hospital." January 23. Available at www.abc.net.au/news/2014-01-22/nt-elders-concede-to-mistakes-in-ritual-circumcision/5213526.

ABC "The Drum." 2014. "Circumcision Reports Were Culturally Insensitive." March 6. Available at www.abc.net.au/news/2014-03-06/mclaughlin-abc-circumcision-reports-were-culturally-insensitive/5301240.

Aboriginal Peak Organisations Northern Territory (APO NT). 2013a. "Grog in the Territory: Central Australian Summit on Alcohol Policy and Its Impact on Aboriginal People and Communities." Available at www.amsant.org.au/apont /wp-content/uploads/2015/02/Central-Australian-Grog-Summit-Report -FINAL-7-November-20131.pdf.

——. 2013b. "Strong Aboriginal Governance Report." May. Retrieved on February 5, 2015, from www.amsant.org.au/apont/publications/reports/.

——. 2014. *Submission to the Northern Territories New Domestic and Family Violence Strategy.* February. Available at www.amsant.org.au/apont/wp-content /uploads/2015/02/141102-APO-NT-Submission-Domestic-and-Family -Violence-Northern-Territory-Government.pdf.

——. 2016. Aboriginal Governance and Management Program. Website. Available at http://aboriginalgovernance.org.au/.

Aboriginal Resource and Development Service (ARDS). 2008. *An Absence of Mutual Respect.* Darwin: ARDS.

Aboriginal and Torres Strait Islander Commission (ATSIC) News Room. 2001. "Yara Ngaukunu—My Story: ATSIC News interviews Commissioner Alison Anderson." Retrieved on May 2, 2005, from www.atsic.gov.au.News_Room/ATSIC _News/February_2001/yarangaukunu.as.

Adams, Douglas. 1979. *The Hitchhiker's Guide to the Galaxy.* London: Pan Macmillan Books.

Agamben, Georgio. 1998. *Homo Sacer: Sovereign Power and Bare Life.* Stanford, CA: Stanford University Press.

——. 2005. *State of Exception.* Chicago: University of Chicago Press.

Alice Springs Correctional Centre. "For Visitors" pages. Retrieved on May 19, 2015, from www.correctionalservices.nt.gov.au/CorrectionalCentres/AliceSprings CorrectionalCentre/ForVisitors/Pages/default.aspx.

Alice Springs News online. 2012. "The Ties That Bind." August 7. Kieran Finnane. Available at www.alicespringsnews.com.au/2012/08/07/the-ties-that-bind/.

——. 2014. "Alison Anderson: Rebel with a Cause." Erwin Chandla. May 19. Available at www.alicespringsnews.com.au/2014/05/19/alison-anderson-rebel-with -a-cause/.

——. 2014. "Pilger's Polemic Fails Australia and Aborigines." Kieran Finnane Reviews, January 27. Available at www.alicespringsnews.com.au/2014/01/27 /pilgers-polemic-wide-of-the-mark-on-australia-and-aborigines/.

——. 2015a. "CLP Fiasco: Now Oz Is Laughing about Us, Not with Us." Irwin Chandla. February 9. Available at www.alicespringsnews.com.au/2015/02/09 /clp-fiasco-now-oz-is-lauging-about-us-not-with-us/.

———. 2015b. "Rosalie Kunoth-Monks Not Welcome in Her Community." May 6. Retrieved on September 18, 2015, from www.alicespringsnews.com.au/2015 /05/06/rosalie-kunoth-monks-not-welcome-in-her-community/.

Alice Springs Women's Shelter, 2013. *Stronger and Stronger Every Day. Evaluation Report of Alice Springs Women's Centre Outreach Service.* Unpublished report.

Allison, F., Chris Cunneen, M. Schwartz, and Larissa Behrendt. 2012. *Indigenous Legal Needs Project: Northern Territory Report.* Cairns, Qld: James Cook University.

Alpher, Barry. 1993. "Out of the Ordinary Ways of Using Language." Chapter 7 in M. Walsh and C. Yallop, eds., *Language and Culture in Aboriginal Australia,* 97–106. Canberra: Aboriginal Studies Press.

Altman, Jon. C. 1987. *Hunter Gatherers Today: An Aboriginal Economy in North Australia.* Canberra: Australia Institute of Aboriginal Studies.

Altman, Jon C., and Melinda Hinkson. 2007. *Coercive Reconciliation: Stabilise, Normalise, Exit Aboriginal Australia.* Melbourne: Arena Publications.

———, eds. 2010. *Culture Crisis: Anthropology and Politics in Aboriginal Australia.* Sydney: UNSW Press.

Altman, Jon C., and S. Kerins. 2012. *People on Country: Vital Landscapes, Indigenous Futures.* Melbourne: Federation Press.

American Anthropological Association. 1995. *Committee for Human Rights Guidelines.* Retrieved on July 6, 2012, from www.aaanet.org/cmtes/cfhr/Committee -for-Human-Rights-Guidelines.cfm.

Anaya, James. 2009. "The Right of Indigenous Peoples to Self-Determination in the Post-Declaration Era." In C. Charters and R. Stavenhagen, eds., *Making the Declaration Work: The United Nations Declaration on the Rights of Indigenous Peoples,* 184–199. Document No. 127. Copenhagen: IWIGIA.

———. 2010. *Promotion and Protection of All Human Rights, Civil, Political, Economic, Social and Cultural Rights, Including the Right to Development. Report by the Special Rapporteur on the Situation of Human Rights and Fundamental Freedoms of Indigenous People. Addendum: The Situation of Indigenous People in Australia.* March 4. New York and Geneva: United Nations General Assembly A/HRC/15/.

Anderson, Michael Ghillar. 2015. "First Nations Asserting Sovereignty." Retrieved on August 20, 2015, from www.sovereignunion.mobi/content/why-deafening -silence-constitutional-recognition.

Anthony, Thalia, and Robert Chapman. 2008. "Unresolved Tensions: Warlpiri Law, Police Powers and Land Rights." In *Indigenous Law Bulletin.* 7(5, May): 9–18.

Arabena, Kerry. 2005. "Not Fit for Modern Society: Aboriginal and Torres Strait Islander People and the New Arrangements for the Administration of Indigenous Affairs." Research Discussion Paper 16. Canberra: Australian Institute of Aboriginal and Torres Strait Islander Studies (AIATSIS), Available at https://

aiatsis.gov.au/sites/default/files/products/discussion_paper/arabena-dp16-not
-fit-for-modern-australian-society-administration-indigenous-affairs_0.pdf.

Arendt, Hannah. 2003. *The Portable Hannah Arendt*, 2nd edition. Edited and with an introduction by Peter Bahhr. New York: Penguin Books.

Aretino, B., P. Holland, D. Peterson, and M. Schuele. 2001. *Creating Markets for Biodiversity: A Case Study of Earth Sanctuaries Ltd*. Canberra: Productivity Commission Staff Research Paper, AusInfo. Available at www.pc.gov.au/research /supporting/creating-biodiversity-markets/cmbiod.pdf.

Atkinson, Judy. 2002. *Trauma Trails Recreating Song Lines: The Transgenerational Effects of Trauma in Indigenous Australia*. Melbourne: Spinifex Press.

Attwood, Bain. 2003. *Rights for Aborigines*. NSW: Allen and Unwin.

Attwood, Bain, and A. Markus. 1997. *The 1967 Referendum, or When Aborigines Didn't Get the Vote*. Canberra: Aboriginal Studies Press.

Austin-Broos, Dianne. 1996. "'Two Laws,' Ontologies, Histories: Ways of Being Aranda Today." *Australian Journal of Anthropology* 7(1): 1–20.

———. 2010. "Quarantining Violence: How Anthropology Does It." In J. Altman and M. Hinkson, eds., *Culture Crisis: Anthropology and Politics in Aboriginal Australia*, 136–150. Sydney: UNSW Press.

———. 2011. *A Different Inequality: The Politics of Debate about Remote Aboriginal Australia*. Sydney: Allen and Unwin.

The Australian. 2016. "Abbott Era Indigenous Cuts Went Too Far, Senate Inquiry Told." March 18. Available at www.theaustralian.com.au/national-affairs /indigenous/abbottera-indigenous-cuts-went-too-far-senate-inquiry-told /news-story/499eb0eaec6848352734717a22b23778.

Australian Bureau of Statistics (ABS). 2011. Census QuickStats. Papunya: ABS. Available at www.censusdata.abs.gov.au/census_services/getproduct/census/2011 /quickstat/SSC70153.

———. 2013. *Prisoners in Australia: Northern Territory*. Available at www.abs.gov.au /ausstats/abs@.nsf/Lookup/4517.0main+features100002013.

Australian Electoral Commission. nd. "Indigenous Electoral Participation Program." Retrieved on September 15, 2015, from www.aec.gov.au/indigenous/.

———. 2016. "Non Voting." Available at www.aec.gov.au/FAQs/Voting_Australia .htm#not-vote.

Australian English Dictionary, 4th edition. 1999. Collins Gem. Sydney: HarperCollins Publishers.

Australian Government. 2011. "National Plan to Reduce Violence Against Women and Their Children." Available at www.dss.gov.au/our-responsibilities/women /programs-services/reducing-violence/the-national-plan-to-reduce-violence -against-women-and-their-children-2010-2022.

———. 2013 (revised). *Cross Borders Indigenous Family Violence Program. Men's Program Manual: Talking in a Group about Stopping Family Violence.* Unpublished, Alice Springs.

———. 2014. *Overcoming Indigenous Disadvantage: Key Indicators 2014 Report.* Available at www.pc.gov.au/research/ongoing/overcoming-indigenous-disadvantage /key-indicators-2014/key-indicators-2014-report.pdf.

Australian Government, Attorney-General's Department. 2011. *Australia's Universal Periodic Review.* Available at www.ag.gov.au/RightsAndProtections/Human Rights/United-Nations-Human-Rights-Reporting/Documents/Universal PeriodicReview.PDF.

Australian Government. Workplace Gender and Equality Agency. 2015. *Gender Composition of the Workforce by Occupation. April 2015.* Retrieved on January 3, 2018, from www.wgea.gov.au/sites/default/files/Gender-composition-of-the -workforce-by-occupation.pdf.

Australian Human Rights and Equal Opportunity Commission (HREOC, now the Australian Human Rights Commission). 1998. "Bush Talks." Available at www .humanrights.gov.au/sites/default/files/content/pdf/human_rights/bush_talks .pdf.

———. 2002. *Social Justice Report 2002.* Retrieved on August 12, 2013, from www .humanrights.gov.au/publications/hreoc-social-justice-report-2002.

———. 2003. *Submission to the Northern Territory Law Reform Committee Inquiry into Aboriginal Customary Law in the Northern Territory.* Sydney: The Sex Discrimination Commissioner of the Australian Human Rights and Equal Opportunity Commission. Available at www.humanrights.gov.au/sage-submission-inquiry -aboriginal-customary-law-nt.

———. 2005. *Social Justice Report.* Sydney: Aboriginal and Torres Strait Islander Social Justice Commissioner.

———. 2006. *Social Justice Report.* Sydney: Aboriginal and Torres Strait Islander Social Justice Commissioner. Available at www.humanrights.gov.au/publications /social-justice-report-2006-0.

———. 2007. *Social Justice Report* 2007. Sydney: Aboriginal and Torres Strait Islander Social Justice Commissioner.

Australian Human Rights Commission. (AHRC) 2008. "The Suspension and Reinstatement of the RDA and Special Measures in the NTER." Retrieved on May 12, 2016, from www.humanrights.gov.au/publications/suspension-and -reinstatement-rda-and-special-measures-nter-1.

———. 2010. *Community Guide to the UN Declaration on the Rights of Indigenous Peoples.* Available at www.humanrights.gov.au/our-work/aboriginal-and-torres -strait-islander-social-justice/publications/community-guide-un.

———. 2011a. *President's Speech, Current Issues in Human Rights*. Charles Darwin University. May 30. Catherine Branson, Q.C. Retrieved on May 25, 2016, from www.humanrights.gov.au/news/speeches/president-speech-current-issues-human-rights-2011.

———. 2011b. *Social Justice Report*. Sydney: Aboriginal and Torres Strait Islander Social Justice Commissioner. Available at www.humanrights.gov.au/sites/default/files/content/social_justice/sj_report/sjreport11/pdf/sjr2011.pdf.

———. 2012a. *Australia's Universal Periodic Review: Progress Report Prepared by the Australian Human Rights Commission on Behalf of the Australian Council of Human Rights Agencies*. Retrieved on March 2, 2016, from www.humanrights.gov.au/sites/default/files/document/publication/ACHRA_UPR_Progress_Report_2012.pdf.

———. 2012b. "Rant against Racism." Retrieved on February 20, 2015, from www.rantagainstracism.com.au/.

———. 2012c. *Social Justice Report*. Sydney: Aboriginal and Torres Strait Islander Social Justice Commissioner. Available at www.humanrights.gov.au/sites/default/files/document/publication/social_justice_report_2012.pdf.

———. 2013. Declaration Dialogue Series Paper No. 2, "Self-Determination: The Fundamental Rights of Aboriginal and Torres Strait Islander Peoples to Shape Our Own Lives." Sydney.

———. 2015. *Australia's Second Universal Periodic Review: Submission by the Australian Human Rights Commission under the Universal Periodic Review Process*. Available at www.humanrights.gov.au/sites/default/files/WEB_Australias_Second_UPR_Review_2015.pdf.

Australian Indigenous Governance Institute. 2013. Available at www.aigi.com.au/.

Australian Institute of Health and Welfare. 2017. "Child Protection Australia 2015–16." *Child Welfare Series no. 66*. Cat. no. CWS 60. Canberra: AIHW. Available at www.aihw.gov.au/getmedia/bce377ec-1b76-4cc5-87d9-d0541fca586c/20479.pdf.aspx?inline=true.

Australian Law Reform Commission. 1986. *Recognition of Aboriginal Customary Laws. Report 31*. Canberra: Australian Government. Available at www.alrc.gov.au/publications/report-31.

Australian Local Government Association. 2013. "50/50 Vision Councils for Gender Equity Program." Retrieved on February 5, 2016, from www.5050vision.com.au/ and www.algwa.org.au/docs/5050ge.pdf.

"Australia's Top Aboriginal Organisations Announced." 2014. Reconciliation Australia media release, October 30.

Bagnall, Geoff. 2015. "What about Lore and Culture, Rosalie Kunoth-Monks." *The Stringer* on-line news, February 18. Available at http://thestringer.com.au/what-about-lore-and-culture-rosalie-kunoth-monks-9584#.Wk7JtDBx1PY.

Bandler, Faith. 1989. *Turning the Tide: A Personal History of the Federal Council for the Advancement of Aborigines and Torres Strait Islanders.* Canberra: Aboriginal Studies Press.

Bardon, Geoffrey, and James Bardon. 2004. *Papunya: A Place Made after the Story: The Beginnings of the Western Desert Art Movement.* Melbourne University Publishing, Victoria: The Miegunyah Press.

Barrett Meyering, I. 2010. "Victim Compensation and Domestic Violence." *Stakeholder Paper 8, Australian Domestic and Family Violence Clearing House.* Sydney: University of NSW,

Bassnett, Susan, and Harish Trivedi, eds. 2002. "Introduction." In *Post-Colonial Translation: Theory and Practice.* Routledge. London and New York.

Batty, Phillip, ed. 2011. *Colliding Worlds: First Contact in the Western Desert 1932–1984.* Melbourne: Museum Victoria, Tandanya National Aboriginal Cultural Institute.

Bauman, Toni. 2002. "'Test 'im blood': Subsections and Shame in Katherine." *Anthropological Forum* 12(2): 205–220.

Bearman, S., N. Korobov, and A. Thorne, A. 2009. "The Fabric of Internalized Sexism." *Journal of Integrated Social Sciences* 1(1): 10–47.

Beck, U., and E. Beck-Gernsheim. 2002. *Individualization: Institutionalised Individualism and Its Social and Political Consequences.* London; Thousand Oaks, CA; and New Delhi: Sage Publications.

Becker, Julia, C. 2010. "Why Do Women Endorse Hostile and Benevolent Sexism? The Role of Salient Female Subtypes and Internalization of Sexist Contents." *Sex Roles* 62(7–8, April): 453–467.

Behrendt, Larissa. 2002. "Lessons from the Mediation Obsession: Ensuring That Sentencing 'Alternatives' Focus on Indigenous Self-Determination." In Heather Strang and John Braithwaite, eds., *Restorative Justice and Family Violence*, 178–190. Cambridge, UK: Cambridge University Press.

——. 2005. "The Relevance of the Rights Agenda in the Age of Practical Reconciliation." In Hunter and Keyes, eds., *Changing Law: Rights, Regulation and Reconciliation*, 137–153. Aldershot, UK: Ashgate.

——. 2007. "The Emergency We Had to Have." In Jon C. Altman and Melinda Hinkson, eds., *Coercive Assimilation: Stabilise, Normalise, Exit Aboriginal Australia*, 15–22. Melbourne: Arena Publications.

——. 2009. "As Good as It Gets or as Good as It Could Be? Benchmarking Human Rights in Australia." *Balyai: Culture, Law and Colonisation* 10: 3–11.

——. 2011. "An Introduction to Global Perspectives on Social Justice and Human Rights." In D. Barnes, ed., *Nelson Aboriginal Studies*, 137–152. South Melbourne, Victoria: Cengage Learning Australia.

Bell, Dianne. 1983. *Daughters of the Dreaming*. Sydney: McPhee Gribble/George Allen & Unwin.

———. 1991. "Intra-racial Rape Revisited: On Forging a Feminist Future beyond Factions and Frightening Politics." *Women's Studies Int. Forum* 14(5): 385–412.

———. 1992. "Considering Gender: Are Human Rights for Women Too? An Australian Case." In A. A. An-Na'im, ed., *Human Rights in Cross Cultural Perspectives: A Quest for Consensus*. Philadelphia: University of Pennsylvania Press.

Bell, Dianne, and Topsy Nelson Napurrula. 1989. "Speaking about Rape Is Everyone's Business." *Women's Studies Int. Forum* 12(4): 403–416.

Benhabib, Seyla. 2002. *The Claims of Culture: Equality and Diversity in the Global Era*. Princeton, NJ, and Oxford, UK: Princeton University Press.

Bern, John. 1979. "Ideology and Domination: Toward a Reconstruction of Aboriginal Social Formation." *Oceania* 50(2): 118–132.

Berndt, Catherine H. 1965. "Women and the 'Secret Life.'" In R. M. Berndt and C. H. Berndt, eds., *Aboriginal Man in Australia*, 236–282. Sydney: Angus and Robertson.

———. 1970. "Digging Sticks and Spears, or, the Two Sex Model." In F. Gale, ed., *Woman's Role in Aboriginal Society*, 39-48. Canberra: Australian Institute of Aboriginal Studies.

Berndt, Donald, and Catherine Berndt. 1999. *World of the First Australians: Aboriginal Traditional Life Past/Present*, 5th ed. Canberra: Aboriginal Studies Press for the Australian Institute of Aboriginal and Torres Strait Islander Studies.

Bhabha, Homi. 2003. "On Writing Rights." In M. J. Gibney, ed., *Globalizing Rights*, 162–183. Oxford, UK: Oxford University Press.

Biddle, Nick. 2013. "CAEPR Indigenous Population Project: 2011 Census Papers. Paper 8. Education: Part 2 School Education." Available at http://caepr.cass.anu .edu.au/research/publications/education-part-2-school-education.

Blagg, Harry. 1998. "Restorative Visions and Restorative Justice Practices: Conferencing, Ceremony and Reconciliation in Australia." *Current Issues in Criminal Justice* 10(1): 5–14.

———. 2008. "Colonial Critique and Critical Criminology: Issues in Aboriginal Law and Aboriginal Violence." In Thalia Anthony and Chris Cunneen, eds., *The Critical Criminology Companion*, 129–143. Sydney: Hawkins Press.

Bolger, Audrey. 1991. *Aboriginal Women and Violence*. Darwin: ANU, North Australian Research Unit.

Brady, Maggie. 2005. "Submission to the Enquiry into Petrol Sniffing in Remote Communities." December 8. Retrieved on September 1, 2013, from http://caylus.org .au/caylusresources/.

Brenkert, G. G. 1986. "Marx and Human Rights." *Journal of the History of Philosophy* 24(1, January): 55–77.

Brennan, Sean, Larrisa Behrendt, Lisa Strehlin, and George Williams. 2005. *Treaty.* Sydney: The Federation Press.

Brooks, David, and Shaw, Gill. 2003. *Men, Conflict and Violence in the Ngaanyatjarra Region.* Ngaanyatjarra Council, unpublished report.

Brown, Michael F. 2007. "Sovereignty's Betrayals." In Marisol De la Cadena and Orin Starn, eds., *Indigenous Experience Today,* 171–194. Oxford, UK: Berg.

Brown, Wendy. 2000. "Suffering Rights as Paradoxes." *Constellations* 7(2): 230–241.

———. 2004. "'The Most We Can Hope for...': Human Rights and the Politics of Fatalism." *The South Atlantic Quarterly* 103(2–3): 451–463.

———. 2006. *Regulating Aversion: Tolerance in the Age of Identity and Empire.* Princeton, NJ, and Oxford, UK: Princeton University Press.

Bunch, Charlotte. 1990. "Women's Rights as Human Rights: Towards a Re-Vision of Human Rights." *Human Rights Quarterly* 12(4, November): 486–498.

———. 2009. "Listen Up: UN Must Hear Women on Violence." *On the Issues Magazine. Spring 09 edition: Lines in the Sand.*

Bunda, Tracey. 2007. "The Sovereign Aboriginal Woman." In *Sovereign Subjects: Indigenous Sovereignty Matters,* 75–85. Sydney: Allen and Unwin.

Burbank, Victoria C. 1994. *Fighting Women: Anger and Aggression in Aboriginal Australia.* Berkeley, Los Angeles, and London: University of California Press.

Bush Heritage Australia. 2017. "Land Clearing." Available at www.bushheritage.org.au/about/about-us/our-challenge/land-clearing.

Butler, Judith. 1990. *Gender Trouble: Feminism and the Subversion of Identity.* New York and London: Routledge,

Byrnes, Andrew, Hillary Charlesworth, and G. McKinnon. 2009. *Bills of Rights in Australia: History, Politics and Law.* Sydney: UNSW Press.

Caffery, J., Patrick McConvell, and Jane Simpson. 2009. *Gaps in Australia's Indigenous Language Policy: Dismantling Bilingual Education in the Northern Territory.* AIATSIS Discussion paper 24. Canberra. Retrieved on April 3, 2016, from http://aiatsis.gov.au/publications/products/gaps-australias-indigenous-language-policy-dismantling-bilingual-education-northern-territory.

Calma, Tom. 2007. "Tackling Child Abuse and Inequality." In J. C. Altman and M. Hinkson, eds., *Coercive Reconciliation: Stabilise, Normalise, Exit Aboriginal Australia,* 273–286. Melbourne: Arena Publications.

Campbell, D., and Janet Hunt. 2012. "Achieving Broader Benefits from Indigenous Land Use Agreements: Community Development in Central Australia." *Community Development Journal.*

Carothers, Thomas. 1998. "The Rule of Law Revival." *Foreign Affairs* 77(2, March–April): 95–106.

Cass, Bettina. 2005. "Contested Debates about Citizenship Rights to Welfare: Indigenous People and Welfare in Australia." In D. Austin Broos and G. Macdonald, eds., *Culture, Economy and Governance in Aboriginal Australia*. Sydney: Sydney University Press.

Cavanagh, Greg. 2015. *Inquest into the death of Perry Jabanangka Langdon* [2015] NTMC 016. August 14, 2015. Northern Territory Coroners Court. Available at https://justice.nt.gov.au/__data/assets/pdf_file/0009/208962/d00752015-perry -langdon.pdf.

Central Australian Aboriginal Family Legal Unit (CAAFLU). 2010. "Submission into the Enquiry of the Child Protection System of the Northern Territory." Available at https://childprotectioninquiry.nt.gov.au/__data/assets/pdf_file/0019/242515 /No70_CAAFLU_Aboriginal_Corporation.pdf.

Central Australian Youth Link-Up Service (CAYLUS). 2012. "About CAYLUS." Available at https://caylus.org.au/about-caylus/#about.

Central Land Council (CLC). nd. Website: Building the Bush: Community Development. Retrieved March 2, 2016, from www.clc.org.au/articles/info/community -development.

———. 2003. "Making Peace with the Past: Remembering the Coniston Massacre 1928–2003." Available at www.clc.org.au/index.php?/publications/content /making-peace-with-the-past-remembering-the-coniston-massacre-1928-2003.

———. 2007. "Submission to Senate Committee on Legal and Constitution Affairs: Inquiry into NTER Bills Inquiry into Commonwealth Emergency Response Bills." August 10. Retrieved on February 11, 2017, from www.clc.org.au/index .php?/publications/content/submission-to-senate-standing-committee-on -legal-and-constitution/.

———. 2008. "Reviewing the Northern Territory Emergency Response: Perspectives from Six Communities." July. Retrieved on February 11, 2017, from www.clc .org.au/index.php?/publications/content/reviewing-the-northern-territory -emergency-response-perspectives-from-/.

———, 2012. Monitoring Report of the Central Land Council Community Development Program, July 2011. Alice Springs: Central Land Council. Retrieved on January 3, 2018, from www.clc.org.au/files/pdf/CLC_CDU_2011_Monitoring _Report_compressed.pdf

———. 2016. *Council News.* April. Available at www.clc.org.au/files/pdf/Council _News_April_2016.pdf

Central Land Council Community Development News. 2013. Summer. Retrieved on January 3, 2018, from www.clc.org.au/index.php?/publications/content /community-development-news-2013-summer.

Centralian Advocate. 2012. "Man Sought about Death." March 9.

Chappells, H., and E. Shove. 2004. "Comfort: A Review of Paradigms and Philosophies." Retrieved on January 10, 2013, from www.lancaster.ac.uk/fass/projects /futcom/fc_litfinal1.pdf.

Charles, C. 2009. "The National Cross Border Justice Scheme." *Indigenous Law Bulletin* 23(7): 12.

Charlesworth, Hillary. 1994. "What Are Women's International Human Rights?" In R. J. Cook, ed., *Human Rights of Women: National and International Perspectives*, 58–84. Philadelphia: University of Pennsylvania Press.

Charlesworth, Max, Howard Morphy, Dianne Bell, and Kenneth Maddock, eds. 1984. *Religion in Aboriginal Australia: An Anthology*. Saint Lucia, Brisbane: University of Queensland Press.

Chesterman, John, and Calligan, Brian. 1997. *Citizens without Rights: Aborigines and Australian Citizenship*. Cambridge, UK, New York, and Melbourne: Cambridge University Press.

Chesters, Timothy, ed. 2009. *Land Rights: The Oxford Amnesty Lectures 2005*. Oxford, UK: Oxford University Press.

Childwise. 2017. "State Legislation and Reporting: Northern Territory" Available at www.childwise.org.au/page/48/state-legislation-reporting-nt.

Cribbin, John. 1984. *The Killing Times: The Coniston Massacre 1928*. Sydney: Fontana Books.

Christen, Kimberly. 2009. *Aboriginal Business: Alliances in a Remote Australian Town*. Santa Fe, NM: School for Advanced Research Press.

Christie, Michael. 2010. "The Ethics of Teaching from Country." In S. Holcombe and M. Davis eds., Contemporary Ethical Issues in Research with Australian Indigenous Peoples, special edition of *Journal of Australian Aboriginal Studies*, 2: 69–80.

———. 2014. "Indigenous Governance in the Era of 'Good Governance.'" *The Conversation*. Retrieved on October 14, 2015, from http://theconversation.com /indigenous-australia-in-the-era-of-good-governance-29316.

Cianci, R., and P. A. Gambrel. 2003. "Maslow's Hierarchy of Needs: Does It Apply in a Collectivist Culture?" *Journal of Applied Management and Entrepreneurship* 8(2): 143–161.

Clarke, Simon. 2005. "The Neo-liberal Theory of Society." In Alfredo Saad-Filho and Deborah Johnston, eds., 50-59. *Neo-liberalism: A Critical Reader*. London and Ann Arbor, MI: Pluto Press.

Clastres, Pierre. 1989 [1974]. *Society against the State: Essays in Political Anthropology*. New York: Zone Books.

Clendinnen, Inge. 2003. *Dancing with Strangers: Europeans and Australians at First Contact*. Cambridge, UK, and New York: Cambridge University Press.

Coker, Donna. 2002. "Transformative Justice: Anti-Subordination Processes in Domestic Violence Cases." In Heather Strang and John Braithwaite, eds., *Restorative Justice and Family Violence*, 128–152. Cambridge, UK: Cambridge University Press.

Coker, Donna, and Ahjane Macquoid. 2015. "Why Opposing Hyper-Incarceration Should Be the Work of the Anti-Domestic Violence Movement." *University of Miami Race and Social Justice Law Review* 5(2): 585–618.

Collard, K. S., A. D'Antoine, D. G. Eggington, B. R. Henry, C. A. Martin, and G. H. Mooney. 2005. "'Mutual' Obligation in Indigenous Health: Can Shared Responsibility Agreements Be Truly Mutual?" Policy Debate for Debate. In *MJA* 182(10) 502–504.

Cook, R. J., ed. 1994. *Human Rights of Women: National and International Perspectives.* Philadelphia: University of Pennsylvania Press.

Combined Aboriginal Nations of Central Australia (CANCA). 1998. *Submission to the House of Representatives Standing Committee on Aboriginal and Torres Strait Islander Affairs: Inquiry into the Recommendations on the Review of the Aboriginal Land Rights (Northern Territory) Act 1976.* Available at www.aph.gov .au/parliamentary_business/committees/house_of_representatives_committees ?url=atsia/reeves/sub39.pdf.

Commonwealth of Australia. 2009. *National Human Rights Consultation Report.* Canberra.

———. 2010. Australia's Human Rights Framework. April. Retrieved on January 4, 2017, from www.ag.gov.au/Consultations/Documents/Publicsubmissionson-thedraftbaselinestudy/AustraliasHumanRightsFramework.pdf.

———, 2015. *Parliamentary Joint Committee on Human Rights. Guide to Human Rights.* Available at www.aph.gov.au/Parliamentary_Business/Committees/Joint /Human_Rights/Guidance_Notes_and_Resources.

———. 2016. "Commonwealth Indigenous Advancement Strategy Tendering Process." Camberra: The Senate Finances and Public Administration References Committee.

Concerned Australians. 2010. *This Is What We Said: Australian Aboriginal People Give Their Views on the Northern Territory Intervention.* East Melbourne, Victoria: Concerned Australians.

———. 2011. *Opinion: NTER Evaluation 2011.* Melbourne. Available at http://www .concernedaustralians.com.au/media/NTER-Evaluation-Opinion-2011.pdf

———. 2012. *A Decision to Discriminate; Aboriginal Disempowerment in the Northern Territory.* Melbourne: Concerned Australians.

Council of Australian Governments (COAG). 2011. "National Indigenous Reform Agreement (Closing the Gap)." Available at www.federalfinancialrelations.gov .au/content/npa/health/_archive/indigenous-reform/national-agreement _sept_12.pdf.

Cowan, A. 2013. "UN DRIP and the Intervention: Indigenous Self-Determination, Participation, and Racial Discrimination in the Northern Territory of Australia." *Pacific Rim Law & Policy Journal* 22(2): 247–310.

Cowan, Jane K. 2001. "Introduction." In J. K. Cowan, M. B. Dembour, and R. A. Wilson, eds., *Culture and Rights: Anthropological Perspectives*. Cambridge, UK: Cambridge University Press.

———. 2006. "Culture and Rights after Culture and Rights." *American Anthropologist* 108(1): 9–24.

———. 2014. "The Universal Periodic Review as a Public Audit Ritual: An Anthropological Perspective on Emerging Practices in the Global Governance of Human Rights." In H. Charlesworth and E. Larking, eds., *Human Rights and the Universal Periodic Review*, 42–62. Cambridge, UK: Cambridge University Press.

Cowlishaw, G. 1982. "Socialisation and Subordination among Australian Aborigines." *Man, New Series* 17(3, September): 492–507.

———. 2004. *Blackfellas Whitefellas and the Hidden Injuries of Race*. Oxford, UK, and Melbourne: Blackwell Publishing,.

———. 2007. Indigenous Rights: AAS Statement. *Australia Anthropological Society Newsletter*. December. Retrieved on June 17, 2012, from www.aas.asn.au /Newsletter/Archive/156%20R%20&%20P%20Issue%20108%20-%20December %202007.pdf.

Cripps, Kyllie, and C. S. Taylor. 2009. "White Man's Law, Traditional Law and Bullshit Law: Customary Marriage Revisited." *Balayi: Culture, Law and Colonisation*.10: 59–72.

Cripps, Kyllie, and Hannah McGlade. 2008. "Indigenous Family Violence and Sexual Abuse: Considering Pathways Forward." *Journal of Family Studies* 14(2–3): 240–253.

Cunneen, Chris. 2007. "Riot, Resistance and Moral Panic: Demonising the Colonial Other." In Scott Poynting and George Morgan, eds., *Outrageous: Moral Panics in Australia*, 20–29. Hobart, Australia: ACYS Press.

Cunneen, C., and Baldry, E. 2011. "Contemporary Penality in the Shadow of Colonial Patriarchy." Paper Presented at the 5th Annual ANZ Critical Criminology Conference, Cairns Australia, July 6–7.

Curran, Georgia. 2011. "The Expanding Domain of Warlpiri Initiation Rituals." In Y. Musharbash and M. Barber, eds., *Ethnography and the Production of Anthropological Knowledge: Essays in Honour of Nicolas Peterson*, 39–50. Canberra: ANU E Press, Australian National University.

Da Cunha, M. C. 2009. *"Culture" and Culture: Traditional Knowledge and Intellectual Rights*. Chicago: Prickly Paradigm Press, University of Chicago.

D'Abbs, Peter. 1990. "Restricted Areas and Aboriginal Drinking." Retrieved on February 11, 2017, from www.aic.gov.au/media_library/publications/proceedings/01 /dabbs.pdf.

Damousi, J., K. Rubenstein, and M. Tomsic, eds. 2014. *Diversity in Leadership: Australian Women, Past and Present.* Canberra: ANU Press, Australian National University.

Davis, Megan. 2007. "Arguing over Indigenous rights: Australia and the United Nations." In J. Altman and M. Hinkson, eds., *Coercive Reconciliation: Stabilise, Normalise, Exit Aboriginal Australia.* Melbourne: Arena Publications.

——. 2008. "'A Home at the United Nations': Indigenous Peoples and International Advocacy." In W. Maley and A. Cooper, eds., *Global Governance and Diplomacy Worlds Apart?* 211–223. Basingstoke, UK: Palgrave Macmillan.

——. 2009 "A Woman's Place." *Griffith Review* 24: 156–162.

——. 2012. "An Alternative Framework for Re-Imagining Self-Determination." The NAARM oration, Melbourne University, November 2012. Retrieved on September 12, 2013, from http://sheilas.org.au/2012/12/an-alternative-framework/.

Day, Andrew, and Kevin Howells. 2008. "Psychological Treatments for Rehabilitating Offenders." In Andrew Day, Martin Nakata, and Kevin Howells, eds. *Anger and Indigenous Men,* 6–19. Sydney: The Federation Press.

Day, Andrew, Martin Nakata, and Kevin Howells, eds. 2008. *Anger and Indigenous Men.* Sydney: The Federation Press.

Daylight, Phyliss, and M. Johnson. 1986. *Women's Business: Report of the Aboriginal Women's Taskforce.* Canberra: Australian Government Publishing Services.

Dean, Mitchell. 2002. "Liberal Government and Authoritarianism." *Economy and Society* 31(1): 37–61.

De Costa, Ravi. 2006. *A Higher Authority: Indigenous Transnationalism and Australia.* Sydney: UNSW Press.

De Tocqueville, A. 1964. *Democracy in America,* 2nd ed. Volume 1. Translated by Henry Reeve. New York: Schocken Books.

Department of Community Services (DCF) Annual Report, 2013–14. Available at www.childrenandfamilies.nt.gov.au/library/scripts/objectifyMedia.aspx?file=pdf/94/58.pdf&siteID=5&str_title=DCF Annual Report 2013 - 14.pdf.

Dietz, M. G. 1987. "Context Is all: Feminism and Theories of Citizenship." Special issue: Learning about Women: Gender, Politics and Power. *Daedalus* 116(4, Fall): 1–24.

Dillon, Michael C., and Neil D. Westbury. 2007. *Beyond Humbug: Transforming Government Engagement with Indigenous Australia.* South Australia: Seaview Press.

Diplomacy Training Program. "Australian Indigenous Programs." Retrieved on January 15, 2016, from www.dtp.unsw.edu.au/australian-indigenous-programs

Doctrinal Statements and Theological Opinions of the Lutheran Church of Australia. 2001. *Volume 2. Ethical and Social Issues: Human Rights.* Adopted by the Commission on Theology and Inter-Church Relations, April 20, 1994. Edited

September 2001. Retrieved on October 3, 2016, from www.lca.org.au/doctrinal -statements--theological-opinions-2.html.

Dodson, Michael. 1998. "Linking International Standards with the Contemporary Concerns of Aboriginal and Torres Strait Islander Peoples." In Sarah Pritchard, ed., *Indigenous Peoples, the United Nations and Human Rights*, 18–31. Zed Books. Sydney: The Federation Press.

"Domestic Violence Will Not Be Tolerated." 2014. *Centralian Advocate* August 22.

Donnelly, Jack. 1982. "Human Rights and Human Dignity: An Analytic Critique of Non-Western Conceptions of Human Rights." *The American Political Science Review* 76(2, June): 303–316.

Dorough, Dalee Sambo. 2015. "Dalee Sambo Dorough: UNPFII End of Year Message 2014." March 9. Available at http://unpfip.blogspot.com.au/2015/03/i-am -writing-this-holiday-message-after.html.

Douzinas, Costas. 2007. *Human Rights and Empire*. Cavendish, UK: Routledge.

Dumont, L. 1986. *Essays on Individualism: Modern Ideology in Anthropological Perspective*. Chicago and London: University of Chicago Press.

Dussart, Francois. 2000. *The Politics of Ritual in an Aboriginal settlement: Kinship, Gender and the Currency of Knowledge*. Washington, DC, and London: Smithsonian Institution Press.

Edmunds, Mary. 2010. *The Northern Territory Intervention and Human Rights: An Anthropological Perspective*. Whitlam Institute, University of Western Sydney. Retrieved on October 15, 2012, from www.whitlam.org/__data/assets/pdf_file /0005/162932/Perspectives_-_Dr_Mary_Edmunds_Nov_2010.pdf.

Englund, Harri. 2006. *Prisoners of Freedom: Human Rights and the African Poor*. Berkeley: University of California Press.

Englund, Harri, and James Leach. 2000. "Ethnography and Meta-Narratives of Modernity." *Current Anthropology* 41(2, April): 225–248.

Essential Oxford English Dictionary (Australian Edition), 4th ed. 2010. Australia and New Zealand: Hinkler Books.

Etzioni, Amitai. 2013. "Communitarianism: Political and Social Philosophy." Retrieved on January 1, 2017, from www.britannica.com/topic/communitarianism.

———. 2015. "Communitarianism." In Michael T. Gibbons, Diana Coole, Elisabeth Ellis, and Kennan Ferguson, eds., *The Encyclopedia of Political Thought*. John Wiley and Sons. Available at https://icps.gwu.edu/sites/icps.gwu.edu/files /downloads/Communitarianism.Etzioni.pdf.

Evans, Nicolas, and David Wilkins. 2000. "In the Mind's Ear: The Semantic Extensions of Perception Verbs in Australian Languages." *Language, the Linguistic Society of America* (76)3: 546–592.

Evatt Foundation. "Doc Evatt: A Brilliant and Controversial Character." Retrieved on February 15, 2016, from http://evatt.org.au/about-us/doc-evatt.html.

Faine, Jean. 1993. *Lawyers in the Alice: Aboriginals and Whitefella's Law*, 2nd edition. Melbourne: The Federation Press.

Fanon, Frantz, 2004 [1961]. *The Wretched of the Earth*. London: Penguin.

Farmer, Paul. 2003. *Pathologies of Power: Health, Human Rights, and the New War on the Poor*. Berkeley: University of California Press.

Ferguson, A. 2012. "Reflections on the 2012 UN Permanent Forum on Indigenous Issues." *Indigenous Law Bulletin* 8(3): 24–25.

Fitz-Gibbon, Kate. 2013. "Submission on the Partial Defence of Provocation." To the New South Wales Government, Crimes Amendment Provocation Bill. Available at https://blogs.deakin.edu.au/criminology/kate-fitz-gibbon-responds-to-nsw-provocation-law-reform/.

First Nations People's Party. 2013. "Official Launch of Australia's First Aboriginal Political Party Near the Aboriginal Tent Embassy in Canberra." Available at www.abc.net.au/news/2013-01-28/official-launch-of-first-aboriginal-political-party/4487324).

Fleming, J., and R. Sarre. 2011. "Policing the NPY Lands: The Cross Border Justice Project." *Australasian Policing: A Journal of Professional Practice and Research* 3(1): 31–33.

Fletcher, Christine. 1996. "Trapped in Civil Society: Aborigines and Federalism in Australia." North Australian Research Unit (NARU) Discussion Paper 4/1996. Casuarina, N.T.: Australian National University.

Forster, C., and V. Jivan. 2005. "Opportunity Lost: In Search of Justice for Victims of Sexual Assault; A Note on Victims Compensation Fund Corporation v GM." *UNSW Law Journal* 28(3): 758–779.

Fraser, Malcolm. 2015. *The Age Newspaper* February 4.

Fred Hollows Foundation. 2012. *"Making Things Happen": Sharing the Outcome of the Indigenous Peoples, Human Rights and Advocacy Training Program for Remote Indigenous Participants Using the Most Significant Change Technique*. April. Unpublished Report.

Freire, Paulo. 1985. *The Politics of Education: Culture, Power, and Liberation*. Massachusetts: Bergin & Garvey Publishers.

———. 1993 [1970]. *Pedagogy of the Oppressed*. London: Penguin Books.

Frost, Malcolm. 2014. "Three Rules for Being Aboriginal: Anxiety and Violence in Central Australia." *Australian Aboriginal Studies* 1: 90–98.

Ganter, Elizabeth. 2011. "Representatives in Orbit: Livelihood Options for Aboriginal People in the Administration of the Australian Desert." *The Rangeland Journal* 33: 385–393.

Geertz, Clifford. 1957. "Ritual and Social Change: A Javanese Example." *American Anthropologist* LIX: 32–54.

Georgatos, Gerry. 2014. "National Indigenous Human Rights Awards." *The Stringer on-line News*. September 14. Available at http://thestringer.com.au/national -indigenous-human-rights-awards-10836#.Viq4xbcrKyY/TheStringer/September.

Gibson, Patraic. 2015. "Removed for Being Aboriginal. Is the Northern Territory Creating Another Stolen Generation?" *The Guardian*, March 4.

Gibson, Patraic, and Larissa Behrendt. 2014. "Submission to Senate Standing Committees on Community Affairs—Out of Home Care." Submission 79. University of Technology, Sydney. Jumbunna.

Giddings, Franklin. 1922. *Studies in the Theory of Human Society*. New York: Macmillan.

Glaskin, Katie. 2012. "Anatomies of Relatedness: Considering Personhood in Aboriginal Australia." *American Anthropologist* 114(2): 297–308.

Goankar, D. P., and Elizabeth A. Povinelli. 2003. "Technologies of Public Forms: Circulation, Transfiguration, Recognition." *Public Culture* 15(3); 385–397.

Gordon, S., K. Hallahan, and D. Henry. 2002. "Putting the Picture Together: Inquiry into Response by Government Agencies to Complaints of Family Violence and Child Abuse in Aboriginal Communities," Department of Premier and Cabinet, Western Australia. Available at www.slp.wa.gov.au/publications/publications .nsf/DocByAgency/FEB7D71FB3A6AF1948256C160018F8FE/$file/Gordon +Inquiry+Final.pdf.

Goodale, Mark. 2006. Introduction to "Anthropology and Human Rights in a New Key." *American Anthropologist* 108(1): 1–8.

———. 2009. *Surrendering to Utopia: An Anthropology of Human Rights*. Stanford, CA: Stanford Studies in Human Rights, Stanford University Press.

———. 2012. "Human Rights." In Didier Fassin, ed., *A Companion to Moral Anthropology*, 468–481. West Sussex, UK: Wiley Blackwell.

Gondolf, E. W. 1997. "Batterer Programs: What We Know and Need to Know." *Journal of Interpersonal Violence* 12(1): 83–98.

Goot, Murry, and Tim Rowse. 2007. *Divided Nation? Indigenous Affairs and the Imagined Public*. Melbourne: Melbourne University Press.

Gordon, A. 2012. "The Cross Border Justice Project: Enhancing Victim Services in the Central Desert Region." Retrieved on March 6, 2015, from www.victimsof crime.org.au/wp-content/uploads/2012/11/Inspector-Ashley-Gordon.doc.

Gottlieb, E. E., and T. J. La Belle. 1990. "Ethnographic Contextualisation of Frieres' Discourse: Consciousness-Raising, Theory and Practice." *Anthropology & Education Quarterly* 21(1, March): 3–18.

Graham, Chris. 2012. "Aboriginal Voters Vent Their Fury . . . and Change Government." *Tracker News*.

Grayling, A. C. 2013. *The Good Book: A Humanist Bible*. New York: Walter Publishing Company.

Green. Jenny. 2012. "The Altyerre Story: Suffering Badly by Translation." *The Austra-lian Journal of Anthropology* 23(2): 158–178.

Greenfield, P. M. 2009. "Linking Social Change and Developmental Change: Shifting Pathways of Human Development." *Developmental Psychology* 45(2): 401–418.

The Greens. 2015. "First Nations Doing It for Themselves." John Barry, August 3. Retrieved on November 12, 2015, from https://greens.org.au/magazine/national/first-nations-doing-it-themselves.

Gundogdu, A. 2012. "'Perplexities of the Rights of Man': Arendt and the Aporias of Human Rights." *European Journal of Political Theory* 11(1): 4–24.

Gusfield, J. R. 1975. *Community: A Critical Response.* New York: Harper Colophon.

Hage, Ghassan. 2012. "Truncating Anthropology's Political Imagination: Critical Review Essay." *The Australian Journal of Anthropology,* 23: 406–412.

Hage, Ghassan, and R. Eckersley, eds. 2012. *Responsibility.* Melbourne: Melbourne University Press.

Hale, C. R. 2009. "Comment on Merlan, F., Indigeneity: Global and Local." *Current Anthropology* 50(3, June): 322–324.

Hamilton, Annette. 1980. "Dual Social Systems: Technology, Labour and Women's Secret Rites in the Eastern Western Desert of Australia." *Oceania* 51: 4–19.

———. 1981. "A Complex Strategical Situation: Gender and Power in Aboriginal Australia." In N. Grieve and P. Grimshaw, eds., *Australian Women: Feminist Perspectives,* 69–85. Oxford, UK: Oxford University Press.

———. 1982. "Descended from Father, Belonging to Country: Rights to Land in the Australian Western Desert." In E. Leacock and Lee, eds., *Politics and History in Australian Band Societies,* 85–108. Cambridge, UK: Cambridge University Press.

Hansen, Ken C., and Lesley E. Hansen. 1992. *Pintupi/Luritja Dictionary,* 3rd. ed. Alice Springs: IAD Publications.

Hargaden, Kevin. 2013. "Karl Marx and the Trouble with Human Rights." *The Other Journal: An Intersection of Theology and Culture. 22: Marxism Issue.* Retrieved on April 25, 2016, from http://theotherjournal.com/2013/05/16/karl-marx-and-the-trouble-with-rights/.

Harris, J. W. 2013. *One Blood: Two Hundred Years of Aboriginal Encounter with Christianity.* Brentford Square, Australia: Concilia.

Hart, N. 2009. "An Interview with Les Malezer." *Indigenous Law Bulletin* 7(11): 9–12. Retrieved on May 20, 2016, from www.austlii.edu.au/au/journals/IndigLawB/2009/12.html.

Hatch, E. 1997. "The Good Side of Relativism." *Journal of Anthropological Research* 53(3): 371–381.

Havnen, Olga. 2012. *Office of the Northern Territory Coordinator-General for Remote Services Report: June 2011 to August 2012.* Northern Territory

Coordinator General for Remote Services. Retrieved on August 8, 2013, from www .territorystories.nt.gov.au/bitstream/handle/10070/241806/NTCGRS_full report_2012.pdf?sequence=1.

Henson, Barbara. 1994. *A Straight-Out Man: F. W. Albrecht and Central Australian Aborigines*. Melbourne: Melbourne University Press.

Hernandez-Castillo, R. Aida. 2010. "The Emergence of Indigenous Feminism in Latin America." *Signs* 35(3): 539–545.

Hiatt, Lester. 1965. *Kinship and Conflict: A Study of an Aboriginal Community in Northern Arnhem Land*. Canberra: Australian National University Press.

Hill, Barry. 2002. *Broken Song: T. G. H. Strehlow and Aboriginal Possession*. Australia: Knopf, Random House.

Hill, Lisa, and Kate Alport. 2010. "Voting Attitudes and Behaviour among Aboriginal Peoples: Reports from Anangu Women." *Australian Journal of Politics and History* 56(2): 242–258.

Hilliard, Winifrid. 1968. *The People in Between: the Pitjantjatjara People of Ernabella*. Adelaide: Hodder and Stoughton.

Hindess, Barry. 2002. "Neoliberal Citizenship." *Citizenship Studies* 6(2): 127–143.

Hinkson, Melinda. 2007. "Introduction: In the Name of the Child." In J. C. Altman and M. Hinkson, eds,. *Coercive Reconciliation: Stabilise, Normalise and Exit*. Melbourne: Arena Publications.

———. 2010. "Introduction: Anthropology and the Culture Wars." In J. C. Altman and M. Hinkson, eds., *Culture Crisis: Anthropology and Politics in Aboriginal Australia*: 1–13. Sydney: UNSW Press.

Hobson, J. A. 1938. *Imperialism: A Study*, 3rd edition. London: Allen and Unwin.

Hockey, Joe. 2014. "Post Budget Address." May 14. Canberra: National Press Club.

Hodgson, D. L. 2011. "Introduction: Gender and Culture at the Limit of Rights." In D. L. Hodgson, ed., *Gender and Culture at the Limit of Rights*. Philadelphia: University of Pennsylvania Press.

Holcombe, Sarah 1989. Contextualising Koorie Women: Reserve and Urban Profiles. Unpublished Anthropology Honours thesis. University of Sydney, Australia.

———. 1997. "Ritual and the Central Australian Gender Debate." *Journal of Interdisciplinary Gender Studies* (JIGS) 2(2): 26–41.

———. 1998. "Amunturrgu: An Emergent Community in Central Australia." Unpublished PhD thesis, University of Newcastle, NSW.

Holcombe, S. 2004a. "The Politico-Historical Construction of the Pintupi-Luritja and the Concept of Tribe." *Oceania* 74(4): 257–275.

———. 2004b. "The Sentimental Community: A Site of Belonging." *The Australian Journal of Anthropology*: 163–184.

———. 2005. "Luritja Management of the State." In Special Edition, Oceania, M. Hinkson and B. Smith, eds. *Figuring the Intercultural in Aboriginal Australia* 75(3): 222–233.

———. 2015. "The Ontologies and Ecologies of Hardship: Past and Future Governance in the Central Australian Arid Zone." Chapter 9 in J. P. Marshall and L. H. Connor, eds., *The World and Its Futures: Ecologies, Ontologies, Mythologies*, 145–160. London: Routledge.

———. 2016. "Human Rights, Colonial Criminality, and the Death of Kwementyaye Briscoe in Custody: A Central Australian Case Study." *PoLAR: Political and Legal Anthropology Review* 39: 104–120. 10.1111/plar.12174.

Holcombe, S., and T. Janke. 2012. "Patenting the Kakadu Plum and the Marjarla Tree: Biodiscovery, Intellectual Property and Indigenous Knowledge." Chapter 11 in M. Rimmer and A. McLennan, *Intellectual Property and Emerging Technologies in the Life Sciences*, 293–319. Cheltenham, UK, and Northampton, MA: Edward Elgar Publishing.

Holcombe, Sarah, and Patrick Sullivan. 2013. "Indigenous Australian Organisations." In Douglas Caulkins and Ann Jordan, eds. *A Companion to Organisational Anthropology*, 493–518. West Sussex, UK: Wiley-Blackwell.

hooks, bell. 2000. *Feminism Is for Everybody: Passionate Politics*. Cambridge, MA: South End Press.

Howe, Adrian. 2002. "Provoking Polemic: Provoked Killings and the Ethical Paradoxes of the Postmodern Feminist Condition." *Feminist Legal Studies* 10: 39–64.

Howells, K. 2008. "The Treatment of Anger in Offenders." In A. Day, M. Nakata, and K. Howells, eds., *Anger and Indigenous Men*, 20–30. Sydney: The Federation Press.

Howes, D., ed. 1991. *The Varieties of Sensory Experience: A Sourcebook in the Anthropology of the Senses*. Toronto: University of Toronto Press.

Hubbard, Elbert. 1908. *Little Journeys to the Homes of Great Teachers*. New York: The Roycrofters.

Huggins, Jackie, J. Willmott, I. Tarrago, K. Willetts, L. Bond, L. Holt, E. Bourke, M. Bin-Salik, P. Fowell, J. Schmider, V. Craigie, and L. Levi-McBride. 1991. Letters to the Editor: Editorial. *Women's Studies Int. Forum* 14(5): 505–513.

Hugman, Richard. 2013. "Human Rights and Social Justice." Chapter 24 in Mel Gray, James Midgley, and Stephen A. Webb, eds. *The Sage Handbook of Social Work*: 372–385. London and Thousand Oaks, CA: Sage.

Human Rights and Equal Opportunity Commission (HREOC). 1999. *"Bush Talks" Report*. Commonwealth Government. Available at www.humanrights.gov.au /sites/default/files/content/pdf/human_rights/bush_talks.pdf.

Hunt, Janet, Diane Smith, William Sanders, and Stephanie Garling, eds. 2008. *Contested Governance: Culture, Power and Institutions in Indigenous Australia*. Canberra: Australian National University, ANU e press.

Hunt, Lyne. 2007. *Inventing Human Rights: A History*. New York and London: W. W. Norton and Company.

Hunter, Ernest. 1998. "Considering Trauma in an Indigenous Context." *Aboriginal and Islander Health Worker Journal* 22(5, September/October): 9–1.

Ignatieff, Michael. 2001. *Human Rights: As Politics and Idolatry*. Princeton, NJ, and Oxford, UK: Princeton University Press.

Jamieson, G. 2008. "The Cross Border Justice Scheme: A Story about Hats." Paper presented at the 5th Australasian Legislative Drafting Conference, Brisbane. Retrieved on March 12, 2015, from www.nt.gov.au/justice/crossborder/documents/A%20Story%20About%20Hats%20-%20Cross%20Border%20Justice%20Scheme.pdf.

Johns, Gary. 2011. *Aboriginal Self Determination: The Whiteman's Dream*. Victoria: Connor Court Publishing.

Johnson, Vivienne. 2010. *Once upon a Time in Papunya*. Sydney: Newsouth.

———. 2015. *Streets of Papunya: The Re-Invention of Papunya Painting*. Sydney: Newsouth.

Jolly, Margaret. 1996. "Devils, Holy Spirits and the Swollen God: Translation, Conversion and Colonial Power in the Marist Mission, Vanuatu, 1887–1934." In P. van der Veer, ed., *Conversion to Modernities: The Globalisation of Christianity*, 231–262. New York and London: Routledge.

———. 2015. "When She Cries Oceans: Navigating Gender Violence in the Western Pacific." In A. Biersack, M. Jolly, and M Macintyre, eds., *Gender Violence and Human Rights in the Western Pacific*, 341–380. Canberra: ANU Press.

Jordan, K., and L. Fowkes, eds. 2016. "Job Creation and Income Support in Remote Indigenous Australia. Moving Forward with a Better System." Centre for Aboriginal Economic Policy Research (CAEPR) Topical Issue No. 2/2016. Canberra: Australian National University. Available at http://caepr.anu.edu.au/sites/default/files/Publications/topical/CAEPR%20Topical%20Issues%202_2016.pdf.

Joseph, Sarah. 2015. "On the Ground at Australia's Universal Periodic Review." *The Conversation*, on-line site. Retrieved on May 1, 2016, from http://theconversation.com/on-the-ground-at-australias-universal-periodic-review-50525.

Kaberry, Phyliss. 1939. *Aboriginal Woman: Sacred and Profane*. London: Routledge.

Keen, Ian. 1997. "The Western Desert vs the Rest: Rethinking the Contrast." In F. Merlan, J. Morton and A. Rumsey, eds., *Scholar and Sceptic: Essays in Honour of L.R Hiatt*, 65–93. Canberra: Aboriginal Studies Press.

———. 2004. *Aboriginal Economy and Society: Australia at the Threshold of Colonisation*. South Melbourne: Oxford University Press.

Kent, Lia. 2010. *Assessing the Human Rights Training Program: Oxfam Australia Partnership and the Long Term Impact of the DTP Training Courses. An Independent Evaluation*. Retrieved on April 2, 1014, from www.oxfam.org.au/wp-content /uploads/2011/08/OAUS-ATSIPP-DTP-Evaluation-1110.pdf.

Kerley, K., and Cunneen, C. 1995. "Deaths in Custody in Australia: The Untold Story of Aboriginal and Torres Strait Islander Women." *Canadian Journal of Women and the Law* 531.

Kimber, R. G. 1981. *The Pintupi of the Kintore Range*. Report for the Department of Aboriginal Affairs, unpublished.

Kleinman, Daniel. 1987. "Anthropology and Psychiatry: The Role of Culture in Cross Cultural Research on Illness." *The British Journal of Psychiatry* 151: 447–454.

Kolig, Eric. 1982. "An Obituary for Ritual Power." In M. C. Howard, ed., *Aboriginal Power in Australian Society*, 14-31. St Lucia, London, and New York: University of Queensland Press.

Koori Mail 1992. "No Electricity for Papunya despite Government Backdown." July 1: 4.

Kral, Inge. 2012. *Talk, Text and Technology: Literacy and Social Practice in a Remote Indigenous Community*. Bristol, UK; Buffalo, NY; and Toronto: Multilingual Matters.

———. 2017. "Submission to the Inquiry into the Appropriateness and Effectiveness of the Objectives, Design, Implementation and Evaluation of the Community Development Program (CDP)." May 31. Senate Enquiry, Parliament of Australia. Available at www.aph.gov.au/Parliamentary_Business/Committees/Senate /Finance_and_Public_Administration/CDP/Submissions.

Kukutai, Tahu, and John Taylor, eds. 2016. *Indigenous Data Sovereignty: Towards an Agenda*. Research Monograph 38. Australian National University Press. Available at http://press-files.anu.edu.au/downloads/press/n2140/pdf/prelims.pdf.

Kymlicka, William. 2007. *Multicultural Odysseys: Navigating the New International Politics of Diversity*. Oxford, UK: Oxford University Press.

———. 2009. Comments on F. Merlan's article "Indigeneity: Global and Local." *Current Anthropology* 50(3, June): 323–325.

Land Rights News. 2012. Central Australian edition. 2(1, April). Available at www.clc .org.au/publications/viewer/land-rights-news-central-australia.

———. 2015. "Translating Rights for All." Central Australian edition. 5(2, August). Available at www.clc.org.au/land-rights-news/publication/land-rights-news -august-2015/.

Langford, Ruby. 1988. *Don't Take Your Love to Town*. Brisbane, Qld: Penguin Books.

Langton, Marcia. 2007. "Trapped in the Aboriginal Reality Show." *Griffith Review Edition 19: Reimagining Australia.*

———. 2008. "The End of Big Men Politics." *Griffith Review: Money, Sex, Power*: 13–38.

———. 2010. "The Shock of the New: The Post-Colonial Dilemma for Australian Anthropology." In Jon C. Altman and M. Hinkson, eds., *Culture Crisis: Anthropology and Politics in Aboriginal Australia*, 91–115. Sydney: UNSW Press.

———. 2012. "Comment: It's a Knockout: How the Aboriginal Vote Won the NT Election." *The Monthly, The Nation Reviewed.* October.

La Trobe University. n.d. Social Work Course. Available at www.latrobe.edu.au /courses/social-work.

Lawless, Elaine J. 1992. "'I was afraid someone like you . . . an outsider . . . would misunderstand': Negotiating Interpretive Differences between Ethnographers and Subjects." *Journal of American Folklore* 105(417): 302–314.

Lawrence, Kate. 2006. "Aboriginal Women Working in Vocational Education and Training: A Story from Central Australia." *Journal of Vocational Education and Training* 58(4): 423–440.

Lawrence, Rebecca, and Chris Gibson. 2007. "Obliging Indigenous Citizens?" *Cultural Studies* 21(4–5): 650–671.

Leene, G. J. F, and T. M. N. Schuyt. 2008. *Power of the Stranger: Structures and Dynamics in Social intervention—A Theoretical Framework.* Aldershot, UK: Ashgate Publishing.

Levitt, Peggy, and Sally Engle Merry. 2011. "Making Women's Human Rights in the Vernacular: Navigating the Culture/Rights Divide." In D. L. Hodgson, ed., *Gender, Culture and the Limit of Rights*, 81–100. Philadelphia: University of Pennsylvania Press.

Lloyd, Arthur S. 1972. "Freire, Conscientization, and Adult Education." *Adult Education Quarterly* 23(1): 3–20.

Lloyd, Jane. 2014. "Violent and Tragic Events: The Nature of Domestic Violence–Related Homicide Cases in Central Australia." *Australian Aboriginal Studies* (1): 99–110.

Lorde, Audre. 1984. "The Masters Tools Will Never Dismantle the Master's House." In Cherrie Moraga and Gloria Anzaldua, eds., *This Bridge Called by Back: Writings by Radical Women of Colour*, 94–101. New York: Kitchen Table Press.

Luke, A. 2000. "Critical Literacy in Australia: A Matter of Context and Standpoint." *Journal of Adolescent and Adult Literacy* Special issue: Re/mediating Adolescent Literacies 43(5, Feburary): 448–461.

MacDonnell Shire Council. 2014. Media Release. "13 New Local Authorities across the MacDonnell Regional Council." May 28. Retrieved on August 7, 2015, from http://macdonnell.nt.gov.au/uploads/misc/MR140528-IMMEDIATE-13-Local -Authorities-for-MacDonnell-Council.pdf.

Macknight, David. 2002. *From Hunting to Drinking: The Devastating Effects of Alcohol on an Australian Aboriginal Community*. London and New York: Routledge.

Maddock, Kenneth, 1984. "The World Creative Powers." In Max Charlesworth, Howard Morphy, Dianne Bell, and Kenneth Maddock, eds, *Religion in Aboriginal Australia: An Anthology*, 85–106. Saint Lucia, Brisbane: University of Queensland Press.

Maffie, James. 2008. "'In the End, We Have the Gatling Gun, and They Have Not': Future Prospects of Indigenous Knowledge." *Futures* 41: 53–65.

Maher, Kyam. 2016. "State Government Announces Intention to Enter into Treaty Discussions with Aboriginal South Australians." News releases, December 14. Available at www.premier.sa.gov.au/index.php/kyam-maher-news-releases /1599-state-government-announces-intention-to-enter-into-treaty-discussions -with-aboriginal-south-australians.

Male Champions of Change. 2017. "Progress Report 2016 Male Champions of Change." Available at malechampionsofchange.com/wp-content/uploads/2017/03/MCC -Progress-Report-2016-FINAL.pdf.

Manago, A. M., and P. M. Greenfield. 2011. "The Construction of Independent Values among Maya Women at the Forefront of Social Change: Four Case Studies." *ETHOS* 39(1): 1–29.

Marcus, Julie. 1993. "The Beauty, Simplicity and Honour of Truth: Olive Pink in the 1940s." In J. Marcus, ed., *First in Their Field: Women in Australian Anthropology*, 111–135. Melbourne: Melbourne University Press.

Marmion, D., K. Obata, and J. Troy. 2014. *Community, Identity, Wellbeing: The Report of the Second National Indigenous Languages Survey*. Canberra: AIATSIS. Available at http://aiatsis.gov.au/sites/default/files/products/report_research _outputs/2014-report-of-the-2nd-national-indigenous-languages-survey.pdf.

Martin, David F. 2001. "Is Welfare Dependency 'Welfare Poison'? An Assessment of Noel Pearson's Proposals for Welfare Reform." *Centre for Aboriginal Economic Policy Research Discussion Paper 213*. Canberra: Australian National University.

———. 2003. "Rethinking the Design of Indigenous Organisations: The Need for Strategic Engagement." *Centre for Aboriginal Economic Policy Research Discussion Paper No 248/2003*. Canberra: Australian National University.

Martin, David F., Frances Morphy, William G. Sanders, and John Taylor, eds. 2002. *Making Sense of the Census: Observations of the 2001 Enumeration in Remote Aboriginal Australia*. CAEPR Research Monograph 22. Australian National University. Canberra: ANU E. Press.

Maruna, S. 1999. "Desistance and Development: The Psychosocial Process of 'Going Straight.'" *The British Criminology Conferences: Selected Proceedings*, 2.

Maslow, A. 1954. *Motivation and Personality*. Harper: New York.

McCann, Joy, and Janet Wilson. 2014. "Representation of Women in Australian Parliaments 2014." Parliament of Australia Research Papers. Available at www.aph.gov.au/About_Parliament/Parliamentary_Departments/Parliamentary_Library/pubs/rp/rp1415/WomanAustParl.

Meggitt, M. J. 1962. *Desert People: A Study of Walbiri Aborigines of Central Australia.* Sydney: Angus and Robinson Publishers.

Memmott, Paul, C. Chambers, C. Go-Sam, and L. Thomson. 2006. *Good Practice in Indigenous Family Violence Prevention—Designing and Evaluating Successful Programs.* Issues Paper 11. UNSW, Sydney: Australian Domestic and family Violence Clearing House.

Memmott, Paul, and the Staff of Tangentyere Council. 1993. *Mwerre Anetyeke Mparntwele* (Sitting Down Good in Alice Springs). Unpublished report. Available at www.aic.gov.au/media_library/publications/proceedings/21/memmott.pdf.

Menzies, P. 2008. "Developing an Aboriginal Healing Model for Intergenerational Trauma." *International Journal of Health Promotion and Education* 46(2): 41–48.

Merlan, Francesca. 1992. "Male–Female Separation and Forms of Society in Aboriginal Australia." *Cultural Anthropology* 7(2): 169–193.

———. 2007. "Indigeneity as a Relational Identity: The Construction of Australian Land Rights." In Marisol Cadena and Orin Starn, eds., *Indigenous Experience Today*, 125–150. Oxford, UK, and New York: Berg.

———. 2009a. Indigeneity: Global and Local. *Current Anthropology* 50(3, June): 303–333.

———. 2009b. More than Rights. *Inside Story.* Retrieved on October 18, 2012, from http:/inside.org.au/more-than-rights/.

Merry, Sally Engle. 2003. "Rights Talk and the Experience of Law: Implementing Women's Human Rights to Protection from Violence." *Human Rights Quarterly* 25: 343–381.

———. 2006a. *Human Rights and Gender Violence: Translating International Law into Local Justice.* Chicago and London: University of Chicago Press.

———. 2006b. "Transnational Human Rights and Local Activism: Mapping the Middle." *American Anthropologist* 108(1): 38-51.

———. 2011. "Measuring the World: Human Rights Indicators and Global Governance." Supplement: Corporate Lives: New Perspectives on the Corporate Form. *Current Anthropology* 53(S3, April): S83–S95.

Mohanty, C. T. 1988. "Under Western Eyes: Feminism Scholarship and Colonial Discourses." *Feminist Review* 30 (Autumn): 61–88.

Moore, Henrietta. L. 1994. *A Passion for Difference: Essays in Anthropology and Gender.* Bloomington and Indianapolis: Polity Press.

Moran, Mark, and Ruth Elvin. 2009. "Coping with Complexity: Adaptive Governance in Desert Australia." Special Issue: Desert Knowledge, Jocelyn Davies and Sarah Holcombe, eds. *GeoJournal* 74(5): 415–428.

Morphy, Frances. 2007. "The Language of Governance in a Cross-Cultural Context: What Can and Can't Be Translated." In *Ngiya: Talk the Law. Volume 1. Governance in Indigenous Communities*, 93–102. Sydney: University of Technology.

———. 2008. "Whose Governance, for Whose Good? The Laynhapuy Homelands Association and the Neo-Assimilationist Turn in Indigenous Policy." In Janet Hunt, Diane Smith, William Sanders, and Stephanie Garling, eds. *Contested Governance: Culture, Power and Institutions in Indigenous Australia*, 113–152. Canberra: Australian National University, ANU e press.

Morphy, Howard, and Frances Morphy. 2013. "Anthropological Theory and Government Policy in Australia's Northern Territory: The Hegemony of the 'Mainstream.'" *American Anthropologist* 115(2): 174–187.

Moreton-Robinson, Aileen. 2000. *Talkin' up to the White Woman: Indigenous Women and Feminism*. Brisbane: University of Queensland Press.

———. 2003. "Resistance, Recovery and Revitalisation." In M Grossman (ed.), *Blacklines: Contemporary Critical Writing by Indigenous Australians* Melbourne: Melbourne University Press.

———. 2004. "Whiteness, Epistemology, and Indigenous Representation." In Aileen Moreton-Robinson, ed., *Whitening Race: Essays In Social And Cultural Criticism*. Canberra: Aboriginal Studies Press.

———, ed. 2007. *Sovereign Subjects: Indigenous Sovereignty Matters*. Sydney: Allen and Unwin.

———. 2013. "Towards an Indigenous Women's Standpoint Theory." *Australian Feminist Studies* 28(78): 331–347.

Morton, John. 1988. 'Géza Róheim's Contribution to Australian Ethnography'. Introduction to Géza Róheim's *Children of the Desert, II: Myths and Dreams of the Aborigines of Central Australia*, edited and introduced by W. Muensterberger & J. Morton, pp. vii–xxx. Sydney: Oceania Publications.

Moten, Fred. 2008. "The Case of Blackness." *Criticism, Vol 50. No.2* Spring, 177–218.

Mullighan Enquiry. 2008. *Children in State Care and Children in APY Lands Commission of Enquiry to the South Australian Parliament*. The Hon. E.P. Mullighan QC Commissioner. Available at: https://www.childprotection.sa.gov.au/sites/g /files/net691/f/cisc-complete.pdf

Murray, Neil. 2012. *Blackfella Whitefella*. One Day Hill. Camberwell, Victoria.

Myers, Fred. 1976. To Have and to Hold: A Study of Persistence and Change in Pintupi Social Life. Unpublished PhD thesis, Bryn Mawr College.

———. 1986. *Pintupi Country, Pintupi Self: Sentiment, Place and Politics among Western Desert Aborigines.* Washington, DC, and London: Smithsonian Institution Press; and Canberra: Australian Institute of Aboriginal Studies.

———. 1988. "Burning the Truck and Holding the Country: Property, Time and the Negotiation of Identity among Pintupi Aborigines." In T. Ingold, D. Riches, and J. Woodburn, eds., *Property, Power and Ideology in Hunting and Gathering Societies.* Berg: London.

Nancarrow, Heather. 2006. "In Search of Justice for Domestic and Family Violence: Indigenous and Non-Indigenous Australian Women's Perspectives." *Theoretical Criminology* 10(1): 87–106.

Nathan, P., and D. Leichleitner Japanangka. 1983. *Settle Down Country: Pmere Arlaltyewele.* Victoria: Central Australian Aboriginal Congress and Kibble Books.

National Aboriginal and Torres Strait Islander Legal Services (NATSILS) Peak Body. 2015. *NATSILS Submission for Australia's Universal Periodic Review.*

National Aboriginal Community Controlled Health Organisation (NACCHO). 2013. "Healing the Fault Lines: Uniting Politicians, Bureaucrats and NGOs for Improved Outcomes in Aboriginal Health." Olga Havnen speech to NACCHO conference. Available at www.naccho.org.au/download/aboriginalhealth/Olga%20Havnen%20Speech%20Danila%20Dilba%20Healing%20the%20Fault%20Lines.pdf.

National Australia Day Council. 2016. "Australian of the Year 2016. David Morrison AO." Available at www.australianoftheyear.org.au/honour-roll/?view=fullView&recipientID=1348.

National Congress of Australia's First Peoples. 2010. *National Congress of Australia's First Peoples Constitution.* Available at https://nationalcongress.com.au/wp-content/uploads/2016/10/2.6_National-Congress-Constitution.pdf.

———. 2013. *National Congress Report 13 (NC 13 Report).* Sydney.

———. 2014. "YouTube 2 UNPFII Day 1" (Katie Kiss, Lez Melzer, and Tennille Lamb). May 15. Retrieved on November 5, 2016, from www.youtube.com/watch?v=guOJ3TpG2EY

———. 2015. *Universal Periodic Review Australia.* Available at info@nationalcongress.com.au.

National Human Rights Consultation Report. 2009. Commonwealth of Australia. Sydney.

National Indigenous Times (NIT). 2014. "Freedom Summit." October 29.

National Report of Australia, 2015. "Universal Periodic Review: Second Cycle." Department of the Attorney General. Available at www.ag.gov.au/RightsAndProtections/HumanRights/United-Nations-Human-Rights-Reporting/Documents/UPR-National-Report-of-Australia-2015.pdf.

Neocosmos, Michael. 2006. "Can a Human Rights Culture Enable Emancipation? Clearing Some Theoretical Ground for the Renewal of a Critical Sociology." *South African Review of Sociology* 37(2): 356–379.

New Matilda.com. 2013. "Why Crossin Must Bow Out." January 24. Available at https://newmatilda.com/2013/01/24/why-crossin-must-bow-out/.

Newman, Peter, Dora Marinova, R. Armstrong, Margaret Raven, J. Marley, N. McGrath, and Fred Spring. 2008. *Desert Settlement Typology: Preliminary Literature, DKCRC Research Report 35.* Alice Springs: Desert Knowledge CRC.

Newman, Saul. 2007. "Anarchism, Poststructuralism and the Future of Radical Politics." *SubStance* 36(2): 3–19.

New South Wales Aboriginal Land Council. 2011. *Annual Report 2010–2011.* Retrieved on May 20, 2016, from http://alc.org.au/publications/annual-reports.aspx.

New Tactics in Human Rights. 2009. "Using Shadow Reports for Advocacy." March 8. Retrieved on May 12, 2016, from www.newtactics.org/using-shadow-reports-advocacy/using-shadow-reports-advocacy.

News.Com.Au. 2015. "Transgender Woman Starlady Explains Why She Moved to the Desert Six Years Ago." Rohan Smith, *Real Life True Stories*, May 22. Retreived on August 8, 2015, from www.news.com.au/lifestyle/real-life/transgender-woman-starlady-explains-why-she-moved-to-the-desert-six-years-ago/story-fnq2o7dd-1227363958569.

Ngaanyatjarra, Pitjantjatjarra and Yankunyjatjarra (NPY) Women's Council. 2010. *Fact Sheet 8: Domestic and Family Violence Service.* Available at www.npywc.org.au/wp-content/uploads/2012/01/08-Domestic-and-Family-Violence-Service.pdf.

———. 2011. "History." Available at www.npywc.org.au/d-and-fv-service-intro/history.

Niezen, Ronald. 2003. *The Origins of Indigenism: Human Rights and the Politics of Identity.* Berkeley and Los Angeles: University of California Press.

———. 2009. *The Rediscovered Self: Indigenous Identity and Cultural Justice.* Montreal and Kingston: McGill-Queens University Press.

———. 2011. The Social Study of Human Rights Review Essay. *Comparative Studies in Society and History* 53(3): 682–691.

No More. 2008. "Domestic Violence Campaign: A Challenge to Men." Catholic Care NT. Available at www.nomore.org.au/news/domestic-violence-campaign-challenge-men.

No to Violence (NTV) Manual 13. nd. Not available on-line. See "Taking Responsibility for your Violent Behaviour." Available at www.ntv.org.au/about-family-violence/what-men-can-do/.

North Australian Aboriginal Justice Agency (NAAJA). 2014a. "'Paperless Arrest' Laws Belong in a Police State, Not the NT." Retrieved on February 20, 2016, from www.naaja.org.au/2014/10/31/paperless-arrest-laws-belong-in-a-police-state-not-the-nt/.

———. 2014b. "NAAJA and CAALAS' Concerns with Paperless Arrests." Retrieved on February 20, 2016, from www.naaja.org.au/wp-content/uploads/2014/12/NAAJA-CAALAS-concerns-on-paperless-arrests.pdf.

Northern Territory Board of Enquiry into the Protection of Aboriginal Children from Sexual Abuse. 2007. *Ampe Akelyerenmane Meke Mekarle* ["Little Children Are Sacred Report"]. Darwin: Northern Territory Government.

Northern Territory Criminal Code Act. Schedule I Criminal Code of the Northern Territory of Australia. Available at www5.austlii.edu.au/au/legis/nt/consol_act/cca115/sch1.html.

Northern Territory Government. 2014. Department Children and Families (DCF), Annual Report 2013-2014. Retrieved on October 7, 2015, from https://territory families.nt.gov.au/__data/assets/pdf_file/0005/238667/Annual-Report2013-14.pdf.

———. 2015. *Mandatory Reporting PHC Guideline*. Department of Health. Available at http://remotehealthatlas.nt.gov.au/mandatory_reporting_overview.pdf.

Northern Territory Law Reform Committee. 2003. *Report of the Committee of Enquiry into Aboriginal Customary law.* Northern Territory law Reform Committee. Available at https://justice.nt.gov.au/__data/assets/pdf_file/0011/238619/ntlrc_final_report.pdf.

Northern Territory News. 2013. "Wife Killer Sent to Prison." March 1. Available at ntnews.com.

———. 2014. "Alison Anderson and Larissa Lee to Quit Palmer United Party." November 29.

Northern Territory Police Association (NTPA). 2012. *Submissions on Behalf of the NTPA: Coronial Inquest into the Death of Terrence Briscoe at Alice Springs Police Watch House on 5 January 2012.* Retrieved on September 28, 2013, from www.pfa.org.au/files/uploads/Submissions_20062012_Final.pdf.

Northrup, Solomon. 2013 [1853]. *Twelve Years a Slave.* UK: Eakin Films and Publishing.

Nussbaum, Martha. 2000. *Women and Human Development: The Capabilities Approach.* Cambridge, UK, and New York: Cambridge University Press.

Ohliger, John. 1995. "Critical Views of Paulo Freire's Work." Madison, WI: Basic Choices. Available at www.bmartin.cc/dissent/documents/Facundo/Ohliger1.html.

Okin, S. M. 1998. "Feminism, Women's Human Rights and Cultural Differences." *Hypatia* 13(2, Spring): 32–52.

Ortner, Sherry. 1974. "Is Female to Nature as Male Is to Culture?" In M. Z. Rosaldo and L. Lamphere, eds., *Woman, Culture and Society*, 67–87. Stanford, CA: Stanford University Press.

———. 1996. *Making Gender: The Politics and Erotics of Culture*. Boston: Beacon Press.

———. 2005. "Subjectivity and Cultural Critique." *Anthropological Theory* 5(31): 31–52.

Palmer, Dave. 2010. *Ngapartji Ngapartji: The Consequences of Kindness*. Evaluation. Available at www.bighart.org/wp-content/uploads/2017/03/BIghART _Evaluation_ConsequencesofKindness.pdf.

Papunya Community. 1992. Media Release. October 15. Unpublished.

Parliament of Australia. 2008. "Apology to Australia's Indigenous Peoples." Prime Minister Kevin Rudd. Available at http://www.australia.gov.au/about-australia /our-country/our-people/apology-to-australias-indigenous-peoples

Payne, Helen. 1989. "Rites for Sites or Sites for Rites? The Dynamics of Women's Cultural Life in the Musgraves." In P. Brock, ed., *Women: Rites and Sites*, 41–55. Sydney: Allen and Unwin.

Pearson, Noel. 2000. *Our Right to Take Responsibility*. Cairns, Qld: Noel Pearson and Associates.

Pennycook, Alistair. 1998. *English and the Discourses of Colonialism*. London and New York: Routledge.

———. 1994. *The Cultural Politics of English as an International Language*. London and New York: Longman.

Peterson, Nicolas. 1993. "Demand Sharing: Reciprocity and the Pressure for Generosity among Foragers." *American Anthropologist*, New Series 95(4, December): 860–874.

———. 2000. "An Expanding Aboriginal Domain: Mobility and the Initiation Journey." *Oceania* 70(3): 205–218.

———. 2010. "Other People's Lives: Secular Assimilation, Culture and Ungovernability." In J. C. Altman and M. Hinkson, eds. *Culture Crisis: Anthropology and Politics in Aboriginal Australia*, 248–258. Sydney: UNSW Press.

———. 2013. "On the Persistence of Sharing: Personhood, Asymmetrical Reciprocity and Demand Sharing in the Indigenous Australian Domestic Moral Economy." *The Australian Journal of Anthropology* 24(2): 166–176.

Peterson, Nicolas, and Marcia Langton, eds. 1983. *Aborigines, Land and Land Rights*. Canberra: Aboriginal Studies Press.

Peterson, Nicolas, and Fred Myers, eds. 2016. *Experiments in Self-Determination: Histories of the Outstation Movement in Australia*. Canberra: Australian National University Press.

Phillips, Anne. 2007. *Multiculturalism* without *Culture*. Princeton, NJ, and Oxford, UK: Princeton University Press.

Piff, K., M. W. Kraus, S. Cote, B. H. Cheng, and D. Keltner. 2010. "Having Less, Giv-ing More: The Influence of Social Class on Prosocial Behaviour." *The Journal of Personality and Social Psychology* 99(5): 771–784.

Pilger, John. 2014. *Utopia.* Documentary Film. UK release 2013, Australia release 2014.

Pilkington, James. 2009. *Aboriginal Communities and the Police Taskforce Themis: Case Studies in Remote Aboriginal Community Policing in the Northern Ter-ritory.* Darwin: North Australian Aboriginal Justice Agency and the Central Australian Aboriginal Legal Service.

Pitarch, Pedro. 2008. "The Labyrinth of Translation: A Tzeltal Version of the Univer-sal Declaration of Human Rights." In P. Pitarch, S. Speed, and X. L. Solano, eds., *Human Rights in the Maya Region,* 91–121. Durham, NC, and London: Duke University Press.

Poirier, Sylvie. 1992. "'Nomadic' Rituals: Networks of Ritual Exchange between Women of the Australian Western Desert." *Man* 27(4): 757–776.

Povinelli, Elizabeth A. 2001. "Radical Worlds: The Anthropology of Incommensura-bility and Inconceivability." *Annual Review of Anthropology* 30: 319–334.

———. 2002. *The Cunning of Recognition: Indigenous Alterities and the Making of Aus-tralian Multiculturalism.* Durham, NC, and London: Duke University Press.

———. 2011. *Economies of Abandonment: Social Belonging and Endurance in Late Lib-eralism.* Durham, NC, and London: Duke University Press.

Power, M. 1999. *The Audit Society: Rituals of Verification.* Oxford, UK: Oxford Uni-versity Press.

Pritchard, Sarah. 1998. "Working Group on Indigenous Populations: Mandate, Stan-dard Setting Activities and Future Perspectives." In Sarah Pritchard, ed., *In-digenous Peoples, the United Nations and Human Rights,* 40–65. Sydney: Zed Books. The Federation Press.

Productivity Commission. 2014. *Overcoming Indigenous Disadvantage.* Australian Government. Available at www.pc.gov.au/research/recurring/overcoming -indigenous-disadvantage/key-indicators-2014.

Pyne, A. 2012. "Ten Proposals to Reduce the Over-Imprisonment of Aboriginal Men in Northern Territory Prisons." *Australian Indigenous Law Review* 16(2): 2–17.

Quinn, Naomie, and Wendy Luttrell. 2004. "Psychodynamic Universals, Cultural Particulars in Feminist Anthropology: Rethinking Hua Gender Beliefs." In *Ethos* 32(4): 493–513.

Rafael, V. L. 1988. *Contracting Colonialism: Translation and Christian Conversion in Tagalog Society under Early Spanish Rule.* Ithaca, NY, and London: Cornell University Press.

Rajagopal, B. 2007. "Introduction: Part Four. Encountering Ambivalence." In M. Goodale and S. Engle Merry, eds., *The Practice of Human Rights: Tracking Law between the Global and the Local*, 273–284. Cambridge, UK: Cambridge University Press.

Ranciere, Jacques. 2004 "Who Is the Subject of the Rights of Man?" *The South Atlantic Quarterly* 103(2/3): 297–310.

Raphael, D. 1965. The Liberal Western Tradition of Human Rights. United Nations Educational, Scientific and Cultural Organisation. Roundtable meeting on Human Rights. Oxford, UK, November 11–19, 1965. Retrieved on June 11, 2013, from http://unesdoc.unesco.org/images/0016/001632/163279eb.pdf.

Read, Peter. 1999. *A Rape of the Soul So Profound: The Return of the Stolen Generations*. Sydney: Allen and Unwin.

Reeves, John. 1998. *Building on Land Rights for the Next Generation. Report on the Review of the Aboriginal Land Right; (Northern Territory) Act, 1976*. Canberra: Aboriginal and Torres Strait Islander Commission.

Relationships Australia. Homepage. Retrieved on May 18, 2015 from www.nt .relationships.org.au.

Reynolds, Henry. 1996. *Aboriginal Sovereignty: Three Nations, One Australia?* Sydney: Allen and Unwin.

Rigney, Lester Irribina. 1999. "Internationalisation of an Indigenous Anti-Colonial Cultural Critique of Research Methodologies: A Guide to Indigenist Research Methodology and Its Principles." Reprinted in *WICAZO SA Review: Journal of Native American Studies* 14(2, Fall): 109–122.

Roche, Chris, and James Ensor. 2014. *Independent Evaluation of the Central Land Council's Community Development and Governance Programmes*. Alice Springs: Central Land Council.

Roheim, Geza 1974, *Children of the Desert: The Western Tribes of Central Australia*. New York and London: Harper and Row.

———. 1988. *Children of the Desert, II: Myths and Dreams of the Aborigines of Central Australia*. Sydney: Oceania Publications, University of Sydney.

Roof, J., and R. Wiegman, eds. 1995. *Who Can Speak? Authority and Critical Identity*. Urbana and Chicago: University of Illinois Press.

Roosevelt, Eleanor. 1958. "In Our Hands." Speech delivered on the tenth anniversary of the Universal Declaration of Human Rights, New York: United Nations. Available at www.vmps.us/eleanor-roosevelt-and-united-nations-universal-declaration -human-rights.

Rorty, Richard. 1989. *Contingency, Irony, and Solidarity*. New York: Cambridge University Press.

———. 1993. "Human Rights, Rationality and Sentimentality." In Steven Shute and Sue Hurley, eds., *On Human Rights: The Oxford Amnesty Lectures 1993*, 111–134. New York: Basic Books.

Rosaldo, Michele Z. 1974. "Woman, Culture, and Society: A Theoretical Overview." In M. Z. Rosaldo and L. Lamphere, eds., *Woman, Culture and Society*, 17–42. Stanford, CA: Stanford University Press.

Rose, Debbie B. 1985. "Christian Identity versus Aboriginal Identity in the Victoria River District. Research Communications." *Australian Aboriginal Studies* 2: 58–61.

———. 1996. "Land Rights and Deep Colonising: The Erasure of Women Aboriginal." *Law Bulletin* 3(85, October): 6–13.

———. 2004. *Reports from a Wild Country: Ethics for Decolonisation*. Sydney: UNSW Press.

———. 2005. "An Indigenous Philosophical Ecology: Situating the Human." *The Australian Journal of Anthropology* 16(3): 294–305.

Rose, Nikolas. 1996. "The Death of the Social? Refiguring the Territory of Government." *Economy and Society* 25(3): 327–356.

———. 1999 [1989]. *Governing the Soul: The Shaping of the Private Self*. London and New York: Free Association Books.

Ross, C., D. Mallard, and S. Fisher. 2010. *Model of Practice for Mediation with Aboriginal Families in Central Australia*. Alice Springs: Relationships Australia Family Relationships Centre.

Ross, David. 2013. "Taking Power: Taking Responsibility—Achieving Strong Aboriginal Governance and Self-Determination." Speech to the Aboriginal Governance Summit, April in Tennant Creek. Retrieved on July 20, 2013, from www .clc.org.au/publications/content/taking-power-taking-responsibility -achieving-strong-aboriginal-governance-a.

Rowse, Tim. 1998. "Indigenous Citizenship and Self-Determination: The Problem of Shared Responsibilities." In N. Peterson and W. Sanders, eds., *Citizenship and Indigenous Australians: Changing Conceptions and Possibilities*, 79–100. Cambridge, UK, and Melbourne: Cambridge University Press.

———. 2005. "The Indigenous Sector." In D. Austin-Broos and G. Macdonald, eds., *Culture, Economy and Governance in Aboriginal Australia*, 207–223. Sydney: Academy of Social Sciences and the Department of Anthropology, University of Sydney Press.

———. 2007. "The National Emergency and Indigenous Jurisdictions." In J. Altman and M. Hinkson, eds., *Coercive Reconciliation: Stabilise, Normalise, Exit Aboriginal Australia*, 47–62. Melbourne: Arena Publications Association.

Sandel, Michael. 1998. *Liberalism and the Limits of Justice*. Cambridge, UK: Cambridge University Press.

Sanders, William. 2001. "Delivering Democracy to Indigenous Australians: Aborigines, Torres Strait Islanders and Commonwealth Electoral Administration." In

M. Sawer, ed., *Elections: Full, Free and Fair*, 158–174. Sydney: The Federation Press.

———. 2005. "CDEP and ATSIC as Bold Experiments in Governing Differently—but Where to Now?" In D. Austin-Broos and G. Macdonald, eds., *Aborigines, Culture and Economy: The Past, Present, and Future of Rural and Remote Indigenous Lives*, 203–212. Sydney: University of Sydney Press.

———. 2007. "The Political Economy of Self-Government." In J. Altman and M. Hinkson, eds., *Coercive Reconciliation: Stabilise, Normalise, Exit Aboriginal Australia*, 63–72. North Carlton, Australia: Arena Publications.

———. 2008. "Regionalism That Respects Localism: The Anmatjere Community Governance Council and Beyond." In J. Hunt, D. E. Smith, S. Garling, and W. Sanders, eds., *Contested Governance: Culture, Power and Institutions in Indigenous Australia*, 283–309. Canberra: ANU ePress.

———. 2012. "W(h)ither the Super Shires: Reflections on the 2012 Local Government Elections in the NT." May 9. CAEPR Seminar, Australian National University. Retrieved on September 18, 2012, from http://caepr.anu.edu.au/sites/default /files/Seminars/presentations/Sanders%20NT%20shires.pdf.

Sanders, William, and Sarah Holcombe. 2008. "Sustainable Governance for Small Desert Settlements: Learning from the Multi-Settlement Regionalism of Anmatjere Community Government Council." *The Rangeland Journal* 30(1): 137–147.

Santos, Boaventure De Souza. 1996. *Toward a Multicultural Conception of Human Rights*. Working Paper series on Political Economy and Legal Change, No. 2, Global Studies Program, International Institute, University of Wisconsin.

———. 2002. "Toward a Multicultural Conception of Human Rights." In Berta Hernandez-Truyol, ed., *Moral Imperialism. A Critical Anthology*: 39–60. New York: New York University Press.

———. 2006. *The Rise of the Global Left: The World Social Forum and Beyond*. London and New York: Zed Books.

———. 2007. "Human Rights as Emancipatory Script? Cultural and Political Conditions." Chapter 1 in B. D. S. Santos, ed., *Another Knowledge Is Possible: Beyond Northern Epistemologies*. London and New York: Verso,

Sapir, Edward. 1985 [1949]. *Selected Writings of Edward Sapir in Language, Culture and Personality*, 5th edition. D. G. Mandelbaum, ed. Berkeley: University of California Press.

Saussure, F. De. 1966 [1959]. *Course in General Linguistics*. C. Bally and A. Sechehaye, eds. New York: McGraw-Hill Book Co..

Sawer, Marian. 1995. "Locked out or Locked in: Women and Politics in Australia." In B. J. Nelson and N. Chowdhury, eds., *Women and Politics Worldwide*, 73–91. New Haven, CT, and London: Yale University Press.

Scheper-Hughes, Nancy. 1995. "The Primacy of the Ethical: Propositions for a Militant Anthropology." *Current Anthropology* 36(3): 409–440.

Schwarz, C., and F. Dussart, eds. 2010. "Engaging Christianity in Aboriginal Australia." Special Edition. *The Australian Journal of Anthropology* 21(1).

Schwarz, M. 2010. "Building Communities, Not Prisons: Justice Reinvestment and Indigenous Over-Imprisonment." *Australian Indigenous Law Review 2* 14(1): 2–17.

Scott, John C. 2009. *The Art of Not Being Governed: An Anarchist History of Upland Southeast Asia.* New Haven, CT: Yale University Press.

Scullion, Nigel. 2014. "Strengthening Governance to Support Effective Services for Indigenous Australians." Media Release, August 7. Available at https://ministers .pmc.gov.au/scullion/2014/strengthening-governance-support-effective -services-indigenous-australians.

Sen, A. 1999. *Development as Freedom.* Oxford, UK, and New York: Oxford University Press.

Sharp, Jared. 2014. "Tackling Family Violence in the Northern Territory." Presentation at the North Australian Aboriginal Justice Agency. Retrieved on February 22, 2015, from www.aic.gov.au/media_library/.../2014.../tue-103-1600-Jared -Sharp.pdf.

Shaw, Gillian. 2002. "An Ethnographic Exploration of the Development of Child Rearing Style among Ngaanyatjarra People from the Pre-Contact Era to the Present." Unpublished Treatise for MA in Public Health. University of New South Wales.

Shweder, Richard. A. 1990. "Ethical Relativism: Is There a Defensible Version?" *Ethos:* 205–218.

Sibthorpe, Beverly, Ian Anderson, and J. Cunningham. 2001. "Self-Assessed Health among Indigenous Australians: How Valid Is a Global Question?" *American Journal of Public Health* 91(10, October): 1660–1663.

Simpson, Audra. 2014. *Mohawk Interruptus: Political Life across the Borders of Settler States.* Durham, NC, Duke University Press.

Simpson, Jane. 2008. "Language Rights and Human Rights." *Endangered Languages and Cultures Blog* Archive. December 10. Retrieved on February 7, 2014, from www.paradisec.org.au/blog/2008/12/language-rights-and-human-rights/.

Skelton, Russell. 2010. *King Brown Country: The Betrayal of Papunya.* Sydney: Allen and Unwin.

Smith, Andrea. 2005. "Native American Feminism, Sovereignty, and Social Change." *Feminist Studies* 31(1): 116–132.

Smith, Benjamin R., and Frances Morphy, eds. 2007. *The Social Effects of Native Title: Recognition, Translation, Co-existence.* Canberra: ANU Press. Centre for

Aboriginal Economic Policy Research Monograph 27. Australian National University.

Smith, Diane. 2008. "Cultures of Governance and the Governance of Culture: Transforming and Containing Indigenous Institutions in West Arnhem Land." In Janet Hunt, Diane Smith, William Sanders, and Stephanie Garling, eds., *Contested Governance: Culture, Power and Institutions in Indigenous Australia*, 75–112. Canberra: Australian National University, ANU e press.

Smith, K. 2012. "From Dividual and Individual Selves to Porous Subjects." *The Australian Journal of Anthropology* 23: 50–64.

Southwood, Stephen. 2007. "Equality of the Law and the Sentencing of Aboriginal Offenders under the Sentencing Act (Northern Territory)." Paper presented to "Rule of Law: The Challenges of a Changing World Defending and Preserving the Rule of Law in a Climate of Global and Regional Uncertainty." Symposium Brisbane, August 31–September 1, 2007.

Sovereign Union. 2011. "Act of Sovereign Union between First Nations and Peoples in Australia." Retrieved on August 21, 2015, from http://nationalunitygovernment .org/content/act-sovereign-union-between-first-nations-and-peoples-australia.

Speed, Shannon. 2006. "At the Crossroads of Human Rights and Anthropology: Towards a Critically Engaged Activist Research." *American Anthropologist* 108(1): 66–76.

———. 2007. "Exercising Rights and Reconfiguring Resistance in the Zapatista Juntas de Buen Gobierno." In Mark Goodale and Sally Engle Merry, eds., *The Practice of Human Rights: Tracking Law Between the Global and the Local*, 163–192. Cambridge and New York: Cambridge University Press.

Spivak, Gayatri. 1988. "Can the Subaltern Speak?" In C. Nelson and L. Grossberg, eds., *Marxism and the Interpretation of Culture*, 271–313. Chicago: University of Illinois Press.

Spolsky, B., and P. Irvine. 1982. "Sociolinguistic Aspects of the Acceptance of Literacy in the Vernacular." In F. Barkin, E. A. Brandt, and J. Ornstein-Galicia, eds., *Bilingualism and Language Contact: Spanish, English and Native American Languages*. New York and London: Columbia University Teachers College Press.

Strang, Heather, and John Braithwaite. 2002. *Restorative Justice and Family Violence*. Cambridge: Cambridge University Press.

St Denis, V. 2007. "Feminism Is for Everybody: Aboriginal Women, Feminism and Diversity." In J. Green, ed., *Making Space for Indigenous Feminism*, 33–52. Halifax, NS: Fernwood Publishing.

Stanner, W. E. H. 1965. "Religion, Totemism, and Symbolism." In R. M. and C. H. Berndt, eds., *Aboriginal Man in Australia*. Sydney: Angus and Robertson.

———. 1966. "On Aboriginal Religion." *Oceania Monograph* 11, University of Sydney.

———. 1979. *White Man Got No Dreaming: Essays 1938–1973*. Canberra: Australian National University Press.

Stark, Evan. 2007. *Coercive Control: How Men Entrap Women in Personal Life*. New York: Oxford University Press.

Stavenhagen, Rodolfo. 2009. "Making the Declaration Work." In Claire Charters and Rodolfo Stavenhagen, eds., 352–371. *Making the Declaration Work. The United Nations Declaration on the Rights of Indigenous Peoples*. Copenhagen: International Working Group for Indigenous Affairs (IWGIA).

Strathern, Marilyn. 1988. *The Gender of the Gift: Problems with Women and Problems with Society in Melanesia*. Berkeley, Los Angeles, and London: University of California Press..

———, ed. 2000. *Audit Cultures: Anthropological Studies in Ethics, Accountability and the Academy*. London and New York: Routledge.

Sullivan, Patrick, ed. 1996. *Shooting the Banker: Essays on ATSIC and Self-Determination*. Darwin: North Australian Research Unit, Australian National University.

———. 2011. *Belonging Together: Dealing with the Politics of Disenchantment in Australian Indigenous Policy*. Canberra: Aboriginal Studies Press.

Sutton, Peter. 1995. *Country: Aboriginal Boundaries and Land Ownership in Australia*. Aboriginal History Monograph Series. Canberra: Australian National University (ANU).

———. 1997. "Summer School Notes on Aboriginal Land Tenure." University of Adelaide, South Australia. Unpublished.

———. 2009. *The Politics of Suffering: Indigenous Australia and the End of the Liberal Consensus*. Melbourne: Melbourne University Press.

Sydney Morning Herald. 2014. "Alison Anderson, Clive Palmer's Mercurial Leader in the NT." November 8. Stuart Rintoul. Available at www.smh.com.au/good -weekend/alison-anderson-clive-palmers-mercurial-leader-in-the-nt-20141106 -11c9o5.html.

Taylor, Charles. 1985. "Atomism." In C. Taylor, *Philosophy and the Human Sciences: Philosophical Papers 2*. Cambridge, UK, and New York: Cambridge University Press.

———. 1992. "The Politics of Recognition." In A. Gutman, ed., *Multiculturalism and the Politics of Recognition*, 25–73. Princeton, NJ: Princeton University Press.

———. 2002. "Modern Social Imaginaries." *Public Culture* 14(1, Winter): 91–124.

Taylor, John. 2008. "Indigenous Peoples and Indicators of Well-Being: Australian Perspectives on United Nations Global Frameworks." *Social Indicators Research* 87: 111–226.

Ting, Inge. 2011. "Aboriginal Crime and Punishment: Aboriginal Incarceration Rates Rise under Neo-Liberalism." *Crikey*, December 15. Retrieved on

September28,2013,fromwww.crikey.com.au/2011/12/15/aboriginal-prison-rate
-continues-t-rise-is-neoliberalism-at-play/.

Thomas, Nicolas. 1991. *Entangled Objects: Exchange, Material Culture and Colonialism in the Pacific.* Cambridge, MA, and London: Harvard University Press.

Thompson, F. 2014. *Northern Territory Midwives' Collection. Mothers and Babies 2011.* Darwin: Department of Health, Northern Territory. Available at http://digitallibrary.health.nt.gov.au/prodjspui/bitstream/10137/596/4/Mothers%20and%20Babies%202011.pdf.

Thompson, Richard. 1997. "Ethnic Minorities and the Case for Collective Rights." *American Anthropologist, New Series* 99(4, December): 786–798.

Tjitayi, K. and S. Lewis. 1988. "Ideology and Domination in Aboriginal Australia: A Western Desert Test Case." In Tim Ingold, David Riches, and James Woodburn, eds., *Hunters and Gatherers 2: Property, Power and Ideology*, 150–164. New York: Berg.

———. 2011. "Envisioning Lives at Ernabella." In Ute Eickelkamp, ed., *Growing Up in Central Australia: New Anthropological Studies of Aboriginal Childhood and Adolescence*, 49–62. New York: Berghan Books.

Tonkinson, Robert. 1991[1978]. *The Mardu Aborigines: Living the Dream in Australia's Desert.* Case Studies in Cultural Anthropology. Fort Worth: Holt, Rinehart and Winston.

Tonnies, F. 2001 [1887] *Community and Civil Society*, edited by Jose Harris. Cambridge, UK: Cambridge University Press.

Trigger, David. S. 1992. *Whitefella Comin': Aboriginal Responses to Colonialism in Northern Australia.* Cambridge, UK, and Melbourne: Cambridge University Press.

Trudinger, David. 2004. Converting Salvation: Protestant Missionaries in Central Australia, 1930s–1940s. Unpublished PhD thesis Canberra: Australian National University.

Tsey, Komla, and A. Every. 2000. "Evaluating Aboriginal Empowerment Programs: The Case of Family Wellbeing." *Australian and New Zealand Journal of Public Health* 24(5): 509–514.

Tsing, Anna. L 2005. *Friction: An Ethnography of Global Connection.* Princeton, NJ: Princeton University Press.

———. 2007. "Indigenous Voice." In Marisol Cadena and Orin Starn, eds., *Indigenous Experience Today*, 33–68. Oxford, UK, and New York: Berg.

Tucker, Margaret. 1977. *If Everyone Cared: Autobiography of Margaret Tucker.* Sydney: Ure Smith.

Turner, Terence. 1993. "Anthropology and Multiculturalism: What Is Anthropology That Multiculturalists Should Be Mindful of It?" *Cultural Anthropology* 8(4): 411–429.

——. 1997. "Human Rights, Human Difference: Anthropology's Contribution to an Emancipatory Cultural Politics." *Journal of Anthropological Research* 53: 273–291.

United Nations. 1979. "Convention on the Elimination of All Forms of Discrimination against Women (CEDAW). Available at www.un.org/womenwatch/daw /cedaw/.

United Nations Commission on the Status of Women. 2013. "Press release: Indigenous Women Speak out about Violence against Women and Children." Available at http://aippnet.org/press-release-indigenous-women-unite-to-speak-out -about-violence/.

United Nations Declaration on the Rights of Indigenous Peoples. 2007. Retrieved on July 2, 2012, from www.un.org/esa/socdev/unpfii/documents/DRIPS_en.pdf.

United Nations Development Program (UNDP). 2004. *Human Development Report: Cultural Liberty in Today's Diverse World*. Available at www.unic.un.org.pl /hdr/hdr2004/hdr04_complete.pdf.

United Nations Economic and Social Council, Commission on the Status of Women. 2013. 57th Session, March 4–15. *Elimination and Prevention of All Forms of Violence against Indigenous Women and Girls*. E/CN.6/2013/L.5.

United Nations Human Rights Office of the High Commissioner. nd. Special Rapporteur on the Rights of Indigenous Peoples. "Introduction." Retrieved on May 18, 2016, from www.ohchr.org/EN/Issues/IPeoples/SRIndigenousPeoples/Pages /SRIPeoplesIndex.aspx.

——. 2009. "The Universal Declaration of Human Rights in 370 Languages." News and Events. Retrieved on January 4, 2018, from www.ohchr.org/EN/News Events/Pages/UDHRin370languages.aspx.

——. 2010. "A New World Record: Universal Declaration in 370 Languages." Retrieved on February 7, 2014, from www.ohchr.org/EN/NewsEvents/Pages /AnewworldrecordUDHR.aspx.

——. 2012. *Human Rights Indicators: A Guide to Measurement and Implementation*. New York and Geneva: HR/PUB/12/5.

——. 2014. "Press Release: A Best Seller: The User's Manual for the Implementation of Human Rights Indicators." Available at www.ohchr.org/EN/NewsEvents/Pages /HumanRightsIndicators.aspx#sthash.H31fkPzL.dpuf.

——. 2015. "Universal Declaration of Human Rights: Pintupi-Luritja." Retrieved February 2, 2016, from www.ohchr.org/EN/UDHR/Pages/Language.aspx?Lang ID=piu.

United Nations Office of the Special Advisor for Gender Issues and the Advancement of Women, and the Secretariat of the UN Permanent Forum on Indigenous Issues. 2010. *Gender and Indigenous People's: Briefing Note 1*. Available at www .un.org/esa/socdev/unpfii/documents/BriefingNote1_GREY.pdf.

United Nations Permanent Forum on Indigenous Issues (UNPFII), Economic and Social Council. 2012. "Combating Violence against Indigenous Women and Girls: Article 22 of the United Nations Declaration on the Rights of Indigenous Peoples." *Report of the International Expert Group Meeting*. E/C.19/2012/1.

———. 2013. "Study on the Extent of Violence against Indigenous Women and Girls in Terms of Article 22 (2) of the United Nations Declaration on the Rights of Indigenous Peoples." E/C. 19/2013/1.

United Nations Universal Periodic Review. 2011. Retrieved on May 18, 2016, from www.ohchr.org/EN/HRBodies/UPR/Pages/UPRMain.aspx

Universal Declaration of Human Rights. 1948. Retrieved on July 2, 2012, from www.un.org/en/documents/udhr/index.shtml.

UPR. 2014. *Beyond Promises: The Impact of the UPR on the Ground*. Retrieved on May 12, 2016, from www.upr-info.org/sites/default/files/general-document/pdf/2014_beyond_promises.pdf.

Urbis. 2013. *Literature Review on Domestic Violence Perpetrators*. Retrieved on May 8, 2015, from www.dss.gov.au/sites/default/files/documents/09_2013/literature_review_on_domestic_violence_perpetrators.pdf.

Venkateswar, S., and E. Hughes, eds. 2011. *The Politics of Indigeneity: Dialogues and Reflections of Indigenous Activism*. London and New York: Zed Books.

Viveiros de Castro, Eduardo. 2004. "Perspectival Anthropology and the Method of Controlled Equivocation." *Tipití: Journal of the Society for the Anthropology of Lowland South America* 2(1): Article 1.

Von Sturmer, J. 1984. "The Different Domains." In *Aborigines and Uranium. Consolidated Report on the Social Impact of Uranium Mining on the Aborigines of the Northern Territory*, 218–237. Canberra: Australian Institute of Aboriginal Studies.

Wacquant, Loic. 2010. "Crafting the Neoliberal State: Workfare, Prisonfare and Social Insecurity." *Sociological Forum* 25(2): 197–219.

Waltja Tjutangku Palyapayi. nd. "About Us." Available at www.waltja.org.au/about-us/service-area/.

———. nd. "Constitution." Available at www.waltja.org.au/about-us/constitution/.

———. nd. "History and Origins." Available at www.waltja.org.au/about-us/history-and-origins/.

———. nd. "Sharing Our Grandmother's Stories." Available at www.waltja.org.au/projects/grandmothers-stories/.

———. nd. "Waltja Wins Category A of Indigenous Governance Awards: Australia's Top Aboriginal Organisations Announced." Available at www.waltja.org.au/waltja-wins-category-a-of-indigenous-governance-awards/.

Walzer, Michael. 1990. "The Communitarian Critique of Liberalism." *Political Theory* 18(1, February): 6–23.

Wardlow, Holly. 2006. *Wayward Women: Sexuality and Agency in a New Guinea Society*. Berkeley, Los Angeles, and London: University of California Press.

Warumpi Band. 1983. "Jailanguru Pakarnu (Out from Jail)." Available at http://aso .gov.au/titles/music/jailanguru-pakarnu/clip1/.

Waters, Larissa. 2014. "Australian Women Encouraged to Simply Shake off Entrenched Inequality." *Daily Life* November 11. Available at www.dailylife.com .au/news-and-views/dl-opinion/australian-women-encouraged-to-simply -shake-off-entrenched-inequality-20141110-11k3ox.html.

Watson, Irene. 2005. "Settled and Unsettled Spaces: Are We Free to Roam?" *Australian Critical Race and Whiteness Studies Association Journal* 1: 40–52.

Western Australia Law Reform Commission. 2005. *Aboriginal Customary Laws*. *Project 94*. Perth: Western Australia Law Reform Commission. Available at www .lrc.justice.wa.gov.au/_files/P94_DP.pdf.

White, Isobel. 1975. "Sexual Conquest and Submission in the Myths of Central Australia." In L. R. Hiatt, ed. *Australian Aboriginal Mythology: Essays in Honour of WEH Stanner*, 123–142. Canberra: Australia Institute of Aboriginal and Torres Strait Islander Studies.

———. 1978. "Aboriginal Women's Status: A Paradox Resolved." In F. Gale, ed., *Women's Role in Aboriginal Society*, 36–49. Canberra: Australian Institute of Aboriginal Studies.

Whyte, Jessica. 2012. "On the Politics of Suffering." *Arena Magazine* 118: 37–39.

Wierzbicka, Anna. 1997. *Understanding Cultures through Their Key Words: English, Russian, Polish, German, and Japanese*. Oxford, UK: Oxford University Press.

———. 2006. *English: Meaning and Culture*. Oxford, UK: Oxford University Press.

Wild, Rex, and Pat Anderson. 2007. *Ampe Akelyernemane Meke Mekerle: Little Children Are Sacred*. Report of the Northern Territory Board of Enquiry into the Protection of Children from Child Abuse. Darwin: Northern Territory Government.

Wild, Stephen. 1987. "Recreating the Jukurrpa: Adaptation and Innovation of Songs and Ceremonies in Warlpiri Society." *Oceania Mongraph* 32: 97–120.

Wilkins, David. 1995. "More Than Just Wishful Thinking: The Survival of the Arrernte Worldview Is Historical Fact, Not Romantic Fictions." *Oceania Newsletter* 15 (March).

Williams, George. 2010. "The Future of the Australian Bill of Rights Debate." Alice Tay Lecture on Law and Human Rights, Freilich Foundation, Australian National University. Retrieved on August 20, 2012, from www.gtcentre.unsw.edu .au/sites/gtcentre.unsw.edu.au/files/mdocs/Alice_Tay_Lecture_2010.pdf.

Williams, Raymond. 1961. *The Long Revolution*. London: Chatto & Windus.

Willis, Matthew. 2011. "Non-Disclosure of Violence in Australian Indigenous Communities." *Trends and Issues in Crime and Criminal Justice* 405. Available at www.aic.gov.au/publications/current%20series/tandi/401-420/tandi405.html.

Willis, Matthew, and Sarah Holcombe. 2014. *Evaluation of the Cross Borders Indigenous Family Violence Program.* Australian Government and the Australian Institute of Criminology. Unpublished.

Wilson, R. A., ed. 1997. *Human Rights, Culture and Context: Anthropological Perspectives.* Chicago: Pluto Press.

Wilson, Tim. 2014. "Opening Minds to 'Forgotten' Freedoms." *Weekend Australian* (May): 17–18.

———. 2015. "Property Rights are Human Rights." Institute of Public Affairs. May 10. Available at https://ipa.org.au/publications-ipa/ipa-review-articles/property-rights-human-rights.

Witte, J., and M. C. Green, eds. 2011. *Religion and Human Rights: An Introduction.* New York: Oxford University Press.

Wolterstorff, N. P. 2011. "Christianity and Human Rights." Chapter 2 in J. Witte and M. C. Green, eds., *Religion and Human Rights: An Introduction.* New York: Oxford University Press.

World Bank Group. 2014. "Voice and Agency: Empowering Women and Girls for Shared Prosperity." Washington, DC: Author. Available at https://openknowledge.worldbank.org/handle/10986/19036.

Wright, Alexis, ed. 1998. *Take Power Like This Old Man Here: An Anthology Celebrating Twenty Years of Land Rights in Central Australia, 1977–1997.* Alice Springs: Jukurrpa Books, IAD Press.

Wright, Alyson. and Ruth Elvin. 2011. *Assessing Shared Responsibility at Ali Curung.* Desert Knowledge CRC Working Paper 82. Alice Springs. Available at https://static1.squarespace.com/static/5450868fe4b09b217330bb42/t/54754549e4b0e82083b88d92/1416971593635/Assessing-Shared-Responsibility-In-AliCurung.pdf.

Wundersitz, Joy. 2010. "Indigenous Perpetrators of Violence: Prevalence and Risk Factors for Offending." *Australian Institute of Criminology (AIC) Reports.* Research and Public Policy Series 105. Available at www.aic.gov.au/media_library/publications/rpp/105/rpp105.pdf.

Yallop, C. 1982. *Australian Aboriginal Languages.* London: Andre Deutsch.

Yap, Mandy, and Yu, Eunice 2016a. *Community Wellbeing from the Ground Up: A Yawuru Example.* BCEC Research Report no 3/16. Bankwest Curtin Economics Centre. Retrieved on January 12, 2017, from http://caepr.anu.edu.au/sites/default/files/announce/16/bcec-community-wellbeing-from-the-ground-up-a-yawuru-example-1.pdf

———. 2016b. "Operationalising the Capability Approach: Developing Culturally Relevant Indicators of Indigenous Wellbeing—an Australian Example. *Oxford Development Studies* 44(3): 315–331.

Yeo, Soo See. 2003. "Bonding and Attachment in Australian Aboriginal Children." *Child Abuse Review* 12: 292–304.

Yolngu Nations Assembly. 2012. "Statement Regarding Australian Federal Government Stronger Futures Bills and Northern Territory Policies." April 24. Retrieved on October 19, 2012, from http://stoptheintervention.org/uploads/files_to_download/Stronger-Futures/Yolngu-Statement-2-5-12.pdf.

Index

If God Were a Human Rights Activist
Boaventura de Sousa Santos
2015

Digging for the Disappeared: Forensic Science after Atrocity
Adam Rosenblatt
2015

The Rise and Fall of Human Rights: Cynicism and Politics in Occupied Palestine
Lori Allen
2013

Campaigning for Justice: Human Rights Advocacy in Practice
Jo Becker
2012

In the Wake of Neoliberalism: Citizenship and Human Rights in Argentina
Karen Ann Faulk
2012

Values in Translation: Human Rights and the Culture of the World Bank
Galit A. Sarfaty
2012

Disquieting Gifts: Humanitarianism in New Delhi
Erica Bornstein
2012

Stones of Hope: How African Activists Reclaim Human Rights to Challenge Global Poverty
Edited by Lucie E. White and Jeremy Perelman
2011

Judging War, Judging History: Behind Truth and Reconciliation
Pierre Hazan
2010

Localizing Transitional Justice: Interventions and Priorities after Mass Violence
Edited by Rosalind Shaw and Lars Waldorf, with Pierre Hazan
2010

Surrendering to Utopia: An Anthropology of Human Rights
Mark Goodale
2009

Human Rights for the 21st Century: Sovereignty, Civil Society, Culture
Helen M. Stacy
2009

Human Rights Matters: Local Politics and National Human Rights Institutions
Julie A. Mertus
2009

The authorized representative in the EU for product safety and compliance is:
Mare Nostrum Group
B.V Doelen 72
4831 GR Breda
The Netherlands

www.ingramcontent.com/pod-product-compliance
Lightning Source LLC
Chambersburg PA
CBHW030906270326
41929CB00008B/597

9 781503 606470